TRADING WITH SAUDI ARABIA

TRADING WITH SAUDI ARABIA

A Guide to the Shipping, Trade, Investment, and Tax Laws of Saudi Arabia

LESLIE ALAN GLICK

ALLANHELD, OSMUN Montclair CROOM HELM London

Published in the United States of America in 1980
by Allanheld, Osmun & Co. Publishers, Inc.
19 Brunswick Road, Montclair, NJ 07042
ISBN 0-916672-43-3

Published in the United Kingdom in 1980
by Croom Helm Ltd, 2-10 St John's Road, London SW11
ISBN 0-7099-0409-6

Library of Congress Cataloging in Publication Data

Glick, Leslie Alan
Trading with Saudi Arabia

1. Foreign trade regulation—Saudi Arabia. 2. Taxation—Law and legislation—Saudi Arabia. 3. Maritime law—Saudi Arabia. 4. Investments, Foreign—Law and legislation—Saudi Arabia. I. Title.
LAW 343.53'8087 79-55002
ISBN 0-916672-43-3

Printed in the United States of America

TO MY WIFE, MELISSA AND TO MY PARENTS

TABLE OF CONTENTS

Chapter XV

PART II - INVESTMENT AND TAXATION

PART III - TARIFF, TRADE, AND BOYCOTT LAWS

PREFACE

This book developed in part from my work and experience as an attorney practicing in the areas of international trade and maritime law. Having represented clients doing business in the Middle East and Saudi Arabia, I found that much of the information needed to make decisions and appreciate the legal consequences of those decisions was almost impossible to find. Particularly, whatever information did exist was fragmented and had to be obtained from many sources, some of which were second or third hand. Copies of actual statutes and regulations were difficult to find due to the nature of the Saudi legal system. The Saudi government is one of the last true kingdoms in existence, and perhaps the most important in terms of its economic signifigance and its role in world affairs. Unlike many nominal monarchies, in Saudi Arabia the king, is in effect, the law. While considerable authority has been delegated to ministers, their power exists only as a result of such delegation. While the king may be the law, in the sense that he enforces and interprets it, the Koran is the true source of Saudi law and the rigid tenets of Islamic jurisprudence limit even the authority of the king. Thus, Saudi Arabia is unique in that it is one of the few countries in the world that is both a monarchy and a theocracy.

Despite these deep imbedded institutions, Saudi Arabia has nonetheless had to cope with the problems of an evolving world power. Western technology and investment has had to be accomodated to an eastern religious law which did not provide for many of the problems engendered by today's complex commercial society. Saudi Arabia has managed to strike a balance between the strong demand for traditional adherence to religious tenets and the practical demands for growth and survival in a commercial society.

Realizing these factors, I began to assemble material on various aspects of Saudi law. My intention was to provide as much of the original source material as possible, including the complete text of decrees and regulations. There were two reasons for this. First, for those who hope to engage in Saudi trade, the task of locating and assembling the various laws and regulations would be a monumental one and would consume considerable time and expense. It is my hope that by providing this material in one text, that both practioners and scholars will have a source book which will enable them to find most major commercial laws without difficulty. Second, the task of interpreting Saudi law is a risky one. Both an understanding of Saudi religious law and political factors is needed, and English translations often lead to differing interpretations. By providing original source material, as well as analysis, each practioner will have the opportunity to view the actual decrees and regulations for himself, rather than rely solely on another's interpretation.

As in any work of this size and scope, certain caveats are in order. Whil every attempt has been made to make this work current, developments in Saudi Arabia are rapid, and the king can revoke by decree, what he had mandated only several days before. Also, the time it takes for such decisions to be publishe in the Official Gazette, and translated and communicated to Western sources, ca be considerable. One Minister's Council resolution which was passed November 1 was not published until January 17. Certain judgements also had to be made as to the inclusion and exclusion of certain topics and material. While many actual decrees and regulations are reprinted in their complete text, not every area could be covered. For example, Saudi Arabia has some one hundred and twen two standards for various products. The complete text of these would be suffic for an entire volume in itself, and while some standards would undoubtedly be of interest to some readers, the broad nature of this book does not warrant such detailed treatment. Specific emphasis was placed on shipping and customs laws because of their growing importance and due to the absence of published materials in these areas, compared to the areas of investment and taxation.

While western understanding of Saudi law undoubtedly will remain inadequate for some time, it is hoped that this book will be a part of a bridge that will enable us to move toward both greater knowledge and appreciation of Saudi Arabian jurisprudence and provide the practical knowledge needed to engage in trade, shipping, and commercial activities.

Leslie Alan Glick

TRADING WITH SAUDI ARABIA

PART I

SAUDI ARABIAN MARITIME LAW

BACKGROUND AND INTRODUCTION

The tremendous growth in trade between Middle Eastern nations and the industrialized nations of the world has resulted in an increased interest and awareness of the potential of these Middle Eastern states as maritime powers. With the great potential capital available for financing a merchant marine provided by the exports of oil, the Middle Eastern states have the potential to develop into major merchant marine powers. However, numerous problems have resulted in the slower than anticipated growth in maritime development in these countries. These problems are a combination of economic, socio-religious and legal factors that exist in the Middle Eastern states.

The purpose of this section is to review in detail the development of one of these states, Saudi Arabia, particularly from the viewpoint of the legal and economic requirements pertaining to operating vessels in Saudi Arabia. However, for purposes of background, in order to understand both Saudi Arabian and other Middle Eastern states approach to maritime transport, a discussion of some of the recent economic activities in all of these states is helpful.

While our main focus will be on Saudi Arabia, it should be remembered that, although pan-Arab cooperation has not achieved the results desired by the Middle Eastern states, various joint venture operations have been initiated in the past and it is likely that the future of the Arab merchant marine will include many cooperative efforts among the states as well as individual operations.

DEVELOPMENT OF THE ARAB TANKER FLEET.

Given the tremendous control of the Middle Eastern nations over the outflow of petroleum, it has been anticipated by most observers that this economic power would be used to provide a basis for developing an Arab tanker fleet which would control at least a sizable portion of oil shipped from the Middle East petroleum exporting nations. Although this development has taken place at a much slower pace than expected, those looking to the future can anticipate an increased growth in the Arab tanker fleet. The experience of Saudi Arabia has shown a growth from no tonnage at all to approximately 2,300,000 DWT's in 1976. A number of factors have kept this growth from being even greater.[1]

[1] A 1975 study by the Department of Commerce, Maritime Administration entitled "Recent Developments in the Growth of Arab Tanker Fleets" indicated that as of January 1, 1975, OPEC countries controlled about 1% of the total world fleet. About two-thirds of this was controlled by Arab countries, with Kuwait the largest owner with 793,000 DWT and Saudi Arabia having only 27,000 DWT.

One of these factors has been the lay-up of tonnage and the low rates that are now available for crude carriers. Many Middle Eastern states, including Saudi Arabia, have been cautious about their building plans due to the over-tonnaging situation and the very low world rates. In addition, the present world situation has cooled the interest of Western nations in joint ventures with the Arabs. Nevertheless, some joint venture operations have been set up, although most are not fully operative .

One example is the Saudi Arabian National Tanker Company, which is a joint venture between the Saudis and Western interests.

Another joint venture operation is the Arab Maritime Petroleum Transport Company (AMPTC), which is owned by several members of the Organization of Arab Petroleum Exporting Countries (OAPEC), including Saudi Arabia. In 1973 it began with capital of $100 million. AMPTC owned a fleet of eight tankers registered under various Middle Eastern flags. These include the Saudi-flag vessel AL RIYADH, which has been laid up in Norway. It was originally predicted that by 1982 AMPTC would own a fleet of 10 million DWT costing more than $2 million.

Other Saudi firms operating tankers include Arab International Maritime Company (AIMC), which is partially owned by Mobil; the Red Sea Saudi Maritime Company, which has one tanker; the Saudi Arabian Maritime Company (SAMARCO), which is a joint venture involving the Saudis and American oil companies, which owns four tankers; and the Saudi Arabia Company (SASCO), which is a joint venture with Mitsui of Japan.

There are recent reports that the Saudis are now establishing its own national flag company whose ships will enjoy a cargo preference as well as subsidies on fuel. The new company is to be known as the Saudi Oil Transport Company (SOTC) and it will be 30% owned by the government, 30% by other Saudi transportation companies, and the remaining 40% by private investors. This latest development has resulted in some comment in the maritime industry, since the position of Saudi Arabia as one of the leading Arab exporting nations, with a tremendous amount of capital at its command, would make SOTC a major power in the international tanker fleet if it were to develop as planned.

If the Saudis' plan to subsidize bunkers takes place, it would not only reduce the cost of oil to the consumer, but would also put other tankers at a competitive disadvantage.

Other joint ventures operating in Saudi Arabia include the Saudi International Petroleum Carrier, Inc., which was recently announced as a joint venture with Texaco; Saudinaft Tankers Co., with participation by British and Dutch interests; Red Sea Saudi Arabian Maritime Company, and Saudi Arabian Shipping Company, Ltd. (SASCO)both of which are joint ventures with Japanese interests; and Saudi Arabian International Transport Co., which is a joint venture with Standard Oil of California; and Safina, with the Swedish Salen group.

It is likely that Arab growth in the ownership and operation of tankers will continue. In a study by the U. S. Maritime Administration, it was concluded that the Arab petroleum exporting states "have repeatedly declared their intent to control their oil and its delivery" and quoted one Kuwaiti shipping executive as saying that Arabs should own at least 60% of the world's fleet.[1]

LINER TRADES AND TRAMP STEAMERS

As noted above, the large growth in oil revenues in the Middle Eastern states has generated new capital projects and demand for consumer goods which has resulted in a tremendous increase in the bilateral trade between these countries and the rest of the world. The Middle Eastern states have so far not developed their full capacity in terms of operating their own liner companies.

---

[1] *Supra*, Note 1, p.2

One reason for this is their lack of experience in liner shipping and the Arabs have approached it with some caution, relying primarily on joint ventures and charter arrangements. Moreover, the existing liner operators include many large well-established companies that have been successful in developing a substantial amount of trade over the years. In addition, since much of the trade is one way, going outbound from the U.S. and Europe, shippers have often had a good deal of say in choosing the carrier and have supported domestic carriers in many instances.

The main Middle Eastern effort in the liner shipping trades has been the United Arab Shipping Company (UASC)[1] which was set up in 1977 by Saudi Arabia, and five other Arab states. UASC began by taking over ships owned by the Kuwait Shipping Company and ordered some 43 other vessels with a total of over 60 ships expected soon. Regular liner service between Saudi Arabia and the United States is also provided by Saudi National Lines.[2]

---

[1] UASC advertises U.S. service from Houston, New Orleans, Newport News, Baltimore and New York to Kuwait, Dubai, Abu Dhabi, Bahrain and Dammam. Its advertisements refer to USAC as the national flag line of the Arabian states of Saudi Arabia, UAE, Bahrain, Qatar, Kuwait and Iraq. See, e.g., Journal of Commerce, November 3, 1977.

[2] Leaves New York, Baltimore and Miami to Jeddah, Dammam and other Middle Eastern ports. See, e.g., Journal of Commerce, March 10, 1978, page 14.

A number of joint venture operations between Middle Eastern and Western states also exist in the liner trades. These include the joint container service from the United Kingdom to the Middle Eastern Gulf, named Arabian Peninsular Container Line, the Saudi International Shipping Company, set up by Saudi and Finnish interests and the Saudi-Orient Maritime Company, involving Saudi and Western interests.

OTHER FACTORS AFFECTING THE DEVELOPMENT OF SAUDI ARABIAN MERCHANT MARINE.

There are a number of other factors which have also influenced the development of the Saudi Arabian merchant marine. One of the limitations of a more extensive Saudi fleet has been the lack of development of the Saudi ports. However, there is evidence that this situation is changing and in the future, the ports in Saudi Arabia would be more than adequate to meet the growth in marine commerce, both of Saudi flag vessels and foreign flag vessels. Saudi Arabia itself has allocated approximately four billion dollars to port development. Much of this has been allocated to the development of Jeddah, which presently has 10 deep water berths, each with shoreside cranes and a RO/RO berth. In addition, Jeddah now has a container terminal which is privately owned. The planned port expansion is due to be completed by 1982, at which time the port will have close to 40 berths.

Dammam has been another port development project in Saudi Arabia. At present, there are 24 berths in operation, which include two RO/RO berths. There are plans to add at least an additional 16 berths, and at least four of these are planned to be devoted to container operations. Additional port expansion is planned for Jubail, which is part of the Al Jubail development project. When fully operational, the port will have around 20 berths, including container and bulk cargo capacity.

Facilities for ship construction and repair has also limited growth. The principal facility has been the Arab Shipbuilding and Repair Yard (ASRY) begun in 1968 as a joint venture involving Bahrain, Iraq, Kuwait, Libya, Qatar, Saudi Arabia and the United Arab Emirates. However, individual countries including Saudi Arabia have been developing plans for their own shipyards.

The final limitation on the development of the Saudi merchant marine, which effects not only Saudi Arabia, but also the other Middle Eastern nations, has been the lack of trained personnel to operate aboard these ships. Considerable money and planning has been devoted towards developing merchant marine training facilities in the Middle East in the last few years. and it is anticipated that there will be locally trained officers in the not too distant future. At least one academy is planned for Saudi Arabia and others are presently in existence in Egypt, and other countries.

One problem in training officers is that the lack of national flag vessels has not provided sufficient amount of training capacity at sea. As the Arab fleets develop, this should be less of a problem. However, it may very well be that the Middle Eastern maritime academies might seek increasingly to convince trading partners such as the U.S. and others to take their cadets on training cruises aboard foreign flag vessels.[1]

SAUDI ARABIAN LEGAL SYSTEM.

Before trying to understand the Saudi Arabian maritime law, it is important to give a brief introduction to the Saudi Arabian legal system for those who are not familiar with it. Saudi Arabia, like most Moslem states, has a legal system that is inextricably meshed with the Moslem religion. Although recent efforts have been made to codify laws and to increase the number of commercial statutes, the basic Saudi Arabian jurisprudence is still based on the teachings of Mohammed, as reflected in the Koran.

---

[1] Information about Arab and Saudi fleets changes constantly. Information used herein was obtained from a number of sources including The Journal of Commerce; "Arab Shipping: Poised for a Take Off," a 1975 Seatrade magazine report; Arab Shipping, 1978, also published by Seatrade magazine (which contains specific data for those needing to go beyond this general discussion); and the U.S. Department of Commerce, Maritime Administration.

There are two primary sources of modern Islamic law referred to as "Shariah". These are the Koran and the Al-Sunna, loosely translated as "The Way of the Prophet". These are the seminal documents in the Moslem system of religious law and establish many of the basic principles that are followed today. Further interpretations of Islamic jurisprudence are contained in the "Concensus of Opinion" which consists of agreements reached by Islamic scholars regarding the acceptance of certain principles of jurisprudence that are not explicitly established in either the Al Sunna or the Koran.

The actual administration of the legal system is quite decentralized. Much of the power remains in the local emirs and sheiks. However, in the earlier part of the 20th century a unified judicial system was established.[1] This system generally administered the Shariah law, in addition to enforcing royal decrees. The king can issue royal decrees to supplement the Shariah law when new situations arise that are not covered in the Shariah law. Traditionally, direct appeals to the king in the form of petitions were permitted to seek redress of grievances.

---

1 For more extensive discussion of the court system, see Solaim "Saudi Arabia's Judicial System" reprinted in The Middle East Journal, pp. 403-406 (Summer, 1971).

Today, the traditional Shariah law still governs most legal matters involving the family, criminal conduct, property, and personal injury. The lower court system deals with minor claims and are presided over by Qadis, who are Islamic judges, appointed by a chief Qadi. There are higher courts which handle more difficult matters, and a special appeals court which hears appeals from both.

Generally, jury trials are unknown in the Saudi system. The cases are usually heard by a single Qadi, who acts partially in the role of an investigating magistrate and cross-examines parties and witnesses. The Qadi determines both guilt and innocence and the amount of damages. In certain criminal cases the actual sentence may be determined by a local emir with the advice of judicial and religious advisory groups known as "Ulema".

Because the Shariah legal system was designed to deal with a semi-feudal society that had not yet reached the industrialized age, it has been found somewhat inadequate to deal with the modern commercial problems now facing a growing state such as Saudi Arabia. Therefore, increasingly commercial problems are handled by the issuance of royal decrees and there also have been increasing codification of laws dealing with investment and foreign trade. While royal decrees are not necessarily based on law contained in the

Shariah, in order to be consistent with the religious underpinnings of the law, it is presumed that royal decrees will be consistent with the Shariah. However, it is understood that in case of direct conflicts, the Shariah law would prevail. Decree disputes are often initially decided by emirs and a grievance board has been established to determine appeals in disputes where the government is a party, including the enforcement of foreign judgments. In addition, other government tribunals have been established such as the Commission on Settlement of Commercial Disputes.[1]

SAUDI ARABIAN MARITIME LAWS AND REGULATIONS.

The remaining sections deal with a description and discussion of a number of the main laws and regulations dealing with the regulation of maritime transportation in Saudi Arabia. A number of preliminary caveats are in order.

Firstly, because of the nature of the Saudi Arabian legal system, whereby laws can be created, altered, and modified by royal decree, it necessarily follows that one must continuously check to find whether laws are still

---

[1] The Saudi Council of Ministers, in Decision No. 58, dated June 25, 1963, established that the Grievance Board has jurisdiction over all disputes arising from governmental contracting with a Saudi or foreign party. Conceivably, this decision would mean that the Grievance Board might have jurisdiction despite international arbitration clauses in any contract between Saudis and foreign entities.

in effect or if changes have been made. Therefore, while every attempt has been made to provide the most recent information, persons contemplating activities in Saudi Arabia, are well-advised to check to make sure what current regulations are in effect.

Secondly, it is rather difficult to obtain accurate information about developments in Saudi Arabia. The embassy and consulates in the United States very often do not have copies of decrees relating to maritime matters and one must often rely on Embassy cables and secondary sources in the trade to get up to date information.

Given this situation, plus the absence of available materials in English, and an inaccessible body of case law, it is difficult to keep completely up to date on developments in this area.

A. Regulations for Seaports, Harbors and Lighthouses.

Perhaps the largest single body of codified, accessible, Saudi Arabian maritime law is contained in the regulations for seaports, harbors and lighthouses. These regulations were initially promulgated July, 1974, by royal decree and consolidated a number of prior regulations.[1] The

[1] See Royal Decree, No. 38, May 11, 1958, Royal Order No. 318/218, May 14, 1934, and Council of Ministers Decision No. 934, dated July 9, 1974.

regulations were implemented by the Minister of Communications on October 14, 1975.[1]

The regulations consist of 25 chapters covering many areas of interest relating to maritime law.

SECTION BY SECTION ANALYSIS.

General Discussion.

The regulations for seaports, harbors and lighthouses was formulated by the Council of Ministers, in Decision No. 934, July 9, 1974. A report was initially drawn up by a committee composed of the Minister of Communications, the Minister of Information, the Minister of State, the head of the Disciplinary Board, and the Director-General of the Frontier Force and Coast Guard. It consists of two parts, the actual regulations which would be more akin to what we would consider statutory law and the rules, which would be similar to the rules promulgated by administrative agencies in the United States.

It was determined that the Minister of Communications shall have the power to administer the ports, harbors and lighthouses within the Kingdom of Saudi Arabia, except to the extent that the Council of Ministers shall entrust this power to other agencies. The regulations empowered the Minister of Communications to issue such rules necessary

---

1 See Ministerial Decision No. 181, October 14, 1975.

to implement the regulations, provided that such rules should not be inconsistent with international conventions to which Saudi Arabia is a member, or with international navigation or quarantine regulations. The matters in which the Minister of Communications is authorized to adopt rules include the following:

1. Use by the public of port and harbor facilities, equipment and property and permitting shipping agencies to exercise their activities within port and harbor zones.

2. All operations, formalities and arrangements relating to the loading and unloading of ordinary and dangerous cargo onto and from marine craft, as well as the handling and storage of such cargo within the port or harbor zone, and the withdrawal of such cargo from storage areas, determining responsibility in cases of shortage, damage or loss in accordance with the regulations in force and in conjunction with the agencies concerned, if necessary.

3. Maintaining the safety and cleanliness of ports and harbors and their navigation channels and docks, and securing the safety of lighthouses.

4. The use of lights, call signals and the use of fire.

5. Navigation within the sea limits of ports and harbors and the approaches thereto and to lighthouses, including the entry, anchoring and mooring of marine craft, determining the procedures, times and places of berthing, the arrangements for their operations, as well as the sailing and departure of such craft.

6. Obtaining from incoming and outgoing marine craft (and their agents, if any) all information pertaining to such craft as is necessary to arrange the procedures for their admission into, berthing at and departure from any port or harbor.

7. Use of whistles, alarm horns and wireless apparatus by marine craft within the limits of ports and harbors.

8. Taking the necessary actions to ascertain that marine craft fulfill safety and security requirements, and examining their documents and certificates.

9. Recording title to marine craft and (subsequent) conveyances of such title, as well as any distraints, mortgages or liens thereon, and regulating the formalities for hoisting the Kingdom's flag on such craft.

10. Registration of ocean-going ships and steamers carrying the Kingdom's flag; determining their registered tonnage, their international tonnage and designating the load lines (draught) of such ships and steamers and the issuance of the certificates and documents in this respect.

11. Issuance of safety and seaworthiness certificates to ocean-going ships and steamers in accordance with the requirements of customary maritime rules, and issuance of seaworthiness certificates in respect of other marine craft, including fishing boats operating in the territorial waters and within the ports and harbors of the Kingdom, as well as pleasure boats of all kinds, and the registration and matriculation of said craft and issuing their licenses on the basis of such certificates.

12. Piloting operations and the profession of pilots.

13. Ship chandlery operations and the activities of peddlers and others, such as stevedores and porters working within the boundaries of ports, and issuing their necessary licenses.

14. Procedures to be followed in cases of marine collision and other marine disasters such as fire or sinking, including investigation of accidents in conjunction with the agencies concerned, and drawing up the necessary reports and endorsing marine reports.

15. Salvage and wrecks within the boundaries of ports and harbors.

16. Specifying the conditions for the exercise of the profession of Master, Officer, Engineer, Stoker, Seaman,

Fisherman, Diver and other persons working at sea, and issuing their necessary licenses.

17. Issuance of seamans' passports after referring to the security agencies concerned.

The Minister of Communications is also empowered to prescribe penalties for violation of these rules consistent with the penalty provisions in the regulations.

An enforcement procedure was set up to ensure compliance with the regulations and rules. The Minister of Communications has the power to appoint those persons with the responsibility for reporting violations of the regulations and the rules and investigating such violations in cooperation with the Frontier Force and Coast Guard and the Customs authorities. The results of the investigations are reported to the Minister of Communications or his representative, with recommendations of an Investigations Committee as to the dosposition of the case. This Investigations Committee has the power to detain persons accused of committing a violation of the rules and regulations, and to prevent that person from leaving Saudi Arabia for a period necessary to complete the proceedings, or a maximum of three days. This period can be extended at the request of the Investigations Committee by written request, including a summary of the charges and a reason justifying the request. This extended period ranges from 30 to 90 days, depending on the type of offense involved. If the offense would be punishable by imprisonment for more than six months, then the detention can last for more than 30 days, but not longer than 90 days. In addition, the Investigations Committee has the power to require the person accused under the rules and regulations to post bail up to the amount of the maximum penalty provided for under the rules and regulations, in lieu of detaining that person within the Kingdom.

In addition, the Investigations Committee has the power to order the release of a person from detention at its discretion. It is interesting that the amount of the ultimate sentence or fine is reduced by any amount of time spent in detention or bail that had been paid. Interestingly, if the final determination involve a fine only, it can be reduced by the amount of 100 _riyals_ for each day of detention.

Generally, the Minister of Communications has the final say as to whether a violation of the rules and regulations has occurred. However, where the recommendation of the Investigations Committee is that of imprisonment, then the accused is entitled to further recourse before a special commission.

The special commission is a quasi-judicial body formed to try those who contravene provisions of the regulations, and of rules and decisions implementing them. The special commission consists of an advisor chosen by the Minister of Communications, an advisor chosen by the Minister of the Interior, and an advisor chosen by the Minister of Finance and National Economy.

If the trial involves a violation relating to maritime law, then the Minister of Communications may appoint a maritime expert to sit upon the commission. A maritime violation is one that involves a violation of the rules of maritime navigation within the boundaries of the port or harbor or its approach channels or during the entry into the port or harbor or movement or anchorage therein, sailing or departure therefrom or from a violation of the rules of pilotage or safety and security relating to the ship.

The special commissions also are empowered, with the assistance of the maritime expert, to determine responsibility in case of collisions occurring in Saudi territorial waters and determine whether or not the rules and regulations have been violated during the course of the collision. However, this power is not exclusive and does not prevent other agencies of the Saudi government from inflicting their own penalties. The commission's main responsibility is to determine responsibility for the collision and not to determine individual claims and disputes which would be handled by the judiciary or administrative agencies.

Certain procedural safeguards are provided for those who are subject to possible criminal penalties before a commission. These include the right to be assisted in the defense by legal counsel authorized to practice within Saudi Arabia; the right to review reports, investigation transcripts, and contents of case files and to reproduce these; the right to cross-examine witnesses; call witnesses; and to present oral and written defenses before the commission. However, the regulations do require the accused to attend his trial in person and the commission is empowered to order the arrest and detention of a person if he fails to attend his trial hearing after being duly summoned. The decisions of the commissions must be by at least absolute majority vote.

Chapter I.

Comments

Chapter I contains definitions of various terms used throughout the text of the regulations.

Chapter I

Article 1 - Definitions

(A) "Regulations" are the Regulations for Ports and Harbors issued by Royal Decree No. M/27, dated 24 Jumada II 1394 (14 July 1974).

(B) Directorate

Is the body of officials appointed for administering the affairs of the whole facilities of a port or a harbor, and for supervising the smooth and orderly running thereof.

(C) Port or Harbor Director

Means the head of the body of officials who are appointed to administer the affairs and activities of the port or harbor, as well as the person who acts on his behalf within the limits of the powers vested in him.

(D) Traffic Director

Means the person assigned for managing the Traffic Division of the port or harbor, or the person who acts on his behalf within the limits of the powers vested in him.

(E) Port or Harbor Controller

Means the person appointed to supervise the activities of the Marine Division of the port, and to implement the regulations and rules relative to marine affairs, or the person who acts on his behalf within the limits of the powers vested in him.

(F) Persons

Means corporeal persons (individuals) and juridicial persons (companies, public and private establishments.)

(G) Captain

Means any qualified person whom the owner of a ship assigns for commanding the ship.

(H) Pilot

Means any qualified person who is officially appointed or authorized by the Ministry of Communications to undertake the guidance of ships in the Saudi ports and harbors.

(I) Berth

Means the place within the port which the Directorate assigns to a ship for the purposes of loading, unloading, disembarking, embarking, bunkering, watering, etc.

(J) Dangerous Goods

Means the dangerous goods included in the Inter-Governmental Maritime Consultative Organization (IMCO)'s classification, which are unloaded or loaded in the port, and against which IMCO's classification number is given.

(K) Owner in Relation to a Ship

Is the person who has legal title to the ship in accordance with the registration certificate. The charterer, the mortgagee in possession of the ship, and the owner's agent, shall each have the status of "owner".

(L) Owner in Relation to Goods

Is the person who has legal possession of the bill of lading or of the shipping documents, whether he be the consignor or the consignee.

(M) Port Zone

Includes all berths, quays, places allocated for loading and unloading operations, and other places located within the port limits.

(N) Port Limits

Are the maritime boundaries of the port in accordance with the latitudes and longitudes approved by the Ministers of Interior and Communications with regard to each port.

(O) Day

Is fixed from six o'clock A.M. (0600) up to six o'clock A.M. of the following day.

(P) Master

Means any qualified person who commands a floating craft and is in charge of it.

(Q) Navigation Officer

Means any person, not being a pilot, who actually steers, and who is responsible for steering, a ship, during his duty period.

(R) Ship's Chief Engineer

Means any person who is continuously responsible for operating the mechanical driving power of the ship.

(S) Ship's Marine Engineer

Means any person who actually operates the ship's engines and who is responsible for the shift.

(T) Outfitter

Is the person who is entrusted by the owner to administer the affairs of the ship.

(U) Ship

Is any floating craft which is used in marine transport operations in accordance with the internationally applied regulations.

Chapter II

Comments

Chapter II deals with general rules, mostly relating to activities in the port zone that effect safety and security.

Chapter II

General Rules

Article 2 The port or harbor directorate shall declare the times assigned for loading, unloading, carrying, storage and withdrawal of the goods from the ware - and storehouses, as well as the times of entry of the ships into, and their departure from, the port or harbor.

Article 3 The Directorate's divisions shall be closed Fridays and official holidays of the Kingdom. Work at the divisions concerned shall continue in the port at the request of those concerned, subject to collection of such overtime charges as are prescribed by the regulations.

Article 4 The port or harbor zone shall be considered a closed area for the public (individuals), the entry of which shall be prohibited except by a special permission from the Port Directorate.

Article 5 Entry into and exit from the port zone shall be through the entrances and exits fixed therefor.

Article 6 Vehicles and marine craft shall follow the instructions issued by the Port Directorate.

Article 7 Nobody other than the ship's crew and the passengers may board the ships that are berthed in the port save by a special permit from the Port Directorate.

Article 8 Photographing within the port limit is prohibited save by a special permission from the authorities concerned.

Article 9 Swimming or fishing within the port zone is prohibited.

Article 10 Smoking and fire kindling within the storehouses or storage yards are not permissible.

<u>Article 11</u> Permits shall be issued by the Port Directorate after completion of the necessary formalities with the competent authorities as required.

<u>Article 12</u> Vehicles and inland means of transportation shall be subject to search by the competent authorities on entry or exit through the port's gates.

<u>Article 13</u> The competent authorities shall have the right to search persons within the port zone and on their entry or exit in the event of suspicion.

<u>Chapter III</u>

<u>Comments</u>

Chapter III is concerned with specific port rules and is divided into a number of parts relating to such areas as entry into the port, pilotage, towage and unloading of goods. The rules require 24 hours advance notice of arrival. This rule apparently applies to both Saudi and non-Saudi vessels. A curious provision, which on its face applies to all vessels, requires a ship to hoist the Saudi Arabian flag upon entering the port zone and to fly the flag until it exits, perhaps to reaffirm Saudi control over the vessel while in port. Pilotage is compulsory for all non-governmental merchant vessels. Priorities for berthing are established and safety regulations are prescribed.

The rules provide for the documentation which must be provided upon entry. The documents are similar in many respects to those required by U.S. Customs. Some of these documents (and comparable U.S. requirements) are: Notice of Arrival[1], cargo declarations [2], Declaration of non-dutiable supplies[3], Declaration of crews' effects [4] and Passenger Lists.[5]

Chapter III

Rules for Ports

Part 1 - Entry into and Exit from Ports

Article 14 Ships which are bound for a Saudi port or harbor shall notify the Port Directorate, either by wireless or through their agents, at least twenty-four hours before their expected time of arrival.

Article 15 The notice of arrival shall include the following particulars:

1) The approximate draught of the ship upon arrival at the port.

2) The quantity and nature of the cargo the ship will unload or load at the port.

3) The quantity and kind of the required fuel and fresh water.

4) Number of passengers on board.

5) The dangerous goods on board (if any).

---

[1] See 19 USC 1433 for comparable U.S. Customs regulations.

[2] See 19 USC 143.

[3] See 19 CFR §4.7(a) - U.S. Customs Form 1303.

[4] See 19 CFR §4.7(b) - U.S. Customs Form 5123.

[5] See 19 CFR 4.50.

<u>Article 16</u> Ships which enter the port in the cases of:

1) Emergency refuge.

2) Force majeure.

3) Medical aid request.

shall be excepted from the provisions of Articles 14 and 15.

<u>Article 17</u> A ship on her way to port shall, on arrival at the pilotage zone, hoist her identification letters and the flag of the State to which she belongs.

<u>Article 18</u> Upon entering the port zone, a ship shall hoist the flag of the Kingdom of Saudi Arabia. This flag shall remain hoisted as long as the ship remains in port and until her exit from the zone.

<u>Article 19</u> Ships in tow shall, before entering a port, obtain a permit from the Directorate.

<u>Article 20</u> A ship which is infected, or which carries a patient suffering from a contagious disease, or which is suspected of carrying a contagious or epidemic disease, shall give the port authorities, by wireless, at least a twelve-hour prior notice of her time of arrival. It shall wait at the anchorage zone until the quarantine medical officer comes on board. She shall not be allowed entry except by permission of the competent authorities.

<u>Article 21</u> A ship which carries dangerous goods shall notify the pilot when he boards the ship to provide pilotage service.

<u>Article 22</u> During their movement within the port limits, all ships shall follow the international rules for the prevention of collision at sea.

Article 23 A ship may not leave port before completing the departure formalities and obtaining a departure permit from the competent authorities.

Part 2 - Pilotage

Article 24 Pilotage shall be compulsory in the ports of the Kingdom for all ships on their entry into, movement within, or exit from, the pilotage zone, against payment of the prescribed fee.

Article 25 The pilotage zone for each port of the Kingdom shall be defined by a decision to be issued by the Minister of Communications.

Article 26 As an exception from the provisions of Article 24, the following shall be exempted from compulsory pilotage:

1) Saudi warships.

2) Ships of the Saudi Arabian Government which are not assigned for commercial activities.

3) Ships whose net tonnage is less than one hundred and fifty (150) tons.

4) Marine craft belonging to ports.

5) Pleasure yachts.

Article 27 Any ship which is subject to compulsory pilotage shall, on her entry into, or movement within, the pilotage zone, hoist on her mast the signal for calling a pilot.

Article 28 The ship's captain shall advise the pilot of the information pertaining to the ship's draught, length, width, maneuverability under various draught and speed conditions. These particulars shall be displayed in a conspicuous place in the wheel house.

Article 29 The Port Directorate shall not be liable for any loss or damage occurring to the ship or to a third party as a result of the employment of the pilot.

<u>Article 30</u> The ship shall be liable for any loss or damage occurring to a third party during pilotage operations.

<u>Article 31</u> A ship shall be liable for any loss or damage occurring to the pilot's boat during the pilot's boarding or leaving the ship.

<u>Article 32</u> In case the pilot is obliged to depart with the ship by reason of bad weather conditions or at the request of the captain, the ship shall be liable for all his expenses arising from such departure until his return to the port, in addition to her paying one hundred <u>riyals</u> for each day of the pilot's absence from the port.

<u>Article 33</u> The ship's captain shall prepare the pilot's ladder in accordance with the specifications and conditions required in the International Convention for Safety of Life at Sea.

Part 3 - Berthing

<u>Article 34</u> The ship's captain shall, before entry into the quay zone, notify the pilot of any technical defects which impair the ship's maneuverability for docking at her assigned berth.

<u>Article 35</u> The Port Directorate shall fix the ship's berth. The captain may not change the ship's berth, whether at dockside or at anchorage, without the permission of the Port Directorate, except for the cases when the safety of the ship, persons or properties is vulnerable.

<u>Article 36</u> Priority of admission to the quays shall be determined in the following order:

1) Ships in distress.

2) Passenger/pilgrim ships.

3) Cargo ships:

   a) Ships carrying livestock.

   b) Ships carrying frozen goods.

   c) Ships carring general cargo.

Article 37 The Port Directorate assumes no responsibility for any loss or damage occurring to a ship by reason of, or during her presence at berth.

Article 38 The ship shall be liable for any loss or damage occurring to third parties or to the port's property as a result of unsafe or improper berthing.

Part 4

Safety of Persons and Property

Article 39 A ship berthed alongside the quay shall place rat screens on her mooring ropes and wires.

Article 40 A ship at anchor in the port may not send down divers to perform any work on her keel without prior permission from the Directorate.

Article 41 The ship's propellers may not be tested whilst the ship is berthed alongside a quay.

Article 42 Use of wireless sets is prohibited during the ship's presence in the port.

Article 43 All launches, sail boats and fishing boats shall not obstruct the passage of ships in the navigation corridor within the port.

Article 44 Ships at anchor in the port shall not carry out any repairs in, or lower any persons into the fuel or ballast tanks of the ship without first obtaining a certificate from the competent authorities at the Port Directorate that such tanks are free of any gas.

Article 45 A ship carrying dangerous goods shall abstain from any act which may cause a fire. Smoking shall be prohibited on her deck throughout her presence in the port.

Article 46 Passengers shall embark or disembark at the points assigned for this purpose.

Article 47 The Port Directorate shall have the right to detain any ship which has caused injuries or damages to the quays or installations until compensation is paid or guarantee of payment is provided by the ship's owner or agent.

Part 5

Towage

Article 48 Requests for towage shall be submitted to the Port Directorate at least two hours before the service is needed.

Article 49 The captain of the tugboat shall act under the supervision of the ship's captain or of the pilot.

Article 50 The ship in tow shall not be liable for the damage occurring to tugboats during towage operations.

Article 51 The ship's captain shall be considered responsible for accidents which occur to his ship during towage operations.

Part 6

Special Declarations (to be submitted) Upon Entry into and Exit from Ports

Article 52 Every ship shall, upon entry into a port of the Kingdom, submit the following declarations which are attached to the Rules:

1) General declaration (arrival)

2) Cargo declaration

3) Declaration of supplies not subject to customs duties

4) Declaration of the crew's personal effects

5) List of the names of the ship's crew

6) List of the names of passengers on board

7) Documents pertaining to the carriage of mail (if any is carried), in accordance with the International Postal Convention.

Article 53 The ship's captain shall upon his arrival at the port notify the local authorities of the passengers aboard his ship.

Article 54 Passengers may not disembark from the ship before completion of the health formalities and issuance of the necessary permission by the competent authorities.

Article 55 The documents which a ship is required to submit with the arrival declaration are:

1) Certificate of registration of the ship.

2) Marine health declaration.

3) Certificate of deratization or of freedom from rats.

4) Certificate of grain shipment, if the ship is carrying a shipment of grain.

Article 56 The documents which a ship is required to submit in order to obtain a departure permit are:

1) Certificate of registration of the ship.

2) International Load Lines Certificate.

3) Certificate of safety equipment for cargo ships.

4) Certificate of safe construction for cargo ships.

5) Certificate of safety for passenger ships.

6) Certificate of safety of the wireless telegraph equipment.

7) Certificate of safety of the radio-telephone equipment.

8) Certificate of deck cargo (if the ship is carrying cargo on deck).

9) Receipt for customs duties, port dues and health fees paid.

10) Cargo declaration and goods manifest.

Chapter IV

Comments

Chapter IV deals with internal port regulations relating to unloading of goods, port services and safety. Unladen goods are required to be moved from the pier area within three days, apparently in an effort to avoid port congestion. A distinction is drawn between ordinary goods and valuable goods, the latter necessitating a special shipping declaration. Dangerous goods are subject to the rules established by the International Maritime classification of dangerous goods issued by the Intergovenmental Maritime Consultive Organization (IMCO). Particular safety precautions are prescribed relating to the inspection of holds of tankers to prevent gassing accidents.

Chapter IV

Goods

Part 1 - Loading and Unloading of Goods

Article 57 It is prohibited to commence loading and unloading operations before (obtaining) the permission of the Port Directorate.

<u>Article 58</u> The Port Directorate shall have the right to refuse the loading or unloading of goods which it considers to be potentially dangerous to life or property.

<u>Article 59</u> The Port Directorate shall have the right, after notifying the customs and the competent authorities, to dispose of or destroy damaged goods which may cause injury to the installations or to public health.

<u>Article 60</u> Goods may not be loaded on a ship before completion of the customs formalities.

<u>Article 61</u> The Port Directorate shall have the right to ascertain the safe loading and stowage of the goods, as well as the ship's equilibrium and seaworthiness.

<u>Article 62</u> The Port Directorate shall have the right to issue an order to the ship to vacate the wharf in the event of the loading and unloading operations falling short of the port's average.

<u>Article 63</u> The Port Directorate's responsibility shall be limited to the particulars recorded in the bill of lading.

<u>Article 64</u> Packages on which there are reservations or which are loose shall have their conditions determined in the presence of representatives of the port and the customs, and the ship's representative or agent.

<u>Article 65</u> Goods shall be unloaded according to their marks which are recorded in the manifest.

<u>Article 66</u> With the exception of valuable goods, the receipt voucher relates only to the outward appearance of the packages, and not to their contents, conditions, weights, measurements or costs.

<u>Article 67</u> The receipt voucher in respect of the goods that have been unloaded on the quay in accordance with the original number of packages shall be handed over to the captain or agent, after settlement of the reservations, if any, and after reconciliation with the ship's manifest.

Article 68 A tallyman shall be assigned to record the number of unloaded packages, and the reservations, if any, in special statements for delivery to the Port Directorate and to the customs.

Article 69 Goods may not be left on the quay for more than three days. The Port Directorate shall, without any liability on its part, have the right to move the goods thereafter to the storage yards, and to charge the agent or the owner of the goods with all expenses.

Article 70 The Port Directorate is not responsible for the goods which remain on the barges at the request of the captain or of the agent.

Article 71 The Port Directorate is not responsible for what would occur to the goods which the ship's agent receives on the quay and moves to the bonded warehouses. He shall be responsible for delivery of the goods to the storehouse according to the cargo manifest submitted by the ship.

Article 72 Livestock may not be off-loaded or brought for loading except at the time of delivery or loading.

Article 73 The Port Directorate is not responsible for injuries which occur to the goods and which are attributable to war risks, weather conditions, self-deterioration, leakage or bad packing after the receipt thereof.

Article 74 No goods that are bound for other ports may be unloaded save by a written permission from the Port Directorate and from the customs.

Part 2 - Valuable Goods

Article 75 A separate shipping declaration shall be submitted in respect of valuable goods. These shall be recorded in a special register which shall be signed by the competent official at the port, the ship's representative and the customs representative.

Article 76 Loading or unloading of valuable packages shall only take place during daytime hours.

Article 77 The value, marks and number of the contents, and the names of the consignor and the consignee, shall be recorded in the manifest.

Part 3 - Dangerous Goods

Article 78 The International Maritime Classification of Dangerous Goods issued by the Inter-Governmental Maritime Consultative Organization (IMCO) and the amendments thereto which were issued by the said Organization shall be applied in all activities relating to the loading, unloading or storage of dangerous goods on ships or in the Saudi ports.

Article 79 All ships carrying dangerous goods shall notify the port authorities at least forty-eight hours before their arrival, save in emergency cases. The Port Directorate shall, after agreement with the public security and other authorities concerned at the port, fix the minimum limit of the quantities of dangerous goods which arrive on ships and which must be declared, on the basis of the circumstances and nature of each port. A notice to this effect shall be published.

Article 80 The Port Directorate shall lay down instructions for the local pilots and the ships' captains for regulating the pilotage, movement and anchorage of ships which carry dangerous goods.

Article 81 Unloading of dangerous goods shall commence immediately on arrival of the ship, after submission of the dangerous goods declaration, copy attached, to the port authorities, together with a list of the dangerous goods on board, the loading plan thereof, the quantities that will be unloaded at the port and the quantities that will remain on board.

Article 82 Storage of dangerous goods shall not be allowed save in the places assigned therefor.

Article 83 The period of stay of dangerous goods that are stored in the places assigned therefor in the ports shall not exceed seven days. The Port Directorate shall organize daily inspection of these places by trained and qualified persons.

Article 84 The instruments and equipment used in handling dangerous goods shall meet the specifications and terms issued by the International Labor Organization.

Article 85 If the unloading is on the quay, a temporary enclosure shall be made around the unloading area. The safety distance should be kept between the ship carrying the dangerous cargo and the other ships. The international signs indicating the unloading of dangerous goods shall be hoisted and the dangerous goods shall be moved forthwith to the places assigned to them.

Article 86 Smoking or the use of fire in the unloading area shall be prohibited.

Article 87 Unloading of dangerous goods shall be stopped at night or during inclement weather conditions.

Article 88 The use of transmission sets, radar, cooking ranges and ovens shall be stopped during the loading and unloading of dangerous goods.

Article 89 The workmen who undertake the loading and unloading of dangerous goods shall be fully conversant with the safe methods for handling such goods.

Article 90 The ship's captain is responsible to see to it that all dangerous goods which will be unloaded at the port are numbered and marked in accordance with the International Maritime Classification of Dangerous Goods.

Article 91 The tallymen of the dangerous goods that are unloaded from the ship shall be available at all times.

Article 92 Where the dangerous goods are discharged on floating craft, the person in charge of the craft shall be handed a statement of the number, type, quantity and figure of the goods that have been discharged on the craft in accordance with IMCO's classification. A copy of the statement shall be delivered to the representative of the Port Directorate.

Article 93 Where there is a possibility of danger, the port authorities shall forthwith provide all necessary means and precautions, including evacuation of the place and moving the adjacent or nearby ships away during the acts of loading, unloading and transporting the dangerous goods.

Article 94 The port authorities shall notify the civil service (authority) before unloading dangerous goods in the port, whether on the quay or at the anchorage.

Article 95 The port authorities shall protect the safety of life and property when dangerous goods are being unloaded.

Article 96 Entry of persons into the ship's holds and other parts containing bulk shipments which are oxidizable or which cause heat or any similar factor that may lead to lack of oxygen or may develop poisonous gases, shall not be allowed save after ascertaining that the ship's captain or the officer in charge has taken all necessary safety precautions, and after making sure that the safety of the persons entering the said holds is guaranteed.

In emergency cases, only persons who are trained in (entering) such holds shall be allowed entry, provided they should wear automatic respirators and protective clothing.

Part 4 - Services

Article 97 Applications for watering or bunkering shall be submitted at least twenty-four hours before they are required.

Article 98 Application for the installation of a telephone in the ship shall be submitted as soon as the ship lays anchor at the berth.

Article 99 Applications for hire of loading and unloading tools and equipment shall be submitted to the Port Directorate in accordance with procedures laid down by the Directorate.

Article 100 Invoices in respect of services performed for the ship shall be settled within a maximum period of fifteen days. The Directorate may take all appropriate proceedings in the event of non-settlement, including refusal of future service of ships belonging to the failing party.

Article 101 Local launches available at the port shall be used. Ships may not use their launches save in emergency cases and after the approval of the competent authorities.

Part 5 - Fire

Article 102 Every ship shall as soon as it enters the port prepare the fire fighting equipment for use.

Article 103 In the event of fire breaking out during its anchorage within the port, a ship shall call for help from the port authorities through the port's signalling tower by means of light signals, international flags or by any other means available at the port.

Article 104 The ship's captain shall see to it that a sufficient number of the crew is available while the ship is lying at the port.

Article 105 The ship's captain shall cooperate with the port authorities and execute their directions with regard to fire fighting on the ship.

Article 106 In the event of its berthing alongside the wharf, the ship's captain shall call for help from the Civil Service Division at the port.

Article 107 In the case of fire breaking on a ship, the boarding of workmen or non-interested persons, shall be prevented save by permission of the ship's captaiun or his representative.

Chapter V

Comments

This chapter sets out general provisions relating to use of marine pilots in Saudi ports. It provides that minor offenses committed by pilots are under the jurisdiction of the port director while major offenses involving loss of life or property come within the jurisdiction of the Special Commissions.

Chapter V

Marine Pilots

Article 108 No one shall practice the profession of pilot in the ports of the Kingdom except after obtaining a pilots' qualification certificate in accordance with the conditions to be laid down by the Ministry of Communications.

Article 109 The certificate of qualification shall be issued over the signature of the Minister of Communications.

Article 110 Pilots (certificates of qualification) shall be of three grades:

(1) First Grade: entitles the holder to pilot ships of any tonnage.

(2) Second Grade: entitles the holder to pilot ships of a gross tonnage of 6000 - 10000 tons.

(3) Third Grade: entitles the holder to pilot ships of a gross tonnage of less than 6000 tons.

Article 111 The pilot's task shall be limited to advising the ship's captain.

Article 112 Pilotage in all ports of the Kingdom shall be subject to the supervision of the Ministry of Communications.

Article 113 The Directorate of the port in which the pilots operate is the competent authority to which they are attached both technically and administratively.

Article 114 Pilots shall be subject to medical examination at the time of their appointment, and once every two years.

Article 115 The Port Directorate shall be competent to examine administrative offenses committed by the marine pilots attached to it. Gross errors which entail loss of life or property, and any offense provided for in the Ports Regulations, in the Council of Ministers' Decision and the Rules thereof, or in international regulations, shall however come under the jurisdiction of the Special Commissions mentioned in Articles Sixth and Seventh of the (Council of Ministers' Decision accompanying the) Ports Regulations.

Chapter VI

Comments

Chapter VI sets out general rules for the performance of stevedoring operations in Saudi ports, including licensing requirements. The rules provide that only Saudi Nationals may be licensed as stevedores.

Chapter VI

Stevedores

Part 1 - General Rules

Article 116 The loading and unloading operations include the loading of goods on, and their unloading from, ships, including the provision of all equipment and workmen necessary for the performance of these operations. They also include restowage of the goods in the ship's holds, or their movement from one hold to another in accordance with the directions and guidance of the ship's captain.

<u>Article 117</u> Agreement regarding stevedoring operations shall take place between the stevedore on the one part and the ship's agent or captain on the other part, in accordance with the following bases and responsibilities:

1. Contracting shall be on the basis of a metric ton of weight/measurement according to the kind of goods, as is recorded in the bill of lading, and to the applicable tariff fixed by the Port Directorate.

2. The contractor, his workmen and subordinates shall be subject to the instructions and directions of the Port Directorate in all stevedoring operations, particularly with regard to goods of a special nature (such as dangerous goods).

3. Loading and unloading operations may not be carried out save after the approval of the competent authorities at the port.

<u>Part 2 - Conditions for Licensing</u>

<u>Article 118</u> No person may practice the profession of a stevedore save after obtaining a license to do so from the competent authorities and after payment of the prescribed fee.

<u>Article 119</u> The granting of a license to practice the profession of a stevedore shall be subject to the following conditions:

(1) That the applicant for a license should be of Saudi nationality.

(2) That his age should not be less than twenty-two years.

(3) That he should be of good character and behavior.

(4) That he should possess all the means necessary for undertaking the operations of loading and unloading.

(5) That he should not have been convicted of a crime or misdemeanor, or subjected to a Shariah punishment, unless he has been rehabilitated.

(6) That the public security authorities should approve the application for license.

Article 120 The application for license, which should be accompanied by the documents confirming the (fulfillment of) the conditions referred to in the next preceding article, shall be submitted to the Port Directorate.

Article 121 The period of the license shall be one full year, and shall be renewable for a similar period, after ascertaining the continuity of the conditions referred to in Article 119, and after payment of the prescribed fee.

Article 122 The application for renewal shall be submitted at least thirty days prior to the expiration of the period of license.

Part 3 - Contractor's Duties and Obligations

Article 123 The ship shall be liable or the stevedoring contractor and his workmen's error with regard to the unloading of goods.

Article 124 The stevedoring contractor shall unload and load the goods according to the arrangement contained in the ship's loading plan.

Article 125 The stevedoring contractor shall classify and sort out the goods on the quay according to their marks and identification signs.

Article 126 The contractor shall supply a sufficient number or workmen to carry out the work in more than one hold, in accordance with the directions of the ship's captain and with the approval of the competent authority at the port.

Article 127 The contractor shall undertake that the rate of loading and unloading shall not be less than ten (10) tons per hour for each gang in the ship's holds.

Article 128 The members of the gang shall not be less than eight persons. Each gang shall be headed by a master who is experienced in loading and unloading operations.

Article 129 The contractor shall observe the following with regard to the workmen:

(1) That priority in engaging workmen should be given to those who carry the Saudi nationality.

(2) That his relationship with them shall be subject to the Labor and Workmen's Regulations and to all other regulations in force in the Kingdom.

Article 130 The contractor shall be responsible for the safety of the packages during loading and unloading operations, and during the presence of his workmen inside the ship's holds, until their final delivery on the quay.

Article 131 The contractor's liability in respect of the loose or damaged packages shall cease on his notifying the ship's captain about their condition and number. These shall be unloaded in accordance with the directions and guidance of the Port Directorate's representative.

The contractor shall however be responsible for the packages found to be defective on the quay.

Article 132 In all cases where the contractor is deemed to be liable for shortage or damage of the contents of packages, he shall be obligated to pay the customs and other fees payable in respect of such shortage, in addition to the compensation due.

Article 133 The contractor shall be obligated to compensate any injuries caused to the port installations by his workmen

Article 134 The loading and unloading tariff currently applicable in every port shall be applied. It may not be amended save on the basis of an application to be submitted to the Minister of Communications, which shall be considered by a committee consisting of a representative of the Port Directorate concerned, a representative of the Ministry of Commerce, and a representative of the Ministry of Labor.

The decision of the committee shall, after the approval of the Minister of Communications, be binding.

Chapter VII

Comments

Regulations for licensing shipping agents and the conduct of their activities are set forth.

Chapter VII

Shipping Agencies and Ship Chandlery

General Rules

Article 135 The shipping agent shall be considered as a trustee of the operations relating to the ship and to its cargo in the port.

Article 136 The shipping agent shall, in respect of the port operations, perform the following acts:

(1) Carry out all operations relating to the goods on behalf of the ship, its owners, outfitters or charterers, as well as on behalf of the owners of the goods.

(2) Supervise the stevedoring operations, prepare the necessary clerks and controllers to tally the packages of each consignment, record their condition and note down the necessary reservations, particularly those pertinent to damage or shortage, and take such proceedings as are necessary in such cases.

(3) Receive the goods coming from the ship, safeguard them and deliver them to the customs warehouses or to the persons concerned directly in accordance with the rules and conditions stipulated in the Customs Regulations, and perform the necessary financial and administrative formalities relating to such goods.

(4) Forward the incoming and outgoing goods manifests to the customs within the statutory periods.

(5) Prepare the loading and unloading reports, and attend inspections and repairs of damaged packages.

(6) Receive damage or shortage claims and take necessary action thereon.

(7) Notify the Quarantine or the Agricultural Quarantine departments and the competent authorities in the event of arrival of consignments that are subject to their supervision.

(8) Notify the Port Directorate about the times of arrival of the ships belonging to him, the cargoes which they carry and those which will be discharged at the port, and the dangerous goods that are coming with the ship.

(9) Receive transit goods and transhipment goods, and delivery them to the customs warehouses until they are transhipped to their destination.

Supply of Foodstuffs to Ships

Article 137 The shipping agency license includes the license to supply the ships with foodstuffs. The shipping agency shall with regard to these operations be subject to the supervision and requirements of the Ministry of Commerce and Industry and of the Ministry of Health.

Conditions for Licensing

Article 138 A shipping agent shall fulfill the following conditions:

(1) He must have a commercial register.

(2) He must have previous experience in marine business operations and in ports services. This should be certified by the chamber of commerce in the place of his work.

Application for License

Article 139 The license shall be issued by the Ministry of Communications after payment of the prescribed fee.

<u>Article 140</u> Persons who are presently undertaking the business of shipping agencies and of ship chandlery must apply to the Ministry of Communications for a license therefor within three months from the date of issuance of these rules.

<u>Article 141</u> The Ministry of Communications shall notify the Port Directorates and the Coast Guard Department of the shipping agencies in respect of which licenses have been issued. Dealing with unlicensed persons shall be prohibited.

<u>Chapter VIII</u>

<u>Comments</u>

Chapter VIII sets forth the marine inspection requirements for both Saudi and foreign flag vessels. Inspection of foreign flag vessels is limited to standards prescribed in the International Convention for Safey of Life at Sea and the International Load Lines Convention. Safety and exemption certificates issued by the nation of registry are honored. Ships not meeting safety specifications may be detained, after appropriate notification of the Consulate of the State of registry of the detained ships. Appeal of a detention order to the Minister of Communications is permitted.

Part 2 of the chapter discusses the operations of the Marine Inspection Office. The office is divided into two divisions: the Ships Registration Division, which performs functions akin to those of the United States Coast Guard relating to the registry of vessels; and a Seaman's Division which has quasi-judicial powers to settle employment disputes. Labor disagreements that cannot be settled by the Seaman's Division are referred to the Primary Commission for Settlement of Disputes.

Chapter VIII

Part 1 - Control and Inspection of Ships

Article 142 A marine inspection office shall be established in every port.

Article 143 Branch marine inspection offices shall be established in secondary ports and harbors.

Article 144 The marine inspection offices and their branches shall be technically attached to the Marine Department of the Ministry of Communications.

Article 145 The marine inspection authorities at the ports shall have the right to inspect Saudi and foreign ships which enter the ports of the Kingdom.

Article 146 Control and inspection shall include verification of the following:

First - Saudi Ships

(1) Ship's registration;

(2) Ship's navigation license;

(3) Availability and validity of international safety certificates on board;

(4) Seaworthiness of the ship and its engines;

(5) Fulfillment of the statutory provisions with respect to the number and qualifications of the crew;

(6) Compliance with the allowable number of passengers on board ship;

(7) Serviceability and efficiency of rescue and life-saving equipment and conformity with the requirements of the International Convention For the Safety of Life at Sea;

(8) Compliance with the terms of the International Load Lines Convention in force;

(9) Compliance with the international requirements and rules for Special Trade Passenger ships (Pilgrims ships) in accordance with the international conventions and treaties.

Second - Foreign Ships

(1) Fulfillment of the conditions prescribed in the International Conventions for the Safety of Life at Sea;

(2) Fulfillment of the conditions prescribed in the International Load Lines Convention in force.

Article 147 In carrying out the inspection, care shall be taken to avoid impeding the commercial operations of the ship.

Article 148 All valid international safety certificates and exemption certificates issued by the government of the country of the ship's flag shall be accepted.

Article 149 Where it is ascertained that the condition of the ship and its equipment do not conform with the specifications recorded in the certificates of safety, the marine inspection authorities shall take action to prevent the sailing of the ship until the safety conditions are fulfilled and until it is ascertained that its sailing will not pose any danger to the passengers of the crew.

Article 150 The Consul of the State to which the ship belongs shall be notified, immediately and through the legal channels, of all the circumstances which led to the detention of the ship or to delaying its sailing. The Ministry of Communications shall also be notified accordingly.

Article 151 Decisions preventing departure of ships must be grounded. Such decision shall be communicated to the ship's captain as soon as it is issued, provided that the decision shall state the circumstances and reasons justifying such prevention.

<u>Article 152</u> The aforementioned decisions may be appealed to the Minister of Communications within one week from the date of issuance of the decision. The final decision on the appeal shall be issued within two weeks, otherwise the appeal shall be considered accepted.

Part 2 - Powers of Marine Inspection Offices and Branch Offices

<u>Article 153</u> The Marine Inspection Office shall consist of two divisions:

(1) Ships Registration Division

(2) Seamen Division

<u>Article 154</u> The Ships Registration Division shall be competent to:

<u>First</u>: (a) Register Saudi ships and the documents relating thereto

(b) Issue registration certificates and title deeds for Saudi ships

(c) Issue international safey certificates to Saudi ships

(d) Issue navigation licenses to Saudi ships

(e) Issue departure permits to Saudi and foreign ships

<u>Second</u>: Carry out control and inspection of the ships mentioned in Part I of this Chapter.

<u>Third</u>: Control and inspect pilgrims' ships.

<u>Article 155</u> The Seamen's Division shall:

(a) Legalize marine labor contracts

(b) Appoint, discharge and register ship crews

(c) Settle disputes relating to seamen's employment contracts, discharge and appointment.

Article 156 If the Marine Inspection Office is unable to reconcile the contracting parties, a report to this effect shall be drawn up, and referred to the competent Primary Commission for Settlement of Disputes at the Labor Offices, provided for under the Labor and Workmen's Law promulgated by Royal Decree No. M/21 dated 6 Ramadan 1389 (15 November 1969).

Article 157 Subject to the application of the provisions pertaining to the marine labor contract included in the Labor and Workmen's Law referred to in the preceding Article, a copy of the seamen's employment contract shall be filed with the Marine Inspection Office.

Article 158 A special register called "Ships' Register" shall be kept at the Martine Inspection Offices of the ports authorized to register ships. Its pages shall be numbered and stamped with the Office seal. One page shall be assigned for each ship.

Article 159 A general register, identical to the Ships' Registers of the Marine Inspection Offices and Branch-Offices, shall be kept at the Marine Department of the Ministry of Communications.

Article 160 A book called "The Journal" shall be kept at the Marine Inspection Offices, in which the applications for registration and their supporting documents shall be entered under serial numbers in the chronological order of their receipt. The applicant for registration shall be given a receipt on which the number and date of the entry shall be recorded.

Article 161 Registers shall be kept at the Marine Inspection Offices and Branch-Offices for recording feluccas, boats, launches, fishing boats and floating craft which are not subject to registration in the ships' register.

Chapter IX

Chapter IX covers the important area of registration of ships. In order for persons interested in registering ships under the Saudi flag to be able to compare the Saudi requirements with those of other nations, we have provided some discussion of the registry provisions in the United States and Liberia as a focal point of comparison and contrast.

Ships may be registered at either the Port of Jiddah or the Port of Dammam. In order to be entitled to registry under the Saudi flag the owner of the vessel must be a Saudi national or Saudi company.

A company registered in Saudi Arabia with at least 51% Saudi capital can qualify. Apparently the sole test of citizenship for a Saudi corporation is the 51% Saudi capital requirement, even if the majority of officers and directors are non-Saudis. In contrast, the U.S. Coast Guard will not document a vessel under U. S. flag, to a corporate owner unless it is incorporated under the laws of the United States or a State and the President or other Chief Executive Officer, and the Chairman of the Board of Directors are U.S. citizens, and so long as "no more of its directors than a minority of the number necessary to constitute a quorum shall be non-citizens."1/

1/ 46 C.F.R. §67.03-5. See also, §2, Shipping Act, 1916 46 U.S.C. §802.

Moreover, the U. S. imposes even more stringent requirements if a vessel is to be documented for use in the domestic Coastwise trade.1/ The Saudi's do not appear to have any special requirement for eligibility of the vessel to engage in the coasting trade. Liberia, which also requires corporations registering vessels to be citizens, provides for a waiver of this requirement by the Deputy Commissioner of Maritime Affairs under certain circumstances.2/

The documents required for registration are set out in Article 169 and are comparable to those of the U.S. and Panama. Section 170 appears to require that the applicant for registry shall submit an official certificate that the vessel has been struck from the rolls of registered ships in the foreign country where it was previously registered. If strictly enforced this would require an applicant to give up foreign registry prior to ascertaining whether Saudi Arabian registry would be granted. Since foreign registry could not be dispensed with while at sea, the

---

1/ See §2, Shipping Act, 1916 supra which requires 75 percent of the interest in a corporation to be owned by citizens if the vessel is to be used in Coastwise trade.

2/ See "List of Requirements for Liberian Ship Registration, Office of Deputy Commissioner of Maritime Affairs, (Revised, Nov. 1974), Part I (A) (2).

vessel would have to enter a Saudi port and then arrange for its documents to be surrendered in the country of registry. This is quite awkward compared, for example, to the Liberian requirement that registration applications include an "Affidavit re Surrender of Foreign Documents" which merely says that the applicant has "ordered and instructed the Master . . . when he receives the Liberian Certificate of Registry . . . (to) surrender the vessel's outstanding documents."1/ U. S. regulations require proof that the transfer of registry is approved by the foreign government concerned, 2/ a requirement not contained in the Saudi regulations. Provisional registration, for vessels acquired abroad, may be granted by Saudi consulates or embassies, for one voyage to enable the vessel to arrive at the first port in the Kingdom, as provided in §181.3/ And if a vessel wished to surrender its foreign documents, it could travel to Saudi Arabia under this provisional registration.

A noteworthy provision in the Saudi regulations, is a requirement that applications are reported and published in two local daily newspapers at the applicant's expense.

1/ Id., Part II (A)(5) and Annex 5.

2/ See 46 C.F.R. §67.63-3(b) and 46 C.F.R. 67.65.5. Liberia requires either the consent of the country of registry or a Certificate of Cancellation. See supra Note 3 at Part II (A)(9).

3/ The U.S. permits provisional registration for a maximum of six months, which would permit a vessel to engage in foreign trade en route to the U.S. See 46 C.F.R. Subpart 67.05.

An "interested party," a term not defined in the regulations, may object to the registration of the ship within 90 days. This objection would then be submitted to the Commission for Settlement of Disputes. This procedure, which is more akin to the practice in registering trademarks than ships, does not set out any grounds for objections nor standards by which the Commission for the Settlement of Disputes makes its decision.1/

Chapter IX

Registration of ships and marine craft

Part 1 - Registration of Ships

Article 162 The ports approved for registration of ships in the Kingdom are:

1. The port of Jiddah.
2. The port of Dammam.

Hoisting the Flag of the Kingdom.

Article 163 No ship may hoist the Flag of the Kingdom of Saudi Arabia unless it is registered in one of the ports thereof.

1/ Section 180 of the regulations provides for a provisional Certificate of Registration for six months (renewable up to two years). This would apparently allow a vessel to operate while publication was taking place and even while an objection was being adjudicated. This type of provisional certificate apparently can only be obtained in Saudi Arabia after full application has been made.

<u>Article 164</u> No ship may change the flag of the State which it hoists, whether during the voyage or during its stay at the port, except in the cases of alteration of its registration or of transfer of its ownership.

<u>Article 165</u> The conditions required for the registration of ships in the Kingdom are:

1. That the owner of the ship should be a Saudi national.

2. Or that the ship should be owned by a Saudi company, establishment or organization.

3. Or that the ship should be owned by a company, establishment or organization which is registered in the Kingdom, provided that the proportion of the Saudi capital contributing therein should not be less than 51%.

<u>Article 166</u> A ship is not deemed to be of Saudi nationality unless it is registered in one of the ports of the Kingdom.

<u>Article 167</u> The marine inspection authorities shall have the right to detain a ship which does not submit its certificate of registration.

Ships and Marine Craft Which are Exempted From Registration

<u>Article 168</u>

1. Warships.

2. Marine craft working within the ports zones.

3. Fishing boats and feluccas, whether sail-or motor driven, whose gross tonnage does not exceed thirty tons.

4. Pleasure boats whose gross tonnage does not exceed ten tons.

Registration Procedures

Article 169 A ship is registered on the basis of an application submitted by its owner to one of the marine inspection offices at the approved ports of registration in the Kingdom.

The application for registration shall include the following particulars:

1. The present name and the previous names of the ship.
2. Date and place of the ship's construction.
3. The present port of registration of the ship (unless it is new and had not been registered).
4. The manner of transfer of her ownership.
5. Type of the ship (sail or motor-driven; the power and type of the motor).
6. Dimensions of the ship.
7. Tonnage of the ship (gross and net).
8. The name of the owner or names of the joint owners, and their nationality.
9. The share of each joint owner.
10. Name, nationality and domicile of the outfitter.
11. Name and nationality of the captain.
12. Real rights attaching to the ship.
13. Past and present liens on the ship.
14. Certificate of construction.
15. Certificate of survey.
16. The deed of sale.

The application shall be accompanied by all documents that are necessary to prove the authenticity of the aforementioned particulars.

Article 170 The applicant for registration shall submit an official certificate that the ship has been struck-off the shipping register at the foreign port in which the ship had been registered.

Article 171 The marine inspection office shall keep the originals or certified copies of the aforementioned documents. The preceding particulars shall be recorded in the ship's folio of the ships' register at the Marine Inspection Office.

Article 172 A ship may be registered in the name of one owner or in the names of several owners.

Article 173 A ship may be registered in the name of an organization, company or establishment registered in the Kingdom, subject to the provisions of Article 165.

Article 174 The shares of a ship shall consist of twenty-four parts.

Article 175 Before registration, a ship shall be surveyed by one of the international classification agencies which are recognized by the Government of the Kingdom, and its tonnages shall be determined in accordance with the terms of the international conventions in force to which the Government of the Kingdom has acceded.

Article 176 The following identification marks, shall be written on the ship:

1. The name of the ship shall be written on both sides of the bow.

2. The name of the ship and its port of registry shall be written on her stern.

3. The ship's official number, and the figure indicating its net tonnage recorded at the Marine Inspection Office shall be be carved on a main beam of the control room (the walkway).

4. The ship's draught shall be graded in feet or meters on both sides of its bow and stern, in latin letters or in figures.

Article 177 The ship's identification marks, mentioned in the preceding Article shall be written clearly and indelibly. They may not be amended or cancelled except after notifying the Marine Inspection Office at the port of registry, re-surveying it and recording the amendments in the certificate of registration. In the event of violation, the ship may be detained by the competent authorities, and its owner or captain may be inflicted with one of the penalties provided for in these Rules.

Article 178 A report shall be drawn up at the Marine Inspection Office in the port of registry, in which a summary of the particulars mentioned in Article 169 shall be recorded. The report shall be signed by the Office Director and by the applicant for registration.

Article 179 A summary of the report shall be published in two local daily newspapers at the expense of the ship's owner. An announcement to this effect shall be put up in the bulletin board at the port of registry of the ship.

Article 180 The ship shall be given a provisional certificate of registration valid for one or more voyages or for a period of six months renewable for a maximum period of two years.

Article 181 If the ownership of a vessel has been acquired abroad, and the conditions for her registration in the Kingdom are applicable to it, the ship shall be granted a provisional certificate of registration by a Consulate or Embassy of the Kingdom abroad, which shall be valid for one voyage to enable it to arrive at the first port in the Kingdom which has a registration office. The Ministry of Communications shall be sent a copy of this certificate.

Objection to the Registration of Ships

Article 182 Any interested party may object to the registration (of a ship) within three months from the date of publication thereof. The application for objection shall be submitted to the Marine Inspection Office at the port of registry.

Article 183 The objector shall institute the objection case before the Commission for Settlement of Disputes within two weeks from the date of submission of the objection to the Marine Inspection Office, otherwise the objection shall be deemed not to have existed.

Article 184 The Commission for Settlement of Disputes shall notify the Inspection Office of the institution of the case, with a copy to the Ministry of Communications.

Article 185 After the expiration of the three-month period without the Marine Inspection Office having received any objection; or after a judgment is passed by the Commission for Settlement of Disputes on the objection submitted, the Marine Inspection Office shall issue a permanent certificate of registration to the ship.

Article 186 The certificate of registration is considered a legal document necessary for the ship's navigation. It may not be withdrawn by reason of debt, mortgage or lien, and it shall not be transferable.

Article 187 The certificate of registration shall be submitted to the competent authorities immediately upon their request.

Loss of the Certificate of Registration

Article 188 If the certificate of registration is lost or damaged, the Marine Inspection Office at the port of registry thereof may give the person concerned a certificate in its stead within ten days of the (date of) submission of an application therefor. This should be marked "certificate in lieu of a lost or damaged one". The same remark should be noted down on the ship's folio in the shipping register.

Article 189 If the certificate of registration is lost while the ship is abroad, the Consulate or Embassy of the Kingdom may issue a provisional certificate of registration to the ship, which shall expire on the arrival of the ship at the first port of the Kingdom in which there is a registry office, provided that the validity of the provisional certificate shall not exceed six months.

Transfer of Registration of a Ship

Article 190 Registration of a ship may be transferred to any other port approved for the registration of ships in the Kingdom. In this case the ship shall be given a new registration number, provided that this should take place on the basis of a letter approved by the former port.

Amendments in the Certificate of Registration

Article 191 The owner of the ship shall notify the Marine Inspection Office of the port in which the ship is registered about any amendment to the particulars recorded in the certificate of registration.

Article 192 The application for amendment shall be submitted within thirty days from the date of amendment. It shall be accompanied by the documents necessary to establish the authenticity of the new particulars.

Article 193 The amendments shall be recorded by the Marine Inspection Office in the port of registry in the ship's certificate of registration and in the ships' register. This shall be authenticated by the office seal and the signature of the office director.

Cancellation of a Ship's Registration

Article 194 The registration of a ship shall be cancelled in the following cases:

1. If the ship is wrecked or captured by the enemy.

2. If the ship loses the nationality of its owner.

3. If a court judgment is passed to that effect.

Article 195 In case the registration of a ship is cancelled, the particulars of registration shall remain in the ship's register for the protection of civil rights.

Article 196 The application for cancellation shall be submitted by the owner, outfitter or captain of the ship within thirty days from the date when the cause for cancellation first arose. The application shall include the following particulars:

1. Name of the ship and its registration number.

2. The ground for cancellation and the documents in support of its authenticity.

3. The name of the applicant for cancellation.

Article 197 The Marine Inspection Office shall, after ascertaining the validity of the grounds for the application for cancellation, note down the cancellation on the ship's folio in the register, as well as on the certificate of registration. The applicant shall be given a certificate to the effect that cancellation has been made.

Article 198 The preceding two articles shall be applied in cases where cancellation of the real rights attaching to the ship is applied for.

Part 2 - Recording of Boats and Floating Craft That Are Exempt from Registration.

Article 199 The marine inspection offices shall enter these units in special registers, and they shall be given a serial number according to priority of registration.

Article 200 — A marine title deed shall be given to these units, in which the name of the owner, his nationality and address, the type of the unit, its dimensions and name, and the selling price, shall be recorded. The number of the marine title deed shall be the number of its registration.

Article 201 — The marine title deed shall be given only after the submission of evidence of ownership and of payment of customs duties, in case the craft is subject to such duties.

Article 202 — An operating licence shall be issued to these units, in which the number of the marine title deed, the name, type and dimensions of the craft, the name of its owner and the number of persons whom it is allowed to carry, shall be recorded.

Article 203 — The operating licence shall not be issued unless technical inspection (of the unit) has been conducted by the competent authorities, and after its serviceability and efficiency have been proven.

Article 204 — Each craft shall be equipped with at least one life buoy, and a number of safety belts, according to the number of persons it is allowed to carry.

Article 205 — The operating licence authorizes the floating craft to operate inside the ports and within the limits of the territorial waters of the Kingdom of Saudi Arabia only.

Article 206 — No marine craft may operate inside the ports or within the limits of the territorial waters of the Kingdom without having obtained an operating licence.

Article 207 — The operating licence shall be renewed annually.

Article 208 — The name and number of the floating craft shall be written on both sides of its bow and on its stern in a permanent and clear manner.

Article 209 With regard to pleasure boats and launches which are owned by Saudi or foreign nationals, the owner shall obtain a security clearance from the Coast Guard Department, authorizing him to cruise for pleasure in the territorial waters before he is issued with the operating licence.

Article 210 Old boats which had not been recorded at the time these Rules are issued by reason of their having outstanding matters with the Customs shall be granted a provisional operating licence valid for six months in order to finalize their outstanding matters with the Customs. The licence shall be considered null and void after the expiration of the said period.

Chapter X

Comments

Chapter X concerns ship safety and is divided into six parts. Part 1 deals with the issuance of navigation licenses based on the seaworthiness of the vessel. Ships surveyed by one of the international classification societies such as the American Bureau of Shipping or Bureau Veritas is exempted from a new survey. Part 2 covers safety certification and the international convention relating to safety. Part 3 lists the foreign survey bureau recognized by the Saudi government to issue inspection and survey certificates and Part 4 deals with the requirements of the International Load Lines Certificate. Part 5 deals with vessel admeasurement. Finally, Part 6 deals with a problem peculiar to Saudi Arabia, the regulation of ships carrying pilgrims to Mecca.

Chapter X

Safety of Ships

Part 1 - Navigation Licence

Article 211 Every ship registered in the ports of the Kingdom shall obtain a navigation licence. An application therefor shall be submitted to the Marine Inspection Office of the port of registry.

Article 212 The navigation licence shall be granted after inspecting the ship and ascertaining its seaworthiness and its compliance with the provisions of the international conventions and agreements.

Article 213 A ship previously surveyed by one of the international agencies for supervision and classification that are recognized by the Government of the Kingdom within the limits of the authorizations given to such agencies shall be exempted from any new survey. The survey reports of such agencies shall be submitted to the Marine Inspection Office at the port.

Article 214 The navigation licence shall be valid for one year effective as of the date of its issuance, unless the ship loses one or more prerequisites for granting the licence.

Article 215 If during the term of the licence a ship sustains a damage which exposes it to danger, the owner, outfitter or captain of the ship shall notify such damage to the Marine Inspection Office of the port of registry. In this case the validity of the navigation licence shall be suspended, and it may not be put into effect again save after a new survey is carried out.

Article 216 If the term of the navigation licence of a Saudi ship expires while it is abroad, the Consul of the Kingdom shall extend the licence until the ship arrives at the first port of the Kingdom. If no Embassy or Consulate exists for the Kingdom at the foreign port, the validity of the licence shall be extended by force of the law until the ship arrives at the first port in which an Embassy or Consulate of the Kingdom exists, or at the first port in the Kingdom.

Article 217 If the term of the navigation licence of a foreign ship expires while it is lying in one of the ports of the Kingdom, it shall be required to have the licence renewed by the Consul of the State whose flag it hoists. If such renewal is impossible because of the non-existence of a diplomatic Consul for its State at the port, the ship shall be allowed to leave, subject to its being notified of the necessity of renewing the licence, and that it would not be admitted to any Saudi port unless the licence is renewed.

Article 218 The term of renewal of the licence may under no circumstances exceed sixty days.

Article 219 The Embassy or Consulate of the Kingdom abroad may in the case of necessity grant a Saudi ship a provisional navigation licence to make a particular voyage, after it is surveyed by an expert of an international agency for supervision and classification which is recognized by the Kingdom. The validity of such licence shall expire on the arrival of the ship at the first port of the Kingdom. The naval inspection offices may issue such a licence to a Saudi ship for making a particular voyage, subject to compliance with the conditions for survey, provided that the validity of the licence shall expire with the completion of that voyage.

Part 2 - Safety Certificates

Article 220 The provisions of the International Convention For Safety of Life at Sea, 1960, shall apply to Saudi ships.

Article 221 Every ship registered in the Kingdom which makes international voyages shall obtain international safety certificates in accordance with the provisions of the International Convention For Safety of Life at Sea, 1960.

Article 222 The safety certificates are:

1. Safety Certificate for a Passenger Ship.
2. Safety Certificate of Construction for a Freight Ship.
3. Safety Equipment Certificate for a Freight Ship.
4. Safety Certificate of the Wireless Set for a Freight Ship.
5. Safety Certificate of the Wireless Telephone Set for a Freight Ship.
6. Exemption Certificate.

Article 223 Safety certificates shall be issued in Arabic and English by the marine inspection offices of the ports approved for registration of ships on the basis of a request to be submitted therefor. The certificate shall be in accordance with the form attached to the Convention.

Article 224 The safety certificate shall be granted only on the basis of the survey and inspection report pertinent to each certificate and issued by an international agency for supervision and classification recognized by the Government of the Kingdom.

Article 225 The reports of survey and inspection shall be kept in the ship's register at the Marine Inspection Office.

Article 226 The safety certificate shall be suspended if the ship sustains a damage that would expose it to danger, or if it violates one of the conditions required for the issuance of the certificate. It may not be put again into effect save after a new survey is made.

<u>Article 227</u> The validity period of a safety certificate for a passenger ship or for a wireless telephone or telegraph set shall not exceed twelve months.

<u>Article 228</u> The validity period of a certificate of safety of equipment for a freight ship shall not exceed twenty-four months.

<u>Article 229</u> The validity period of the certificate of exemption shall not exceed that of the basic certificate for which the exemption was granted.

<u>Article 230</u> The validity period of the safety certificate may be extended by the Marine Inspection Office if it expires while the ship is lying at a port other than the port of registry thereof. Provided that the extension shall be for the purpose of enabling the ship only to arrive at her port of registration, or at the port where it is possible to carry out an inspection thereon.

<u>Article 231</u> The validity of the safety certificate may not be extended for a period exceeding five months. In the event of a ship arriving at her port of registration or at the port where it surveyed during the effective period of the extension, it may not leave the said port unless it has obtained a new safety certificate.

<u>Article 232</u> The validity of a safety certificate which has not been extended in accordance with the last preceding Article may be allowed to extend for a period not exceeding one month.

<u>Article 233</u> Ships which are exempted from the application of the terms of the International Convention For Safety of Life at Sea, 1960, and which are not issued with safety certificates are:

1. Warships.

2. Freighters whose gross tonnage is below five hundred (500) tons.

3. Wooden vessels of rudimentary construction.

4. Pleasure boats which do not engage in trade.

5. Vessels not mechanically driven.

6. Fishing vessels.

Article 234 No Saudi ship which does not satisfy the conditions of safety may leave or attempt to leave a Saudi port. She should be in possession of the following valid certificates, or of valid exemption certificates:

A. If it is a passenger ship

1. Navigation licence.

2. Safety certificate for a passenger ship.

3. Passengers certificate.

B. If it is a freighter

1. Navigation Licence.

2. Safe Construction Certificate for a Freight Ship.

3. Safety Equipment Certificate for a Freight Ship.

4. Safety Certificate for the Telephone and Wireless Telegraphy Systems.

Article 235 A medical service in accordance with the International Sanitary Convention, 1969, shall be available on every Saudi ship.

Part 3 - International Non-Governmental Agencies For Supervision and Classification.

Article 236 The following agencies are authorized to conduct survey and inspection work on Saudi ships, and to issue survey and testing certificates therefor on behalf of the Government of the Kingdom, unless an amendment is issued (otherwise):

1. American Bureau of Shipping.

2. Bureau Veritas.

3. Die Norske Veritas.

4. Germanischer Lloyd.

5. Lloyd's Register of Shipping.

6. Nippon Kajei Kukai.

Part 4 - International Load Lines Certificate, 1966

Article 237 A ship registered in the Kingdom may not make an international voyage unless it has been subjected to the tests stipulated for by the International Load Lines, 1966, and unless it has been marked and issued with the International Load Lines Certificate, 1966, or when necessity arises and it is provided with an exemption certificate for International Load Lines, 1966, in accordance with the provisions of the said Convention.

Article 238 The provisions pertaining to the International Load Lines shall not apply to the following ships:

1. Warships.

2. New ships (whose keel was laid down, or which are in a similar stage of construction at or after the effective date of the Convention), and whose length is less than twenty-four (24) metres (seventy-nine (79) feet).

3. Existing ships (not mentioned in item 2), whose gross tonnage is less than one hundred and fifty (150) tons.

4. Pleasure yachts which do not engage in trade.

5. Fishing vessels.

<u>Article 239</u> No ship may sail from a port of the Kingdom unless it fulfills the conditions and provisions of the International Load Lines in accordance with the conventions in force.

<u>Article 240</u> Every Saudi ship to which the International Load Lines Convention, 1966 applies shall abide by the requirements of the said convention in the zones indicated in Supplement II of the Convention.

<u>Article 241</u> The load lines on both sides of the ship which correspond to the season of the year and to the zone in which the ship is located shall at no time be submerged on the ship's departure from the port, or during the voyage, or on its arrival at the port.

<u>Article 242</u> The act of survey, inspection and marking which is undertaken in execution of the terms of the Convention shall be carried out by one of the International agencies for supervision and classification that are recognized by the Government of the Kingdom.

<u>Article 243</u> The international agencies for supervision and classification which are recognized by the Government of the Kingdom, and which are mentioned in Article 236 of Part 3 of this Chapter are authorized to issue certificate of international load lines for Saudi ships, and to issue exemption certificates in accordance with the terms of the said convention (Ministerial Decision No. 93, dated 13.5.95 (5.23.75).

<u>Article 244</u> The International Load Lines Certificates for the year 1966 shall be cancelled by the marine inspection authorities in the following cases:

A. Alteration of the materials of the hull or of the superstructures of the ship, which involves an increase in the water line of the ship.

B. Failure to maintain the following fittings and equipment:

1. Hatch protection facilities.

2. The ship's railing.

3. The hatches.

4. Passage facilities to the forecastle (Crew accommodations).

C. Absence of any record on the certificate to the effect that the periodical surveys mentioned in the convention have been conducted.

D. Change of nationality of the ship.

Article 245 The marine inspection authorities shall have the right to inspect Saudi and foreign ships in the ports of the Kingdom with regard to the international load line rules to ascertain:

1. That the ship is not loaded in excess of the limits allowed in the International Load Lines Certificate granted to the ship.

2. The location of the ship's load line which corresponds to what is recorded in the certificate.

3. That no alteration has been made in the ship's construction materials, which would make the ship unsuitable to take to sea without endangering life.

Article 246 If a ship carries a load lines exemption certificate, the purpose of the inspection will be to confirm that the conditions recorded in the certificate are adhered to.

Article 247 Inspection shall be conducted to the extent required to ensure that the ship will not take to sea unless it is certain that the passengers or the crew will not be exposd to danger.

Article 248 In case there is cause to detain the ship because of its violation of the terms of the International Load Lines Convention, the marine inspection authorities which had inspected the ship shall notify the Consul or the diplomatic representative of the State whose flag is hoisted by the ship, and the ship's captain, of the detention decision and the whole circumstances which have led to making the said decision. The Ministry of Communications shall be notified accordingly.

Article 249 The International Load Lines Certificate, 1966, shall be issued in Arabic and English in accordance with the form attached to the Convention, Supplement No. 3. The same applies to the load lines exemption certificate.

Part 5 - Measurement of Ships' Tonnage

Article 250 Measurement of Saudi ships' tonnage (gross and net tonnage) shall be in accordance with the terms of the International Convention for Measurement of Ships' Tonnage, 1969.

Article 251 Ships which are exempted from the terms of this Convention are:

1. Warships.

2. Ships which are less than twenty-four (24) meters (seventy-nine (79) feet) long.

Article 252 Determination of gross and net tonnage of Saudi ships shall be through the international supervision and classification agencies which are recognized by the Government of the Kingdom.

Article 253 The International Tonnage Certificate of a Saudi ship shall be issued in Arabic and English, in accordance with the form attached to the Convention under Supplement No. (2).

Article 254 The International Tonnage Certificate shall be considered null and void in the following cases:

1. In the event of amendments being made in the ship's outfit, or in the hull or in the volume of spaces used.

2. In the event of amendments being made in the total number of passengers the ship is allowed to carry in accordance with her passengers' certificate.

3. In the event of amendment being made in the load line specified for the ship.

4. In the event of amendment being made in the permissible draught, if such amendment has caused an increase in the gross or net tonnage of the ship.

Article 255 The Tonnage Certificate shall become ineffective by the mere change of the flag of the State which the ship hoists. The validity of the certificate may in that case be extended for a period not exceeding three months, or until the other State issues a new Tonnage Certificate for the ship, whichever is less.

Article 256 The Tonnage certificates issued by the governments of other States shall have the same effect as those issued by the Government of the Kingdom.

Article 257 The marine inspection authorities may with regard to Tonnage Certificates inspect foreign ships during their stay at the ports of the Kingdom within the following limits:

1. To ascertain that the ship carries an International Tonnage Certificate.

2. (To ascertain) that the main specifications of the ship are identical with the particulars recorded in the Tonnage Certificate.

Article 258 The inspection proceedings mentioned in the preceding Article shall in no case cause any delay to the ship.

Article 259 If the inspection reveals that the main specifications of the ship are different from those recorded in the tonnage certificate to an extent that would lead to an increase in the gross or net tonnage of the ship, the marine inspection authorities may give an order to prevent the ship from leaving the port, and may forthwith notify the Consul of the State whose flag is hoisted by the ship, as well as the Ministry of Communications, stating the reasons for giving such order.

Article 260 The International Agencies for Supervision and Classification which are recognized by the Government of the Kingdom and which are mentioned in Article 236 of Part 2 of this Chapter are authorized to issue the International Tonnage Measurement Certificate to Saudi ships in accordance with the 1947 Convention, until the 1969 Convention shall come into effect. (Ministerial Decision No. 63 dated 13.5.95 (5.24.75).

Part 6 - Special Trade Passenger Ships, and Open Space Requirements For Such Ships.

Special trade passenger ships are those ships which carry large numbers of passengers on deck in international voyages within the limits of the zone shown in Rule (2), Paragraph (6) and on the map of Supplment No. (1) of the Special Trade Passenger Ships Convention, 1971, such as pilgrim-carrying ships.

First: Special Trade Passenger Ships Convention, 1971.

Article 261 The provisions of the said Convention shall be applied to Saudi pilgrim-carrying ships which hold a Safety Certificate for Passenger Ships in accordance with the International Treaty For Safety of Life at Sea, 1960.

<u>Article 262</u> The provisions of the International Treaty for Safety of Life at Sea, 1960, concerning passenger ships shall be applied to pilgrim-carrying ships in addition to the provisions of the said Convention.

<u>Article 263</u> The provisions of this Convention shall be applied to the existing and the new pilgrim-carrying ships, unless otherwise provided.

<u>Article 264</u> In addition to the Safety Certificate for a Passenger Ship, and to the Certificate of Exemption provided for under the International Convention For Safety of Life at Sea, 1960, a certificate called "Safety Certificate for Special Trip Passenger Ships, 1971" shall be issued for pilgrim-carrying ships. It shall be written in Arabic and English in accordance with the Form included in Supplement No. (2) of the Convention.

<u>Article 265</u> The said certificate shall be issued to Saudi ships by one of the International Agencies for Supervision and Classification which are recognized by the Government of the Kingdom, in accordance with the terms provided for in the said Convention. (Ministerial Decision No. 63, dated 13.5.95 (5.24.75)).

<u>Article 266</u> A ship which carries pilgrims to the ports of the Kingdom shall be obligated to apply the rules of the International Convention For Safety of Life at Sea, and the open space requirements relating to pilgrims.

<u>Article 267</u> No ship shall be allowed to leave a Saudi port if it carries a number of pilgrims in excess of its tonnage fixed by the Safety Certificate.

<u>Article 268</u> Carriage of pilgrims on sail boats is not allowed.

<u>Article 269</u> The validity period of a Safety Certificate for Special Trade Passenger Ships which are issued to Saudi ships shall not exceed five months per year (the pilgrimage season).

Second: Protocol on Open Space Requirements For Special Trade Passenger Ships, 1973.

Article 270 This Protocol shall be applied to Saudi passenger ships which make special voyages and which hold a valid Safety Certificate for a Passenger Ship in accordance with the Convention For Safety of Life at Sea, 1960, and a valid Safety Certificate for a Special Trade Passenger Ship, 1971.

Article 271 The said ships shall be issued with a certificate called "Open Space Certificate for a Special Trade Passenger Ship", after a survey for the ship has been made by one of the International Agencies for Supervision and Classification which are recognized by the Government of Kingdom in accordance with the provisions of the Protocol. The certificate shall be (written) in Arabic and English in accordance with the Form attached with the Protocol.

Article 272 The validity period for the said certificate shall not exceed five months per year (the pilgrimage season).

Article 273 A Special Trade Passenger may not be carried in the following places:

1. On any deck below the one immediately next to the farthest additional load line.

2. Anywhere in an open space on a tweendeck the height of the ceiling of which is less than 1.90 metres (6 feet 3 inches).

3. In front of the collision bulkhead or of its upper extension, according to the limit prescribed by Rule (9), Chapter II of the Convention for Safety of Life at Sea, 1960.

4. On any lower tweendeck within a distance of 10% of the ship's length measured from the front shaft.

5. On any open deck that is not covered according to the conditions laid down by the competent authorities.

6. During seasons of inclement weather, the spaces on an open deck are not to be considered as accommodation spaces for the special trade passengers, but they may be considered as recreation spaces.

Article 274 The number of special trade passengers in any voyage shall not exceed the number allowed in accordance with the Special Trade Passenger Ships Convention, 1971.

Article 275 Spaces that are not furnished with beds for special trade passengers, and which are assigned for their accommodations shall be calculated on the basis of the schedule of Supplement No. (1) of the Protocol, taking into consideration the locations of these spaces, the duration of the voyage, and the effects of the temperate and bad weather.

Article 276 Recreation spaces shall be assigned on the open decks, of a minimum area of 0.37 square metres (4 square feet) for each tweendeck or lower deck passenger, on which the words "Recreation Space for Special Trade Passengers only" shall be written clearly.

Article 277 Where the period of the voyage is 24 hours or more, the number of special trade passengers allowed to be carried in accordance with this Rule in any space shall not exceed the quotient of the total volume of that space in cubic meters (or in cubic feet) divided by 3.06 m^3 (108 cubic feet).

Article 278 When calculating the number of passengers who may be accommodated in a space not furnished with beds, the following areas shall be deducted:

1. 5% of the total area of the space shall be assigned for the passengers' accompanied baggage.

2. An area extending for a distance of 0.75 metres (2 feet 6 inches) from the entrance until the first staircase, lavatory, water closet, faucet or hydrant.

3. The area of any hatch on deck.

4. The area necessary for operating the life boats and buoys.

5. Any area which the expert surveyor considers unsuitable for accommodating the passengers.

Article 279 Every ship which makes a voyage of a duration of 72 hours or more in normal conditions shall be furnished with one bed for each special trade passenger.

The following conditions shall be met:

1. The size of the bed shall not be less than 1.90 metres (6 feet 3 inches) long x 0.70 metres (2 feet 3 inches) wide.

2. Each bed shall directly lead to a passage. These passages shall be arranged so that they would directly lead to the escape route.

3. The width of these passages shall not be less than 0.7 metres (2 feet 3 inches) each.

Article 280 All spaces including passages, stairs and staircases allocated for the accommodation or use of the special trade passengers shall be provided with sufficient lighting systems, and where practicable, with natural lighting facilities.

Article 281 Every ship shall be provided with a suitable mechanical ventilation system for distribution of fresh air in all closed parts allocated for the accommodation or use of special trade passengers. The system shall be capable of changing the air and of admitting fresh air ten times per hour.

Article 282 Every ship shall be provided with an approved cloth awning for the protection of the following parts against weather conditions:

1. The open parts of the deck which are assigned for the use of special trade passengers.

2. The open parts of the deck which are located directly above the spaces assigned for the accommodation or use of special trade passengers.

Article 283 Special trade passengers are not allowed to cook on board the ship.

Article 284 The hatches on the deck (when open) shall be provided with an enclosure of a minimum height of 0.9 metres (3 feet). They should be properly covered with netting when they are opened for ventilation purposes.

Article 285 Spaces assigned for special trade passengers, including the recreation spaces, shall be kept free of goods.

Article 286 Medical service in accordance with the terms of the International Health Rules, 1969, shall be available on every ship. Ships shall abide by the terms of the said Convention, taking into consideration the nature of the voyage.

Article 287 The said certificate shall be issued to Saudi ships by one of the International Agencies for Supervision and Classification which are recognized by the Government of the Kingdom, in accordance with the terms provided for in this Protocol. (Ministerial Decision No. 63 of 13.5.95 (5.24.75)).

Chapter XI

Comments

Chapter XI covers technical provisions such as navigation aids, channel markers and collision avoidance. Reference is again made to IMCO standards.

Chapter XI

Safety of Navigation in Saudi Arabia's Ports and Territorial Waters

Part I: Navigation Aids and Publications

Article 288 The Ministry of Communcations is the agency responsible for determining the locations of navigation aids and for placing such aids in the ports and territorial waters of the Kingdom for the purpose of ensuring the safety of maritime navigation.

Article 289 It is prohibited to install navigation aids in the ports or on the shores of the Kingdom, or to alter such aids or change their location or specifications, save after obtaining the approval of the Ministry.

Article 290 It is prohibited to conduct any hydrographic survey on the shores, or in the territorial waters of the Kingdom, without obtaining a licence to do so from the Ministry and from the Frontiers Force.

Article 291 The Port Directorate may, in case an accident occurs which affects the safety of navigation (such as a ship wreck) place the international signs at the scene and thereafter notify the Ministry.

Article 292 Notices to mariners shall be issued by the Ministry of Communications.

Article 293 In ports which are operated by private companies (such as oil ports), the latter shall give the Ministry sufficient advance notice before conducting hydrographic surveys or placing navigation aids, so that the Ministry may study the action and issue the necessary notices. This provision shall not apply where delay may expose ships bound for the said ports to navigational hazards, in which cases the companies concerned may undertake such work, provided that they notify the Ministry accordingly.

Article 294 When navigational accidents occur to ships while they are in the ports or within the territorial waters of the Kingdom, the agency which receives information on the matter shall forthwith notify the Ministry of Communications of the accident.

Part 2 - Channel Separation Schemes

Article 295 The Ministry of Communications is the agency responsible for laying down channel separation schemes in the ports and territorial waters of the Kingdom, and for issuing the necessary Notices to Mariners on such schemes after approval of the scheme by the Inter-Governmental Maritime Consultative Organization (IMCO).

Article 296 All captains of Saudi ships shall on all seas and in all ports strictly observe the traffic rules relative to channel separation schemes that are issued by IMCO.

Article 297 International rules in force for the prevention of collision shall be applied during navigation within channel separation schemes.

Article 298 Channel separation schemes shall be used day and night, and in all weather conditions.

Article 299 Channel separation schemes are reserved for the passage of all ships, unless it is otherwise stated.

Article 300 Deep channels are reserved for ships which, by reason of their draughts and of the nature of the seabed in the area, can pass only through these channels. All other ships shall avoid passing through such channels.

Article 301 Ships' captains shall, during passage through deep channels, pay attention to possible changes-as a result of weather conditions or other causes-in the depths shown on the maps.

<u>Article 302</u> Ships' captains shall, during passage through channel separation schemes, observe the following:

1. Proceed in the appropriate lane in the general direction of traffic flow in that lane.

2. So far as practicable keep clear of traffic separation lines or separation zones.

3. Join or leave a traffic lane at the termination of the lane.

4. When joining or leaving a traffic lane from the side (i.e., not at its termination) do so at as small an angle to the general direction of traffic flow as practicable.

<u>Article 303</u> Ships shall so far as practicable avoid crossing traffic lanes, but if obliged to do so shall cross as nearly as practicable at right angles to the general direction of traffic flow.

<u>Article 304</u> Inshore traffic zones (near the coast) must not be used for through traffic which can safely use the appropriate traffic lane within the adjacent traffic separation scheme.

<u>Article 305</u> A ship (other than a crossing ship) shall not enter a traffic separation zone or cross a traffic separation line except in the following cases:

1. In cases of emergency to avoid immediate danger.

2. To engage in fishing within the channel separation zone.

<u>Article 306</u> When navigating near the terminations of traffic separation schemes, ships shall do so with extreme caution and care.

Article 307 Except in cases of emergency, ships shall not anchor within a traffic separation scheme or in areas near its terminations.

Article 308 A ship which will not use a traffic separation scheme shall avoid it by as wide a margin as is practicable.

Article 309 Arrows appearing on maps indicate the approximate general direction of traffic. Ships shall not proceed in the exact direction of the arrows.

Article 310 The international signal letters YG mean: "You are contravening traffic within the channel separation scheme."

Chapter XII

Comments

Chapter XII is of particular interest to those planning to operate in Saudi waters. It encompasses the important area of prevention of oil pollution. Saudi Arabia has adopted the conditions prescribed by the International Convention For the Prevention of Pollution of the Sea by Oil, 1954, as amended in 1962. Many parts of the chapter parallel the United States Oil Pollution Act, 1961 as amended 1/ which is the U.S. law implementing the Convention. In general, however, the U.S. law and the regulations implementing it are more detailed and encompassing than the Saudi's. For example, the U.S. regulations specify 12 items

---

1/ 33 U.S.C. §1001-1010.

that must be kept in the oil record book aboard a tanker1/ while Article 320A only covers eight.

Chapter XII

Prevention of Pollution of the Sea by Oil and Disposal of Ship Waste and Refuse

Part 1: Prevention of Pollution of the Sea by Oil.

Article 311 The conditions prescribed in the International Convention for the prevention of pollution of the Sea by Oil, 1954 as amended in the year 1962, shall be applicable to Saudi ships.

Article 312 "Oil" means crude oil, lubricating oil and heavy diesel oil. "Oily mixture" means a mixture with an oil content of 100 parts or more in every million parts of the mixture.

Article 313 Oil tankers of a gross tonnage of 150 tons or more and other vessels of a gross tonnage of 500 tons or more shall be prohibited from discharging oil or oily mixture within a distance of 100 nautical miles from the Kingdom's coasts, measured from the base line of measurement.

Article 314 Saudi oil tankers of a gross tonnage of 150 tons or more and other vessels of a gross tonnage of 500 tons or more shall be prohibited from discharging oil or oily mixtures in the seas or in the prohibited zones of the seas as mentioned in Annex A to the said Convention.

Article 315 Without prejudice to the preceding Articles, ships to which the provisions of the above-mentioned Convention apply shall be prohibited from discharging oil or oily mixture in the sea except when the following conditions are satisfied:

1/ 33 C.F.R. § 151.35.

A) <u>For vessels other than oil tankers:</u>

1. The ship is proceeding en route.

2. The rate of oil or oily mixture discharge does not exceed 60 liters per mile.

3. The oil content of the oily mixture is less than 100 parts per million parts of the mixture.

4. The discharge is made as far as possible from the coast.

B) <u>For Oil Tankers:</u>

1. The oil tanker is proceeding en route.

2. The rate of oil or oily mixture discharge does not exceed 60 liters per mile.

3. The total quantity discharged by the tanker on a ballast voyage does not exceed 1/15000 of its total cargo-carrying capacity.

4. The tanker is more than 50 miles from the nearest land.

<u>Article 316</u> The preceding Article shall not apply to the discharge of clean ballast water which does not leave any traces of oil on the surface of the water when the tanker is stationary in calm water on a clear day.

<u>Article 317</u> The provisions of Paragraph (A) of Article 315 shall apply to the discharge of oil or oily mixture from the ship's machinery space bilges, except where an oily water separator is available which is approved by the authorities concerned, so that such discharge does not leave any traces of oil on the surface of the sea.

<u>Article 318</u> Saudi ships must avoid putting ballast water in bunker fuel tanks.

<u>Article 319</u> The building specifications of Saudi oil tankers to be registered after the first of January 1977, must comply with the conditions prescribed in Annex (C) of the Convention mentioned above.

<u>Article 320</u> Saudi oil tankers of a tonnage of 150 tons or more and other Saudi ships of a tonnage of 500 tons or more must keep a special record book in the form specified in Annex (B) to the Convention, which form is attached to the rules for the implementation hereof. This book shall be known as the "Oil Record Book" in which information on the following operations shall be registered whenever such operations take place:

A) <u>With respect to oil tankers:</u>

1. Loading of the oil shipment.

2. Transfer of oil from one tank to another during the voyage.

3. Offloading of the oil shipment.

4. Filling cargo tanks with ballast water.

5. Cleaning of cargo tanks.

6. Discharge of ballast water containing oil.

7. Discharge of oily residues.

8. Discharge of water containing oil from machinery space bilges and the method followed in such discharge.

B) <u>With respect to other ships:</u>

1. Filling bunker fuel tanks with ballast water or cleaning such tanks.

2. Discharge of ballast water or cleaning water containing oil from bunker fuel tanks.

3. Discharge of oily residues.

4. Discharge of ballast water containing oil and machinery space bilges, and the method followed in such discharge.

Article 321 Oil escapes or emergency discharges must be recorded in the Oil Record Book, indicating the reasons for and the circumstances of such escape or discharge, as well as the precautionary measures taken to reduce or stop the escape. Emergency cases are as follows:

1. The discharge of oil or oily mixture for the purpose of securing the safety of the ship, preventing damage to the ship's cargo or saving life (at sea);

2. The escape of oil or oily mixture resulting from damage to the ship or from a cause beyond control;

Provided that appropriate and reasonable action be taken after the occurrence of the damage or leakage to prevent or minimize the escape of oil.

Article 322 The Master of the ship must notify the port authorities of any oil escape from the ship while the latter is in the Kingdom's ports or territorial waters, immediately upon the occurrence of such escape. He must further indicate the circumstances of the occurrence of the escape and the measures he has taken to stop or restrict the escape.

Article 323 The marine inspection authorities shall, in cooperation with the competent agency at the Ministry of Petroleum and Mineral Resources, have the right to examine the oil record books of all Saudi and foreign ships in the ports of the Kingdom.

<u>Article 324</u> In cooperation with the competent agencies of the Frontier Force and Coast Guard, ships shall be observed while at anchor in the Kingdom's ports or during their presence in its territorial waters and incidents of pollution of water by oil shall be communicated to the port authorities. Port authorities may detain the ship which commits a violation.

<u>Article 325</u> Agencies which supervise and are responsible for the operation of oil loading terminals in the Kingdom and offshore floating installations and platforms for oil pumping and producing operations, shall be responsible for any oil escaping from such installations or terminals to the sea and for the elimination of pollution, and shall be liable for appropriate compensation for damages.

<u>Article 326</u> In cooperation with the Ministry of Petroleum and Mineral Resources, studies and arrangements shall be made in order to provide oil loading terminals in the Kingdom with adequate facilities to receive oily residues from tankers.

<u>Article 327</u> Arrangements are to be made to provide ship repair ports and other ports in the Kingdom with necessary facilities for the reception of oily residues and oily mixtures from ships. Such facilities are to be adequate to the requirements of ship traffic at the port.

<u>Article 328</u> Oil loading terminals in the Kingdom must be provided with adequate instruments and equipment to eliminate any pollution of the sea water by oil at such terminals or at the facilities attached thereto.

<u>Article 329</u> Ports in the Kingdom, particularly ship repair ports and ports which supply vessels with bunker fuel, must be equipped with instruments and equipment for the elimination of pollution of water by oil.

<u>Article 330</u> Barges and boats which carry fuel to ships at ports must keep a special record in which the following operations and the time of their performance shall be registered:

1. Loading of the barge with fuel.

2. Quantities discharged to ships.

3. Name of ship and her anchorage location.

Article 331 There shall be established in the Ministry of Communications a center for receiving information relating to pollution in the Kingdom's ports and territorial waters.

Article 332 Naval ships shall be exempt from the conditions prescribed in this chapter, provided they shall, on their part, take such precautions as may be necessary to prevent pollution of sea water.

Part 2: Discharge of ship waste and refuse

Article 333 All ships are prohibited from throwing waste matter, food leftovers and ship refuse in the ports,navigation channels or territorial waters of the Kingdom of Saudi Arabia.

Article 334 Arrangements must be made at each port to collect waste matter, food leftovers and ship refuse from ships lying at anchor in the port, and to dispose of such waste and refuse in accordance with instructions issued by the Ministry of Health.

Article 335 Saudi ships are prohibited from releasing waste matter or ship refuse at sea within a distance of 12 miles from the coast.

Chapter XIII

Comments

Chapter XIII concerns the conditions for issuance of Seamen's passports for employment aboard Saudi flag vessels.

Chapter XIII

Seamen's Passport

Article 336 No person may practice any profession on Saudi ships which make sea voyages outside the territorial waters of the Kingdom unless he obtains a seaman's passport.

Article 337 Those who work in warships shall be excepted from the preceding Article.

Article 338 The medical examination requirements for the various marine professions shall be laid down by a decision of the Minister of Communications.

Conditions Necessary For Granting a Seaman's Passport.

Article 339 The granting of a seaman's passport shall be conditional upon the following:

1. That according to a medical report the applicant's vision, health and physical condition qualify him for the kind of profession which he will practice on the ship under various weather conditions.

2. That the applicant should not have been convicted of a crime, misdemeanor or any immoral act, unless he has been rehabilitated.

3. That the applicant should meet the academic standards and possess the technical experience required for practicing the profession for which the passport is granted.

4. That the applicant should not be under eighteen (18) years of age.

Article 340 The seaman's passport may not be used except for working on ships. The seaman's passport takes the place of an ordinary passport in case the holder travels to join the ship or to return to the Kingdom.

Particulars to be recorded in the Seaman's Passport.

Article 341 The following particulars shall be recorded in the seaman's passport:

1. Particulars of the holder's identification.

2. Particulars of the names, numbers, gross tonnages of the ships, the dates and places where they are joined, and the dates and places of service thereon.

3. Limits of the voyage and type of the job.

4. Evaluation of efficiency and behavior.

Article 342 The said particulars shall be recorded by the Marine Inspection Offices in the Kingdom, or by the Consul of the Kingdom if the ship is abroad.

Article 343 The seaman's passport shall be cancelled if the holder thereof loses any one of the conditions required for granting it.

Procedure For Obtaining a Seaman's Passport.

Article 344 The application for a seaman's passport shall be submitted to the Port Director.

Article 345 The application shall be accompanied by the following documents:

1. Educational qualifications and the experience required for the profession, or evidence of the applicant's possession of a marine certificate.

2. Certificate of birth or an official extract therefrom.

3. Police record, provided that not more than three months should have passed since it was issued.

4. Eight recent photographs of the applicant, 4 x 6 cms. in size.

Article 346 A seaman's passport shall be valid for a period of five years from the date of its issuance, and it may be renewed for a similar period.

Article 347 Application for renewal of a seaman's passport shall be submitted at least one month before its expiration date.

Article 348 If the period of validity of a seaman's passport expires while the holder is outside the Kingdom, the Embassy or Consulate of the Kingdom abroad shall extend it for a maximum period of six months, renewable for a similar period.

Article 349 The format of the seaman's passport shall be determined by a decision of the Minister of Communications.

Chapter XIV

Comments

Chapter XIV sets out the conditions for licencing of officers and manning of vessels. Saudi officials have the right to inspect licences of officers of foreign flag vessels and may detain a ship that is not in compliance.

Chapter XIV

Conditions for Practicing Seamanship

Article 350 No person may work in the following jobs on Saudi ships unless he is the holder of a Certificate of Seamanship Qualification which qualifies him for performing the duties of the said job:

1. Captain.
2. Duty Officer.
3. Chief Engineer.
4. Duty Engineer.

Article 351 A decision of the Minister of Communications shall determine the conditions governing the issuance of Certificates of Seamanship Qualification for the jobs listed in the preceding Article.

Article 352 The following certificates of seamanship qualification shall empower their holders to occupy the jobs mentioned against each one of them:

1. Certificate of Captain of the High Seas qualifies its holder for commanding ships of any tonnage and type and in any voyage.

2. Certificate of First Navigation Officer of the Ocean-Going Ships qualifies its holder to occupy the following jobs:

   a) First Navigation Officer of an ocean-going ship.

   b) Commanding an ocean-going freighter whose gross tonnage is less than 500 tons.

   c) Commanding coastal navigation vessels.

3. Certificate of Second Navigation Officer of the High-Seas qualifies its holder to occupy the following jobs:

a) Second Navigation Officer of an ocean-going ship.

b) First Navigation Officer of a coastal navigation vessel (passenger or freighter).

c) Commanding coastal passenger or freight vessels of a gross tonnage below two hundred (200) tons.

4. Certificate of a Captain of Coastal Navigation qualifies its holder to occupy the following jobs:

   a) Commanding coastal vessels.

   b) Second Navigation Officer of an ocean-going ship.

5. Certificate of Coastal Navigation Officer: qualifies its holder to occupy the following jobs:

   a) Navigation Officer of a coastal vessel.

   b) Commanding coastal freighters of a gross tonnage below one hundred and fifty (150) tons.

6. Certificate of Chief Marine Engineer (Steam/Diesel) qualifies its holder to occupy the position of Senior Marine Engineer in ocean-going ships and coastal navigation vessels of any tonnage, taking into account the type of engine of the ship and of its certificate.

7. Certificate of Marine Engineer (Steam/Diesel) qualifies its holder to occupy the position of Shift Engineer in ocean-going ships and in coastal navigation vessels of any tonnage, taking into account the type of engine of the ship and of his certificate.

8. Certificate of Marine Master qualifies its holder to occupy the following jobs:

a) Commanding a sailboat (with or without auxiliary engine).

b) Commanding a tugboat within the limits of the port.

c) Commanding launches of any type.

Article 353 No person may sail launches or motor-driven floating craft within Saudi ports unless he obtains a licence to do so from the marine inspection authorities at the port.

Article 354 The number of holders of marine certificates on Saudi ships shall not be less than the following, according to the tonnage of each ship.

		Number
A) Marine Officers		
	1. Ships of a gross tonnage below 700 tons.	Two
	2. Ships of a gross tonnage of 700-2000 tons.	Three
	3. Ships of a gross tonnage over 2000 tons.	Four
B) Marine Engineers		
	1. Ships of a gross tonnage over 700 tons, or of a total engine power exceeding 800 H.P.	Three, one of whom to be the holder of a certificate of Chief Engineer.

Article 355 It is permissible to engage one or more persons who do not possess the job qualifications stated in the preceding Articles, provided that they shall not be in charge of shifts.

Article 356 An unqualified person may not replace a qualified one in taking over a shift save in cases of force majeure.

Seamen

Article 357 The number of qualified seamen on Saudi ships shall not be less than the following, according to the ship's tonnage:

	Number of Seamen
1. Ships of a gross tonnage of 700-2000 tons.	Six
2. Ships of a gross tonnage exceeding 2000 tons.	Nine

Article 358 A qualified seaman is one whose actual marine service on deck is not less than three years.

Article 359 The number of qualified seamen in each shift shall not be less than three.

Wireless Officers

Article 360 The number of wireless officers on Saudi ships shall not be less than the following limits:

A) Passenger Ships (equipped with automatic alarm system	No. of Wireless Officers
1. Passenger ships carrying or authorized to carry 250 or more passengers.	One (provided that the number of hours of moni toring the call for hel frequency shall not be less than 8 per day.)
2. Passenger ships carrying or authorized to carry 250 passengers or more, and whose sailing time between two consecutive ports exceeds 16 hours.	Two, one of whom shall be the holder of a Wireless Certificate of the first degree (provided that the minimum number of hours of monitoring the call for help frequency shall be 16 hours per day.

3. Passenger ships mentioned in Paragraph (2) above, whose sailing time between two consecutive ports is less than 16 hours.	One (provided that the minimum number of hours of monitoring the call for help frequency shall be 8 hours per day).

B) Freighters (equipped with automatic alarm system)	No. of Wireless Officers
1. Ships of a gross tonnage of 1600 tons or more.	One (provided that the minimum number of hours of monitoring the call for help frequency shall be 8 hours per day)
2. Ships of a gross tonnage of 300-1600 tons (if equipped with a wireless telegraph system and an automatic alarm system)	One (provided that the minimum number of hours of monitoring the call for help frequency shall be 8 hours per day)

Article 361 If the ship is equipped with a wireless telephone system only, it shall have on board at least one person who holds the certificate of wireless telephone operator. (He may be the Captain, an officer or a seaman of the ship).

Article 362 By "Wireless Officer" is meant the person who is in possession of a wireless certificate of the first or second degrees.

Article 363 The marine inspection authorities of the Saudi ports shall have the right to inspect the certificates of the captains, navigation officers, marine engineers and wireless officers on Saudi or foreign ships during their presence in the Saudi ports.

Article 364 The marine inspection authorities may prevent any ship, whether Saudi or foreign, to depart in case it does not meet the minimum number required of the holders of marine certificates in accordance with the provisions of this Chapter.

Chapter XV

Comments

Chapter XV contains provisions for penalties resulting from violations of other articles of the Rules and Regulations. These penalties can include both fines and imprisonment, as well as the revocation of licences, and even confiscation of a vessel.

Chapter XV

Penalties

Article 365 Any violation of the provisions of Chapter II shall make the perpetrator liable to a fine not exceeding one thousand Saudi riyals or the equivalent thereof.

Article 366 Any violation of the provisions of Part 1 of Chapter III - with the exception of Article 23 thereof - shall make the perpetrator liable to a fine not exceeding one thousand Saudi riyals or the equivalent thereof.

Article 367 Any violation of the provisions of Article 23 of Part 1, in Chapter III shall make the proprietor liable to a fine not exceeding ten thousand Saudi riyals or the equivalent thereof.

Article 368 In the event of a ship leaving the port after issuance of a decision prohibiting her departure, the captain thereof shall be punished with imprisonment for a period not exceeding three months, and with a fine not exceeding ten thousand Saudi riyals or the equivalent thereof, or with either one of the said penalties.

Article 369 Any violation of the provisions of Part 2 of Chapter III - with the exception of Article 24 thereof - shall make the perpetrator liable to a fine not exceeding five hundred Saudi riyals or the equivalent thereof.

<u>Article 370</u> Any violation of the provisions of Article 24, Part 2 of Chapter III shall make the perpetrator liable to a fine not exceeding one thousand Saudi riyals or the equivalent thereof, and the pilotage fees shall be doubled.

<u>Article 371</u> Any violation of the provisions of Parts 3 and 4 of Chapter III shall make the perpetrator liable to a fine not exceeding three hundred Saudi riyals or the equivalent thereof.

<u>Article 372</u> The Port Directorate shall have the right to withdraw or to refuse renewing the licence to practice the profession of stevedore in the following cases:

1. If it is established that the stevedore had committed a breach of the contracts concluded with the captains or agents of the ships.

2. If the stevedoring tariff laid down by the Port Directorate is contravened.

3. In cases dictated by the public interest.

<u>Article 373</u> The Port Directorate shall have the right to suspend the licence referred to in the next preceding Article for a period not exceeding three months in the following cases:

1. Non-abidance by the minimum loading and unloading averages provided for.

2. Contravention of the Port Rules (and) Regulations.

3. Contravention of the Customs Regulations and of the Customs Instructions.

4. Contravention of the port instructions regarding loading and unloading.

<u>Article 374</u> The Port Directorate may withdraw the licence or refuse to renew it in case of repetition of contraventions, provided that the second contravention is committed before the lapse of six months from the first contravention.

<u>Article 375</u> A penalty of imprisonment for a period not exceeding one year, and of a fine not exceeding ten thousand Saudi riyals or the equivalent thereof, or any one of the said penalties, may be inflicted:

1. On every owner, outfitter or captain of a ship who hoists the flag of the Kingdom on a ship not registered in the Kingdom.

2. On every owner, outfitter or captain of a ship who does not register it in accordance with the provisions of Chapter IX.

3. On every owner, outfitter or captain of a ship who forges the ship's registration certificate or alters its particulars.

The Commission for Settlement of Dispute may order confiscation of the ship with due regard to international marine practice in such cases.

<u>Article 376</u> A penalty of imprisonment for a period not exceeding three months and a fine not exceeding five thousand Saudi riyals, or the equivalent thereof, or any one of the said penalties, may be inflicted:

1. On the owner of a ship who fails to file the application for registration of the ship within the prescribed time in accordance with the terms provided for in Chapter IX.

2. On the owner of the ship who fails to file an application for recording the modifications made to the ship in the registration certificate thereof in accordance with the terms provided for in Chapter IX.

3. On the owner of the ship who fails to file an application for cancellation of the ship registration in accordance with the terms provided for in Chapter IX.

4. On the owner of the ship who uses the provisional registration certificate otherwise than is provided in Chapter IX.

5. On the owner or captain of the ship who alters the figures and marks of the ship's draught, or the ship's distinguishing marks, unless the purpose of the violation is to avoid capture.

6. On the owner or captain of a ship who refuses to submit the ship's registration certificate to the authorities concerned.

Article 377 Any violation of the provisions of Part 2 of Chapter IX shall make the proprietor liable to a fine not exceeding one thousand Saudi riyals or the equivalent thereof.

Article 378 Any violation of the provisions of Parts 1 and 2 of Chapter X shall make the perpetrator punishable as follows:

1. If it is a passenger ship

   By a fine not exceeding ten thousand Saudi riyals or the equivalent thereof.

2. If it is a freighter

   By a fine not exceeding five thousand Saudi riyals or the equivalent thereof.

Article 379 Any person who alters or modifies the position of the load lines on the ship or who obliterates the same with the intent of fraud shall be punished with imprisonment for a period not exceeding two years, and with a fine not exceeding thirty thousand Saudi riyals or the equivalent thereof, or with either one of the said penalties.

<u>Article 380</u> Any captain, owner or outfitter of a ship who attempts or orders to get it out of the Saudi ports while she is loaded in excess of the authorized load prescribed for her in accordance with the International Load Line Certificate which she carries shall be liable to the following fines:

1. A fine not exceeding one thousand Saudi riyals, or the equivalent thereof.

2. An additional fine of one thousand Saudi riyals or the equivalent thereof for each inch of draught in excess of what is prescribed for the ship.

<u>Article 381</u> Any ship which enters the Saudi ports carrying on board a number of pilgrims in excess of the load prescribed in accordance with the International Safety Certificate issued to it shall be punished with the following penalties:

1. The owner of the ship shall bear the expenses of retransporting the excess number on aircraft or other ships after the end of the pilgrimage season.

2. The ship shall be punished with the fines prescribed by the Regulations and mentioned in the Quarantine Regulations, namely, fifty riyals or the equivalent thereof for each passenger in excess of the passenger load prescribed for the ship.

<u>Article 382</u> Every ship shall be obligated to retransport the pilgrims who had come on her, with the exception of the illegal number in excess of her load, to which the provisions of the next preceding Article applies.

<u>Article 383</u> Any owner, agent or captain of a ship who issues tickets for passengers in excess of the legal number of the ship's load which is prescribed for the type of the voyage and recorded in the International Safety Certificate issued to the ship, shall be punished with a fine equal to double the price of the tickets sold. The owner shall bear the sojourn expenses of the ticket holder at the port until the procuration of a means of transportation for him at the expense of the ship's owner.

<u>Article 384</u> The captain of the ship shall be punished with a fine not exceeding two thousand Saudi riyals or the equivalent thereof if he violates the rules pertaining to the channel separation schemes and the rules of traffic therein in any zone having such channel separation schemes.

<u>Article 385</u> Any violation of the provisions of Articles 313 and 314 of Chapter XII shall make the captain or the owner of the ship liable to imprisonment for a period not exceeding one year, and to a fine not exceeding twenty thousand Saudi riyals or the equivalent thereof, plus reimbursement of the pollution, remove expenses, or to any one of these two penalties. The authorities concerned may detain the ship until payment of the prescribed fine has been effected.

<u>Article 386</u> Any violation of the provisions of Article 320 shall make the captain of the ship liable to a fine not exceeding three thousand Saudi riyals, or the equivalent thereof.

<u>Article 387</u> Any captain of a ship who prevents the competent authorities from inspecting the oil register, or who refuses to submit same to the said authorities shall be punished with imprisonment for a period not exceeding six months, and with a fine not exceeding three thousand Saudi riyals, or the equivalent thereof, or with any one of the said two penalties.

<u>Article 388</u> Any violation of the provisions of Article 321 shall make the captain of the ship liable to a fine not exceeding five thousand Saudi riyals or the equivalent thereof.

Article 389 Any violation of the provisions of Articles 333 and 335 shall make the captain of the ship liable to a fine not exceeding ten thousand Saudi riyals or the equivalent thereof.

Article 390 Any owner, outfitter or captain of a Saudi ship who contravenes the provisions of Chapter XIV shall be punished with imprisonment for a period not exceeding one year, and with a fine not exceeding ten thousand Saudi riyals, or the equivalent thereof, or with any one of the said two penalties.

Article 391 Any person who by way of fraud or by using forged documents succeeds in occupying the position of captain, marine officer or marine engineer in a Saudi ship shall be punished with imprisonment for a period not exceeding two years, and with a fine not exceeding ten thousand Saudi riyals or the equivalent thereof, or with any one of the said two penalties.

B. Miscellaneous Decrees and Regulations Affecting Shipping.

The regulations governing seaports, harbors and lighthouses discussed in the preceding sections is a general set of rules covering a wide range of areas. However, periodically additional rules are issued to cover specific problems. Original texts of these rules are often difficult if not impossible to obtain. Often the best or only sources are unclassified cables received from embassies and newspaper accounts. Realizing that these sources may not always be satisfactory, and the changing nature of such regulations in a royal kingdom, some of the more significant of these miscellaneous rules, regulations and decrees are set out below.

(1) Stevedoring and Unloading Tariffs for Jeddah (Jidda).* (Source: Unclassified Cable from American Embassy, Jeddah to Department of State November 15, 1977).

---

* Text uses Saudi spellings. Headnotes use American spellings.

In September the Ports Authority for Saudi Arabia announced its intention to take over stevedoring and unloading functions at Jidda Seaport, which until now have been performed by private firms, for the purpose of speeding up and reducing the cost of port operations.

The new system is scheduled to go into effect November 15, 1977. The basic stevedoring tariff will be SR 15 per metric freight ton (compared to SR 20 or more charged previously by private firms), (SR 3.52 = $1.00) while specific unloading charges are calculated according to size, weight or type of cargo. A complete schedule of the new tariff for Jidda Islamic Seaport, as published in the local press, is attached. According to port regulations, all owners or operators of vessels are required to deposit the estimated amount of stevedoring charges with the Jidda Port Administration finance department, against a proforma invoice, prior to berthing of the vessel and commencement of discharge operations. Payment for cargo to be unloaded on weekends (Thursdays and Fridays) must be made prior to the closing of banks on weekends.

The stevedoring tariff represents about 40 percent of actual stevedoring costs according to Ports Authority President, Dr. Fayez Badr. The reduced costs for stevedoring and unloading reflect the Saudi Government's continuing effort to reduce the costs of imported goods and to improve the operation of the Kingdom's port operations. The Ports Authority, in a recent press conference, stated it expects shipping conferences and shippers to reciprocate by reducing ocean freight rates charged on Jidda-bound cargo.

The Port Authority has not yet taken over stevedoring responsibilities in Dammam or other Saudi seaports but it intends to do so eventually.

Stevedoring and Unloading Tariffs for Jidda Islamic Seaport

Effective November 15, 1977

I.	Stevedoring, including the following:	Tariff
	Pilotage; vessel towage, except LASH barges; mooring and unmooring; opening and closing of hatches; stevedoring, and use of associated gear and mechanical equipment (except heavy lift cranes); tallying and prompt production of outturn report; ship and shore supervision; continuous work seven days a week; use of port barges; and no overtime or shift premium:	SR 15 per ton
II.	Unloading tariff:	
	A. The following cargo is rated on a per ton (1000 kilograms) deadweight basis:	
	1. Bagged cement and lime and other bagged cargo; cargo in drums; iron and steel; liner-board and newspring in rolls; temperature controlled/chilled/frozen cargo	SR 15/ton
	2. Packaged timber and plywood	SR 9/ton
	B. All other general cargo will be rated on measurement tonnage, as follows:	
	1. Up to 2.5 measurement/weight ratio:	SR 15 per cubic meter
	2. 2.5 to 5.0 measurement/weight ratio:	SR 11 per cubic meter
	3. Over 5.0 measurement/weight ratio:	SR 8 per cubic meter
	C. The following cargo will be charged a per unit rate:	
	1. Cars, landrover-type vehicles, vans/minibuses, and other vehicles up to three tons weight:	SR 25 per unit
	2. Any wheeled or tracked vehicle from three to ten tons weight:	SR 100 per unit

Any wheeled or tracked vehicle from ten to twenty tons:	SR 300 per unit
Any wheeled or tracked vehicle over twenty tons:	SR 450 per unit
3. Mobile homes up to 20 meters long:	SR 300 per unit
Mobile homes from 20 to 40 meters long:	SR 600 per unit
Mobile homes over 40 meters long:	SR 900 per unit
4. Containers, 20-meter length (charge includes terminal charge and outward loading of an equivalent-sized empty unit) (Stevedores' responsibilities start and finish at ship's hook.)	SR 200 per unit
Containers, 40-meter length:	SR 300 per unit

D. Other charges. The above-listed stevedoring charges do not include the following:

Handling of fire and water-damaged cargo:	Special quotations
Idle time for which vessel or consignee is responsible:	SR 200 per gang hour or part thereof
Restowing cargo on board vessel which is not for Jidda discharge.	SR 400 per gang hour or part thereof

E. The following terminal charges will be levied on cargoes landed at Jidda port but not handled by Jidda Port Administration stevedores:

1. Containers/mafis/flats up to 20-meter length:	SR 60 per unit
Containers/mafis/flats over 20-meter length:	SR 90 per unit

2.	Trailers, up to 20-meter length:	SR 60 per unit
	Trailers, over 20-meter length:	SR 90 per unit
3.	Other ro-ro units, up to 20-meter length:	SR 60 per unit
	Other ro-ro units, over 20-meter length:	SR 90 per unit
4.	Cars, landrover-type vehicles and other vehicles up to three tons:	SR 8 per unit
5.	All other passenger vehicles over three tons:	SR 25 per unit

(2) Regulations Governing Carriage and Import of Cement Through the Port of Jeddah (Source: Unclassified Cable from American Embassy Jeddah to Department of State Dated January 12, 1977)

Regulation P/A/2/76

PURPOSE: To prescribe rules governing the import of cement cargo through the Port of Jidda in order to expediate discharge, to minimize loss of cargo in handling and to accelerate supply of cargo to the market.

SCOPE:

These regulations shall apply to all members of the trade and all government agencies involved in the shipment, stowage, carriage, discharge, distribution and import of cement cargoes moving through the Port of Jidda, and to all vessels commencing to load cargo for Jidda on or after December 1, 1976.

Berths at the Port of Jidda will only be given to such vessels which have fully observed the conditions of loading and discharge as outlined hereunder in these regulations.

CONDITIONS OF CARRIAGE:

A. The contract of affreightment or charter party should specify that the vessel carrying cement has sufficient cranes or cargo handling gear at each hatch with a safe working load of 3 tons or more.

B. All cargoes of bagged cement intended for discharge at the Port of Jidda are to be bagged in 5-ply bags with an inner vapour barrier bag of polyethylene or similar waterproof material.

C. Stowage of cement is to conform to the following conditions wherever possible:

1. In the ends of the hatches, stowage of bags should be fore and aft.

2. In the wings of the hatches, stowage of bags should be fore and aft.

3. In the square of the hatch right from the bottom layers to the top within a square of 20'x30', all bags must be left in pre-slung state in nylon straps having either a canvas or polyethylene base capable of standing the load which it is required. The weight of each sling is not to be less than 2 N/T and not more than the safe workload of the crane/derrick which plumb the hatch.

D. All broken/torn bags must be rejected and contents rebagged at the Port of loading prior to stowing.

E. Cement shall be discharged at the Port of Jidda through the use of forklifts in the holds as much as possible.

F. Stevedores and other contractors are required to guarantee a discharge rate of not less than 2000 tons per day.

G. Importers or contractors are to guarantee an adequate supply of flat-bed trailers for towing heads and lorries to sustain and clear the specified rate of discharge.

H. No trailer/trucks, loaded or empty are to be left in the Port area. Program for the movement of cement from the Port are to be given by the importers to the Port Administration prior to the commencement of discharge.

I. Discharge of cement is to continue without any stoppage for 24 hours a day and 5 days in the week.

J. Vessels loaded with cement cargo in excess of 500 tons shall be prohibited from carrying any other commodity for discharge at the Jidda Port. This prohibition includes steel, timber and all general cargo unless all cargo is pre-slung in units of not less than 2 tons.

K. The Port will cancel the registrations of any vessel which does not conform to the regulations. A survey will be conducted and a recognized surveyor on all cement vessels and any vessel which does not adhere to the foregoing conditions will not be allowed to discharge at the Port of Jidda.

(3) Information and Documents to be Supplied by Vessels Prior to Berthing at Saudi Seaports. (Source: Unclassified Cable from American Embassy, Jeddah to U.S. State Department Dated April 24, 1977)

All vessels calling at Saudi Arabian ports to discharge cargo are required to produce, prior to berthing, copies of cargo plan, manifests and cargo summary. Any vessel failing to do so will not be allowed to discharge. As an exception to the above, and to facilitate shipowners, vessels will be allowed to discharge (without producing the aforementioned documents) provided the Ports Authority at Port of Discharge has received by telex details of manifests prior to vessel's arrival. In such case, however, failure by the shipowner/agent to submit all documents required, i.e., cargo plan, manifests and cargo summary within 36 hours of commencement of discharge, will result in a withdrawal of this concession for subsequent vessels of shipowner/ operator calling at Saudi Arabian port.

The information required by telex will be:

Port of loading.
Bill of lading number.
Marks and number on bill of lading.
Description of cargo on bills of lading.
Hazardous cargo specified by bill of lading.
Heavy lifts and abnormal sizes, if any, to be specified.

Total number of bills of lading from each port. LASH operators will identify bills of lading to specific barge numbers.

(4) Rules Relating to Container Traffic in Jeddah (Release by Fayez I. Badr, President Ports Authority 1977)

KINGDOM OF SAUDI ARABIA
PORTS AUTHORITY JEDDAH SEA PORT

TO: All Shipping Agents handling Containers Traffic in the Port of Jeddah.

It is imperative to obtain at the earliest possible moment an improvement in the present situation of the container traffic, both in relation to the Port of Jeddah and outside this Port. The present imbalance of containers shipped out as compared to those which come into the Port, the resulting excessive number of containers in the Port, the large number of containers in the most disparate parts of the Kingdom which remain abandoned and unclaimed, all these are unacceptable.

I wish to ask your cooperation for immediate measures on your part to correct this situation within the month of March 1977 and with this target in mind, I hereby require you to comply to the following:

1. In order to encourage consignees to return the containers quickly a deposit of S.R. 1500 is to be requested by you for each container delivered.

   In addition, a rental of S.R.75 is to be charged to the consignees for each day beyond 15 days starting from date of landing from the ship.

2. Consignees must be advised by you of the expected date of arrival and name of ship, of their containers, by hand delivered or registered letter at least one day before arrival to enable consignees to make their arrangements in time for withdrawal of their container.

3. You are to establish a proper Container Control System which must enable you to know at any time, the situation of each container from date of landing in the Port until it is reshipped giving all details such as: consignees name, serial number date of landing, date of delivery to consignee and date of reshipment.

   This container control system is first of all essential to you to enable a quick turnaround of the containers, but this information must be available to our Authority at any time we may require it.

4. You are to make the necessary arrangements for the proper staff and equipment to enable you to move the containers fast from Pier to Terminal, and then from Terminal to outside the Port.

5. You are to cable to this Authority at the beginning of each week, the following informations:

   A) Number of containers landed in the Port.

   B) Number of containers you delivered inland, out of the Port.

   C) Number of containers you reshipped from Port and out of the Kingdom.

   D) Number of containers you have in Port at the end of the previous week.

   E) Detailed list with their full addresses of consignees whose containers have been lying in the Port for a period of more than 15 days.

6. Please arrange for us to receive the information under paragraph NO 5 for the period of November, December and January not later than 10 days from the date of this circular.

7. I shall review your figures at the end of each three months period and shall expect to see the figures of containers you receive into the Kingdom, balance (give or take a maximum of 5 percent), with the figures of containers you reship out of the Kingdom.

8. It will be your responsibility to withdraw any containers lying abandoned and unclaimed in the Country, which with a proper Container Control System, you should now be able to trace. Your urgent attention and action is requested.

   I am very confident that with your full cooperation this situation can be improved quickly and satisfactorily. If you have any inquiries regarding any point, please contact the Director General of the Port.

5) Rule Restricting Vessels Over 15 Years Old (Source: Saudi Arabian Port Authority Circular, 1976; Journal of Commerce)

   1. No vessel which is of more than 15 years as of December 1st, 1976 and having commenced the loading of cargo for Saudi Arabia on or after December 1st, 1976, which date will be determined by the date of the first bill of lading issued for a Saudi Arabian port, will be permitted to discharge cargo at a Saudi Arabian port.

      a) The exception to this regulation will be granted if upon request by the shipper or charterer a condition survey establishes that the vessel is cargoworthy in every respect and that the deck machinery is adequate to meet the standard of discharge in the ports of Saudi Arabia.

      b) The cost and expense for such survey shall be borne by the shipowner or charterer but the appointment of the surveyor has to be approved by the Kingdom of Saudi Arabian ports.

      c) Merchants and/or importers are to specify in their Letter of Credit that the vessel carrying their cargo to Saudi Arabia is not more than 15 years old on the date of commencement to load or that an exemption has been granted by the Kingdom of Saudi Arabian ports.

d) Any vessel entering a port in Saudi Arabia which does not meet the foregoing requirements shall not be discharged.

2. The stowage of all cargo shall be surveyed on the arrival of the vessel. All cargo damaged by any means shall not be discharged and shipowner shall be responsible for the disposal.

JEDDAH PORT ADMINISTRATION

CIRCULAR

1st November 1976

(6) To: All Stevedoring Companies
operating in the Port of Jeddah

Working hours for discharge of cargo

Stevedoring companies shall immediately arrange their labour personnel into permanent work gangs. The names and position in the gang for each Company shall be presented to the Port Office by 15th Zualkaidah, 1396 (November 17th, 1976).

One hour after the commencement of each shift the stevedores representative shall deliver to the Berth Superintendent the personnel composition of each gang working on the vessel. Failure to submit the required list of each shift shall be considered a violation of this Circular.

Each gang shall consist of the following minimum number of personnel:

3 Winchmen

1 Signalman

8 Hatchmen

1 Foreman

1 Tally Clerk

When discharging general cargo consisting of several Bills of Lading, the number of hatchmen required shall be increased to 12. Each gang as described shall remain intact each day and on every vessel. No change in the composition of work-gang shall be tolerated unless it results from workers illness or resignation, which case must be substantiated.

Fayez I. Badr, Ph.d.

President, Port Authority

JEDDAH PORT ADMINISTRATION

CIRCULAR

2nd November 1976

(7) To: All Shipping Agents, Shedkeepers, Customs Employees at Gates, Yards and Sheds and Chamber of Commerce in Jeddah, Riyadh, Mecca, Medina and Taif

Deliveries of Cargo and Bills of Lading

Effective from the date of this Circular consignees are not permitted to remove their cargo from the Port of Jeddah in less than Bill of Lading lots, unless the total weight or volume exceeds the capacity of a vehicle described below. Deliveries in part lots of small loads by merchants utilizing the Port as a Storage warehouse will not be permitted.

Bills of Lading covering a large tonnage or volume which cannot be delivered by one truck load shall be removed from the Port in vehicles with a capacity of not less than 15 tons weight or not less than 30 cubic meters in volume.

Any violation of this order will subject to consignee or merchant to a review of his license or prohibit the violator from importing goods through the Port of Jeddah.

Fayez I. Badr, Ph.d.

President, Ports Authority

JEDDAH PORT ADMINISTRATION

CIRCULAR

5th November 1976

To: All Ships Agents and the Chamber of Commerce of Jeddah, Mecca, Medina, Taif and Riyadh

Surveys of Cargo prior to discharge

The quantity of cargo currently being landed at Jeddah Sea Port in a damaged condition due to inadequate packing, bad stowage or inefficient stevedoring methods has reached proportions which are impeding the working of the Port. Effective from the date of this Circular a survey of the cargo on-board each ship or barge will be carried out by a responsible officer of the Jeddah Port Administration before the commencement of discharge.

1) The discharge of particular consignments will not be permitted if such a survey indicates that their further handling will cause:

a) An unacceptable degree of damage to the goods

b) Delay to the working of the ship

c) Delay to their subsequent orderly delivery to consignees

2) The Ship Agent will be informed by the Port Administration of the date and time of the survey and is to ensure that the surveyor is given full facilities onboard the ship. The Ships Agent can if he so wishes attend the survey but the carrying out of a survey will not be dependent on his presence.

3) In addition to the initial survey further inspections will be carried out during the working of the ship and the discharge of cargo which is not up to acceptable standards refused.

4) The landing of repaired or recoopered packages will be at the discretion of the Port Administration and permission will be given only if:

a) A reasonable rate of discharge can be maintained.

b) The packages are marked in such a manner as to allow them to be identified against the Bill of Lading or manifest.

c) The number and description of the items in each package are clearly indicated.

d) They are landed at a time acceptable to the Port Administration.

5) If during the working of a ship the quantity of damaged or otherwise unacceptable packages or the time required to make them fit for discharge is such as to slow down the overall discharge rate the ship will be removed from the berth until corrective measures are complete to the satisfaction of the surveyor. The completion of the ships discharge at anchor or alongside will be at the discretion of the Port Administration.

Fayez I. Badr, Ph.d.
President, Port Authority

CIRCULAR

9th October 1976.

(9) TO: SHIPPING AGENTS AND MEMBERS OF CHAMBER OF COMMERCE

The loss, the damage, and the lack of care in separating to Bill of Lading from transhipped cargo is preventing the Ports from clearing the cargo.

1. Commencing October 20, 1976 no vessel loaded with the

original cargo and cargo from another vessel regardless of the manner of transhipment shall be granted a berth in Ports of Kingdom of Saudi Arabia.

2. Prior to berthing all vessels will be surveyed to establish the condition of all cargo. All vessels carrying unmarketable cargo shall not be permitted to discharge.

Dr. Fayez I. Badr, President
Ports Authority, Kingdom of
Saudi Arabia.
Jeddah Islamic Sea Port.

CIRCULAR

(10) TO ALL AGENTS AND MEMBERS OF CHAMBER OF COMMERCE

Rules and Regulations for all Lighters and Barges engaged in the discharge of vessels at anchorage in the Port of Jeddah

1. Commencing November 15, 1976 (Zualkaidah 23/1396) the following procedures shall be enforced:

   a) The Ship Agents shall prepare tallies for all cargo loaded on barges, showing the following:-

      1) Bill of Lading number
      2) Number of packages
      3) Condition of cargo
      4) Barge number under load
      5) Ship's name, date and rotation number

   b) Tally sheets signed by Ships Master or Agent shall be submitted to the Barge Traffic Manager immediately on completion of loading. No Barge discharge shall be permitted until complete tally record is submitted.

   c) The Barge cargo shall be tallied during discharge by an employee of the Shipping Agent. Full accountability of cargo is the sole responsibility of Shipping Agent.

   d) The Port Authority shall survey the Barge cargo prior to discharge and the Shipping Agent shall be notified of any damage. Repetition of such damages shall result in possible cancellation of the license given to the Shipping Agent by the Jeddah Port Administration.

   e) The cleanliness of the Barge is the sole responsibility of the Shipping Agent.

   f) All barge owners are to produce a certificate describing the seaworthiness and condition of the barge. The Port Marine Staff shall survey all barges and those unsafe or unfit for the carriage of cargo shall be rejected and the operator shall be required to make repairs within 2 months. Any barge which is determined to be unseaworthy shall not be given permission to load. All barges to be equipped with safe ropes and tackle.

   g) Condition of the cargo loaded on a barge shall be the sole responsibility of the Shipping Agent.

   h) The Port shall make available Pallets for cargo suitable for palletization. The Shipping Agent shall be responsible for the return of these Pallets in like good order and condition.

i) The tugs operated by Private Companies shall assist in the movement of barges upon request by the Port Management. Failure of these companies to conform to the instructions of the Port Administration could lead to cancellation of the operating licenses issued by the Port Administration.

j) Forklift for work at anchorage will not be supplied by the Port.

k) The Port Administraton will not permit the discharge of barge cargo in the Port unless the Ships Agents show proof that the Consignees have been notified of the availability of their cargo at the Port.

JEDDAH PORT ADMINISTRATION CIRCULAR

1st November, 1976

(11) TO: ALL SHIPPING AGENTS AND MEMBERS OF THE CHAMBER OF COMMERCE

Working hours for Discharge and Delivery of Cargo

Commencing (November 15th, 1976) 23rd Zualkaidah 1396 all vessels will discharge cargo on a 24-hour basis. No exception shall be considered; refrigerated warehouses, cement merchants/receivers and all consignees receiving direct discharge cargo shall make immediate arrangements to supply sufficient vehicles and labour at the inland terminus to effect continuous discharge of cargo.

Fayez I. Badr, Ph.d.
President, Ports Authority

7th November, 1976

(12) TO: ALL SHIPPING AGENTS AND MEMBERS OF CHAMBER OF COMMERCE

Effective from the date of this Circular importers, merchants and dealers of machinery, automobiles, trucks and mobile units of any type shall not be permitted to sell or transfer the ownership of the vehicle nor be permitted to transfer the Bill of Lading or any part of the Bill of Lading to individuals or Companies until the vehicle is removed from the Port of Jeddah.

Vehicles remaining in the Port beyond the 15 days free storage period shall be subject to immediate auction by the Customs.

Fayez I. Badr, Ph.d.
President, Ports Authority

1st November, 1976

(13) TO: ALL SHIPPING AGENTS AND MEMBERS OF THE CHAMBER OF COMMERCE

Separation of cargo to Bills of Lading

The Shipping Agents acting on behalf of the Shipowners are required by International Law relating to the Ocean carriage of goods to separate the cargo into Bills of Lading at the Port of discharge.

Shipping Agents shall instruct their Stevedoring Contractors to execute the complete separation to Bills of Lading in accordance with the Ship's manifest. This requirement shall commence on November 10th, 1976 - 18th Zualkaidah 1396 and the Shipping Agent shall be held responsible for the non-adherence to this order.

All General Cargo shall be separated and loaded onto pallets in the ships hold and all bagged cargo shall be separated into brand names. All cargo designated in the ships manifest as dangerous, corrosive or toxic shall be isolated and discharged only on the approval of the Berth Superintendent.

Fayez I. Badr, Ph.d.
President, Ports Authority

KINGDOM OF SAUDI ARABIA PORTS AUTHORITY
PRESIDENT OFFICE

(14) CLARIFICATION

To clarify the circular issued by the Ports Authority NO 256 dated 5.11.96 dealing with the basic requirements for cargo vessels calling at Saudi Ports, the Ports Authority would like to confirm that: the exception granted for vessels more than 15 years of age shall also apply to those vessels which have a valid certificate for cargo gear and tackle provided that such a certificate is issued by one of the following societies approved by the Government of Saudi Arabia. The certificate's date or its renewal should conform with the date of sailing from Port of shipment.

1. AMERICAN BUREAU OF SHIPPING
2. BUREAU VERITAS
3. DET NORSK VERITAS
4. GERMANISHER LLOYDS
5. LLOYD REGISTER OF SHIPPING
6. NIPPON KAIJI KYOKAI

(15) Regulation on Handling of Octel Anti-Knock Compounds in Saudi Ports

(May, 1979)

Owing to the highly dangerous nature of this cargo, the following rules must be strictly adhered to:

1. Cargo must be stowed on deck and must be readily available for immediate discharge. Block stowage is advisable when practical.
2. Fire fighting equipment on board vessels should be ready for immediate use. This equipment should include a spray attachment for hoses.
3. Uninterrupted direct delivery must be effected. The cargo must not be discharged onto the quay.
4. The consignee must provide a safety surveillance team to be present from the time the vessel berths until the goods have been removed from the port area.
5. The safety team must report their presence to a port official on arrival, and they must wear distinguishing clothing to allow all concerned to easily recognize them.
6. The safety team must have readily available all necessary safety equipment to inspect and isolate an area in the event of an accident.
7. The consignee must deposit with the Port Safety Department at least one spare safety kit.
8. Vehicles taking delivery of the cargo must be maintained to a high standard of efficiency and, in the case of carriage of I.S.O. Modular Tanks, the vehicles must be fitted with appropriate twist-lock securing devices in good working order.
9. Vehicles carrying the subject substance must travel through the Port area under escort and with an accompanying safety team.
10. Passage through the Port will not be allowed during the peak hours. Any vessel/person contravening these rules will be subject to penalties.

Fayez I. Badr, Ph.D.
President and Chairman of the Board Ports Authority
Kingdom of Saudi Arabia

(16) Ras Al Mishab - Port Information

(July, 1979)

Ras Al Mishab is a new deep water sea port with 2,400 ft. of berthing space.

Vessels calling at Ras Al Mishab are requested to contact Ras Al Mishab Harbour Office on VHF Channel 16 prior to arrival at Pilot buoy, (buoy No. 5 of Ras Al Mishab approach channel) which is loacted at 28 13' N. and 48 43' E. Do not proceed beyond this point before consulting with Ras Al Mishab Harbour Office, with services available from 0600 to 1700 hours every day except Friday.

Pilotage is compulsory and available during daylight hours (0600 to 1700), 7 days a week, with short notice prior to vessels arrival.

Dredged channel of 4 miles is well marked by buoys and two pairs of range lights that lead vessels in and out of the port.

Maximum allowed draft at present time is 33 ft. . However, after completion of works on expansion of the port we expect to accommodate vessels up to 35 ft. draft regardless of length and/or tonnage.

The port has two tugboats available to assist vessels in docking and undocking, or in case of need or assistance. Each tugboat is capable of generating 2,000 h.p. by main engine.

The turning basin of 1,250 ft. radius provides safe maneuvering for any size of the vessel not exceeding 34 ft. draft.

The pier is 18 ft. above water level and accordingly not suitable for Ro/ Ro cargo operation; however, the harbour is well equipped for receiving any type and size of cargo including heavy lifts and bulk cement up to 24,000 tons.

The harbour is fully equipped with forklifts, discharging gear, spreaders for 20 ft. and 40 ft. containers, and portable cranes up to 300 tons capacity, all handled by professional stevedores.

The supply of bunkers, water and/or provisions is not available at this port, and we suggest that vessels calling at Ras Al Mishab secure their needs at other ports. Only emergency medical attention can be provided, if requested by Master.

No shore leave is permitted in this port, except for the Master for business purposes. Port regulations must be strictly observed by all vessels.

Any other particulars such as crew changes, emergency repairs, provisions, etc., are handled through local Agents.

We hope that the above information is of help to all concerned and we welcome any questions or explanations not covered above.

Harbour Master
Ras Al Mishab

(17) Marad Advisory No. 79 - 1 (February 9, 1979)

TO: U.S. Flag Steamship Operators

Subject: Saudi Arabia; anti-pollution port regulations

The Department of State advises:

In the past few weeks the Saudi Port Authorities, particularly at Jidda, have adopted a policy of strict enforcement of regulations with regards to dumping of garbage and flushing oil tanks in the harbor areas and at anchorages in the immediate area of the open roadstead. Fines of up to SR 20,000 have been assessed to ship's captains who have been negligent about their vessel's pollution control practices. Saudi flag vessels have not been exempted from these pollution fines.

Burt Kyle
Director, Office of Domestic Shipping
U.S. Maritime Administration

(18) Ras Tanura Port Regulations

The following regulations and special notes are promulgated for the use of ships Masters entering and leaving Ras Tanura and Dammam ports:

Inbound Vessel:

1. Vessels fitted with the appropriate VHF radio equipment are requested to monitor Channel 16 when in the vicinity of Ras Tanura channel and anchorage area.

2. Vessels shall report time of passing Beacon No. 3 to Ras Tanura Pilot Station.

3. Vessels shall report time of passing Buoy No. 7 to Ras Tanura Pilot Station.

4. Vessels proceeding within the area bound by Channel Buoy No. 9 and the southern extremity of Ras Tanura anchorage should limit speed to a maximum of 5 knots.

5. No overtaking is permitted in the Ras Tanura arrival channel after passing Buoy No. 9.

6. A minimum distance of one mile shall be maintained between vessels proceeding in the same direction after passing Buoy No. 9.

7. Vessels passing Buoy No. 17 must navigate with extreme caution and give way to vessels departing from the berths.

8. Freighters transmitting the Ras Tanura port area, bound for Dammam, should alter course Eastward after passing clear of Buoy No. 17 and keep to the eastern sector of the tanker anchorage.

9. Under no circumstances shall inbound vessels navigate in the buoyed deep water departure channel.

Outbound Vessels:

1. All vessels are to monitor Channel 16 when in the vicinity of Ras Tanura channel and anchorage area.

2. Vessels departing from Ras Tanura anchorage must advise Ras Tanura Pilot Office of their intentions thirty minutes before departing.

3. Freighters outbound from Dammam shall, when passing Dammam Channel Beacon No. 1, alert Ras Tanura Pilot Office of their estimated time of arrival at the southern extremity of the tanker anchorage. Freighters should keep to the eastern sector of the tanker anchorage and avoid the maneuvering area from the anchorage to the piers.

4. Vessels maneuvering within the area bound by the southern extremity of the Ras Tanura anchorage and the entrance to the departure channel (Buoy 17 & 18) should limit speed to a maximum of 5 knots.

5. Any departing vessel shall not overtake any vessel ahead until both vessels have passed clear of Buoy No. 5.

6. A minimum distance of one mile is to be maintained between vessels proceeding in the same direction until clear of Buoy No. 5.

7. Under no circumstances shall outbound vessels navigate in the arrival channel.

C) INTERNATIONAL CONVENTIONS & TREATIES

The text of the Seaport and Harbor regulations refer to, and often incorporate by reference, various international maritime conventions. Saudi Arabia is a signatory to the following international agreements relating to shipping matters:

1. International Convention of Load Lines, 1966.
2. International Convention of the International Maritime Consultive Organization
3. International Convention for Safety of Life at Sea, 1960
4. International Convention for the Prevention Pollution of the Sea by Oil (with reservation)

Saudi Arabia is not a participant in a number of other significant maritime agreements, such as the Convention of the International Regulations for Preventing Collisions at Sea; Convention of the High Seas; Convention of the Continental Shelf; Convention for the Unification of Certain Rules of Law with Respect to Assistance and Salvage at Sea; International Convention for the Unification of Certain Rules Relating to Bills of Lading for the Carriage of Goods by Sea and the Convention on Facilities of International Maritime Traffic.

Saudi Arabia also has numerous bi-lateral treaties with the United States and other countries, mostly dealing with economic and technical cooperation.

Listed on the following pages are the bi-lateral treaties between the United States and Saudi Arabia.

SAUDI ARABIAN TREATIES WITH UNITED STATES

Cultural Relations

Agreement for Cultural Exchange, July 25, 1968 TIAS 6746

Economic and Technical Cooperation

Economic Assistance Agreement for Expansion of the Port of Dammam, May 1, 1958, TIAS

Agreement on Cooperation in the Field of Economics, Technology, Industry, and Defense June 8, 1974, TIAS 7974

Technical Cooperation Agreement, February 13, 1975, TIAS 8072

Project Agreement for Technical Cooperation in Statistics and Data Processing, September 27, 1975, TIAS 8490

Project Agreement for Technical Cooperation in the Procurement of Electrical Power, November 23, 1975, TIAS 8495

Project Agreement for Technical Cooperation in Agriculture and Water, November 23, 1975, TIAS 8494

Project Agreement for Technical Cooperation in Electrical Power Planning, February 29, 1976, TIAS 8614

Project Agreement for Technical Cooperation in Science and Technology, February 29, 1976, TIAS 9019

Project Agreement for Technical Cooperation in Manpower Training and Development, June 12, 1976, TIAS 8673

Project Agreement for Technical Cooperation in Procurement of Electrical Equipment, March 26, 1977, TIAS 9027

Project Agreement for Technical Cooperation in Upgrading and Improving the Scientifi Capability of the Consumer Protection Department in the Saudi Arabian Ministry o Commerce, May 3, 1977, TIAS 8876

Project Agreement for Technical Cooperation in Establishing an Information Center, May 3, 1977, TIAS 8875

Project Agreement for Technical Cooperation in Desalinization, May 3, 1977, TIAS 8878.

Project Agreement for Technical Cooperation in Highway Transport, August 16 and 26, 1977, TIAS 8991.

Project Agreement for Technical Cooperation in the Field of Solar Energy, October 30, 1977, TIAS 9077.

Project Agreement for Technical Cooperation in Audit Administration and Training, May 16, 1978

Project Agreement for Technical Cooperation in Customs Administration and Training, June 11 and 22, 1978

Project Agreement for Technical Cooperation in Supply Management Development, July 13, 1978.

Project Agreement for Technical Cooperation in Increasing the Electrical Power Generating Capacity of the Nasseriah Power Station, November 9 and 13, 1978.

Investment Guaranties

Agreement on Guaranteed Private Investment, February 27, 1975, TIAS 8045.

Trade and Commerce

Project Agreement in Regard to Diplomatic and Consular Representation, Juridical Protection, Commerce and Navigation., November 7, 1933, 48 STAT 1826.

D) SAUDI INCOME TAX & INVESTMENT REGULATIONS

While it is beyond the scope and purposes of this book to give a detailed and comprehensive treatment of the Saudi tax and investment laws, it is nevertheless an important tangential area for those interested in operating ships under the Saudi flag and engaged in trade and commerce with Saudi Arabia, and a brief discussion is warranted.

INCOME TAX

The original Saudi tax regulations were contained in the Royal Decree issued on November 2, 1950. [1] The regulations established a tax on personal income and capital gains. Income was defined as all personal income either earned or resulting from investment of capital within Saudi Arabian territory. The initial regulations were revised several times. [2] In its current form the law exempts Saudi nationals and Saudi companies (wholly owned by Saudis) from the tax. However, non-Saudis, including foreign corporations which operate in Saudi Arabia are subject to taxation. Profits distributed to non-Saudi individuals from profits of companies jointly owned by Saudi and non-Saudi nationals, are also subject to taxation. Income is considered derived "inside" the Kingdom if it is earned or results from investments in the territory of Saudi Arabia, its territorial waters, its air space and the national zones between Saudi Arabia and Iraq and Kuwait respectively. For purposes of taxation of capital investments, transport vehicles and ships are specifically included in the definition of property subject to the tax. The first 5,000 Riyals of personal income is exempted from the tax. If income is derived solely from

---

1) Royal Decree No. 17/2/28/3321.

2) Royal Decree No. 17/2/28/8955, May 7, 1951.
Royal Decree No. 17/2/28/576, November 19, 1956.
Royal Decree No. 102, May 4, 1966.

capital investments the first tax exemption is prorated if the taxpayer resides in Saudi Arabia for less than one year.

The tax rates applying to both earned and investment income are as follows (after deduction of the exemption):

5% - up to 20,000 Riyal
10% - 20,000 to 50,000 Riyal
20% - over 50,000 Riyal

Corporate profits are subject to a separate tax. Corporate profits subject to taxation include net profits claimed by non-Saudi companies operating inside Saudi Arabia and the total portion of the non-Saudi partners share of net profits of Saudi companies. The corporate tax rate is as follows:

20% - up to 100,000 Riyal
30% - 100,000 - 500,000 Riyal
35% - 500,000 - 1,000,000 Riyal
40% - over 1,000,000 Riyal

Foreign companies operating both inside and outside of Saudi Arabia are only subject to taxation on revenues realized by the company from sources within the country. Where the company has revenue from non-Saudi operations, it must apportion revenues that are attributable to Saudi sources.*

Amounts paid by U.S. companies to Saudi Arabia under Royal Decree 17/2/28/3321 (See text on the following page) were held not to be a creditable income tax within the meaning of Sections 901 and 903 of the U.S. Internal Revenue Code. See <u>Rev. Ruling</u> 78-63, which revoked <u>Rev. Ruling</u> 55-296.

---

* At present there is no tax treaty between the United States and Saudi Arabia.

ROYAL DECREE NO. 17/2/28/3321

IN ITS ORIGINAL FORM

21 MUHARRAM 1370 (2nd. NOVEMBER 1950)

WITH THE HELP OF GOD.

WE 'ABDUL 'AZIZ 'ABDUL RAHMAN AL FAISAL

KING OF SAUDI ARABIA,

In consideration of what has been submitted to Us by our Minister of Finance regarding the necessity of increasing the income of the Government to enable it to carry the burden of general reforms, and to promote the general welfare of the country, and to improve the standards of living, We have agreed to the introduction of an income tax in accordance with regulations, the text of which follows, and which We have approved and for exesution of which We have issued our Order :

ARTICLE I

SUBJECT TO TAX

These Regulations prescribe a tax on personal income of individuals and on the income or profit yielded by the investment of capital.

The word "income", wherever it occurs in these Regulations, means all personal income earned or resulting from the investment of capital within the Kingdom of Saudi Arabia and where it has rights in the two Neutral Zones between it and both Iraq and Kuwait.

ARTICLE II

PERSONAL INCOME

Personal income in these Regulations shall mean all kinds and descriptions of compensation for personal services which an individual receives as wages from the person or the company employing him, or from someone acting on their behalf. These Regulations also apply to the salaries of the employees of the Saudi Arabian Government.

There shall be considered as personal income everything paid in cash, and likewise the amount of the value, according to a reasonable estimate, of chattels or other things given in lieu of any salary, or the amounts deducted from salary or wages to settle debts.

ARTICLE III

TAXABLE PERSONAL INCOME

Taxable personal income is that which exceeds annually 20,000 Saudi Arabian riyals.

ARTICLE IV

THE TAX RATE APPLICABLE TO PERSONAL INCOME

The tax rate applicable to personal income is 5% of the taxable income as defined in these Regulations; and the amount shall be collected by the means specified in instructions to be issued by the Minister of Finance.

ARTICLE V

COLLECTION OF TAXES ON PERSONAL INCOME AND THE OBLIGATIONS OF EMPLOYERS RELATING THERETO

Any one who employs a person or persons liable to personal income tax shall deduct the amount of the tax from the wages and salaries of these persons and shall pay the deducted amounts to the authority to be designated by the Ministry of Finance, on or before the 15th of the month following the month for which deduction was made. He shall also record the matter on the required form under the supervision of the official to be delegated by the Ministry of Finance.

In case of his delay or failure to pay the tax on behalf of the person or persons whom he employs, he will become responsible for payment of such amount and the Ministry of Finance shall have the right to collect it from him by means which it may decide.

Any one employing a person or persons shall give them notice of the amount of tax deducted from their wages or salaries, and that shall be recorded on the proper form.

Companies which are registered — in accordance with the Regulations for the Registration of Companies, approved by Royal Decree No. 144 — shall have the right to deduct the amounts of the taxes due from the wages of their workmen and the salaries of their employees and pay them at one time for a period not exceeding three months, on or before the 15th of the month following the period for which the taxes were deducted.

In case any employer of a person or persons delays paying the taxes due from them within 5 days from the legal date of payment, he shall be fined an additional amount of 10% of the original amount due. And if the period of delay exceeds 15 days the fine shall be 25%.

ARTICLE VI

INCOME TAX ON THE INVESTMENT OF CAPITAL

Income from capital, according to these Regulations, shall mean all income or profit, including the profits resulting from any enterprise or transaction in which capital is used, such as the purchase and sale of different kinds and descriptions of goods, the products from lands, the exchange of any kind of money, and the hiring and letting of any properties whether movable or immovable. This shall include animals, trucks, ships, other means of transportation, machinery, and equipment. Capital shall not include the necessary tools which an individual workman owns and uses in performing his work or trade.

ARTICLE VII

NET PROFIT ON THE INVESTMENT OF CAPITAL

The net profit resulting from the investment of capital, subject to income tax under these Regulations, shall be considered to be all income, proceeds, and profits, meaning thereby the gross income, for commercial transactions completed during the year (gross income shall include all amounts, incoming in money, in addition to properties and acquisitions which may be acquired without money), there being deducted therefrom the cost of goods sold, and the ordinary and necessary running expenses of the enterprise, and a reasonable amount for depreciation, but not including therein the personal expenses of the owner of the enterprise.

The net profit resulting from the investment of capital shall be considered to be 15% (fifteen percent) of the gross income, unless the taxpayer is able to convince the responsible official otherwise by force of adequate documents and accurate records.

ARTICLE VIII

THE RATE OF INCOME TAX ON THE NET PROFIT FROM THE INVESTMENT OF CAPITAL

The income tax on the net profit resulting from investment of capital shall be collected at the rate of ten percent (10%) after deduction of the sum of the twenty thousand Riyals exempted as provided for in Article III and in paragraph e of Article XVII of these Regulations.

ARTICLE IX

TAX DECLARATIONS ON NET PROFIT FROM THE INVESTMENT OF CAPITAL

Every person liable to the tax on net profit resulting from the investment of capital shall submit declarations therein and pay the tax therein indicated to the official whom the Ministry of Finance shall delegate for the collection of the amount.

Those declarations shall be written on a form the nature of which the aforesaid Ministry shall prescribe; and that shall be completed and the tax indicated in the declaration shall be paid on or before the 15th day of the month following its falling due.

In case of delay or of failure on part of the person subject to the tax to pay what is due from him within five days from the legally prescribad date, he shall be penalised by having to pay the additional amount of 10% of the sum due. If the delay exceeds fifteen days the fine shall be 25% (twenty-five percent).

ARTICLE X

INCOME OF COMPANIES

The word "company" in these Regulations shall mean any company that is registered or that is required to be registered, in accordance with the Regulations for the Registration of Companies (approved by Royal Decree No. 144). This expression shall include also, all companies engaging in all kinds of operations in the Kingdom of Saudi Arabia and where the Kingdom of Saudi Arabia has rights in the two neutral zones between it and both Iraq and Kuwait.

ARTICLE XI

RATE OF TAX

The rate of tax on companies shall be 20% of their net profit, (as that profit is defined in these Regulations). The tax shall be collected annually.

ARTICLE XII

NET FROFIT

The net profit of companies subject to payment of tax shall be the total grass income, as defined, after the deduction of the amounts which these Regulations specify.

ARTICLE XIII

GROSS INCOME

The gross income subject to the tax in accordance with these Regulations shall be considered to be all the proceeds, profits, and earnings of whatever kind and in whatever form paid, resulting from all kinds of industry and commerce such as buying and selling and financial or commercial transactions, and resulting also from dealing with and development of oil or other mineral resources, and from properties movable or immovable, including all proceeds resulting from commissions, or from profits on shares or securities, or any profits or earnings resulting from any commercial transactions the object of which is profit, and earning from any source of wealth whats oever. There shall be considered as gross income for any company incorporated under the laws of any country other than Saudi Arabia, and carrying on its operations at the same time both outside and inside the Kingdom of Saudi Arabia, all the proceeds which that company earns locally from any source whatsoever within the Kingdom. There shall be added thereto that part of the proceeds of the company pertaining to local resources which the company obtains from the carrying on of its joint operations inside and outside the country . The Kingdom of Saudi Arabia, whenever and wherever it occurs in these Regulations, shall include what it has rights to in the two Neutral Zones between it and both Iraq and Kuwait.

ARTICLE XIV

AMOUNTS LEGALLY DEDUCTIBLE UNDER THE REGULATIONS

Amounts which are legally deductible for the determination of the net profits of companies in accordance with these Regulations are as follows :

a. All the ordinary and necessary expenses which the business or the enterprise requires and the expenditure of which takes place during the year, including therein a reasonable amount for the salaries of employees and for any compensation granted for any personal services.

b. Travel expenses which are connected with the business or the enterprise.

c. Rentals for properties rented in connection with the business or the enterprise.

d. Any losses incurred by the business or the enterprise and not compensated for in any way.

e. A reasonable amount for depreciation of properties which are used or employed in the operations.

ARTICLE XV

DECLARATIONS

Every company subject to these Regulations must submit a declaration on the official form and pay the amount shown thereon to the official delegated by the Ministry of Finance for this purpose. The said declaration must be submitted and the required amount paid on or before the fifteenth day of the third month following the end of the year for which the declaration was made.

In case of failure to submit the declaration and to pay the amount within five days from the time limit, there shall be added to the sum due a fine amounting to ten percent of the tax. If the delay exceeds a period of fifteen days, the fine shall become twenty-five percent (25%).

ARTICLE XVI

RULES FOR CALCULATION OF INCOME

The taxpayer must set down in the records of his accounts all the gross income which he receives for the year itself, and likewise the amounts deducted (except for depreciation and loss). When the taxpayer gives proof of the correctness of his records and that they reflect truly his gross income and the deductions, he may submit the declaration on the basis of those records. If an auditor who is legally and internationally recognized certifies to the correctness of those records for any year in which the tax is due, the declarations on the basis of the said records shall be considered as correct.

If the taxpayer declares that he keeps records in a clear manner on the basis of a financial year different from the calendar year, he may request the Ministry of Finance that it permit him to make his declarations in accordance with the financial year which he follows. In such case he shall submit declarations and pay the tax on the fifteenth day of the third month after the end of the financial year which he follows. Penalties for delay in submitting the declarations and in payment of the tax shall be as mentioned in Article XV of these Regulations.

ARTICLE XVII

EXEMPTED FROM THE TAX

There shall be exempt from the provisions of these regulations :

a. The Royal Family.

b. Officers and men of the armed forces, police, and coast guard.

c. Persons officially appointed to religious posts in mosques.

d. Foreign ambassadors, ministers plenipotentiary and other diplomatic representatives, consuls, and consular representatives, on condition of reciprocal treatment and within the limits of this treatment.

e. Persons whose income does not exceed annually twenty thousand Saudi Arabian Riyals.

f. Animals and plants on which the religious tax (zakat) is paid.

g. Contributions and aids paid to the Government, charitable organizations, and institutions for social welfare which are recognised by the Saudi Arabian Government.

ARTICLE XVIII

a. The Minister of Finance shall enforce the income tax regulations, and there shall be formed in the Ministry of Finance a special department for taxes.

b. To facilitate the enforcement of these Regulations the Kingdom shall be divided administratively into not more than six districts, in accordance with what the Minister of Finance deems necessary for the administration and enforcement of these Regulations. There shall be appointed for each district a director, who shall have therein an office where the inhabitants of the district shall submit their declarations and pay the taxes due from them according thereto. The aforesaid director shall receive the taxes due and shall pay them monthly to the Ministry of Finance.

c. There shall be in each district a committee composed of three qualified and expert persons to check the declarations and to decide whether it is necessary to add any amount to them. That committee shall have the right to request the taxpayer that he present himself before it personally, or that he delegate someone to appear before it on his behalf. It shall have the right also to request the taxpayer or his agent to sumbit his records and books for checking, it being provided that those records and books shall be returned to their owner upon his request after the Committee has checked them.

d. When the Committee discovers a tax due and not mentioned in the declaration, or any tax on which declaration was not made, it shall have the right to collect the tax due and a fine amounting to 25% (twenty-five percent) from the properties of the taxpayer, in accordance with instructions which the district director will issue.

e. When the director of the district pays to the Ministry of Finance the taxes collected during any month of the year, he shall send an accompanying list covering names and addresses of the persons who paid the taxes as well as the amount paid by each of them.

f. As for the companies incorporated in countries other than Saudi Arabia and under the laws of the country in which they are incorporated, but carrying on operations both inside and outside of the Kingdom of Saudi Arabia, they shall submit their declarations to the tax department in Jeddah. The head of that department shall appoint a special committee composed of three qualified and expert persons to review and check their declarations. Those companies shall have the right to delegate any of their employees to appear on their behalf before the said committee, if such is requested. They (i.e., the companies) shall have the right to defend the correctness of the taxes about which investigation is in progress. The Committee shall have the right to check the records and accounts of those companies at any time it deems fit, but it shall not have the right to hold those records and accounts for such a period as to hamper the operations of the companies.

g. The committee shall have no right to impose on the companies any additional taxes above the amount of tax which they estimate except after abtaining the approval of the Ministry of Finance or of whoever may be acting on his behalf.

ARTICLE XIX

The Minister of Finance is accorded full authority to take all measures necessary for the enforcement of these Regulations and the collection of the taxes prescribed thereunder. This includes without limitation the employment and training of the necessary employees, the issuing of necessary official forms, instructions, and orders, notification to taxpayers conecerning payment of the taxes and whatever may be connected therewith, and obliging individuals and companies to keep records which will facilitate the collection of these taxes.

ARTICLE XX

The tax prescribed by these Regulations shall be effective for the first time beginning with the first of Muharram 1370. (13 October 1950).

ROYAL DECREE
No. 17-2-28-8955
Dated 30-9-1370 corresponding to 5-7-1951

With the help of God Almighty, We, Abdul Aziz Ibn Abdul Rahman Al-Faisal, Sovereign of the Kingdom of Saudi Arabia, in accordance with what our Finance Minister has referred to us, and after perusal of Royal Decree No. 17-2-28-3321, dated Muharram 21, 1370 (2-11-1950), and Royal Decree No. 17-2-28-7635, dated Rabi' Awal 16, 1370 (26-12-1950), hereby decree the following:

Article III of Royal Decree No. 17-2-28-3321, dated Muharram 21, 1370 (2-11-1950), should be amended as follows: "A foreign employee shall not be entitled to the exemption of the twenty thousand Riyals of his annual income from tax unless he spends a full year in the Kingdom. If he stays for less than a year, the exemption he is entitled to shall be in proportion to the period he spends.

Issued from Our Palace in Riyadh on Ramadhan 30, 1370 (5-7-1951).

Note: This Decree was cancelled by Article (4) of Royal Decree No. 17-2-28-576, dated 14-3-1371 (19-10-1956).

ROYAL DECREE
No. 17-2-28-576, dated 14-3-1376 (19-10-1956)
Amending some rules of the Saudi Income Tax Code

We, Saud Ibn Abdul Aziz, Sovereign of the Kingdom of Saudi Arabia, after perusal of the Income Tax Code issued by Royal Decree No. 17-2-28-3321, dated Muharram 21, 1370 H. (2-11-1950), which was amended by Royal Decree No. 17-2-28-8955 on Ramahdan 30, 1370 H. (5-7-1951), and the resolution of the Council of Ministers No. 31 dated 27-2-1376 H. (2-10-1956), concerning the amendments proposed by the Minister of Finance and National Economy for the above-mentioned Income Tax Code in order to be more in harmony with the development of economic life in the land and the international income tax regulations, hereby decree the following:

The first eleven articles of the Income Tax Code issued by Royal Decree No. 17-2-28-3321 dated Muharram 21, 1370 H. (2-11-1950), and amended by Royal Decree No. 17-2-28-8955 dated Ramahdan 30, 1370 H. (5-7-1951), shall be amended according to the following:

ARTICLE I: **The Persons Covered by the Tax:**

This Code is applicable to the entire earnings of individuals other than Saudis. (Royal Decrees have been issued according the same treatment accorded to the Saudis to citizens of Bahrain, Kuwait and Qatar, from whom the Zakat is taken instead of the income tax.)

A tax is also levied on the profits of non-Saudi companies operating inside the Kingdom or inside and outside the Kingdom simultaneously. A tax is also imposed on the profits distributed to non-Saudi nationals from companies jointly formed with Saudi and foreign capital.

Saudi nationals and Saudi companies, whose capital, partners and shareholders are entirely Saudi, shall not be liable for income tax.

CHAPTER ONE

ARTICLE II : **Personal Income :**

"Personal Income" according to this Code means all the the earnings of an individual in the form of salaries, wages, compensations for services rendered or rewards for any job he undertakes or service he performs inside the Kingdom for an individual, a firm or anybody. This includes the earnings of non-Saudis contracted or employed by the Saudi Government. Also to be considered as personal income are the reasonably evaluated costs of belongings given to an individual in the way of compensation for salaries, wages or rewards due to him for his work, or service; and also the sums deducted from any salary, wage or rewards for the purpose of repayment of debts. The term "inside the Kingdom" shall mean in this Code its land territories, territorial waters, air space and its share of rights in the neutral zones between itself and both Iraq and Kuwait.

ARTICLE III : **Income of Invested Capital :**

By "capital income" in this Code is meant any net profit or profits made by an individual in any operation using movable or immovable property for the purchasing and selling of goods of various kinds and qualities, or the produce of land, or to exchange money, the renting and letting of movable and immovable property, including animals, transport cars, boats and other means of transport and equipment of all kinds. Also to be considered as income or profit from capital are the profits realised by individuals in joint ventures. The necessary tools owned or used by artisans or self-employed professionals for the carrying out of their vocations or professions are not to be considered as capital.

ARTICLE IV :

All the general revenues of operations taking place during the year as a result of capital investment are to be considered net income or profit. The general revenues include all the cash revenues in addition to the properties and possessions obtained without payment and that is after deduction of the value of sold goods and the reasonable costs of administration and consumption. The personal expenses of the taxable person are not to be included.

Also to be considered a net revenue or profit from capital investment is 15 per cent of the general revenues, unless the tax payer convinces the authorities concerned to the contrary by the evidence of sufficient documents and accurate records.

ARTICLE V : **Amount Exempted from Tax :**

1. The first five thousand Riyals of an individual's personal income, or the personal income and the revenues or net profits resulting from capital investment, shall be exempted.
2. If the personal income of an individual is the outcome of capital investment only, the first ten thousand Riyals shall be exempted from tax and he is not entitled to the full annual exemption unless he resides in the Kingdom for a full year or is considered to be resident for a full year. If the period of residence is less or is considered to be less than one year, the amount exempted shall be in proportion to the period he stayed in the Kingdom.

ARTICLE VI : **Ratio of Tax :**

The ratio of tax on the total personal income and net profits and revenues resulting from capital investment beyond the limit of tax exempted amounts in the two cases referred to in Article 7 shall be as follows :

1. Five per cent of the part of the total income in excess of any of the two limited amounts exempted from tax and less than 20 thousand Riyals per annum.

2. Ten per cent of the part of the total income in excess of 20 thousand Riyals and less than thousand Riyals per annum.

3. Twenty per cent of the part of total income which exceeds 50 thousand Riyals per annum.

Any income realised by an individual as a result of investing his capital in one of the companies which previously was subjected to taxation imposed on companies according to this Code shall not be subject to taxation.

ARTICLE VII : **Imposition of Taxes on Personal Income and the Duty of Employers towards this :**

An employer of a person or persons liable to personal income tax must deduct the amount of he tax from the wages or salaries of these individuals and such amounts should be paid to the authorities specified by the Ministry of Finance on or before the fifteenth day of the month following the month for which the tax was withheld. Such tax should be registered in the authorised form under the supervision of an official assigned by the Ministry of Finance. In case of delay or failure to pay the tax for the person or persons employed by him, the employer shall become responsible for the payment of he required amount and the Ministry has the right to collect it as it sees fit.

Anyone who employs another person or persons should inform them of the amount to be deducted from their salaries or wages and to record this in the authorised form.

As for registered companies according to the Companies Law issued by Royal Decree No. 144 the Registration of Companies rules have been cancelled as stated in the preceeding chapters), they hall have the right to withhold taxes due on the wages and salaries of their workers and employees and o pay them together for a period not exceeding three months on or before the fifteenth day of the nonth following the period for which the taxes were collected.

In case of delay on the part of anyone who employs a person or persons in payment of taxes due rom them for five days after the legal date for payment, a fine equivalent to 10 per cent of the amount lue as taxes becomes payable. If the period of delay is in excess of 15 days the fine shall be 25 per cent f the taxes due for payment.

RTICLE VIII : **Collection of Taxes on Incomes of Artisans and Self-Employed Professionals and Incomes resulting from Capital Investment :**

Artisans and self-employed professionals are obliged to submit statements of their incomes, which re subject to taxation, and which they have earned in exercising their professions or from investing heir capital, to the Zakat and Income Tax Department and to pay the taxes due from them during the fteen days following the completion of one year's stay in the Kingdom. Anyone who delays in submitting such statement and the payment of the tax due by the appointed date shall be fined an extra sum equivalent to 10 per cent of the tax, and if the delay is more than fifteen days, the fine shall amount to 25 per cent of due tax.

ARTICLE IX :

Every artisan or self-employed professional, or individuals investing their capitals and at the same time employed by another party, be that an individual, a company or a government or private body, is obliged to add to the above-mentioned statement in the preceeding Article the details of salaries, wages or awards obtained through such a work and the amount of taxation withheld by the employer.

CHAPTER II

Tax on the Profits of Companies

ARTICLE X : **Profits Subject to the Companies' Tax :**

The "companies' profits" in this Code shall mean the following :

1. The net profits made by a foreign company operating inside the Kingdom only or both inside and outside the Kingdom.
2. All the shares of the non-Saudi partners in Saudi companies in the net profits.
3. The total shares of the net profits of non-Saudi partners in companies with limited partnership

ARTICLE XI : **Ratio of Tax Imposed on Companies' Profits :**

1. Twenty per cent of the profits amounting to less than 100 thousand Riyals per annum.
2. Thirty per cent of the part of the profits in excess of 100 thousand Riyals and less than 500 thousand per annum.
3. Thirty-five per cent of the part of the profits in excess of 500 thousand Riyals and less than one million Riyals per annum.
4. Forty per cent of the part of the profits exceeding one million Riyals per annum. The tax shall be collected annually, and the profits of any company shall not be subject to taxation if they have already been taxed according to the provisions of this Code.

Article 2 :

Paragraphs, A, B, C, D, E, F of Article 17 of the previous Code (No. 3321) shall be cancelled

Article 3 :

The regulations of Royal Decree No. 17-2-28-7634, dated Rabi' Awal 16, 1370 H. (26-12-1950) shall continue in force.*

* This concerns oil companies.

Article 4 :

Royal Decree No. 17-2-28-8955, shall expire on Ramahdan 30, 1370 H. (5-7-1951).

Article 5 :

This Decree shall be published and become effective as from the beginning of the current year, 1376 (8-8-1956), and the Minister of Finance and National Economy shall enforce it and he is authorised to issue the necessary decisions to this effect.

Royal Signature

ROYAL DECREE NO. 3321 IN AMENDED FORM

Royal Decree No. 17/2/28/3321 dated 21.1.1370 corresponding to 2.11.1950, amended by Royal Decree No. 17/2/28/8955 dated 30.9.1370 corresponding to 5.7.1951; and Royal Decree No. 17/2/28/576 dated 14.3.1376 corresponding to 19.10.1956; and Royal Decree No. 102 dated 19.11.1380 corresponding to 4.5.1961 and Royal Decree No. 111 dated 26.11.1380 corresponding to 11.5.1961.

With the Help of God Almighty,

We Abdul Aziz Ibn Abdul Rahman Al Faisal, Monarch of the Kingdom of Saudi Arabia,

In view of what our Finance Minister has submitted to us concerning the need to increase the State revenues in order to be able to shoulder the general reforms and to work for the welfare of the country and raise the living standards,

We have approved the creation of income tax in accordance with the accompanied Code, endorsed it and issued our orders for its implementation.

Article I : Those Subject to Taxation

This Code provides for the imposition of a tax on the total income earned by an individual, other than Saudis, (1) from his personal income or any income earned by investment of capitals. It also imposes a tax on the profits of companies whose capital is non-Saudi and which carry out their operations inside the Kingdom only or inside and outside the Kingdom simultaneously. It also provides for the imposition of the tax on the profits distributed to non-Saudi individuals from profits of companies whose partners are both Saudi and non-Saudi nationals.

Saudi nationals and Saudi companies which are totally owned by Saudis shall be exempted from the tax.

CHAPTER I

Article II : Personal Income

For the purposes of this Code, "personal income" means all the earnings of an individual from salaries, wages, compensations or rewards for any work or service he performs inside the Kingdom for another individual, company, or body. This shall include all what the employees and non-Saudi individuals contracted by the Government earn. To be considered as personal income also are the reasonably estimated amounts as value of property, or anything else, given to an individual as compensation for salaries, wages or rewards to which he is entitled for his work or service. Also to be subject to tax are the amounts which are deducted from any salary, wage, compensation or reward to pay the debts of their earners.

---

(1) Several Royal Orders were issued providing for according the citizens of Bahrain, Qatar and Kuwai the same treatment accorded to Saudi subjects by collecting the zakat from them instead c income tax.

The term "inside the Kingdom" shall mean throughout the text the territory of the Kingdom, its territorial waters, its air space and what falls under its jurisdiction in the two netural zones between the Kingdom on the one hand and Iraq and Kuwait on the other.

Article III : Income of Capital Investments

For the purposes of this Code the expression "income accruing from capital" shall mean all net income or profit obtained by an individual as a result of any operation in which he uses movable or immovable property for the purchase and sale of goods of various kinds and qualities or produce of land. for the exchange of money, the rent and lease of movable and immovable property, including animals, transport vehicles, ships, other transportation facilities, and all kinds of machinery and equipment. To be considered as income or profit resulting from capital investment shall be the profits realized by partners in companies of limited liability.

The necessary equipment owned and used by an individual for the exercise of his profession or vocation shall not be considered as capital.

Article IV :

All general revenues which are realized during the year shall be considered as net income or profit resulting from investment of capital. General revenues shall include all the cash revenues in addition to the properties and other possessions obtained without money after deducting the cost of the sold goods, administrative expenses and depreciation costs, which are reasonably estimated. These shall not include the personal expenditures incurred by the tax payer.

To be considered as net income or profit resulting from capital investment is the 15 per cent of the general revenues, unless the tax payer convinces the authorities concerned by means of full documents and accurate records otherwise.

Article V: Tax Exemption Limit

1. The first SR 5,000 (five thousand) of an individual's total personal income, or of total personal income and revenues of capital investment shall be exempted from the tax.
2. If the individual's personal income is the result of capital investment only the first SR 10,000 of his total income shall be tax exempt. The tax payer shall not be entitled to a full year's exemption unless he resides in the Kingdom a full year or considered as staying for one year. If the period of his residence in the Kingdom is less than that, the exemption granted to him shall be in proportion to the period he stayed in the Kingdom or that in which he is considered as resident.

Article VI : Rate of Tax

The tax rate to be applied to the total of personal income and net income, or the profits resulting from investment of capital and which are in excess of the exemption limit referred to in the foregoing Article, shall be according to the following :

1. Five percent (5%) of the part of the total income which exceeds the exemption limit and does not exceed SR 20,000 (twenty thousand) per annum.

2: Ten percent (10%) of the part of the income in excess of SR 20,000 (twenty thousand) and which does not exceed SR 50,000 (fifty thousand) per annum.

3. Twenty percent (20%) of the part of the total income which exceeds SR 50,000 (fifty thousand) per annum.

Any income realized by an individual from investing his capital in a company shall not be subject to the income tax if this income has been subjected to the tax imposed on the profits of companies in accordance with this Code.

Article VII : **Collection of Tax on Personal Income and Duties of Employers Towards This**

Any one who employs an individual or individuals subject to the personal income tax shall deduct the value of the tax from the wages or salaries of these individuals and pay the deducted amount to the authorities designated by the Ministry of Finance on or before the fifteenth day of the month following the month for which the tax was deducted. He shall also record this in the official form under the supervision of the official delegated by the Ministry of Finance.

In case of the employer's failure or delay to pay the tax on the income of the person or persons employed by him, he shall be considered liable for payment of the tax amount and the Ministry of Finance shall be authorised to collect it from him in the manner it deems fit.

Any individual who employs a person or persons shall inform them of the amount of tax deducted from their wages or salaries and shall record this on the official form provided for this.

As for companies which are registered in accordance with the Companies Registration Code, which was approved by Royal Decree No. 144, (1) they are authorized to deduct the amount of the tax due from the wages and salaries of their employees and shall pay them once for a period not exceeding three months on or before the fifteenth day of the month following the period for which the tax was deducted.

In case of any employer's delay in payment of the taxes due on his employee or employees for five days after the legal date of payment, he shall be fined an extra amount of ten percent (10%) of the original amount due for tax. If the period of delay exceeds fifteen days, the fine shall be twenty-five percent (25%).

Article VIII : **Collection of Tax on Incomes of Men of Professions and on Incomes Resulting from Capital Investment**

Individuals of free professions and vocations shall be personally obliged to submit statements on their taxable incomes realized from performing their professions and vocations, or from investing their capitals, to the Zakat and Income Tax Service and to pay the taxes due on them within the fifteen days following the elapse of one year on their stay in the Kingdom. Anyone who delays submitting the abovementioned statement and payment of the due tax on the appointed time shall be fined an extra amount

1. The Companies Registration Code was cancelled by Article 21 of the Commercial Register Code issued by Royal Memorandum No. 21/1/4470 dated 9.11.1375 (June 18, 1956).

of ten per cent (10%) of the tax due. If the delay exceeds fifteen days the imposed fine shall be twenty-five percent (25%) of the tax due.

Article IX :

Any man of profession or vocation or operating in capital investment working simultaneously for any other party, be that party an individual, company, and a governmental or non-governmental body, shall be required to declare in the above-mentioned statement the wages, salaries, compensations, or rewards realized from his work and the amount of tax deducted by the employer thereon.

CHAPTER II

TAX ON CORPORATE PROFITS

Article X : Profits Subject to Corporate Tax

For the purposes of this Code, the term "corporate profits" shall mean the following:

1. The net profits realized by any non-Saudi company which carries out its activities inside the Kingdom only or inside and outside the Kingdom simultaneously.
2. The total portion of the non-Saudi partners' share of the net profits of Saudi companies.
3. The total portion of the non-Saudi partners shares of the net profits of partnerships limited by shares (Societes en Commandite par Actions).

Article XI : Rate of Tax Imposed on Corporate Profits

The tax rate imposed on the net profits of companies shall be in the following manner:

1. Twenty percent (20%) on the portion of profits which does not exceed SR 100,000 (one hundred thousand) per annum.
2. Thirty percent (30%) on the portion of profits in excess of SR 100,000 (one hundred thousand) and which does not exceed SR 500,000 (five hundred thousand) per annum.
3. Thirty-five percent (35%) on the portion of profits in excess of SR 500,000 (five hundred thousand) and which does not exceed SR one million per annum.
4. Forty percent (40%) of the portion of the profits which exceeds one million Riyals per annum.

The tax shall be deducted annually.

The profits realized by any company shall not be subject to taxation if they have been subjected to tax previously in accordance with this Code. (1)

Article XII : Net Profits

All general revenues, as defined hereunder, shall be considered the net profits of the taxable companies after deduction of the amounts provided for by the Code.

---

1. The first eleven articles were amended by Article I of Royal Decree No. 17/2/28/576 dated 14.3.1376 corresponding to 19.10.1956.

Article XIII : General Revenues

For the purposes of this Code, the expression "general revenues subject to taxation" shall mean all the profits, revenues, and gains regardless of their type and the manner in which they are paid and resulting from all kinds of trade and industry, of sale or purchase, or any financial or commercial deals, or the outcome of operations and investments in oil and mineral resources and any other movable or immovable properties, including all the revenues realized through commissions, and profits of stocks, promissory notes and guarantees, or any profits or gains resulting from any commercial deals aiming at making profits from any source of wealth.

The general revenues of any company established under the laws of any country other than those of Saudi Arabia and performs its operations inside and outside the Kingdom of Saudi Arabia simultaneously shall only inc'ude all the revenues realized by the company locally and from any source in the Kingdom.

To this shall be added that portion which is attributed to local revenue sources which the company realizes from its joint operations inside and outside the country. Wherever it appears in this Code, the Kingdom of Saudi Arabia includes its rights in the two neutral zones between itself and each of Iraq and Kuwait.

Article XIV : Amounts to be Deducted According to Code

The amounts to be deducted when estimating the net profits of a company according to this Code are :

1. All the ordinary and necessary expenditures required for the operations of the company and which are incurred during the year, including the provision of a reasonable amount for the salaries of employees and the compensations and rewards paid for personal services.
2. Travel expenses related to the activities of work.
3. Rents of properties rented for the operations of the company.
4. Any losses incurred by the company and for which no compansation is made one way or the other.
5. A reasonable amount for depreciation costs of the properties used during performance of work

Artivle XV : Statements

Every company subject to this Code shall submit a statement on the official form and shall pay the amount stated therein to the official delegated by the Ministry of Finance for this purpose.

The said statement and the payment of the required amount should be submitted on or before th fifteenth day of the third month following the end of the year for which the statement was made.

In case of failure to submit the statement and to pay the said amount within five days of the appointed period a fine of ten percent (10%) of the tax due shall be imposed. If the period of delay exceed fifteen days the fine shall become twenty-five percent (25%).

Article XVI : Rules of Income Definition

All the general revenues received by the tax payer shall be recorded in his account registers fo the same year. The same shall be made for the deducted amounts (except for depreciation and shortage). When the tax payer establishes the authenticity of his records and proves that they give a true picture of his general revenues and the deducted amounts, he may submit the statements on the bases of these records. When a legal and internationally recegnized auditor endorses the authenticity of the records for any year on which the tax should be deducted, the statements submitted on the bases of these records shall be considered correct.

If the tax payer declares that he possesses clear records based on a fiscal year different from the calendar year, he may ask the Ministry of Finance to permit him to submit his statements according to the fiscal year he adopts. In this case he shall submit the statement and pay the tax on the fifteenth day of the third month following the end of the fiscal year he adopts. The precautions against delay in submitting the statements and effecting of payment shall be the same as provided in Article XV of this Code.

Article XVII : Exemptions from the Tax

Those exempted from the provisions of this Code shall be : (1)

D. Ambassadors, Ministers plenipotentiary and other diplomatic representatives, consuls and foreign consular representatives as well as the administrative employees of the foreign legations who are appointed by their respective governments and to which they are subjects, on condition of reciprocal treatment and within the limits of this treatment.

G. Donations and contributions paid to the government, or to charitable societies, social bodies and establishments, which are recognized by the Saudi Arabian government.

Article XVIII :

A. The Minister of Finance shall enforce the Income Tax regulations, and a department for tax shall be established at the Ministry of Finance. (2)

B. To facilitate the enforcement of this Code, the Kingdom shall be divided into administrative areas, not to exceed six in number, according to the discretion of the Minister of Finance and the necessity for administering and application of this Code. A director shall be appointed for each area, who shall set up an office to which the inhabitants of the area submit their income tax statements and pay the taxes due on them accordingly. The said director shall receive the taxes due and pay them every month to the Ministry of Finance.

C. A committee composed of three men, of experience and efficiency, shall be set up in each area to examine the statements and to determine whether additional amounts should be added to the income tax deducted.

The said committee is authorized to request the tax payer to present himself to it in person or deputize some one else to present himself to the committee on his behalf. It is also authorized to request the tax payer or his proxy to submit his records and accounts for auditing on condition

---

. Paragraphs A, B, C, and E of this Article were cancelled by Article II of Royal Decree No. 17/2/28/576 dated 14.3.1376 (Oct. 19, 1956).

The Zakat and Income Tax Service was established by Ministerial Decision No. 394 dated 7.8.1370 (June 14, 1951):

that such records and accounts shall be returned to the owner when he requests them after having been checked.

D. When the committee discovers that a tax is due and have not been mentioned in the statement, or any tax for which no statement was given, it shall be authorized to collect the tax due in addition to a fine of twenty-five percent (25%) of the property of the tax payer, in accordance with the instructions to be issued by the Director of the Area.

E. When the Area Director pays to the Ministry of Finance the taxes collected during any month of the year he shall accompany them with a list of the names and addresses of those who paid the taxes and the amount paid by each one of them.

F. Non-Saudi companies established under the laws of their respective countries and carry out their operations inside and outside the Kingdom of Saudi Arabia shall submit their statements to the Tax Directorate in Jeddah, (1) whose director shall appoint a committee composed of three men of experience and efficiency to examine and check the accuracy of these statements. The companies shall have the right to delegate any of their employees to present himself before the said committee if so requested and to give evidence of the accuracy of the taxes in question. The committee shall have the right to audit and check the registers and accounts of the companies at its convenience, but it shall not have the right to hold such registers and accounts for a period long enough to hinder the operations of the companies.

G. The committee shall not have the right to impose additional taxes on companies before securing the approval of the Minister of Finance or whoever acts for him as to the amount of the tax which it estimates.

Article XIX :

The Minister of Finance shall have sufficient uthority to take all the precautionary measures necessary for the application of this Code and the collection of the taxes imposed in accordance thereof; this includes, without any definition, employment and training of necessary officials, issuance of official forms, instructions and orders, and notification of tax payers to pay their taxes, and any other measure related thereto, and to request individuals and companies to acquire the records which facilitate the collection of such taxes.

Article XX :

The tax provided for in this Code shall be applicable for the first time as from the month of Muharam 1370 A. H. (October 13, 1950) (2)

---

1. The Minister of Finance issued a memorandum to the Assistant Undersecretary of Finance in the Eastern Province No. 9324/4 dated 17.9.1372 (May 30, 1953) to the effect that big companies should settle their taxes in Jeddah.

2. The Minister of Finance issued Order No. 8328 dated 28.8.1370 (June 3, 1951) providing for the enforcement of the Tax Code as from the beginning of January 1950 for companies. As for personal income tax, its collection started as of the date provided for in the relevant Article.

ROYAL DECREE NO. 102

dated

19.11.1380 (May 4, 1961)

With the Help of God Almighty,

We Saud Ibn Abdul Aziz Al Saud, Monarch of the Kingdom of Saudi Arabia,

After perusal of Articles 19-30 of the Council of Ministers Ordinance,

And in accordance with the Council of Ministers Resolution No. 583 dated 15.11.1380 A. H. (April 30, 1961),

And in view of what the President of the Council of Ministers has presented to us,

Decree the following :

1. The salaries and wages earned by contracted employees at the Saudi Arabian embassies and consulates abroad shall be exempted from income tax on the basis of reciprocal treatment for Saudi employees contracted by foreign embassies in the Kingdom.
2. The President of the Council of Ministers and Ministers concerned shall enforce this our Decree.

Royal Signature

● ● ●

ROYAL DECREE NO. 111

dated

26.11.1380 (May 11, 1961)

With the Help of God Almighty,

We Saud Ibn Abdul Aziz Al Saud, Monarch of the Kingdom of Saudi Arabia,

In accordance with Article 30 of the Council of Ministers Ordinance,

And after perusal of the Council of Minister's Resolution No. 690 dated 25.11.1380 A. H. (May 10, 1961),

And in view of what the President of the Council of Ministers has submitted to us,

Decree the following,

1. Paragraph D of Article 17 of the Income Tax Code shall be amended as follows :

   D. Ambassadors and ministers plenipotentiary and other diplomatic envoys, consuls and foreign consular representatives as well as the administrative officials of foreign legations appointed by their respective governments and of which they are subjects, on condition of reciprocal treatment and within its limit.

2. The President of the Council of Ministers and Ministers concerned shall enforce this our Decree.

Royal Signature

E) FOREIGN CAPITAL INVESTMENT CODE

Saudi Arabia has had a code governing foreign capital investment since 1957. T original code was replaced in 1964 [1], and in January, 1979, the 1964 Code was supe seded [2]. The Code applies to investments in securities, equipment, patent and trad mark rights, and to means of transport (which would include vessels). A foreign inv is one who does not enjoy Saudi nationality and in a case of a corporation, one whos equity owners are not all Saudi Arabian [3]. Foreign investment is regulated by an interagency board of six representatives. Under the 1964 law, representatives were required to be at the deputy minister level. However, the 1979 Code changed this tc permit representatives as low as the tenth grade in each ministry.

The Secretary General of the Committee is the head of the Investment Bureau of the Ministry of Industry and Electricity. This function was previously performed by the head of the Foreign Investments Office of the Ministry of Commerce and Industry. The Committee functions include reviewing investment applications and handling complaints by foreign investors. One significant change in the 1979 Code is to permit approved investors to receive a 10 year tax holiday for industrial and agricultural projects. Previously the maximum tax holiday was 5 years for all projects. However in order to participate in the tax exemption, 25% or more of the total capital must come from Saudi nationals. Another significant change in the Code relates to eligil for licensing. Previously it was sufficient to show that the investment was in an economic development project other than petroleum and minerals. Now the applicant m also prove that the investment shall be accompanied by foreign technical know-how. Thus, it would appear that investment of capital will not be permitted unless the project is one where foreign know-how will be used.

---

1) Royal Decree No. 35, February 25, 1965, now superseded.
2) Royal Decree M/4, dated 2.2.1399, (January 1, 1979).
3) The 1964 Code did not define when a corporation was a Saudi national. The 1979 makes it clear that 100% of the equity must be Saudi owned, otherwise it is fore

Once approved, a foreign investment enjoys the same privileges as a domestic investment. The 1979 Code adds, for the first time, the right of a licensed foreign investor to acquire real estate, in accordance with the Regulations for Non-Saudis Taking Possession of Real Estate. The foreign company is also subject to Saudi labor and social security laws.

Foreign investors who violate the Code can have their license revoked or be liquidated. Dissatisfied investors may file an appeal within 30 days after the ministers'decision. Such appeals are final. A 1963 decision of the Council of Ministers prohibits Saudi agencies from submitting disputes to international arbitration, and the grievance board, therefore it is the only source of redress.

FOREIGN CAPITAL INVESTMENT CODE

(Issued by Royal Decree No. M4 dated 2.2.1399 A.H.)

Follows is the full text of the newly promulgated Foreign Capital Investment Code issued under Royal Decree No. M/4 on 2.2.1399 A.H. corresponding to January 1, 1979 A.D.. This code supersedes and cancels the old one issued under royal decree No. 35 of 11.10.1383 A.H. (February 25, 1964).

Article 1: The term "foreign capital" in this code shall be taken to apply to money, funds, bonds, securities, machinery, equipment, spare parts, raw materials, products, means of transport, rights such as patent rights, trade marks, and such value when owned by a natural person who does not enjoy the Saudi Arabian nationality or a corporate person whose equity owners are not all of the Saudi Arabian nationality.

Article 2: Without prejudice to the provisions of other regulations in force, foreign capital investment shall be subject to the license to be issued by a Minister of Industry and Electricity Resolution on the recommendation of the Foreign Capital Investment Committee once it fulfills the following two conditions:

1. It shall be invested in economic development projects, which under this code do not include petroleum and mineral projects.
2. It shall be accompanied by foreign technical know-how.

Article 3: Development projects shall be defined by a resolution issued by the Minister of Industry and Electricity on the proposal of the Investment Committee within the framework of the development plan.

Article 4: A special committee concerned with the investment of foreign capital shall be set up at the Ministry of Industry and Electricity. It shall be formed as follows:

--The Deputy Minister of Industry and Electricity, or his designated representative, as chairman.

--A representative of the Planning Ministry.

--A representative of the Finance and National Economy Ministry.

--A representative of the Ministry of Agriculture and Water.

--A representative of the Ministry of Petroleum and Minerals.

--A representative of the Commerce Ministry.

The rank of each of the above-mentioned representatives shall not be less than the tenth grade. The Head of the Investment Bureau at the Ministry of Industry and Electricity shall function as the Committee Secretary General. The Minister of Industry and Electricity shall appoint a legal counselor for the committee. The committee may hear the viewpoint of any expert provided he is not given a vote in the adoption of resolutions. The committee can meet with a quorum of four members, including the chairman. The committee's deliberations shall be conducted in camera and decisions shall be taken by a majority vote. In case of a tie vote, the chairman's vote shall be determining. The committee's resolutions shall not be final until approved by the Minister of Industry and Electricity.

Article 5: The duty of the committee referred to in the above Article 4 shall be the following:

1. Propose projects that are considered economic development ones.
2. Look into investment applications.
3. Examine whatever complaints submitted by foreign investors, or other competent parties or disputes arising from application of this Code, and forward its recommendations thereon to competent quarters.
4. Recommend penalties which it deems should be imposed against any establishment which violates the provisions of this Code.
5. Consider legislation and draft by-laws for implementation of this Code.

Article 6: The Foreign Capital Investment Bureau at the Ministry of Industry and Electricity shall provide all the necessary information, explanation and statistics which may be requested by anyone wishing to invest foreign capital in the Kingdom.

The said Bureau shall also do all the paper work require when foreign capital investment is licensed to operate in the Kingdom. The Foreign and Interior Ministries shall grant licensed investors and their officers and employees entry and exit visas and residence permits.

Article 7: Foreign capital which has fulfilled the conditions provided for in this Code shall be entitled to the following privileges:

a) All privileges enjoyed by national capital in accordance with the Regulations for Protection and Encouragement of National Industries as far as industrial ventures are concerned.

b) An industrial or agricultural project in which foreign capital is invested shall be exempt from income and corporate tax for a period of ten years. Other projects shall be exempted from these taxes for a period of five years.

Projects enjoying exemption when this Code goes into effect shall benefit from the exemption clause in this paragraph. The exemption shall be subject to the participation of national capital in the project with no less than 25% of the total capital. This percentage shall be maintained throughout the exemption period. The exemption period shall commence from the date on which production starts. The Council of Ministers may amend this paragraph.

c) Acquisition of real estate in accordance with the Regulations for Non-Saudis Taking Possession of Real Estate.

Article 8: Without prejudice to the provisions of this Code, projects enjoying the privileges under this Code shall be subject to the Regulations for Workmen and Social Insurance and other laws and regulations in force in the Kingdom.

Article 9: The provisions of this Code shall not apply to projects in which foreign capital is invested in the following cases:

a) If the projects had already existed before the enforcement of this Code.

If, however, they continue to function or increase their capital, they shall henceforth, be subject to the provisions of this Code.

b) If the projects were licensed to operate in the Kingdom under special codes or agreements.

Article 10: Should any establishment licensed to operate under this Code violate the provisions thereof, the Minister of Industry and Electricity shall issue a warning to the establishment requesting it to conform with these provisions within a period he shall determine. If the establishment fails to comply, and does not respond to the warning the Minister may, on the recommendation of the Investment Committee, revoke the license of the defaulting establishment or completely liquidate it.

The Minister may, on the recommendation of the afore-mentioned committee, instead of revoking the license, decide to deprive the defaulting establishment of all or part of the privileges provided for in this Code.

The parties involved may file a complaint with the Grievances Board within 30 days after the Minister's resolution imposing the penalty on the defaulting establishment had been communicated to them via official channels. The verdict of the Grievances Board shall be categorical and final.

Article 11: The Minister of Industry and Electricity shall issue the rules for implementation of this Code, which shall be published in the Official Gazette.

Article 12: This Code shall be published in the Official Gazette and shall go into force 30 days after it is published. The Foreign Capital Investment Code issued under Royal Decree No. 35 dated 11.10.1383 A.H. shall be cancelled as soon as this Code becomes effective.

F) OTHER REQUIREMENTS PERTAINING TO FOREIGN BUSINESS OPERATIONS

Foreign businesses which wish to establish branch offices in Saudi Arabia must obtain approval prior to establishment of an office. Within one month after commencement of operations, a foreign branch must comply with the provisions of the Statute of Commercial Registration, 1375,(1955) and register with the Ministry of Commerce and Industry, Commercial Registration Offices. A detailed application form along with copies of contracts, if any (in Arabic), must be filed with the application together with a registration fee, which is presently 100 Riyals (about $35 U.S.).

Saudi law requires that agents of foreign companies be either Saudi nationals or Saudi corporations. [1] These local agencies must be wholly Saudi in terms of capital, and local membership. The Ministry of Commerce and Industry maintains a register of agents of foreign firms. The government urges foreign firms to have local representation, if they are doing any business in Saudi Arabia.[2] Companies engaged in import-export trade, but not desiring to manufacture products in Saudi Arabia or to have offices there, can locate representatives through the five Saudi Chambers of Commerce and Industry, listed in Appendix I. The Chambers publish various circulars in which advertisements can be placed. Various newspapers also can be utilized to contact prospective representatives. A list of major newspapers appears in Appendix IV. Another source of contacts is the Commercial Directory, which contains names and addresses of Saudi and non-Saudi businessmen.[3]

---

1) Royal Decree No. 11 of 1382, (1962)
2) The Royal Decree on Service Agents issued in January 1978, requires foreign firms doing business with the Saudi Government to have a "service agent" who is a Saudi national. The text of the decree is set out in the following pag
3) In the United States such information is also available through the United States Department of Commerce, and information is published on a monthly basis.

SERVICE AGENTS REGULATION

Royal Decree No. M/2 of 21/2/1398 (effective January 20, 1978).

Article 1

These regulations shall apply to Saudi agents and foreign contractors and shall govern contracts with the Government of the Kingdom of Saudi Arabia. For the purpose of these regulations, contractors shall include individuals and companies performing consulting or construction work.

Article 2

These regulations shall apply to all contracts entered into between foreign contractors and the Government of the Kingdom of Saudi Arabia.

Article 3

All foreign contractors which have no Saudi partner shall appoint a Saudi national as a service agent. Non-Saudis cannot be appointed as service agents. In the case of foreign contractors which perform consulting work, their service agent must be a Saudi consulting office.

Article 4

Agents shall not be permitted in armament contracts and services related thereto, and shall not be permitted in contracts between the Saudi Government and foreign governments.

Article 5

Service agents must be of Saudi nationality, reside in the Kingdom and hold a commercial registration covering agency activities.

Article 6

A foreign contractor may appoint more than one Saudi service agent in connection with different activities of the foreign contractor. Saudi service agents may represent different foreign contractors, provided they may not represent more than ten contractors.

Article 7

The relationship between a foreign contractor and its Saudi service agent shall be governed by an agency agreement specifying the obligations of the parties.

Article 8

A foreign contractor shall be required to pay its Saudi service agent a fee in consideration of the services performed by the agent. The fee shall be agreed upon by the parties but shall not exceed five percent of the contract price agreed upon between the foreign contractor and the Government of the Kingdom. Foreign contractors must attach to their bids a letter naming their agent and the agent's address. Such letter must be attested to by the agent.

Article 9

A Saudi service agent may not act as agent for foreign companies seeking both consulting and construction work for the same project. However, a Saudi service agent may act as an agent for a consulting contractor in connection with one project and at the same time may act as a service agent for another foreign contractor for construction work in connection with another project.

Article 10

The purpose of the agency shall not be to exercise undue influence or interference.

Article 11

Without prejudice to the provisions of other regulations, the Committee for the Settlement of Commercial Disputes shall have jurisdiction over any dispute arising out of the relationship between a foreign contractor and his Saudi service agent.

Article 12

In the event of his violation of any of the provisions of these regulations, a foreign contractor shall be prohibited from operating in the Kingdom. If a violation is committed by a Saudi agent, his commercial registration shall be cancelled, and he shall be precluded from acting as an agent thereafter.

Article 13

These regulations shall come into force as of the date of their publication in the Official Gazette.

Where licensing of technology is involved, as well as foreign capital, licenses are required from the Secretariat General for Foreign Capital Investment in Riyadh. These applications should include a feasibility report and copies of any contracts, and will be treated in confidence. There is presently no fee required for an application or the license.

G) INCENTIVES TO DEVELOPMENT

A variety of incentives are available to investors. Foreign controlled enterprises can be eligible for these incentives if at least 25% of its capital is Saudi controlled. Capital and earnings have been permitted to be repatriated with minimal government interference. Some of these incentives include exemption from import duties and protective tariffs, tax holidays, and government procurement preferences. The Saudi Industrial Development Fund provides interest free loans to private companies for up to 15 years, and 25% of the total capital.

H) U.S.-SAUDI ARABIAN JOINT COMMISSION ON ECONOMIC COOPERATION

The U.S. - Saudi Arabian Joint Commission was established in June, 1974, to provide U.S. technical expertise and assistance to the Saudi government, and is co-chaired by the U.S. Secretary of the Treasury and the Saudi Minister of Finance and National Economy. Presently, over sixteen projects are in operation, ranging from agriculture to consumer protection. Of particular interest in the trade area is a project agreement relating to technical cooperation in customs administration and training, which is discussed in more detail in the section on customs and tariff laws.

I) PREFERENCES FOR LOCAL GOODS AND RESTRICTIONS ON FOREIGN MANUFACTURING

In order to encourage development of local industries, the Saudis have recently adopted certain resolutions which grant a preference to Saudi manufactured goods in government contracts. On April 7, 1977, it was decreed that Saudi products and manufactured goods are to be preferred over similar foreign goods, as long as they serve the purpose for which they are needed, even if their quality is lower than that of the foreign product.[1)] Where only one Saudi manufacturer of the product exists, the local goods can be purchased directly, without the need for a formal bid.[2)] In drafting specifications for products in government contracts, Saudi officials are also required to give priority to Saudi products "as long as the Saudi products are satisfactory".[3)] There is some indication that these requirements have not been strictly observed and that higher Saudi officials have been exerting increased pressure on those at the ministerial level and below to comply.[4)] Foreign companies working on government projects are similarly prohibited from establishing local manufacturing facilities without a prior license from the Ministry of Industry and Electricity.

---

1) Royal Decree M/14, dated 7.4.1397 (April 17, 1977), Article 1,Section E.
2) Id.
3) Resolution of the Council of Ministers, No. 1977, dated 17.11.1396 (November 17, 1976)
4) For example, the Second Deputy Prime Minister sent a memorandum to the President of the Council of Ministers(No. 18301, dated 27.7.1397) on July 27, 1977, stating that in some cases consultants have specified foreign products, although locally manufactured goods of similar quality were available. All departments were instructed to "fully observe" Article 1, Section E of Royal Decree M/14.

This was originally required by directive of the Second Deputy Prime Minister No. 24851 dated 5.10.1397 (October 5, 1977) and recently supplemented by the ministerial resolution set out on the following page.

Resolution Requiring Foreign Companies to Obtain a License to Open Branch Offices

Text of the Ministerial Resolution No. 680, Dated 9.11.1398 A.H. (October 10, 1978)

"The Minister of Commerce, in view of his prerogatives, and after perusal of the Regulations for Companies issued by Royal Decree No. M/6 dated 22.3.1385 A.H. ; amd following review of Paragraph (9) added to Article 229 of the Regulations for Companies in accordance with Royal Decree No. M/5 dated 13.3.1387 A.H., and in view of the public interest, decides the following:

First: Managers of foreign companies which enter into contract with government departments and agencies in the Kingdom in accordance with special contracts, or those which enter into sub-contracts with such companies after obtaining permission of the competent authorities, must within thirty days after the contract signing, file an application with the Ministry of Commerce to obtain the necessary license to open an office for themselves in one of the cities in the Kingdom in order to undertake implementation of the works assigned to them in accordance with such contracts. They must present all the documents and statements necessary to get said license. Managers of foreign companies operating in the Kingdom and which have not yet obtained the said license must file their applications within thirty days after this resolution goes into effect.

Second: The branches and offices of foreign companies operating in the Kingdom must undertake to prepare for each fiscal year a statement on the financial position of the branch or office and a report on its activities inside the Kingdom wherein should be set down all the activities undertaken during the year under report and the projects carried out or under implementation. The heads of such branches or offices must send copies of these documents to the Companies Department within a month after preparation of said documents.

Third: The said branches and offices must facilitate the mission of the Ministry's representatives in inspecting their documents, books, and records and present to them the statements and information they request.

Fourth: This resolution shall be published in the official gazette and shall become effective from the date of publication.*

---

* The resolution was published in the official gazette on December 15, 1978

In order to promote its "buy Saudi" program, the Ministry of Industry and Electricity has prepared a list of local manufactured goods suitable for government projects. All government contracts are theoretically required to contain a clause obligating contractors to purchase goods on the list (which is supposed to be revised every six months). Contractors are prohibited from importing goods similar to those on the list. [1] Foreign firms are also prohibited from importing supplies and consumer products for their employees. If the goods are not available locally, the foreign firms must request that a Saudi firm import it. [2] As a practical matter the U.S. Embassy in Jedda advises that ministry sources have verbally informed the embassy that listed domestic manufacturers would only be given preference over other products (both foreign and domestic) if they are not more than fifteen or twenty per cent above the cost, or below the quality of the competing goods. [3] The U.S. Embassy has concluded that most U.S. exporters, with the possible exception of those in the truck and air conditioning assembly fields will not be adversely affected by the "buy Saudi" program because most of the listed products "do not figure prominently in U.S. exports", and because of quality differences in U.S. products.

J) STANDARDS

In addition to the "buy Saudi" program, restrictions on use of foreign made products have developed as part of the Saudi effort to develop product standards. While there is no evidence that these standards were intended

---

1) A copy of the list is reproduced in Appendix II
2) Saudi Port Authority release, dated August 1, 1978
3) Unclassified cable, U.S. Embassy Jedda to Dept. of State, August 1, 1977.

as a non-tariff barrier to imports, the practical result is to place an additional burden on foreign manufacturers wishing to sell their products in Saudi Arabia. Saudi Arabia has developed standards for some one hundred and twenty two products ranging from frozen chickens to car radiators. These standards are developed by the Saudi Arabian Standards Ogranization's Board of Directors. Some of these regulations will undoubtedly require foreign exporters to alter their products to comply with Saudi standards. For example, the Saudi standard on labeling of prepackaged foods,[1] requires that Arabic be used on food labels to give the name, net contents, and lists of ingredients. The standards also cover package design and display of information, marking of origin and truth in labeling. A copy of the complete list of Saudi standards is contained in Appendix III.

---

1) 1/1393 H./1973

K) TENDERS REGULATIONS

Since a vast majority of business between foreigners and Saudi Arabia is with the Saudi government, the Tenders Regulations play an important part in Saudi commercial law. The Tenders Regulations were amended in 1977 [1] and supersede, but do not replace, an earlier and more complicated set of regulations. The new regulations take precedence in any areas of conflict. As in the previous rules, there is a preference established by the government for Saudi companies and individuals. A second priority is given to ventures where the Saudi interest is 50% or more. As discussed previously in Section I (" Preference for Local Goods and Restrictions on Foreign Manufacturing") , the government also gives a preference to Saudi manufactured goods, even where their quality is lower. Saudi products are defined as those to which Saudi materials or labor "have contributed a reasonabl percentage". Thus there is considerable administrative flexibility in enforcing this rule.

Also appearing for the first time in the new regulations is a provision (Article 10), for the issuance by the Council of Ministers of form contracts. The new regulations also make certain changes relating to performance bonds and penalti for delays. In April 1977, the Minister of Finance issued rules for implementation of Tenders Regulations [2]. The Rules deal largely with procedural questions, such as the issuance of specifications, announcements of tenders, and preparation of the bids. Also the Rules provide for informal letting of smaller contracts (less than 100,000 Riyals) by informal exchange of correspondence instead of by formal bidding

The complete text of the Tenders Regulations and Rules for Implementation are set out on the following pages:

---

1) Royal Decree No. M/14, dated 7.4.1397, (March 27, 1977)
2) Ministerial Resolution No. 2131/97, dated 5.5.1397, (April 23, 1977)

SAUDI ARABIAN TENDERS REGULATIONS AND RULES FOR IMPLEMENTATION

Issued by Royal Decree M/14 dated 7.4.1397 (March 27, 1977)

TENDERS REGULATION
Basic Rules

Article 1: On procurement of government purchases and implementation of projects and works needed by it, the following basic rules shall be observed:

a) All individuals and establishments wishing to deal with the government and possessing the qualifications to do so shall be given equal opportunity and treated equally.

b) The competing bidders shall be given adequate and standard information about the work required and shall be enabled to obtain such information at the same time and a specific date shall be set for the submission of bids by all of the bidders.

c) In order to secure its puchases and execute its projects and works, the government shall deal with the individuals and establishments licensed to exercise the type of work within which the necessary works or purchases fall, in accordance with the established rules and procedures.

d) Saudi individuals and companies licensed to operate in accordance with the existing laws and regulations shall have priority in dealing with the government followed by establishments consisting of Saudis and non-Saudis whenever Saudi interests in the capital amounts to 50% or more.

e) Manufactured goods and products of Saudi origin shall be preferred over similar foreign goods and products if they serve the purpose for which the tender was announced, even though they possess lower qualities than similar foreign goods and products.

When such goods and products are available, they may be purchased directly if they are produced by a single factory; if more than one factory produces them, a tender shall be arranged among them provided that the Ministry of Industry defines the appropriate purchase price in both cases.

Manufactured goods and products shall not be considered of Saudi origin unless they are produced by a Saudi industrial establishment licensed to operate inside the Kingdom, and the said establishment has submitted a certificate from the Ministry of Industry and Electricity testifying that local raw materials or local manpower have contributed a reasonable percentage to the production of these goods and products.

f) Purchase or implementation of works shall be carried out at fair prices that do not exceed prevailing rates and competition among those working in this area according to the regulations shall be considered the practical method to arrive at this.

g) Offers shall not be accepted and contracts shall not be concluded according to such offers except in accordance with the prescribed conditions and specifications.

Bid Submission Rules

Article 2:

a) Bidders shall be notified by announcement in the Official Gazette twice at least, or by means of official letters addressed to those invited to participate in a tender in case it is restricted to a number of bidders.

b) The soliciting agency may invite bids in two stages:
First: Send invitations to those wishing to compete for the supply of requirements or undertake works from among those in the required activity to select the acceptable bidders.
Second:Ask bidders to submit their offers and the soliciting agency selects those to be invited for the tender in the light of the information it may obtain if the nature of work is within its field of specialization: if not, the invitation is to be sent on nomination by one of the competent departments of the government.

If such information is not available at any government agency, resort may be made to one of the specialized establishments or international bodies.

c) The tender notice shall specify the date and place for the submission of offers. The bids shall be presented in sealed envelopes that shall not be opened except at the specified deadline unless there is a provision in these regulations that allows the submission of open bids.

d) A bid shall be accompanied by a preliminary deposit of 1-2% of its value in accordance with the conditions and specifications. This deposit shall not be necessary in case of direct purchase or open bids referred to hereunder.

e) Offers submitted inside sealed envelopes shall be opened by a committee that meets at the date prescribed for the opening of bid envelopes and the quoted prices shall be announced to the bidders or their representatives attending the session. The committee for opening of bids shall consist of three members at least to be presided over by an employee whose grade shall not be less than the tenth.

f) Bidders may not decrease or increase their quoted prices after the presentation thereof unless in cases wherein negotiations are allowed under these regulations.

Methods of Procurement and Performance

Article 3:

Material purchases and performance of works shall be carried out as follows:

a) Construction Works: No less than five contractors officially classifed within the group qualified to carry out the required work and licensed to operate in the Kingdom in accordance with the established rules shall be invited to present their offers within a period that should not be less than one month. In the invitation shall be specified the day and the hour on which the bids will be opened.

b) Machinery and Equipment of various kinds, including motor vehicles of all types such as passenger, transport and unloading vehicles, special purpose vehicles such as those used for fire-fighting, and transport of garbage; and heavy equipment both stationery and mobile such as agricultural machinery, road equipment, cranes, electric equipment such as generators and transformers, water pumps, wires and cables shall be procured through the selection of three acceptable types that serve the purpose.

Saudi agents of such equipment and machinery licensed to act as their agents shall be invited to submit, after notifying them about the specifications,their open bids within three days at least and 20 days at most according to what the soliciting agency defines. If such equipment does not have an official agent in the Kingdom, purchase may be made from the manufacturing companies.

c) Office equipment and articles including cameras, typewriters, calculating machines, filing cabinets and cupboards, arm-chairs, drapes, floor carpeting, cutting, tying and stapling machines, printed matter and other stationery and interior decoration operations shall be procured by direct purchase from those who deal with them if the value is less than one million Riyals. If the value is more than that, open bids shall be solicited from three individuals who deal in these articles at least.

d) Operation and maintenance works, whether related to electrical or mechanical equipment of building, shall be carried out through invitation of at least three specialized contractors licensed to exercise these activities to present their offers inside sealed envelopes within a period to be determined by the soliciting agency.

e) Supply of food including cooked meals, and foodstuffs, whether the required service is confined to provision of meals only or delivery thereof also, shall take place through invitation of at least three specialized Saudi caterers to submit their respective bids inside sealed envelopes within a period to be specified by the soliciting agency.

f) Drilling of wells shall take place through the invitation of at least three specialized contractors who are licensed to carry out such operations to submit their bids inside sealed envelopes within the period to be specified by the soliciting agency.

g) Spare parts shall be procured through direct purchase from the official agent or other regardless of cost.

h) All kinds of purchases and work whether those in the abovementioned paragraphs or others, shall be carried out by direct purchase if the value of the requirement does not exceed one million Riyals. The minister or the head of the soliciting agency shall exercise this prerogative and shall not delegate authority to exercise it save within the SR 500,000 limit.

i) Consulting operations, studies, drawing up of specifications and supervision of implementation shall be made by direct procurement if within the one million Riyals limit. If the value is in excess of this level, the procurement shall be carried out by inviting at least three consulting bureaus to submit bids within a period to be specified by the government agency concerned and the Minister shall select the best of these offers. Agreement on studies and designs shall be against lump sum amounts. As for supervision of implementation, it may be for lump sum amounts or recurring at a certain percentage of the work value performed.

j) Procurement of medicines shall take place by inviting at least three Saudi agents of international pharmaceutical companies of repute. These international firms shall be selected by a technical committee to be appointed by the competent Minister. The committee shall choose the companies to be invited from the list that is annually endorsed by a decision of the Health Minister.

This committee shall seek the help of an international body to obtain the practical technical information on the said firms.

k) Arms shall be procured by direct agreement with producing firms, and selection from among these firms shall be effected after prior approval of the Council of Ministers.

l) Major projects involving civil engineering and mechanical and electrical operations requiring a high degree of execution or the use of patents or certain scientific methods shall be carried out by inviting at least three specialized international companies in two stages according to the provisions of Article 2-(b) of these regulations.

m) Unless specifically mentioned in this article, anything required by a government department shall be procured by inviting at least three competitors to submit bids and select the best offer made.

Article 4:

The soliciting agency shall give opportunity to the largest number of those qualified parties operating in the field for which the procurement is required so that its dealing is not confined to certain individuals or establishments.

Contract Award Rules

Article 5:

a) A committee or more consisting of three persons at least shall be formed at every ministry or government department to examine the bids. A committee shall be chaired by an official whose grade is not less than the 12th to present its recommendations for the contract award to the best bidder. The committee shall seek the help of a report to be prepared by specialized technicians in making its recommendations for the contract award.

b) If the committee is formed in a place other than the headquarters of a ministry or government department, its chairman may be of a grade less than the 12th.

c) The committee shall adopt its recommendations in the presence of all members. If a member is absent he shall be replaced by an official who acts for him in his absence. If the member is appointed for his person he shall be replaced by a standby member to be appointed by the Minister. The committee's decision shall be by majority of votes and the resolution shall be recorded in the minutes of the session with reference to the opposing viewpoint, if any, and the opinions of each side for submission to the competent authority which will decide on the recommendation.

d) A committee may conduct negotiations with the party with the lowest bid that meets the conditions and specifications, or any other bidder, in the following cases:

1. In case the bids are markedly higher than the market prices, the committee may ask the tenderer with the lowest bid to decrease it. If he declines or does not lower it to a reasonable level, the committee may negotiate with the second lowest bidder, or ask the competing bidders to lower their bids.

2. In case the lowest bid is accompanied with reservations, negotiations may be carried out with the bidder to withdraw his reservations in whole or in part, to reach the acceptable bid. If he refuses, and insists on keeping some or all of them and if such reservations were unreasonable and do not make the bid the best one, the committee may negotiate with the nest bidder and so forth until it arrives at the best offer.

e) A tender or bids may be cancelled when the need no longer exists or when the committee sees that all the bids are unsuitable from the viewpoint of price, conditions or specifications and it was not possible to reach a result by negotiations in accordance with the preceding paragraph.

Bid Award and Contracting Authority

Article 6:

The authority to decide on materials purchase and work implementation whose value exceeds SR 3 million shall rest with the Minister or head of the independent agency, and for lesser amount with the Deputy Minister or whoever acts in his place. Delegation of authority to other officials for lesser amounts may take place provided it is compatible with the authority of the delegated person.

Contract Conditions

Article 7:

a) Whoever enters into contract with the government shall submit a final deposit (performance guarantee) amounting to 5% of the contract value.

b) The final deposit shall not be required in case of contracts for consultancy work, direct purchase, or purchase of spare parts.

c) The final deposit may be gradually reduced in operation and maintenance contracts in accordance with work performance provided it does not become less than the required deposit for the remaining work under the contract.

d) The deposit shall meet any of the methods mentioned in Article (d) above. If the deposit is in the form of a guarantee from an insurance company, it shall not be less than 25% of the contract value.

Advance Payments

Article 8:

a) The soliciting agency may effect to the contractor with whom it enters into contract an advance payment of the amounts due to him within the 20% limit on signing of the contract in exchange for a letter of guarantee equal to this amount. This payment is to be deducted in installments in accordance with the work performance statements.

b) The remaining portion of the amounts due to the contractor shall be paid gradually in installments according to work progress provided that the amount paid to the contractor does not exceed the value of the work performed. Payment of a certain percentage of the value shall be postponed until supply of purchased materials has been completed or on preliminary delivery of works and after presentation of a certificate from the Zakat and Income Tax Department proving that the contractor has paid amounts due from him. The contract shall specify the dates and methods of payments for the contractor.

Delay Fines

Article 9:

a) A contractor to the government shall be subject to a delay fine of not more than 4% of the value of supply contracts and not more than 10% of the value of public works performance, operations and maintenance, or consultancy contracts in accordance with the details specified by the contracts and the Rules of Implementation unless the delay is the result of force majeure, emergency, or an action beyond the contractor's control.

b) The Minister or the head of the soliciting agency may extend the contract period if the delay was the result of the following:

1. Assigning new works to the contractor if he was ordered to do them within a period that does not allow the performance thereof in the remaining period agreed in the contract.

2. A previous order from the department concerned for reasons that are not related to the contractor.

3. If the delay was caused by factors other than those mentioned in the previous paragraph, exemption from the delay fine shall not be granted except with the approval of the Ministry of Finance and National Economy.

Contract Forms

Article 10:

Forms for public works, supply, and other types of administrative contracts shall be issued by a resolution of the Council of Ministers on the recommendation of the Finance and National Economy Ministry. Pending the issuance of these forms, the contract to be concluded by government departments shall specify the conditions that safeguard the rights of the government agency and deal with any disputes that may arise.

Article 11:

Materials that exceed the requirements of the government department may be sold to other government departments after appraising their value by a committee consisting of at least three officials which should first check market prices and provided that the sale price is not less than the estimate made by the said committee. If the value of these materials exceeds SR 100,000, the sale shall only take place by public auction in accordance with the procedures provided for in the Rules of Implementation of these Regulations.

Government employees may not purchase items sold by the Government unless the sale takes place in public auction and the purchased items are for the purchaser's personal use.

Article 12:

If the need arises for consultation over certain provisions of the Regulations, the government department shall refer the matter to a committee consisting of four cabinet ministers, including the Finance Minister and the Minister concerned, who will be nominated by the Council of Ministers. This committee shall submit its recommendations to the Prime Minister or his deputy for issuance of the appropriate resolution.

Article 13:

The Minister of Finance and National Economy shall issue Rules for Implementation explaining the details of these Regulations.

Article 14:

These Regulations shall cancel and supersede all contradictory rules.

RULES FOR IMPLEMENTATION OF TENDERS REGULATIONS

Issued by Ministerial Resolution No.2131/97 dated 5.5.1397 (April 23, 1977)

Article 1:

a) Before inviting bids for the supply of materials or work and other material it may want, a soliciting agency shall prepare detailed and sufficient specifications provided that no reference is made to the type, description or number mentioned in producer's catalogues or to specific trade marks, or draw up specifications that correspond to certain trade mark descriptions.

b) On preparing specifications, soliciting agencies must give priority to products of national industries if they fulfill the desired objective.

Article 2:

Tender conditions and specifications may have a provision allowing the fractioning of offers is such fractioning is in the interest of the soliciting agency. Delivery may also be in accordance with a sample to be designated by the soliciting agency or presented by the bidder.

Article 3:

A specific date and place shall be mentioned in the tender notice for the submission and opening of bids and for bid award. The date for opening of bids may be the closing date for presentation of such bids.

Article 4:

The announcement or notice for tender shall be advertised twice at least in the official gazette, or it may be communicated officially in writing to the invitees. The first announcement or notice shall precede the closing date for presentation of bids by one month at least, unless otherwise provided by the regulations.

Article 5:

Bids shall be delivered to soliciting agencies by registered mail or by hand against a receipt wherein shall be mentioned the date and hour of delivery of the bid. The bids shall be presented on the forms prepared for this purpose which the bidder obtains from the soliciting agency against payment of value thereof and and inside an envelope sealed with wax.

Article 6:

Bids that are delivered or reach the soliciting agency

after opening any bid envelopes shall be rejected.

Article 7:

In preparing the offer, the bidder must observe the following:

a) Prices shall be written in ink, in figures and words, and quoted in Saudi currency, unless the declared tender conditions and specifications allow quotation of the bid value in another currency.

b) It should be mentioned in the quoted price list whether the item to be supplied is produced or manufactured in the Kingdom of Saudi Arabia, any Arab League country or any other foreign country.

c) A bid must be duly signed by the bidder; if it is presented by a company or body, it must be signed by a person who is officially authorized to represent the company or body.

d) No obliteration or erasure may be made in the quotation list. Any correction of prices or other data must be written in ink in both figures and words and duly signed.

e) The soliciting agency shall have the right to check the details and totals of the quotations submitted to it, and make the necessary corrections of material errors herein. If a discrepancy is found between the price shown in figures and that shown in words, the latter shall prevail. If a disparity exists between the unit price and total, the unit price shall prevail.

f) The unit prices fixed by the contractor in the quotation list shall include and cover all expenses and liabilities, of whatever kind, the contractor may incur in respect of any item.

g) No consideration shall be given to any bid based on allowing a certain percentage or amount of discount on the lowest bid submitted by other bidders.

Article 8:

Before submitting his bids on work, maintenance, and operation contracts, a bidder must personally investigate the nature of the work and local conditions and must obtain adequate information on all matters which, in any way, may affect his rates or prices or his risks and obligations. The soliciting agency must, however, provide all such information as may be requested of it in this respect, and which may be available, before the closing date for bids presentation.

Article 9:

A bidder shall accompany his bid with any of the guarantees mentioned in Article 2, paragraph (d) of the Regulations, and such guarantee shall be valid until the date specified for award of the bids.

Article 10:

A bid shall remain open for acceptance and irrevocable until the date of the award and the soliciting agency shall be entitled to ask the bidder to extend the period of its validity. A bidder shall be considered as agreeing to continue his adherence to his bid, if on expiry of the guarantee period, he does not withdraw his offer and regain his guarantee. If the bidder withdraws his offer before the bid award, the soliciting agency shall have the right to confiscate the temporary deposit presented by him without any advance notice or take any other measures.

Article 11:

The Minister or head of the independent government agency shall issue a resolution providing for the formation of the Bids Opening Committee and the Bids Examination Committee in accordance with the provisions of Articles 2-E and 3-A of the Regulations, provided that a standby member is appointed for each committee to replace any of the absent members.

Article 12:

On commencing operation, the Bids Opening Committee shall ascertain the marks of envelopes containing the bids, mention this in its report, set down the number of bids, give each bid a serial number in the form of a fraction whose numerator shall be the serial number of the particular bid and whose denominator shall be the total number of bids. The committee's chairman or any of its members shall then read the name of the bidder, and the total amount of his bid, so that the attending bidders or their representatives may hear this information. The committee's chairman and all members shall sign the bid sheets and the report of its minutes and procedures.

Article 13:

The Bids Opening Committee shall sign the samples and catalogues that are submitted with the bids or the letters of guarantee that are presented during the bids opening session, set them down on a list or include them in the report (minutes) of the meeting.

Article 14:

The bids opening shall take place on the hour and day specified for this purpose provided that the soliciting agency concerned receives the incoming daily mail arriving in the morning of the day designated for bids opening. The committee shall finalize its work on the same day.

Article 15:

The bids, report (minutes) of the Bids Opening Committee and samples shall be delivered to the competent administrative department to analyze the samples if necessary in preparation for presentation thereof to the special committee for bids analysis to carry out its assignment. This shall take place as quickly as possible so that the bids examination committee may adopt the recommendations it deems necessary and present them to the competent authority for bid award before the designated date.

Article 16:

The Bids Examination Committee shall make sure the bids meet the conditions and specifications and it may seek the help of technical experts it sees fit, and recommend the bid that is best from the financial and technical viewpoints after excluding those bids that contradict the conditions and specifications in accordance with the provisions of Article 5 of the Regulations.

Article 17:

On making its recommendation, the Bids Examination Committee shall seek guidance from the prices of previous local or foreign transactions as well as the market prices.

Article 18:

The Bids Examination Committee's deliberations shall be recorded in minutes to be duly signed by its chairman and members for presentation to the person authorized to award the bid.

Article 19:

A single bid shall not be accepted unless endorsed by the competent minister and the urgent nature of the work does not permit another invitation for bids.

Article 20:

Temporary deposits (guarantees) shall be immediately returned to bidders of unsuccessful offers after the bid award without any need on the part of such bidders to file applications for this purpose.

Article 21:

The successful bidder shall, within a period of not more than 10 days following the day on which he was notified by registered letter that his bid has been accepted, deposit any of the guarantees provided for in Article 7 of the Regulations, unless otherwise provided by the rules.

Article 22:

The final guarantee shall not take place if the successful bidder has supplied all the items for which he was given the contract and the soliciting agency has accepted them in final manner within the period specified for deposit of the final guarantee or if he has supplied a part of such items and such part was accepted and its price was sufficient to cover the guarantee's (deposit's) value, provided that no part of this price may be paid to cover the deposit's value until the contractor has fulfilled all his obligations.

Article 23:

If the successful bidder fails to submit the final deposit within the specified period, the soliciting agency may grant him a grace period of not more than 10 days; and if he also fails to deliver within this period, the soliciting agency may confiscate the temporary deposit or implement the contract at the expense of the successful bidder and ask him to pay compensations.

Article 24:

Without prejudice to provisions of Article 7 of the Regulations, the final deposit shall be kept until the contractor or supplier has fulfilled his obligations.

Article 25:

The soliciting agency may increase or decrease the obligations of a contractor or supplier within a limit of 20% of his obligations.

Article 26:

A contractor shall perform his obligations within the specified period including the grace period mentioned in the previous article unless the order to the contractor to perform the contract was issued on a date that does not allow the contractor or supplier to perform within that period, in which case the appropriate grace period shall be added to the performance period for completion of work under the contract.

Article 27:

If the contract's value is less than SR 100,000 exchanged correspondence shall suffice as a binding contract instead of concluding contract; if the contract's value exceeds this amount, a written contract between the soliciting agency and the contractor or supplier shall be drawn up as soon as a notice has been served on the successful bidder and the final deposit is submitted. The contract shall be executed in four copies at least, a copy of which will be handed over to the contractor, another to the accounting authority and a third to the Zakat and Income Department.

Article 28:

A contractor or supplier may not assign the contract in whole or in part without the written approval of the soliciting agency. Nevertheless, the contractor or supplier shall remain jointly responsible with the assignee or sub-contractor for the contract performance.

Article 29:

The soliciting agency and contractor or supplier shall perform the contract in accordance with its terms; if the contractor fails to do so, the soliciting agency may, after serving a notice on him by registered mail and the elapse of 15 days without rectification of this situation, perform the contract at his expense or annul the contract, and in both cases the agency shall be entitled to compensation. If the soliciting agency fails to carry out its commitments, the contractor may claim compensations after serving notice on it by registered letter to correct the situation within 15 days. The contractor may not halt performance of the contract on the grounds that the soliciting agency has failed to fulfull its commitments.

Article 30:

A contractor shall stand answerable for a period of ten years, for any collapse, whether total or partial, that may occur as a result of defective execution in the buildings or structures erected by him, unless it is agreed in the contract that such buildings or structures shall serve for a period of less than ten years.

Article 31:

The contractor shall be held responsible for reviewing in detail the engineering and technical designs and shall notify the soliciting agency about the technical errors he may discover in the designs and which would undermine the structure's safety.

Article 32:

In case work is withdrawn from a contractor, the soliciting agency shall perform, in any way it uses to get its requirements (including direct purchase), the contract at the expense of the contractor.

Article 33:

The soliciting agency may prevent the contractor to retrieve from the work site articles, equipment and materials and use same for completion of work after preparing a report (minutes) wherein shall be set the condition of structures on withdrawal, the articles, equipment and materials existing at the site, provided the contractor is notified about the date for drawing up the minutes to set down his views; if he fails to attend the session, the minutes shall be held against him.

Article 34:

In supply contracts, if the supplier delays performance of his obligations, he shall be subject to a fine of 1% of the delayed item's value for every week provided the fine does not exceed 4% of the contract's value.

Article 35:

In consulting contracts, if a contractor delays performance of his obligations he shall be subject to a fine of 1% of the value of the delayed work for every month of delay, provided the fine does not exceed 10% of the contract's value.

Article 36:

In maintenance and operation contracts, if the contractor fails to fulfill his obligations, he shall be subject to a periodic fine to be specified in the contract, provided that the fine at the end of performance does not exceed 10% of the contract's value.

Article 37:

In public works contracts, if a contractor fails to complete work and deliver it in full on schedule and the soliciting agency does not see a justification for withdrawing the work from him, a fine shall be imposed upon him for the delay of completion beyond the scheduled date, to be calculated on the basis of the average daily costs of the project by dividing the contract's value by its period as follows:

a) A fine on the first part of the delay period amounting to one quarter of the average daily costs for each day of delay until it reaches either 15 days or 5% of the contract period.

b) A fine on the second part of the delay period amounting to half the average daily costs for each day of delay until the delay for the two parts reaches either 30 days or 10% of the contract period.

c) A fine on the third part of the delay period amounting to the full average daily costs for each day of delay until the delay for the two parts reaches the two parts provided for in paragraph (b).

The total amount of fines shall not exceed 10% of the contract value. If the soliciting agency, however, deems that the delayed portion neither precludes full utilization of the work on the specified dates, nor interferes with the use of any other utility or adversely affects the completed portion of the work, the total amount of the fine must not exceed 10% of the value of the delayed portion of work.

Article 38:

Without prejudice to provisions of Article 11 of the Regulations, surplus materials not needed by the soliciting agency shall be sold in auction to be announced in the press and at the offices of the soliciting agency 15 days at least before the auction date.

Article 39:

A bidder in a public auction shall submit a bank guarantee of 1% of the value of his bid to be raised to 5% in the case of the bidder with the best offer at the end of the auction. The remaining value of the bid shall be paid when the award is endorsed.

Article 40:

The bid award result shall be endorsed by the minister or head of the government agency concerned if the value reaches SR 500,000 or more, and by his deputy if it is less than that.

CUSTOMS, TARIFFS AND TRADE LAWS

INTRODUCTION

Saudi Arabian trade policy could generally be described as a liberal one. Due to the large revenues generated from oil imports, the country has considerable foreign exchange and has found little need to adopt protectionist measures. Moreover, the quest to improve the domestic living standard has created a need for industrial development that can only be met by imports of equipment and technology. In fact, Saudi Arabia's tariff structure is perhaps one of the most liberal in the world. In 1974[1] duties on a majority of items were eliminated and most others were reduced to a flat 3 percent ad valorem. The duties that do remain high are generally of a punitive nature and are at the 20% ad valorem level. These duties are generally assessed on goods that compete with local industries that the Saudis wish to protect. Because of the general low rate of duties we have not attempted to provide a complete schedule of all Saudi tariffs. Those that are exempt or at 3% are not listed under the assumption that prospective exporters to Saudi Arabia would not be concerned when items can be admitted duty free or at the 3% ad valorem level. Further duty reductions are provided to members of the Arab League States as part of the Agreement to Facilitate Trade and Exchange and to Organize Transit Between the Arab League States.

1) Royal Decree M/44, 24/7/1394. The full text is set out on the following pages

Imports have increased steadily from 7,444,000,000 in 1975 to approximately 13,000,000 in 1977 (C.I.F., in U.S. dollars). The imports from the United States represented from 20-25% of the total imports. The principal products imported include aircraft, cars and trucks, electric power equipment, construction and mining equipment (including oil drilling equipment), cereal, household furnishings, and medical and office equipment and computers. Saudi exports have exceeded three times the dollar value of imports during the last three years. There is currently an oversupply of consumer goods due to relatively small population and high level of competition between the U.S., Europe and Japan.

In 1975 Saudi Arabia adopted an ambitious $142 billion five-year plan. While steady progress has been made toward the goals of the plan, there have been unforeseen problems including rising inflation. As an effort to control inflation the Government has frozen its budget starting with July 1977 at the level of the two previous years, around 31.5 billion. Development still remains at a high level, particularly such infrastructure projects as the Jubayl and Yaubu developments which will result in hundreds of millions of dollars of new contracts.

Customs Tariff

Updated to 15/11/1396 H. by Resolution No. 1961 published in the Official Journal Um-Al-Qura No. 2657 of 17.1.1397H.

ROYAL DECREE
No. M/9
Date: 6/4/1393H. (1)

With the help of God,
We, Faysal Ibn Abd Al Aziz Al Saud,
King of the Kingdom of Saudi Arabia,
As it is our wish to provide the citizens with a more prosperous life by either cancelling or reducing customs duties on imported commodities, and,

After perusal of Articles Nineteen and Twenty of the Ministers Council's Regulations issued by virtue of Royal Decree No. 38 of 21/10/1377H., and,

After perusal of Royal Decree No. M/5 of 28/2/1388H., concerning the Customs Tariff and its relevant annexes and amendments, and,

According to Ministers Council's Resolution No. 417 of 6/4/1393H., and,

According to the submissions made by the Vice-President of the Ministers Council,

Hereby decree as follows:

(1) Customs duties shall be levied at the rates specified in the appended Customs Tariff and the annexes attached thereto.

(2) The rates of Customs Duties may be amended - for the protection and encouragement of national industries and agrarian products - by virtue of a Ministers Council's Resolution based on a proposal made by the Minister of Finance and National Economy and by the Minister of Trade and Industry after having a committee formed by both Ministries making the relevant study. Such amendment shall come into force on the day following the publication of the Ministers Council's Resolution in the Gazette.

(3) The Minister of Finance and National Economy shall issue the decrees concerning the application of the Customs Tariff according to the provisions of the Customs System and its Executive Regulations. He may also - without amendments to customs duties - introduce modifications concerning the wording of the Customs Tariff Tables and the import procedures referred to therein.

(4) This tariff shall not prejudice the exemptions prescribed for the authorities referred to in the Customs System and its Executive Regulations, nor shall it prejudice the agreements already concluded.

(5) The Customs Tariff issued by Royal Decree No M/5 of 28/2/1388H., its annexes and amendments, as also any provisions conflicting with the provisions of this Decree, shall be cancelled.

(6) This Decree shall be published in the Gazette and shall come into force from Saturday 9 Rabi'II, 1393H.

---

(1) This Decree was published on 8/4/1393H. in the Gazette 'Um Al Qura' edition No. 2471.

ROYAL DECREE
No. M/44
Date: 24/7/1394H. (2)

With the help of God,
We, Faysal Ibn Abd Al Aziz Al Saud,
King of the Kingdom of Saudi Arabia,
As it is our wish to provide the citizens with a more prosperous life by cancelling and reducing customs duties on imported commodities which are not available in the Kingdom and, After perusal of Articles Nineteen and Twenty of the Ministers Council's Regulations issued by Royal Decree No. 38, dated 22 Shawwal, 1377, and,

After perusal of Royal Decree No. M/9 dated Rabi' II, 1393, by virtue of which the Customs Tariff, its annexes and amendments were issued, and,

According to the Ministers Council's Resolution No. 1020 of 19/20 Rajab, 1394,

Hereby decree as follows:

(1) All the rates of Customs duties levied at 10% and 5% in the Customs Tariff by virtue of Royal Decree No. M/9 of 6 Rabi' II, 1393H., are reduced to 3%.

(2) All the commodities listed in the second and third chapters of Section I of the Customs Tariff are exempted from customs duties.

(3) Customs duties imposed on private, public and tourist cars specified in paragraphs (2) & (3) of Item 87/2/1 are reduced to 3%.

(4) Subsidiary charges specified in the annex to the Customs Tariff are cancelled.

(5) This Royal Decree shall be published in 'Um Al Qura' Gazette and shall come into force from the date of its publication.

(6) The Vice-President of the Ministers Council and the Minister of Finance and National Economy are requested to put this Decree into force.

Signed

Faysal

(2) 'Um Al Qura' Gazette No. 2536 of 26/7/1394H.

ROYAL DECREE

No. M/83

Date: 28/11/1395H.

With the help of God,
We, Khaled Ibn Abd Al Aziz Al Saud,
King of the Kingdom of Saudi Arabia,
As it is our wish to reduce the cost of housing, and to encourage construction and building works in order to secure more housing units for the citizens, and,
After perusal of Article Twenty of the Regulations of the Minister Council issued by Royal Decree No. M/38 of 22/10/1377H., and,
After perusal of Royal Decree No. M/9 of 6/4/1393H., concerning the Customs Tariff as amended by Royal Decree No. M/44 of 24/7/139 and,
After perusal of the Ministers Council's Resolution No. 1612 of 14/11/1395H.,
Hereby decree as follows:

(1) Customs duties on certain building materials are to be reduced to 3% of the total value.
(2) The Vice-President of the Ministers Council and the Minister of Finance and National Economy are requested to put this decree into force.
(3) This Decree shall be published in the Gazette 'Um Al Qura' and shall come into force from the date of its publication.

Signed

Khaled Ibn Abd Al Aziz

GENERAL PROVISIONS FOR THE CUSTOMS TARIFF.
No. 1191
Date: 6/4/1393H.

The Minister of Finance and National Economy,
According to Royal Decree No. M/9 of 6/4/1393H., and to Articles (18) and (21) of the Customs System.

DECREE

(1) The Customs Tariff and its relevant amendments shall be applicable, from the date of coming into force, to the goods for which no customs duties were paid.

On the other hand, goods cleared against a deposit prior to the application of the Customs Tariff amendment shall be subject to the duties and charges rates in force on the date the relevant deposit was made.

(2) The value which is to be declared for Customs purposes shall be the actual price already paid or agreed to be paid for the imported goods packed and ready for shipment at the port of origin, plus the relevant additional expenses incurred until delivery to the importing country. Additional expenses shall be taken to mean transport and freight charges, insurance, commission, and brokerage expenses and the like to the port of unloading, except for the cost of air or mail transport for goods. The latter shall be calculated at the rates specified by the Customs Administration by virtue of a decree issued by the Minister of Finance and National Economy.

(3) The value of imported goods declared expressed in foreign currency shall be converted into Saudi currency at the applicable rate of exchange published by the Saudi Arabian Monetary Agency on the date of the registration of the customs declaration. However, if any amendment is made to the published rate of exchange, the said amendment shall apply from the time of its enforcement to the goods for which no customs duties had been paid.

(4) The Customs Administration is empowered to request the production of invoices, packing lists, insurance policies, supporting documents, contracts, correspondence and the like concerning the imported goods without being bound by the contents thereof. The approval of the goods' owner or his representative should be obtained if the Customs findings differ from his statement in the Customs declaration.

If a dispute arises between the Customs and the goods' owner as to their type, origin or value, an official Proces Verbal report shall be drawn up and referred to a committee formed by the Minister of Finance and National Economy to settle such dispute. In this case, and at the request of the goods' owner, the goods may be released against a deposit based on the Customs findings until a settlement is reached by the Committee.

(5) No commodities or goods are to be released from the Customs zone unless all duties and charges stipulated by the Customs Tariff are paid or deposited, or covered by cash or by a Bank guarantee. However, Government imports may be released and the relevant duties may be paid in the manner prescribed by the Minister of Finance and National Economy.

(6) When verified and paid customs duties and subsidiary fees on imported goods are underassessed, whatever the reason may be, the owner of the goods whose name is duly stated on the declaration of customs and the delivery order is held responsible for the payment of the difference to the Customs Administration upon receipt of a written notice from the Customs.

The Customs is authorised to withold goods addressed to the above-mentioned owner up to a quantity equivalent to the value of the amount due. Should the owner fail to pay the difference within three months, the Customs is authorized to offer the with-held goods for sale and to deduct the amount due according to the procedures prescribed in the Customs System and its Executive Regulations.

(7) If verified and paid customs duties and subsidiary fees are over-paid, according to the Customs Tariff, whatever the reason may be, the Customs Administration shall notify the goods' owner to this effect and shall refund the difference according to financial instructions.

(8) The Customs Administration shall act accordingly.

The Minister of Finance and
National Economy.

MINISTERIAL RESOLUTION

No. 4/3062
Date: 27/8/1393H.

The Minister of Finance and National Economy.

According to Royal Decree No. M/9 of 6/4/1393H., and to Article (2) of the General Provisions to the Customs Tariff issued by Ministerial Resolution No. 1191 of 6/4/1393H. to the effect that the value for Customs purposes shall be the actual price already paid or agreed to be paid for the imported goods packed and ready for shipment at the port of origin, plus the relevant additional expenses incurred up to delivery to the importing country, "additional expenses" shall be taken to mean transport and freight charges, insurance, commission, and brokerage and the like up to the port of unloading, except for the cost of the air and mail transport for goods. The latter shall be calculated at the rates specified by the Customs Administration by virtue of a decree issued by the Minister of Finance and National Economy, and,

According to the letter of the Customs Administration No. 4513/7 dated 9/4/1393H., decrees as follows:

(1) Charges of air or mail transport for goods shall be calculated at Fifty Halalas per gross kilogramme or fractions thereof.

(2) This Decree is to be communicated to the Customs Administration to carry out its provisions from the date of issue.

The Minister of Finance and
National Economy

RULES FOR THE INTERPRETATION OF THE CUSTOMS TARIFF

The following principles are to be followed in the interpretation of the Customs Tariff:

(1) The titles of sections, chapters and sub-chapters are provided for ease of reference only; the classification of articles is legally determined according to the text of sections and headings or of chapter notes and according to the following rules, provided that such rules do not contradict the text of the headings or notes.

(2) The text concerning an article in one of the headings of the Customs Tables Tariff covers the said article in its pure or mixed state or when combined with other articles. Likewise, a text concerning a product of a particular substance shall be taken to cover a product which is wholly or partly composed of that substance. Mixed or composite articles shall be classified according to the rules referred to in the following paragraph (3).

(3) If, <u>prima facie</u>, goods could be classified under two or more headings in accordance with the preceding rule or in other cases, classification shall be effected according to the following rules:

(a) The heading which is more specific in its context than other more general headings shall be considered;
(b) Mixed articles or products which are composed of different materials or which are produced by mixing various materials, and which cannot be classified according to sub-paragraph (a) shall be classified according to the substance or material which contributes the most to its main characteristics, if such characteristics can be defined;

(c) In cases where (a) and (b) cannot be applied to a particular article, the heading which provides for the highest rate of duty shall be applied.

(4) If the notes to one of the sections or chapters stipulate the exclusion of certain articles, indicating that such articles are covered by another section or chapter, or by a certain heading, the exclusion shall cover all the articles included or coming under that section or chapter or heading - unless otherwise indicated - regardless of the fact that only some of those articles werereferred to in the said notes.

(5) Articles which are not referred to in any of the headings shall be subject to the heading applied to the most similar articles.

(6) In classifying goods coming under the same heading, the aforementioned instructions (1) to (5) shall also apply to subheadings and paragraphs similarly.

The Ministers Council's Resolution No. 1961 dated 15/11/1396 was issued and published in the Official Gazette 'Um Al Qura', Edition No. 2657 of 17/1/1397, concerning the amendment of certain Customs rates of duty specified in the Tariff for certain articles for the protection of the national economy.

Hereunder are the headings covered by the amendment:

Heading	Articles	Unit of Duty	Rate of Duty
32/8	All articles of the heading	Ad val.	10%
32/9	All articles of the heading	Ad val.	10%
59/4	Twine, cordage, ropes and cables, plaited or not:		
	1. Not plaited	Ad val.	3%
	2. Plaited	Ad val.	10%
84/12	(Subheading 2) Desert coolers	Ad val.	20%

TARIFF CLASSIFICATIONS AND RATES OF DUTY FOR
DUTIABLE ITEMS EXCEEDING 3% AD VALOREM

Tariff No.	Articles and Description	Rates of Duty (% Ad. Val. or in Saudi Halalas)
4/5	Birds' eggs and egg yolks, fresh, preserved, dried or sweetened:	
	1. Eggs in the shell:	
	1. Other than for hatching 100 eggs	200
13/3	Vegetable saps and extracts; pectic substances; pectinates and pectates; agar-agar and other mucilages and thickeners derived from vegetable products:	
	1. Tahinah (sesame juice)	20%
17/4	Sugar confectionery, not containing cocoa:	
	1. Sweetmeats, drops and bonbons	20%
	Minimum duty per 1 kg. net direct packing	50
	2. Toffee (caramels), Turkish delight and nougat	20%
	Minimum duty per 1 kg. net direct packing	50
	3. Almond candy, pistachio candy and the like; all types of marzipan and the like	20%
	4. Fruit Jellies, fruit pastes, and liquorice prepared as confectionery	20%
	5. Chewing-gum, sweetened or sugar-coated	20%
	6. Halava tahiniah	20%
	7. Other	20%
18/6	Chocolate and other food preparations containing cocoa:	
	1. Chocolate, in pieces, moulded shapes, bars or tablets, etc.	20%
	2. Confectionery products (halava candies) containing cocoa	20%
	3. Other food preparations containing cocoa:	
	1. Ice-cream, ready to serve, containing cocoa	20%
	2. Other	20%
19/3	Macaroni, spaghetti, vermicelli, etc;	
	1. Macaroni, vermicelli and similar items such as spaghetti, cannelloni, pastas in the shape of shells, stars or letters, etc	20%

Tariff No.	Articles and Description		Rates of Duty (% Ad. Val. or in Saudi Halalas)
24/1	Unmanufactured tobacco; tobacco refuse:		
	1. Raw or unmanufactured tobacco	1 kg.gross	100
	2. Unmanufactured tumbak	1 kg. gross	100
	3. Refuse:		
	1. Fit for use as tobacco	1 kg. gross	100
	2. Other	1 kg. gross	100
24/2	Manufactured tobacco; tobacco extracts and essences:		
	1. Cigars	1 kg. with immediated packing	800(1,2)
	2. Cigarettes	per 1,000 cigarettes	500(1,2)
	3. Other:		
	1. Chopped or pressed tobacco	1 kg.net	500(1,2)
	1. For smoking(loose)	1 kg.net	500(1,2)
	2. For pipes	1 kg.net	500(1,2)
	3. For retail sale	1 kg.net	500(1,2)
	4. Pressed or liquored tobacco for making snuff	1 kg.net	500(1,2)
	5. Chopped or pressed tobacco for chewing	1 kg.net	500(1,2)
	6. Other	1 kg.net	500(1,2)
	2. Snuff	1 kg.net	500(1,2)
	3. Jirak	1 kg. gross	100(1,2)

(1) The immediate packing of these items in which they sold by retail for consumption should bear, by prior fixation in the factory, a Customs stamp of 3 halalas.

(2) The following warning, in the Arabic language, should be printed on each packet: "Smoking is harmful" (Royal Ordinance No. 31763 of 18/11/1395 H., coming into force from 1/1/1397 H. by virtue of Royal Ordinance No. 62/7,issued on 20/3/1396 H.)

Tariff No.	Articles and Description		Rates of Duty (% Ad.Val. or in Saudi Halalas)
25/6	Quartz (Other than natural sands), quartzite, including quartzite not further worked than roughly split, roughly squared or squared by sawing:		
	1. Other than crude, in the form of unsawn agglomerates		20%
25/20	Gypsum,anhudrite, calcined gypsum and plasters with a basis of calcium sulphate, whether coloured or not, but not including plasters specially prepared for use in dentistry:		
	1. Coloured or uncoloured	1 ton gross	2,100
27/10	Petroleum oils and oils obtained from bituminous minerals, other than crude; preparations not elsewhere specified or included, containing not less than 70% by weight of petroleum oils or of oils obtained from bituminous minerals, such oils being the basic constituents of the preparations:		
	1. Petroleum spirit (gasoline)	1 litre	16(1)
	2. Kerosene, jet fuel and white spirit:		
	1. White spirit	1 litre	16(1)
28/4	Hydrogen, rare gases and other metalloids and non-metals:		
	1. Oxygen		20%
29/1	Hydrocarbons:		
	1. Other:		
	1. Acetylene gas		20%
32/8	Prepared pigments, prepared opacifiers and prepared colours; bitrifiable enamels and glazes; liquid lustres and similar products of the kind used in the ceramic, enamelling and glass industries; engobes (slips); glass frit and other glass, in the form of powder, granules or flakes		10%

---

(1) A consumption fee of 8 Halalas per litre shall be charged.

Tariff No.	Articles and Description	Rates of Duty (% Ad.Val. or in Saudi Halalas
32/9	Varnishes; distempers; prepared water pigments of the kind used for finishing leather; other paints and enamels; pigments in linseed oil, white spirit or turpentine spirits, varnish or other similar elements; stamping foils; dyes or other colouring matter in forms or packings of a kind sold by retail:	
	1. Varnish	10%
	2. Distempers and water pigments	10%
	3. Pigments prepared with oil, varnish or other elements	10%
	4. Dyes in forms or in packings for retail sale	10%
	5. Stamping foils	10%
	6. Other	10%
34/2	Organic surface-active agents; surface-active preparations and washing preparations, whether or not containing soap:	
	1. Organic surface-active agents (such as Clorex, etc.)	20%(1)
	2. Surface-active preparations and washing preparations:	
	1. Dry-powdered (such as Tide,etc.)	20%
39/1	Condensation, polycondensation and polyaddition products, whether or not modified or polymerized and whether or not linear, such as phenoplasts, aminoplasts, alkyds, polyallyl esters and other unsaturated polyesters, silicones, etc.:	
	1. Plates and sheets:	
	1. Porous cellular or foam	20%
	minimum assessment per 1kg.net	60

---

(1) This duty is valid for five years effective from Muharram 3, 1394 H. and thereafter will revert to 3% (Council of Ministers' Resolution No. 1438 of 30/11/1393 H.,published in Um Qura issue No. 2508 of 2/1/1394 H.)

Tariff No.	Articles and Description	Rates of Duty (% Ad. Val. or in Saudi Halalas)
39/2	Polymerization and copolymerization products, such as polyethylene, polytetrahaloethylene, polyisobutylene, polystyrene, polyvinyl chloride, polyvinyl acetate, polyvinyl chloroacetate and other polyvinyl derivatives, polyacrylic and polymethacrylic derivatives, coumarone-indene resins:	
	6. Plates and sheets:	
	1. Porous, cellular or foam	20%
	minimum assessment per 1 kg. net	60
	7. Pipes, tubes and hoses:	
	1. Hardened pipes and tubes of polyvinyl chloride	20%
	minimum assessment per 1 kg. net	70
39/3	Regenerated cellulose; cellulose nitrate; cellulose acetate and other cellulose esters, cellulose ethers and other chemical derivatives of cellulose, plasticized or not (such as collodions, celluloid); vulcanized fibre:	
	6. Plates and sheets:	
	1. Porous, cellular or foam	20%
	minimum assessment per 1 kg. net	60
39/5	Natural resins modified by fusion (fused resins); artificial resins obtained by esterification of natural resins or of resinic acids (ester gums); chemical derivatives of natural rubber (such as chlorinated rubber, rubber hydrochloride, oxidized rubber and cyclized rubber):	20%
	minimum assessment per 1 kg. net	60
39/6	Other high polymers, artificial resins and artificial plastic materials, including alginic acid, its salts and esters; linoxyn:	
	5. Plates and sheets:	
	2. Porous, cellular or foam	20%
	minimum assessment per 1 kg. net	60
39/7	Articles of materials of the kinds described in headings 39/1 to 39/6:	
	1. Sacks, pouches and cones, whether or not printed	20%
	minimum assessment per 1 kg. net	100

Tariff No.	Articles and Description	Rates of Duty (% Ad.Val. or in Saudi Halalas)
39/7 (ctd)	2. Household and culinary implements and utensils	20%
	minimum assessment per 1 kg. net	100
	20. Hardened pipes and tubes of poly-vinyl chloride	20%
	minimum assessment per 1 kg. net	70
40/8	Plates, sheets, strip and rods and pro-file shapes, of unhardened vulcanized rubber:	
	1. Plates, sheets and strip of sponge or cellular rubber	20%
44/24	Household utensils of wood	20%
44/27	Articles of fine joinery (boxes, caskets, receptacles, drawers, pen boxes, racks, lighting fittings, etc.); ornaments and fancy articles, including articles for personal use; parts of all the foregoing, excluding wooden furniture of Chapter 94:	
	6. Beads of wood	20%
44/28	Other articles of wood:	
	1. Articles of wood used in agriculture and animal husbandry, such as rabbit pens, poultry coops, beehives, cages, nests, mangers, barns, etc.	20%
	2. Cash boxes, travel boxes, suitcases and similar articles	20%
	5. Advertisement boards, signboards and road signs	20%
	6. Toothpicks and clothes hangers	20%
	7. Capacity measures and gauges made of wood	20%
	8. Other	20%
48/15	Paper and paperboard, cut to size, for uses other than those specified under headings 48/10 to 48/14	
	8. Toilet paper in rolls or sheets	20%
48/16	Boxes, bags, pouches, cones and other packing containers, of paper or paperboard:	
	1. Boxes, packing containers, cases and covers therefor, whether or not printed	20%
	2. Paper bags for packing cement and the like, whether or not printed	20%
48/18	Registers, exercise books, notebooks, memo-randum blocks, diaries, agendas, files, bin-ders for books and papers; school and station-ery goods; albums of paper or paperboard:	
	4. Files and folders, whether or not printed	
	1. With metal fittings	20%
	2. Other kinds	20%

Tariff No.	Articles and Description	Rates of Duty (% Ad.Val. or in Saudi Halalas)
48/21	Other articles of paper pulp, paper, paperboard or cellulose wadding:	
	1. Table covers, napkins, towels and kerchiefs	20%
58/2	Other carpets, carpeting, "Kelem", "Schumacks" and "Karamanie" rugs and the like, whether or not ready-made	
	2. Carpets and rugs of chenille yarn; prayer rugs	20%
	5. Of cotton:	20%
59/4	Twine, cordage, ropes and cables, plaited or not:	
	2. Plaited	10%
61/1	Men's and boys' outer garments:	
	3. Of wool or of fine hair	20%
61/6	Shawls, scarves, mufflers, veils and the like:	
	2. Of synthetic or artificial fibres:	
	1. "Shamagh"	20%
	4. Of cotton:	
	1. "Shamagh"	20%
62/2	Bed linen, table linen, toilet linen and kitchen linen; curtains and other furnishing articles:	
	4. Of cotton:	
	1. Ordinary towels, pilgrimage towels, bath towels and hand towels	20%
63/1	Clothing, clothing accessories, blankets and traveling rugs, household linen and furnishing articles of textile materials (other than articles of heading 58/1, 58/2 or 58/3), footwear and headgear of any material, showing signs of appreciable wear and imported in bulk, bales, sacks or similar packings:	
	1. Footwear	20%
	2. Headgear	20%
64/1	Footwear with outer soles and upper of rubber or artificial plastic material	20%
64/2	Footwear with outer soles of leather or composition leather; footwear (other than footwear falling within heading 64/1) with outer soles of rubber or artificial plastic material:	
	1. With uppers wholly or mostly of leather:	
	1. Of reptile or fish skin leather	20%
	2. Other:	
	1. For men and boys	20%
	2. For women and girls	20%
	3. For babies	20%
	4. Footwear for household use	20%
	2. With upper of silk or synthetic or artificial fibres or with embroidered uppers	20%
	3. With uppers of other fabrics	20%
	4. Other	20%
64/3	Footwear with outer soles of wood or cork:	
	1. With soles of cork	20%
	2. Other	20%

Tariff No.	Articles and Description	Rates of Duty (% Ad.Val. or in Saudi Halal
64/4	Footwear with outer soles of other materials (cordage, paperboard, textiles, felt, plaited material, etc.)	20%
65/5	Hats and other headgear (including hairnets), knitted or crocheted, or made up from lace, felt or other textile fabric in the piece, but not from strips, with or without accessories therefor:	
	8. Hoods for overcoats or cloaks:	
	1. Shamagh	20%
70/10	Carboys, bottles, jars, tubular containers and similar glass containers used for the conveyance or packing of goods; stoppers and other closures, of glass	20%
73/23	Casks, drums, cans, boxes and similar containers, of sheet iron or steel, for the conveyance or packing of goods	20%
73/39	Iron or steel wool for scouring and cleaning household articles and for similar purposes	20%
73/40	Other articles of cast iron, iron or steel:	
	7. Shelving	20%
	8. Other	20%
74/9	Reservoirs, tanks, vats and similar containers, for any material, of copper, of a capacity exceeding 300 litres, whether or not lined or heat-insulated, but not fitted with mechanical or thermal equipment	20%
76/10	Casks, drums, cans, boxes and similar containers (including rigid and collapsible tubular containers), of aluminum, for the conveyance or packing of goods	20%
76/15	Articles of a kind commonly used for domestic purposes, sanitary ware for indoor use, and parts thereof, of aluminum	20%
79/6	Other articles of zinc:	
	1. Cans, boxes and other similar articles for the conveyance and packing of goods	20%
83/3	Safes, strong-boxes, armoured or reinforced strong-rooms, including strong-room doors and walls, cash and deed boxes and the like, of base metal	20%
83/4	Filing cabinets, racks, sorting boxes, paper trays and similar office equipment of base metal, other than office furniture falling within heading 94/3	20%
84/12	Air-conditioning units, self-contained, comprising a motor-driven fan and elements for changing the temperature and humidity of air:	
	2. Desert coolers	20%

Tariff No.	Articles and Description	Rates of Duty (% Ad. Val. or in Saudi Halalas)
85/12	Electric water heaters of all kinds; electric hair dressing appliances (for example, hair dryers, hair curlers, etc.); electric irons; electro-thermic domestic appliances; electric heating resistors, other than those of heading 85/24:	
	1. Electric water heaters	20%
87/5	Bodies (including cabs), for the tractors and vehicles falling under 87/1 through 87/3	
	2. Bodies of vehicles falling under heading 87/2 or 87/3 and of road tractors	20%
94/1	Chairs and seats (other than those falling within heading 94/2), whether or not convertible into beds, and parts thereof:	
	1. Of wood, and parts thereof	20%
	2. Of straw and rattan, and parts thereof	20%
	3. Of plastic, and parts thereof	20%
	4. Of base metal, and parts thereof	20%
	5. Other	20%
94/3	Other furniture and parts thereof:	
	2. Other:	
	1. Of wood, and parts thereof	20%
	2. Of straw and rattan, and parts thereof	20%
	3. Of plastic, and parts thereof	20%
	4. Of base metal, and parts thereof	20%
	5. Other	20%
94/4	Mattress supports, articles of bedding and the like, fitted with springs or stuffed or internally fitted with any material, including foam rubber or artificial plastic foam material, of all kinds (for example, mattresses, quilts, pillows, cushions, etc.), whether or not covered:	
	1. Mattress supports	20%
	2. Articles of bedding and the like:	
	1. Mattresses	20%
	2. Quilts	20%
	3. Pillows, cushions and puff seats	20%
	4. Other	20%
	3. Other	20%

SAUDI ARABIAN CUSTOM REGULATIONS AND RULES FOR IMPLEMENTATION

The complete text of the Saudi Arabian custom regulations is set out in the following pages. This is followed by the rules for implementation, which are divided into two columns. In the left hand column is the actual text, and in the right hand column is a summary and analysis when considered useful, including comparisons to comparable sections of the custom laws and regulations of the United States. Since the United States has a well developed body of law and regulations pertaining to customs matters, it is hoped that this will provide a point of reference in comparing and analyzing the Saudi law.

Saudi customs regulations are enforced by the Directorate of Customs, the Department of the Coast Guard, and the Administer of Finance who is empowered to issue rules for implementation. The original customs regulations were first issued on June 30, 1930, under Royal Order No. 326. These are now obsolete and have been replaced by Royal Order No. 425, issued in November 1973.

CUSTOMS REGULATIONS

1. These Regulations shall be called the Customs Regulations for Saudi Arabia. (Definitions, Terms, and the Meanings given to them in the Regulations...)

2. The Customs Line is the boundary separating Saudi Arabia, including its rights in the Iraq and Kuwait Neutral Zones, from the neighboring countries and also the shores of the surrounding seas.

3. The Customs Control Zone is the area which extends for a distance of ten kilometers into the Kingdom from the Customs Line, and in the direction of the high seas for two nautical miles beyond the territorial waters of the Kingdom, as defined by Royal Decree No. 6/4/5/3711 dated 1 Sha'ban 1368 [28 May 1949].

4. The Customs Area is any seaport or airport at which there is a Customs post, and is also any other Customs office. The Customs Area shall be established and defined by a decision from the Minister of Finance.

5. Goods may not pass across the Customs Line at night, i.e., between sunset and sunrise, except in cases of pressing necessity, such as the landing of pilgrims, or for operations connected with the Government, or by written authorization from the Minister of Finance.

6. Representatives of both the Directorate of Customs and the Department of Coast Guard shall have the authority to carry out any arrest, seizure, search, or investigation connected with the

enforcement of these Regulations, each within his own jurisdiction. They shall also have, within the Customs Area, the right to search and arrest persons and to inspect and seize goods and means of land, air, and sea transportation. In case suspicion of smuggling arises, they may, with the permission of the Director General of Customs concerned, or the official acting for him, search and detain persons, shops, houses, etc. in any location within the Customs Area, for the purpose of looking for goods smuggled past Customs. However, it shall not be proper for them to inspect search or seize anyone or anything outside this area except in the presence of the Director of Police or the official acting for him. In order to seize goods suspected of being smuggled, the representatives in question have the right also to inspect means of transportation, materials, and persons crossing the Customs Line. They also have this right in the deserts in cases of suspicion or reports from informers, provided that if the information proves to be false, the informer shall be punished in accordance with the provisions of the Regulations.

7. In accordance with the provisions of these Regulations, smuggled goods tracked down by the above-mentioned representatives may be seized wherever they are found, even after they have crossed the boundaries of the Customs Control Zone.

8. No one is permitted to clear any goods on behalf of another, or to practice any profession within the Customs Area except as provided by the Rules for Implementation of the Customs Regulations. The Directorate of Customs or a representative therefrom has the right to keep out of the Customs Area any suspected person or any person having a previous record of smuggling.

9. Captains of steamships, sailboats, and airplanes, and [drivers of] automobiles and other means of transportation arriving from foreign countries are required to submit the original copy of the manifest of the cargo they have with them, which should show the quantities, marks, kinds, numbers, and destination of packages, the name and kind of transportation facility, and the total number of packages in figures and words. This copy should be prepared in accordance with the [established] procedures and approved by the proper authority at the port of export. The manifest formalities, including shortages and overages in the number of packages, their contents, and their various kinds, should be completed in accordance with the instructions set forth in the Rules for Implementation. The representatives of the Customs Department and members of the Coast Guard have the right to board steamships and sailboats, within the Customs Control Zone defined in Articles 2,3, and 4 of these Regulations, and require them to anchor and enter the Customs Zone. Furthermore, Customs representatives alone have the right to board airplanes, automobiles, and other means of transportation whether they are in transit or otherwise, and require them to produce their manifests. All the particulars mentioned in the manifest and other documents must agree with the cargo. However, the above-mentioned representatives may not board military steamships or planes, even in cases of suspicion, except by special permission to be obtained from higher authorities.

10. All of the means of transportation referred to in the previous Article, of whatever kind they may be, whether proceeding to a Saudi seaport or airport, or passing in transit [with destination either] within Saudi Arabia or outside Saudi Arabia shall,

within the limits of the provisions of the Rules for Implementation of these Regulations, be subject to search in accordance with the administrative procedures and formalities applicable to such search, with all the requirements of firmness, accuracy, and reasonableness.

11. Ships are forbidden to anchor except in the Customs Zone. If, owing to an emergency or acts of God, they are forced to anchor elsewhere than in the Customs Zone or make contact with the shore, the captain of the ship must not remove from or add to the cargo anything whatsoever for the purpose of smuggling, and he shall notify the nearest Customs office whenever it is possible to do so.

12. Pilots of aircraft authorized to fly over Saudi Arabia shall in their flight follow the aeronautical route fixed by Saudi Arabia and shall land in the places provided for landing, unless they are forced by an emergency to act otherwise, in which case they shall submit a report to the Customs concerned.

13. Goods to be imported by land shall be directed to the nearest Customs office on the border or to the Customs office designated by the Directorate of Customs; and they shall follow the regular route without any deviation therefrom, and shall comply fully with the formalities set forth in the Rules for Implementation of the Customs Regulations.

14. The unloading of goods of all categories in the Customs Area and the withdrawal of them from it into the Kingdom, and the shipment or removal of them from that area, shall be governed by the limitations and conditions prescribed by the Rules for Implementation.

15. Shipping companies and airlines are required to take good care of the goods unloaded in the Customs Area, and shall be responsible to Customs for any shortage which may occur in such goods, whatever the cause or nature of such shortage may be, until they are actually delivered to the Customs concerned, against an official receipt, in accordance with the provisions of the Rules for Implementation of these Regulations.

16. The bearer of the delivery order issued by the shipping company or airline concerned shall be considered the agent of the owner of the goods for the purpose of completing the formalities for him and in paying the duties and bearing the responsibility on his behalf.

17. Priority shall be given to the Directorate of Customs over creditors and others in collecting its prescribed duties on goods within the Customs Area. Accordingly, it has the right to impound goods on which duties are not paid until the duties on them are paid in accordance with the regular prevailing procedures and formalities.

18. Duties, charges, and all dues payable on goods shall be paid in cash in Saudi Arabian currency, in accordance with the Customs Tariff, and shall be collected in accordance with the terms set forth in the Rules for Implementation.

19. The Directorate of Customs shall not be responsible in any way for any injury or damage which may occur to the goods while within the Customs Area, whether such injury or damage was the result of accidents or the result of negligence on the part of the owners of the goods.

0. While in Customs, goods shall remain at their owners' risk and the latter shall take whatever steps they think necessary

to insure these goods against the risks to which such goods may be exposed, and shall promptly withdraw them from the Customs after making diligence in completing the necessary formalities in respect thereof.

21. The importer must submit to the Customs all the true and correct documents which establish all [the] particulars of the imported goods, as well as the actual prices paid or those agreed upon in the currency of the exporting country plus the freight and insurance charges. However, if the Customs finds that the value shown on the documents does not agree with the F.O.B. price at the Saudi ports of the goods at the time of agreement, it may fix such value computed on the basis of the nearest comparable value that can be ascertained.

22. In accordance with the provisions of the Rules for Implementation of the Customs Regulations, the following shall be exempted from examination procedures, import and export duties of all kinds, and any additional charges with the exception of porterage charges:

    a. Things and belongings of his Majesty the King.

    b. Things for the strict personal use of and personal effects of ambassadors, ministers plenipotentiary, charges d'affaires counselors, secretaries, and attaches of any embassy; also, members of the consular staff accredited to the Government and registered in the list of the diplomatic corps, provided the materials imported are in the name of the office held by these persons or in the name of the corps to which the person enjoying international exemption on a reciprocal basis is attached. The exemption also includes the materials referred to above which are imported in the name of a person who does not enjoy exemption, provided the title to these materials is transferred to and they are taken out of the Customs Areas by someone who this Article provides is entitled to exemption.

c. Things imported directly from abroad for use in embassies, legations, and consulates [provided they are in quantity] within the reasonable limits of usage or consumption, and [provided the exemption is] on a basis of reciprocity. Goods in the Customs warehouse imported for a person who does not have the right to exemption may, before clearance, be exempted if sold to any of the above-mentioned parties, provided the title to such goods is transferred to and they are taken out of Customs by the party who has the right to exemption.

d. Things and materials imported for persons other than those referred to in the above sections, such as educational or technical missions and others. The exemption in such cases is out of courtesy and is applicable if High Orders concerning such goods are issued or if they are covered by a special Ministerial Order issued within the limits of the authority granted by His Majesty the King to the Minister of Finance.

23. In accordance with the Rules for Implementation, the following goods shall be exempt from all kinds of import and export duties including other additional charges with the exception of transportation charges within the Customs Areas:

a. Whatever is imported from abroad for the Great Mosque, the Prophet's Mosque, [other] mosques, Waqfs, charitable establishments, poorhouses, and charities, provided that the approval of the Council of Ministers is obtained.

b. Strictly personal effects of passengers carried by them, and the necessary used household effects accompanied by their owners.

c. Fifty kilograms of food for each pilgrim, together with two garments for making the pilgrimage and the [pilgrim's] used personal effects.

d. Provisions and supplies necessary for ships, aircraft, and automobiles, such as fuel, etc., together with reasonable quantities of foodstuffs and clothing for the use of their crews.

e. Sailboats and steamships used in transport between Saudi and foreign ports, including fishing boats licensed under the Fishing and Shellfishing Regulations in force.

f. Commercial samples and advertisements of industrial firms that are imported and that have no commercial value and are not intended for sale.

g. Goods re-imported from abroad after having been previously exported under circumstances provided for in the Rules for Implementation.

h. Gold ore of all kinds and forms, the manufacturing costs of which do not exceed one per cent of the value of the pure gold [contained therein].

i. Foreign gold and silver coins and foreign currency notes licensed to be imported in accordance with the releveant instructions in the Rules for Implementation.

j. Silver ingots.

k. Copies of the Quran, religious and scientific books of all kinds, and printed matter, after they are examined and inspected by the oommittee concerned, and school note-books of the usual shape and size.

l. Carbolic acid, all forms of D.D.T. and all insecticides of all kinds, including insecticides for tree pests, after they are examined and inspected by the committee concerned.

m. Containers imported for the packing of dates.

n. Necessary household furniture for use by foreigners sent to work for the Government for the first time, if their [employment] agreements provide for [such exemptions].

o. Tractors, ploughs, and agricultural machinery, together with horses, accessories, and spare parts for them as well as well drilling machines that are not usable for other machines.

p. Fire extinguishing materials.

24. Except for the cases mentioned in the previous sections, Customs exemption may not be granted except by High Orders or by a special Ministerial Decision to that effect issued within the limits of authority granted by his Majesty the King.

25. Persons who are regularly subject to inspection as required by the Customs Regulations, whether coming into or going out of the country, shall be given special forms on which their belongings, whether inside their suitcases or in their pockets,

should be listed, so that the Customs may carry out the instructions stipulated in the Rules for Implementation, and take the necessary action in this regard. Persons who meet or escort travelers are subject to inspection in the event of suspicion.

26. First:

Imported goods which are not in demand in the Kingdom may be re-exported, and the duties paid thereon may be refunded subject to the following conditions-

1. The period that has elapsed since the entry of the goods to be re-exported shall not have exceeded one year.
2. The items to be re-exported shall not be other than those imported, the duty on which was previously assessed.
3. They shall not have been used within the Kingdom.
4. The merchant shall have proven by virtue of convincing evidence that the goods to be re-exported are not in demand.
5. The Ministry of Finance [and National Economy] shall have approved the re-export and the refund of duties.

Second:

Goods and items which have entered the Kingdom after the prescrib duties thereon have been paid, and the owners of which request that they be exported for the purpose of overhauling, repairing, decorating, or processing them, or adding something to them, etc. may be exported and then re-imported after the following procedur are carried out:

a. A certificate must be submitted, authenticated by the authori ties concerned who are directly connected with items of that kind, showing the descriptions of the items of the things to be exported together with the reasons for export mentioned above.

b. The descriptions of the items to be exported shall be recorded in the register kept for this purpose, and the necessary markings shall, if possible, be placed on them. The owner shall be given a certificate to that effect.

Third:

At the time the above-mentioned items are returned, a certificate authenticated by the Customs of the exporting country shall be submitted to the Customs of destination, showing the descriptions of the items and any trade-marks they may bear. When these [descriptions and distinguishing marks] are compared with the descriptions recorded by the Customs at the time of the export of the items, the differences occurring to these items, whether [something has been] added or removed, shall be noted, and the Customs duties and additional charges shall be collected on each such [difference] occurring according to its value, as well as on the freight and insurance charges due.

Fourth:

Owners of items imported from foreign countries who wish to re-export such items prior to their leaving the Customs areas and before Customs duties and additional charges are collected on them, shall be permitted to do so under the following conditions, after the storage and transportation charges are collected:

a. If the items are not foodstuffs, clothing, medical supplies, construction materials, or the like, which the country may be in need of.

b. If the items are of the kinds that are not desired in the country, or that have been found not to be in conformity with the order of the merchant with whom the exporter abroad has entered into a [purchase] agreement.

c. If the items have, by mistake, been shipped to or unloaded in a country other than that to which they are exported.

d. If the items, after their arrival, have been found defective or damaged, or otherwise [impaired] so as to make them unsuitable to be placed [on sale] in the local markets.

27. Temporary clearance of the following items without the collection of Customs duties and the various additional charges is permitted under such terms and conditions as the Minister of Finance specifies:

a. Furniture, articles, and other items prepared for the reception of groups and missions coming to Saudi Arabia on official or scientific missions, and likewise those items prepared for use by members of the Saudi diplomatic and consular corps coming from abroad on a temporary basis.

b. Commodities and goods for authorized official exhibits of friendly countries. The exemption [in this case] shall be [valid] until those items are sold within the Kingdom, when duties shall then be collected thereon, or until they are re-exported to the country of origin.

28. The Directorate of Customs may sell by public auction goods which are not withdrawn within twelve months from the date of their unloading, after notifying those concerned or advertising them at least eight days before the date of the sale. If such goods or items are perishable, subject to shrinkage, or dangerous and if they are not withdrawn at the proper time, they may be sold immediately, in accordance with the procedure prescribed in the Rules for Implementation of the Customs Regulations.

29. After the duties, charges, and expenses of all kinds are collected on such goods, the balance of [their] value shall be kept as money in trust for the person concerned.

30. After the goods which are subject to specific duty or to a flat rate of duty become the property of the Government, they shall be sold by public auction; and if their value does not cover the duties due on them, they shall be treated in the following manner:
   a. Tobacco, tumbak, and cigarette paper of all kinds shall be destroyed [and the action recorded] in a regular report prepared in order that the entries on these items may be closed.
   b. All other kinds of foodstuffs, clothing, medical supplies, and other materials which may be used and benefited from shall be distributed to Government departments, asylums, hospitals, and other charitable institutions and shall be officially charged to the account of the State.

31. All goods which cannot be sold after having been offered [for sale] in a public auction at least twice, shall become the property of the Government, free of charge, after the regular report on them has been prepared.

32. The owner of the goods referred to in the previous Article may withdraw them after the payment of Customs duties, storage charges, and additional charges, including all expenses, before the consummation of the sale or the signing of the regular report in accordance with

which the title to the goods is transferred to the Government.

33. The right to claim the balance held by the Government of the value of the goods mentioned in Article 29 shall be forfeited and shall become an earned right of the Government if the owners of the goods do not claim such amounts within a maximum period of five years from the date of sale.

34. Goods imported otherwise than in accordance with the rules for Implementation of the Customs Regulations shall be re-exported at the expense of the importer within the period which the Customs specify. If this period expires and the goods are not exported, they may be destroyed at the expense of the importer, who shall not have the right to claim any compensation [for them].

35. By a decision from the Minister of Finance, permission may be granted for the construction of general warehouses inside and outside the customs areas for storing goods on which duty has not been paid. Upon the approval of the Government to create free zones the Minister of Finance may allow the construction of warehouses or plants in them, in accordance with the provisions and conditions the Minister of Finance [himself] determines.

36. The Minister of Finance has the right to specify [which goods are] transit goods and such conditions as he sees fit for supervising the passage of these goods or preventing their passage and seizing them when necessary, in accordance with the procedures and instructions set forth in the Rules for Implementation.

Contraband Goods

37. Periodical lists of goods that are prohibited for administrative, religious, or economic reasons shall be prepared by the Ministry of Finance and submitted to the High Authority for his approval, and shall then be put into effect.

Smuggled Goods

38. The importation into or exportation from Saudi Arabia, including the Iraq and Kuwait Neutral Zones, of goods, materials, or things of any kind by illegal means without payment of the Customs duties prescribed thereon, shall be considered as smuggling. It shall likewise be considered as smuggling to attempt to import or export, contrary to the provisions of these Regulations or other Rules and Regulations in force, any contraband goods, including those kinds [of goods] which are subject to special arrangements with regard to importation or exportation.

39. All items of all kinds the entry of which is not prohibited, if seized [after having been] smuggled or during the attempt to smuggle them, shall be confiscated and a fine equal to double the amount of Customs duties and the additional charges due thereon shall be collected from the guilty party. Such items are detailed hereunder:

a. Items which pass through locations not specified by Customs, before the official permit is obtained.

b. Items which, prior to their arrival at the first Customs house, are offloaded from the means of transport at other than the officially recognized land or sea boundaries, such offloading having been done for no compelling reason and in a manner which indicates an attempt to smuggle the items.

c. Items which, upon inspection, appear to have been hidden or concealed by any sort of arrangement for concealment, or [are found] within folded articles, such as mattresses and the like, so as to give rise to the suspicion that they have been [deliberately] concealed, or in the corners of hiding places of the means of transport where normally no articles are kept, or among the passengers' luggage or their personal clothing which they carry [with them].

d. Items on which duties have not been paid and the withdrawal of which is attempted under the pretense that duties have been paid thereon, and by using the mark placed on goods on which duties have actually been paid.

e. Items which, upon inspection, prove to be different in quantity, kind, quality, measurement, or weight, from what is shown on the invoice; or items the container of which bears a figure that differs from the actual [number] of the inside contents; or items for which fabricated or fictitious invoices or documents are presented, or which bear counterfeit marks for the purpose of evading [payment of] part or all of the duties.

f. Local goods and things which are smuggled or which an attempt is made to smuggle for export.

g. Things which are brought into Customs storehouses or warehouses under a description other [than that applicable to them although it is prohibited to export or import them.

40. Items that fall under the categories outlined in the sections

of the above Article and that are proved by evidence or by the confession of the smugglers themselves to have been smuggled, but that have not actually been seized, shall have their cost collected in an amount equivalent to the cost of similar items, in addition to the collection of a fine equal to double the Customs duty and the additional charges thereon

41. If means of transport coming from foreign countries by land, sea, or air deviate from the usual route to locations having no Customs houses and unload their cargo for no compelling reasons, this cargo shall be considered as smuggled and shall be subject to the provisions on smuggling as outlined in the previous Article.

42. In case the smuggling is repeated, the smuggled goods shall be confiscated and a double fine shall be collected. The fine shall be collected four-fold if the smuggler smuggles [anything] within five years from the date of expiration of the penalty for the first smuggling.

43. If the smuggler cannot pay the fine imposed on him, he shall be imprisoned one day for each five Riyals [of the amount of the fine], provided the period of imprisonment shall not exceed three months.

44. All kinds of equipment used for smuggling, weapons, and all means of transport, shall be confiscated, with the exception of:

a. Aircraft and ships, unless they have been actually fitted out for smuggling.

b. Means [of transport] which are not owned by the smuggler, if the owner thereof conclusively proves that he was neither aware of the smuggling nor directly or indirectly an accessory thereto, provided such means were used in smuggling for the first time, in which case the value of the means of transport shall be estimated and collected from the smuggler.

c. Means of transport, if the smuggled goods are tumbak, tobacco, or cigarettes, of all kinds, and the quantity [involved] does not exceed five kilograms, or, where goods other than narcotics and liquor are involved, if the value thereof does not exceed SR 500.

45. The Customs Committee concerned, the formation of which is provided for in Article 52, shall conduct regular investigations to consider smuggling cases and decide on the handling of smuggled articles. A decision shall be taken in this respect, supported by the reasons necessitating conviction and the confiscation of goods, or the collection of an amount in lieu of confiscation, or the collection of a cash fine and the confiscation of the means of transport, in accordance with the pertinent Article; provided a copy of the said decision is delivered to the convicted person within twenty-four (24) hours frm the date of issuance of the decision. In case the parties concerned protest against the decision, they shall be granted a period of fifteen days from the date they are notified of the decision and must submit their protest to the administrative governor within that period for transmission to the authority concerned. If the fifteen days elapse and they do not submit their protest, the

Committee's decision shall become effective. If the person convicted refuses to accept the notification, or if he cannot be found, a report shall be made accordingly and the text of the decision shall be presented to the administrative governor for transmittal to the person convicted. Administrative governors must use the quickest means to communicate the decision to the person convicted, through writing, publication, or advertising. If, after the expiration of thirty days from the date of publication or advertising in case the convicted person's whereabouts are not known, or after the expiration of thirty days from the date of writing to him in the event his whereabouts are known, he does not submit his protest, the Committee's decision shall be considered effective.

46. If the person who has actually smuggled contraband or dutiable goods escapes, the Customs officer may chase him and may search for him in the house or place in which he was seen taking refuge. If the owner of the house refuses to surrender him to the officer, provided this is done in the presence of a police representative and the owner of the place or his representative, the governmental instructions issued in this regard shall be enforced.

47. If the owner of the smuggled goods is not present, the party causing them to be smuggled or arranging for their transport shall be considered as their owner.

48. If evidence arises on the presence of smuggled goods in any place or building, the place or building shall be searched in accordance with the usual procedure.

49. The person or persons who seize, discover, or give information about smuggled goods, or assist the responsible officials in any of the above-mentioned instances, shall be rewarded with a portion of the value of the smuggled goods and of the fine, in accordance with the instructions outlined in the Rules for Implementation.

50. If the things that have been smuggled or are being smuggled are in the category of narcotics or intoxicants, they shall be dealt with under the pertinent articles of the Regulations Prohibiting the Use of and Trading in Narcotics, and other applicable Regulations. Articles seized shall be destroyed immediately and the action recorded in a special regular report, and the accused and the go-between shall be referred to the authorities concerned for trial in accordance with the provisions of the applicable Articles of the Regulations and approved Decisions. The fines collected under the law shall be delivered to the Customs Department. If the smuggled goods are arms, weapons, or counterfeit money, the smugglers shall be referred to the courts concerned after the proper fines required from them under these Regulations are imposed.

51. If the things that have been smuggled or are being smuggled are articles or items the import of which is prohibited, they shall be confiscated, and the guilty party shall be penalized by a fine equal to their value locally. The penalty shall be doubled if he repeats the offense .

52. Customs Committees are authorized to consider and decide on all cases of smuggling or attempts to smuggle. The reports of the Committee are considered true unless they are proved

false. The Customs Committee is an administrative court that has the right to hear witnesses, question the person accused of smuggling, collect evidences on the offense, and investigate the arguments the accused presents in his own defense. Each Committee shall be formed, and its areas [of jurisdiction] defined, by a decision from the Minister of Finance.

53. The penalty for smuggling or for attempting to smuggle shall be a fine equivalent to double the Customs duties and additional charges [due on the goods involved] and, in all cases, the materials that are the subject of the offense shall be confiscated. If such materials are not seized, the offender shall have to pay the cost of them as estimated by the Customs, plus a fine equal to double the duties and additional charges due. If the materials that are the subject of the offense are of the kinds on which no Customs duties are levied, or if they are subject to import and export restrictions, the fine shall be equal to their cost. In case of recurrence of the offense , the goods shall be confiscated and the fine shall be doubled. The fine may be made fourfold if the offender commits the offense again within five years from the date of expiration of the penalty for the first smuggling offense.

But, if the goods are in the category of contraband, they shall be confiscated, a fine equivalent to double the duty thereon shall be imposed, and a sentence of imprisonment for a period of from one to twelve months shall be inflicted. In case the fine imposed is not paid, the offender shall be imprisoned one day for every five riyals, provided the period of imprisonment does not exceed three months.

54. Anyone who, for the purpose of escaping payment of part or all of the duties payable, goes so far as to break or change the lead seal, or any of the distinguishing marks and fastening devices placed on the goods by the Customs, shall be punished by imprisonment for a period of from three months to one year, and the rules on smuggling shall be applicable with regard to those goods.

55. Anyone who forges the stamps and distinguishing marks of the Customs for purposes of fraud, or uses them with no right [to do so] while being aware of the forgery, shall be punished by imprisonment for a period of from three months to one year, and the goods released or being released shall be considered smuggled.

56. Where persons agree between themselves and form a gang for the purpose of smuggling goods to escape from payment of Customs duties, the heads of such gangs shall be punished by imprisonment for a period of from four months to two years, and the members of the gang shall be punished by imprisonment for a period of from three months to one year. The goods shall be confiscated or, if they are not seized, the value of them and double the duties due thereon shall be collected from the gang collectively.

57. Any person proved guilty of smuggling who, while in the act of smuggling, has threatened the Customs or Coast Guard officials with arms, shall be punished by imprisonment for a period of from six months to three years, in addition to the other penalties.

58. If an armed person is found among several smugglers during the

occurrence of smuggling, all of them shall be punished by imprisonment for a period of from six months to two years, in addition to the other penalties.

59. The Customs Directorate has the right to dispose of the goods, smuggling equipment, and the means of transporation which are finally pronounced to be confiscated; and has [also] the right to sell them and, in accordance with the rules provided in the Rules for Implementation, distribute a portion of their value and of the amount of the fine among all those who [gave information which] led to the seizure of [the goods involved in] the offense, or those who participated or helped in seizing or discovering them.

60. In cases of emergency, if keeping the seized goods in custody exposes them to shrinkage or loss, the Customs Directorate has the right to sell them in the presence of a member of the Chamber of Commerce and a member of the Municipal Council, and prepare a report of sale. In locations where no Chamber of Commerce or Municipal Council exists, representatives of the Amirate and Police shall act in their place. If an order is issued to return the goods sold to their owner, he shall be entitled to collect the balance of the value of them after the duties, the charges due, and the expenses of sale have been deducted. However, if the seized goods are not contraband the owner of them may request that they be handed back to him after payment to the Customs of their cost plus the duties and additional charges and the maximum fine due [thereon]. These amounts shall be credited to him as a deposit pending a decision in the case.

61. Customs and Coast Guard officials who are proved to have deliberately prepared or assisted in the preparation of untrue seizure reports in connection with goods which, according to law, are not considered smuggled, and to have subjected them to confiscation. or [untrue seizure reports] in connection with goods which are smuggled but on which they do not apply the rules governing smuggling, shall be punished by imprisonment for a period of from six months to one year, in addition to being discharged from their positions. The person concerned shall reserve the right to ask for compensation for the loss he has sustained. If it is proved that the alteration of facts has been done through the influence of an outsider, the person who exerted the influence shall be punished by imprisonment for a period of from three months to one year.

62. Imprisonment for a period of from six months to two years shall be inflicted upon any employee or workman of Customs and upon any person performing the work of a Customs guard entrusted with Customs control, who dares to smuggle or attempts to smuggle goods, whether he is a principal, an accessory, or a go-between. The penalty mentioned [above] shall also be inflicted upon any employee or workman of Customs and upon any person performing the work of a Customs guard entrusted with Customs control who, by committing any act during the performance of his duties or by willful negligence of his duties, attempts to facilitate the avoidance of Customs duties, in whole or in part, on the goods which are subject to such duties, or attempts to facilitate the illegal entry into Saudi Arabia of any goods

the entry of which is prohibited. The sentence of imprisonment referred to above shall not bar the Customs Committees from imposing fines and confiscating [the goods] in the manner prescribed in Articles 39 through 51 of these Regulations.

63. These Articles of the Regulations shall supersede the former Customs Regulations including the subsequent approved Orders, Decisions, and Instructions. Any Article in conflict with the foregoing Articles or with the supplementary Articles of the Rules for Implementation which follow these Regulations, shall be considered as cancelled; and, in all matters, the provisions of these Regulations and the pertinent Rules for Implementation shall prevail.

64. The Minister of Finance shall carry out the provisions of these Regulations and he may, within the competences and powers granted to him by His Majesty the King, issue the Rules for Implementation and the necessary decisions for their enforcement .

65. These Regulations shall become effective as of the date of their ratification and notification to the authorities concerned, who shall circulate and publish them by all means of publication.

IN THE NAME OF GOD, THE MERCIFUL, THE COMPASSIONATE

When the World War was over and the restrictions imposed by the War were relaxed, the world began again to breathe the clean air of freedom and to rise from the ashes of the War's devastation. Quickened by the stirring of this new life, mankind marshalled all its resources and potentialities and turned to the task of rehabilitation and reconstruction in order to set itself once again on the road towards growth and progress.

Since the end of the War this country has been fortunate in achieving progress in many fields of activity. This period has seen the establishment of economic, commercial, public works, and cultural projects each of which shines forth like a beacon light across the land.

Among the most important factors which have encouraged the expansion of commerce are the ports, airports, railroads, and other public works established by His Majesty's Government. In view of the close relationship between commercial circles and the Customs administration, common interest requires that new rules and regulations be drawn up to complement the new Customs Tariff. These new rules and regulations represent a sincere effort to keep pace with the general progress of the country and to meet the present need for streamlining the transaction of official business.

His Majesty the King, while still Crown Prince, therefore issued Royal Order No. 425, dated 5 Rabi' I 1373 [12 November 1953], sanctioning the new Customs Regulations, to supersede the previous Regulations issued under Royal Order No. 326, dated 3 Safar 1349 [30 June 1930], which have become obsolete.

In accordance with Article 64 of the above-mentioned Regulations, which charges us, within the limits of the authority conferred on us, with issuing the rules and decisions necessary for putting these Regulations into effect, we have compiled the Rules for Implementation. In so doing, we have endeavored to make the Rules comprehensive and the procedures simple. We have issued these Rules so that they may be complied with, and trust that God will make them serve the purpose for which they are intended and be beneficial to all.

In the reign of His Majesty King Sa'ud ibn 'Abd al-'Aziz Al Sa'ud, may God prolong his days, safeguard his reign, and crown his endeavors with success.

Minister of Finance

'Abd Allah Al Sulaiman

TEXT

Chapter I

The Customs Organization

Article 1. The Directorate General of Customs, whose function is to supervise all the Directorates of Customs, shall be directly responsible to the Ministry of Finance.

The Directorates of Customs shall be six in number, directly responsible to the Directorate of General of Customs, and there shall be customs offices and customs points attached to each of them.

Directorates of Customs

Directorate of Customs for the Western Province, Jiddah

Directorate of Customs for the Eastern Province, Dammam

Directorate of Customs for the North, Tabuk

Directorate of Customs for the South, Jaizan

Directorate of Customs for the Frontiers, Qaryah

Directorate of Customs for the Northern Frontiers area, Ar'ar

COMMENTARY

The growth in Saudi Arabian imports has greatly taxed the resources of the Saudi Customs Service, and the Saudis recognized the need to modernize and update the training of its personnel. As a result, the Saudi Ministry of Finance and National Economy entered into a project agreement with the United States' Department of Treasury (the parent agency of the U.S. Customs Service) for technical, management, training and manpower advisory assistance. This was one of the projects carried out by the United States-Saudi Arabian Joint Commissi on Economic Cooperation. Up to 80 Saudi Customs officials per year will receive training in the United States under this program. U.S. technical advisers are also provided in Saudi Arabia. The full impact of this program on the development of the Saudi Customs Department has yet to be seen, but it will undoubtedly result in increased use of sophisticated techniques and a general expediting of customs proced

TEXT	COMMENTARY

<u>Customs Offices and Customs Points Attached to the Directorates of Customs</u>

<u>Directorate of Customs for the Western Province</u>

1.	Jiddah Customs Subsidiaries: a. Passengers' Customs b. The Southern fuel wharf	Seaport
2.	Jiddah Airport Customs	Airport
3.	Mecca Customs	Land
4.	Ash-Sharai' Customs Office	Land
5.	al-Lith Customs	Seaport
6.	al-Qunfudhah Customs	Seaport
7.	al-Birk Customs	Seaport
8.	Tuwal and al-Qadhimah Customs	Seaport
9.	Rabigh Customs	Seaport
10.	Yanbu' Customs Subsidiary: a. Yanbu' Airport Customs	Seaport
11.	Amlaj Customs	Seaport
12.	al-Wajh Customs Subsidiary: a. al-Wajh Airport Customs	Seaport
13.	Dhaba Customs a. al-Surah Customs Office (on the coast) b. al-Khuraybah Customs Office (north of Dhaba)	Seaport

TEXT		COMMENTARY
14. Medina Customs	Land	
Subsidiary:		
a. Airport		
15. Hayil Customs	Land	
16. Riyadh Customs	Land	
Subsidiaries:		
a. Airport Customs		
b. Railroad Customs Office		
c. Rumah Customs Office		
d. Umm al-Jamajim Customs Office		
Directorate of Customs for the Eastern Province		
1. King Abd al-Aziz Port Customs (Dammam)	Seaport	
2. Old Dammam Port Customs	Seaport	
3. Ras Tanura Customs	Seaport	
4. Nariya Customs	Land	
Subsidiaries:		
a. Manifah Customs Office	Coastal	
b. Abraq al-kabrit	Land	
c. al-Maqta' Customs Office	Land	
5. al-Khobar Customs	Seaport	
6. Qatif Customs	Seaport	
Subsidiaries:		
a. Darin (Customs located on an island opposited Qatif)	Seaport	
7. Dhahran Airport Customs	Land	
8. Neutral Zone Customs	Seaport	
9. Safaniya Customs Point	Seaport	
10. al-Hasa Customs	Land	

TEXT		COMMENTARY
Subsidiaries:		
a. al-Hasa Airport	Land	
b. al-Hasa Railroad	Land	
c. al-Hazm Gate Customs Point	Land	
d. al-Salihiyah Gate	Land	
e. al-Khabbaz Gate	Land	
f. Al Mulhim Gate	Land	
g. al-Mubarras Gate	Land	
11. Salwa Customs	Land	
12. Jubail Customs	Seaport	
13. al-'Uqayr Customs	Land	
<u>Directorate of Customs for the North</u>		
1. Tabuk Customs	Land	
Subsidiary:		
Airport Customs Office	Land	
2. Al-Bir Customs Office	Land	
3. Haql Customs (the only coastal Customs of the Directorate of Customs for the North, located on the Red Sea at the terminus of the coastal boundary line)	Seaport	
4. Natn Customs Office	Land	
5. ash-Sharaf Customs Office	Land	
6. al-Qulaybiyah Customs Office	Land	
7. al-Burayj Customs Office	Land	
8. al-'Ula	Land	
9. Tayma	Land	

TEXT		COMMENTARY

Directorate of Customs for the South

1.	Jaizan Customs	Seaport
2.	al-Tuwal Customs	Land
3.	al-Mawsim Customs	Seaport
4.	al-khawiyah Customs	Land
5.	al-Jabiri Customs	Land
6.	al-Qahmah Customs	Seaport
7.	Farasan Customs	Seaport
8.	'Ayban Customs	Land
9.	Dhahran al-Yaman Customs and its subsidiary, "Alab Customs Office	Land
10.	Najran Customs and its subsidiaries, Nahuqah, al-Mawfijah and al-Khadra Customs Offices	Land
11.	al-'Aridah Customs	Land
12.	Jaizan Airport Customs	Land
13.	al-Matla' Customs Point	Land

Directorate of Customs for The Frontiers

1. Qaryat Customs Subsidiaries: Land
   a. al-Mafraq Customs Point
   b. Riyadh Customs Point

TEXT	COMMENTARY
c. Kuwait Customs Point	
al-Hafar — Land	
Subsidiary:	
a. Riyadh Customs Point	

toms Area, Free Zone, and Bonded Warehouses

The Customs Area

icle 2. The Customs Area is the area surrounded by a fence, wall or markers and consisting of a Customs house, with its warehouses and wharfs. The Area may be located on the shores of the sea or on the land boundaries that separate Saudi Arabia from the neighboring countries. In general, it is the area where Customs formalities are carried out, whether on the coasts, on the frontiers, at airports, or within the Kingdom.

cle 3. The Customs has the right to search any person, car, passenger or freight vehicle, or anything else that passes through its gates or through the Customs

CUSTOMS AREA
Articles 1 - 6

U. S. Customs collection districts are set out in 19 USC Sections 1 and 2.

Enforcement provisions pertaining to boarding of vessels and search of vehicles are contained in 19 USC Section 1581. These provisions allow customs officers to board any vessel or vehicle at any place in the U.S. or within customs waters. U.S. Customs and Coast Guard, however, are limited by the search and seize provisions of the U.S. Constitution. So-called "border searches" are permitted without probable cause with a "mere suspicion" being sufficient, but are limited to the geographic area surrounding a point of entry. In other cases a search warrant may be required. See 19 USC, 1595. Since Saudi government is a monarchy without a constitution, they are obviously

TEXT

Area, or crosses the Customs line . It may also enforce this at sea on commercial vessels, sailboats, boats, etc., which may be found at a distance of two miles beyond the territorial waters of the Kingdom as defined by Royal Decree No. 6/4/5/3711, dated 1 Sha'ban 1368,May 28,1949. In the event of hot pursuit, the Customs may go beyond this distance, in accordance with the provisions of Article 6 of the Customs Regulation. In all instances, all of the means of transportation in the Customs areas shall remain under Customs surveillance until they depart from the seaport, land station, or airport.

Article 4. Withdrawal of goods and luggage: All kinds of goods crossing the Customs line or the Customs area must be accompanied by an official clearance certificate regardless of whether they are

COMMENTARY

not restricted by the limitations that apply to the U.S.. Both Saudi regulations and those of the U.S. permit the seizure and confiscation of goods concealed to avoid the payment of duties (for example see e.g. 19 USC, Section 1584). Under U.S. law, a ship or vehicle carrying concealed goods is itself subject to forfeiture. The Saudis do not appear to have a comparable provision.

TEXT

COMMENTARY

dutiable or not.

Passengers arriving at night shall be permitted to take only the personal effects they need for the night. The rest of their belongings shall be withheld in order that the formalities on them may be completed the next day.

icle 5. Goods concealed with a view to avoiding payment of duties thereon or escaping from the restrictions laid on their import or export, shall be seized and shall be subject to confiscation.

icle 6. Persons who have work to do inside the Customs area are permitted to enter the area during regular working hours. The Customs administration has the right to expel any person from the Customs area whenever it thinks that his presence in that area is undesirable for justifiable reasons.

TEXT		COMMENTARY
2.	The Free Zone	THE FREE ZONE Articles 7 - 18
	It is to be noted that the Regulations for this zone shall not be considered effective until after the locations and number of such zones have been fixed.	The Saudi free zone is comparable to the U.S. free trade zone discussed in 19 USC, Sections 81A - 81U and 19 CR, part 146.
Article 7.	The Free Zone is the fenced in area which the Government allocates within the Customs area for the purpose of erecting warehouses for lease to licensed individuals in order to store goods listed in the manifest for the Free Zone, and materials necessary for the supply of vessels, or for the purpose of establishing factories therein, in accordance with the provisions set forth hereinafter.	Both countries prohibit residence in the zone (19 USC, Section 1810), and require the keeping of accounts and records (19 USC, 81p). Both countries provide for payment of duties when the goods leave the zone and enter the customs territory. However, unlike U.S. regulations, Saudi law does not explain the customs treatment when two or more products result from the manipulation or manufacture of merchandise in the zone. For example, under U.S. law, when the foreign merchandise is used in combination with U.S. goods to manufacture a new product, duty is payabl
Article 8.	The advantage of this zone is that it is possible to carry out any modification of packages stored within the zone, that there is no time limit for leaving goods there, that the Regulations for unclaimed goods	on the quantity of the foreign merchandise used with an allowance for irrecover waste. Where several products are used, duties are apportioned in regard to the relative value of such products (see 19 U

TEXT		COMMENTARY
	do not apply to the goods stored in it, and that Customs duties and storage charges are not collected on such goods. However, duties and charges shall be collected on materials imported from abroad and used for construction therein.	Section 18c). Saudi regulations are also silent on the procedure for granting licenses in the zone.
[Arti]cle 9.	Residence in this zone is prohibited and, except for ships' supplies, the consumption or sale of goods at retail in this zone is likewise prohibited.	
[Arti]cle 10.	The tenants shall keep regular books to record the movement of imported and exported goods, and such books shall be subject to examination by Customs.	
[Arti]cle 11.	If it appears that some of the goods found in the warehouse are not recorded in these books, the goods shall be considered smuggled goods and shall be subject to the provisions of the Customs Regulations that deal with smuggling. In addition, the	

TEXT	COMMENTARY
lease of the warehouse shall be liable to cancellation.	
Article 12. Unloading and storage in this zone are permitted only after obtaining an order from Customs and under Customs supervision. Likewise, when the goods are to be shipped, the approval of Customs must be obtained.	
Article 13. The storage in this zone of goods whose importation is prohibited, explosives, and inflammable materials is prohibited.	
Article 14. It is not permitted to store in the Free Zone goods shown on the manifest as imports.	
Article 15. Goods to be withdrawn from the Free Zone into the Kingdom must be taken first to the Customs area for completion of the formalities. They shall be considered as newly arrived imports, and shall be subject to the tariff in effect at the time of payment of the duties.	
Article 16. The condition of the goods stored in the Free Zone may be altered	

TEXT		COMMENTARY
	in accordance with the requirements of business fluctuations. Sorting, cleaning, mixing, modification of the form of goods, or any other operation shall not be allowed except by special permission from the Customs.	
cle 17.	The Free Zone shall be subject to guarding and supervision by Customs at all times. Customs employees have the right to enter this zone at any time to search for contraband or smuggled goods, or to carry out any function that the public interest may require.	
cle 18.	The Customs Administration shall fix the working hours in the Free Zone which, in any case, shall fall between sunrise and sunset.	
Bonded Warehousing System		BONDED WAREHOUSING SYSTEM Articles 19 - 37
cle 19.	The construction of general warehouses inside or outside the Customs area, for storing goods imported into Saudi Arabia or exported therefrom, may be permitted after the Customs Depart-	Saudi regulations on bonded warehouses appear to closely parallel those in the United States.

TEXT

ment approves the location, plan, and construction of the warehouses, in accordance with the provisions set forth hereinafter.

Article 20. The owner of the warehouse shall pay a deposit, specified by the Customs Department, to insure the carrying out of the terms of his obligation towards the Customs.

Article 21. The owner of the warehouse shall keep in his books complete records regarding the movement of goods in the warehouse whether the goods are still in the status of imports or have been cleared.

Article 22. The warehouses shall be subject to Customs control, and Customs shall bear no responsibility for the goods stored therein.

Article 23. Personnel required for operating the warehouses shall be appointed by the Customs, and the owner of the warehouse shall assign to them the necessary offices and other facilities.

Article 24. The owner of the warehouse shall be required to pay the salaries

COMMENTARY

Both countries permit goods to remain in the warehouse for a maximum of three (3) years, although U.S. regulatior provide for one (1) year extensions (18 CFR, Section 144.5 and 144.6), while Saudi regulations do not. Saudi regulations are silent on such points as transfer of the right to withdraw merchandise from a bonded warehouse (see U.S. regulations in 19 CFR, Section 144.

TEXT

COMMENTARY

of employees the Customs assigns for control, and likewise 1/12 of the total salaries annually in return for the indemnity or pension which the Government must pay to them upon their leaving the service. The Customs Administration shall compute the total amount of these salaries at the end of each month, and the owner of the warehouse shall remit them to the Customs Treasury for the account of the ministry of Finance.

cle 25. The doors of warehouses shall be locked with two different locks, the key to one of which shall be kept with the Customs, so that they may be opened in the presence of the Customs representative assigned to control the warehouse.

cle 26. Goods found in the warehouse and not recorded in its books shall be considered smuggled, and the proprietor of the warehouse and the owner of the goods shall both

TEXT	COMMENTARY

be jointly responsible for the payment of the fines due.

Article 27. Goods may stay in the warehouse for a period of three years, after which they shall be dealt with as unclaimed goods. After the expiration of this period, they shall be sold at auction in order that the duties and warehouse charges due may be collected. The balance of the proceeds shall be kept in the Customs Treasury as a deposit for a maximum period of five years, after which it shall finally be entered as income in the Treasury's account.

Article 28. Customs duties and additional charges shall become due on goods stored in warehouses at the time such goods are withdrawn into the Kingdom.

Article 29. Goods may not be taken into or drawn out of the warehouse except with permission from the Customs and after completion of the proper formalities.

TEXT	COMMENTARY
icle 30. Contraband goods may not be permitted to be stored in the warehouses. Inflammable and dangerous materials may not be stored except in the places assigned for them.	
icle 31. If contraband goods are found in the warehouses they shall be considered as smuggled and shall be treated accordingly.	
icle 32. The owner of the warehouse shall be responsible to Customs for the carrying out of the formalities required from the owner of the goods.	
icle 33. Warehouses shall be opened only during the Customs official working hours. However, the Customs director or the person noting in his place may authorize work within the warehouses at other times, against the payment of wages for work outside regular working hours. Such authorization must be given in writing.	
cle 34. If an emergency occurs in the warehouse, its owner may take	

TEXT		COMMENTARY
	such precautions as he sees fit to protect the goods stored there without first securing permission from Customs. However, he must notify Customs immediately.	
Article 35.	Customs duties shall be collected on all materials imported from abroad for use in building the warehouses.	
Article 36.	Customs shall examine the books of the company once a month and shall make a partial inventory of the goods deposited in the warehouses three times a year. A complete inventory of the goods shall be taken once a year.	
Article 37	Goods shall be stored in the warehouses through the use of applications for storage to be submitted to Customs. The manifest section in Customs shall, in accordance with the contents of these applications, close the entries relating to these goods. by making an endorsement to the effect that the goods have been transferred to the bonded	

TEXT

warehouses. A manifest section dealing with bonded warehousing only shall be established and it shall enter the applications for storage in a special register wherein the closing entries for goods withdrawn from storage shall be made.

Chapter III

ork Schedules in the Directorate General f Customs and the Directorates of Customs

ticle 38. Work in the Directorate General of Customs and in all the Directorates of Customs shall begin one hour and a half after sunrise and shall continue for six hours and a half. In the Customs areas, warehouses, and wharves, work shall continue for seven hours and a half; and at the Customs gates, for eight hours.

icle 39. The above working hours shall be fixed by the Director General of Customs and by the Directors of

COMMENTARY

CHAPTER III

WORKING HOURS
Articles 38 - 42

The only significant portion of these regulations is the suspension of work in all customs houses on Friday (except for passenger inspection).

TEXT

COMMENTARY

Customs, each within his own field of jurisdiction, and Customs departments and others concerned shall be notified of the schedule.

Article 40. Ships tied up to mooring buoys may, for purposes of transshipment, be unloaded into lighters at any time, provided written authorization is obtained from Customs.

Passenger and Airport Section

Article 41. The Passenger Section shall be open every day including Fridays and holidays, in accordance with the work schedules established by the Directors of Customs. Airports are further bound by the schedules of airplanes.

In the event of the arrival of pilgrims or passengers before the end of the official working hours, work shall continue in the section until the ship's passengers land.

Customs Directors may, at the request of those concerned, order

TEXT

work to be done before or after these work schedules, as well as on holidays, against the payment of charges for work outside the established regular working hours These charges, however, shall not apply to pilgrims' means of transport.

It is understood that employees who work in addition to the official hours of work are entitled to payment for work outside the regular working hours, and payment will be made to them on the basis of the additional hours worked.

Holidays

.cle 42. Work shall be suspended in all Customs houses on Fridays, on the days of 'Id al-Fitr, on the day before the first day 'Id al-Adha, and the days of 'Id al-Adha.

Chapter IV

tions for Practice as Customs Clearing Agent

cle 43. The function of clearing Agents is to complete the Customs formalities outlined in these Regula-

COMMENTARY

CHAPTER IV

CONDITIONS FOR PRACTICE OF CUSTOMS CLEARING AGENTS

Articles 43 - 49

Saudi law, like U.S. law, provides for

TEXT

tions on behalf of merchants. The handing over of the Delivery Order to them to enable them to carry out the Customs Formalities does not give them any title to the goods, unless those are transferred to their names. They can, through clearance, withdraw consignments from the Customs areas as long as they have the clearance certificate in their hands and their names are recorded thereon.

No one is authorized to practice the profession of clearing goods belonging to others except by written authorization from the Department of Customs.

Article 44. The authorization referred to in the previous Article shall be granted subject to the following conditions:

1. The Clearing agent must be a Saudi national not less than eighteen years of age.
2. He must be able to read and write.
3. He must furnish a bond in the

COMMENTARY

licensing of customs house brokers. Both countries restrict licenses to citizens only. In the U.S. a formal examination with a passing score of seventy-five (75%) is required, while the Saudi law merely requires that the applicant be literate. Both states permit corporations to obtain licenses. U.S. regulations are, in general, more detailed and complex. (See 19 CFR, Part 111).

TEXT	COMMENTARY
amount specified by the Customs Directors for the payment of whatever fines may be imposed upon him, and to compensate for whatever damage that may be incurred owing to his practicing clearance work.	
5. He must not have a previous record of smuggling.	
icle 45. A license is valid for a period of one year, and must be renewed at the end of each year against the payment of five riyals for each license upon its renewal.	
icle 46. Merchants may clear their goods themselves or through their agents provided such agents possess the qualifications stipulated for clearing agents, and provided that their names are submitted to the Customs Department at the beginning of each year for authorization and for them to be granted licenses against collection of the amount specified in the previous Article	
cle 47. Organizations may be licensed to	

TEXT | COMMENTARY

establish clearing offices, provided the person in charge of them possesses the qualifications specified in Article 44, in addition to the following:

1. He must furnish a bond of not less than one thousand riyals.
2. He must keep legal registers for consignments cleared, and such registers must be subject to examination by Customs officials.
3. He must submit the names of clearing agents working for him and they must hold the licenses referred to.

Article 48. The owners have the right to endorse the delivery order to public or private clearing agents or to the clearing offices, and in such a case the latter parties will act on behalf of the former in signing all clearance documents, paying duties on the goods, and receiving them. The clearing agents shall assume all responsibilities resulting from

TEXT	COMMENTARY
their duties. The owners may also sign the delivery orders and the clearance documents. In this case, the clearance certificate may be delivered only to the owners themselves who are require to sign for the receipt of the goods. Hence, the duties of the clearing agent shall be to complete the customs formalities only, and the owners shall assume the responsibility for all errors resulting from discrepancies in the declarations.	
icle 49. The Customs director may impose penalties on clearing offices and agents through warning or suspension for a maximum period of one month. If violations call for more severe penalties, the Director General of Customs has the right to extend the period of suspension to six months. In the event the violation is repeated, the suspension may be extended to a full year, or the	

TEXT

clearing agent may be barred from practicing the profession of clearing.

Chapter V

Customs Duties

Duties of Imports

Article 50. Customs duties on imports shall be collected according to the Customs tariff in effect on the day of payment, as specified in the Saudi Customs Tariff and its provisions.

Method of Assessment of Duties

Article 51. Duties on goods which are subject to ad-valorem duties shall be assessed on the basis of the actual price paid or agreed upon in the currency of the exporting country. This price shall be the price of the imported goods, packed and ready for shipment, at the port of export, plus shipping and insurance expenses to the port of destination in Saudi Arabia. When it is not possible to determine this value, the

COMMENTARY

CHAPTER V

CUSTOMS DUTIES

Articles 50 - 55

Both states base assessment of duties (where *ad valorem* duties are involved) on export value. However, Saudi regulations, unlike the U.S., include shipping and insurance in the export price. Thus, although Saudi tariffs are generally lower than those in the U.S., the value upon which *ad valorem* duties are calculated are higher. Both countries provide for alternate methods of valuation where export value cannot be determined (for U.S. regulations see, for example, 19 USC, Section 1401A).

TEXT | COMMENTARY

valuation of imports shall be made on the basis of the closest comparable value that can be determined.

Goods which are subject to duties according to weight shall have such duties collected on them on the basis of their gross or net weight, as stipulated in the Customs Tariff. The gross weight is the weight of the goods with all their outer and inner packing including anything used inside the package for purposes of wrapping, separating, or arranging the goods. The net weight is the exclusive weight of the goods.

Exports

icle 52. All exports of local products (except those covered by special agreements between the Government and other parties) are exempt from Customs duties and additional charges except storage charges, porterage fees, and payments to Customs personnel for work outside regular working

TEXT | COMMENTARY

hours.

Transit Goods

Article 53. Goods in transit are exempt from Customs duties on a basis of reciprocity.

Excise Duties

Article 54. Excise duty shall be collected on the products of Saudi Arabia, in accordance with such Ministerial Decisions as may be issued in this respect.

Duties on Containers

Article 55. As a general rule no special duties are collected on containers which cannot be used again because of the damage done to them on their being opened to remove the goods therein.

Similarly, no special duties are collected on bags used in packing bulk items, or on containers of no commercial value such as the following:

Boxes of cardboard or ordinary wood

Tin cans, sealed or with sealed nozzles

TEXT	COMMENTARY
Baling straps Small barrels used for packing cheese and preserved fish Baskets and crates Canvas covers Wooden boxes and crates used for packing double packages Luggage used for carrying personal effects Bottles and demijohns Frames and inner hangers used for wrapping and transporting velvet and plush Reels for ribbon used in machines, spools for sewing, thread, and the like. If the containers are of the kind that can be used again, such as iron barrels, compressed gas cylinders, or iron bottles for mercury, duties thereon shall be collected at the rate applicable to the material they contain if such material is subject to ad valorem duties. But, if the duties on the item are specific, no duties shall be collected on	

TEXT

the containers.
However, duties on ornamented wooden boxes, varnished boxes, cardboard suitcases, and other unusual containers shall be collected separately in accordance with the Customs Tariff(Section 208 of the General Provisions).

Chapter VI

Additional Charges

1. Wharfage Charges

Article 56. Wharfage charges equivalent to 3 percent of the Customs duties payable are collected on goods in general unloaded at Saudi seaports, and are collected along with the Customs duties.

The following shall be exempt from wharfage charges:

1. Items imported in the name of H.M. the King and the Royal Family.
2. Items imported for the official use of the diplomatic and consular corps, provided this is done on a basis of

COMMENTARY

CHAPTER VI

ADDITIONAL CHARGES

Articles 56 - 94

The Saudi system of assessing various charges and fees in addition to customs duties is different in many aspects from those in the U.S. and other countries. Firstly, the ports are all nationally owned, and thus administered through one central government. Although there are individual port administrations, they are not political separate jurisdictions.

The Saudis have many charges such as wharfage fees that are tacked on to the customs duties. These are figured as a percentage of the customs duties. As discussed earlier, since customs tariffs

TEXT

reciprocity.

3. Items for the personal use of ambassadors, ministers plenipotentiary, consular employees and personnel of the foreign diplomatic and consular corps, provided this is done on a basis of reciprocity.
4. Arms and military supplies imported by the Government.
5. Ordinary personal effects of passengers and household effects of immigrants whom the Government agrees to allow to immigrate and take up residence in the country.
6. Samples of no commercial value.
7. Unwrought gold and silver in their primary form, and ingots scraps, or broken pieces thereof, and permitted currencies and coins.
8. Items such as empty cylinders and barrels which are exported from Saudi Arabia to be filled and returned. However, when items are returned after

COMMENTARY

have generally been reduced to 3%, these additional fees such as wharfage fees which are 3% of the duties, are minimal, even when municipal fees of 6% and a special charitable fee of 1% to Al-Falah Schools is added. Stamp taxes are imposed on cigarettes and tobacco products at the port of entry.

The Saudis also impose further stringent storage charges for goods left on the docks for over ten (10) days. This is largely due to the serious port congestion problem discussed earlier. The Saudis also have a schedule of fees for various supervisory duties performed by customs officials outside of normal working hours. This is a practice followed in other countries, although usually a provision for overtime pay is made without a specific schedule of fees. See e.g., 46 USC Section 382 (b).

TEXT

COMMENTARY

having been sent abroad for repair, the wharfage charges shall be collected in proportion to the duties due on the repairs done.

9. Goods exempted from duties in accordance with the Customs Tariff as provided for in items 01/2.02/2,03/2,01/4, 02/4,01/6,02/6,03/6,and 04/6. These goods are, respectively, medicines, sterilized (absorbent) cotton and gauze, disinfectants, insecticides, books, magazines, school slates, slate pencils, chalk, agricultural implements, water pumps used in agriculture, nursery plants, and fertilizers, as well as seeds for cultivation, tractors, and water well drilling rigs.

10. The exemption from wharfage charges of items exempted from duties in accordance with agreements or special orders shall be restricted by

TEXT

COMMENTARY

the text of the agreement or order and shall only be within the limitations and subject to the terms of that text.

icle 57. Wharfage charges shall not be collected on goods imported or exported by air or by land. Nor shall they be collected on automobiles, livestock, or animals imported or exported by land.

icle 58. Wharfage charges at the rate previously stated, that is 3 per cent of the import duties, shall be collected on tobacco, cigarettes, jurak, and tumbak imported by sea.

cle 59. Wharfage charges shall not be collected on the following exports:

1. Locally made goods
2. Foreign goods (in transit)
3. Foreign goods unloaded by mistake.
4. Foreign goods which have enentered the country and approval for the re-export of which has been issued.

TEXT | COMMENTARY

5. Foreign goods which are in the Customs warehouses and approval for the re-export of which is issued.

2. Municipal Fees

Article 60. Municipal fees at the rate of 6 per cent of the total Customs duties shall be collected on all imported goods.

3. Special Contribution for al-Falah Schools

Article 61. A special contribution for al-Falah schools shall be collected on all goods imported from abroad at the rate of 1 per cent of the total Customs duties.

4. Duties on Licensing and Certification of Automobiles

Article 62. Duties on licensing and certification of automobiles shall be collected in the following manner:

1. 400 riyals on each automobile with a load capacity of 1 ton or less
2. 500 riyals on each automobile with a load capacity of 1 to 2 tons.

TEXT

COMMENTARY

3. On automobiles whose load capacity exceeds two tons, 200 riyals per each extra ton. Fractions of a ton shall be considered a full ton.
   (To be entered in a special column and forwarded to the Ministry of Finance, a separate cash receipt to be issued by the Customs cash office, and a reference made in the examiner's ledger to the number and date of this receipt).

5. Banderole Stamps

e 63. List of the kinds and values of banderole stamps used on tobacco, cigarettes, tumbak, and cigarette paper imported from abroad:

1. One-half qirsh red stamp on each booklet of cigarette paper.
2. One-quarter qirsh green stamp on two-ounce packages of tobacco, on 30-gram to 60-gram packages of cigarettes, and on two-and-ahalf-ounce packages of tumbak.

TEXT	COMMENTARY
3. One-eighth qirsh blue stamp on one-ounce, half-ounce, and quarter-ounce packages of tobacco, and on 10 gram to 40 gram packages of cigarettes.	
4. One-half qirsh red stamp on four-ounce packages of tobacco	
5. Seven-eighth qirsh stamp on seven-ounce packages of tobacco.	
6. One-eighth qirsh banderols stamp duty shall be collected on each net ounce of pipe tobacco, after the net weight of the different sizes is determined. The duty is assessed on the same basis as that on two-ounce packages of loose tobacco.	
7. One-half qirsh banderols stamp duty on each kilogram of Amayidi, Kadhimiyah, or green tobacco imported from abroad, plus one Saudi qirsh for the lead seal affixed to the packages containing these varieties.	

TEXT

COMMENTARY

6. Storage Charges

ticle 64.a. As a general rule storage charges are collected, after the lapse of ten days including Fridays, but excluding holidays, on all goods arriving from outside or inside the Kingdom and passengers' luggage actually received by the Customs. whether in its warehouses or in the places it designates. Storage charges shall be reckoned as of the date the full load of the means of transportation is finally received, and on the basis of the gross weight per package and shall be reckoned daily in accordance with the following list:

. 10 days er day	2nd 10 days per day		3rd 10 days per day		Specification
H.	CQ.	H.	CQ.	H.	
.625	-	1.25	-	2.50	Per package weighing up to 10 kg. gross
1.25	-	2.50	1.	-	Per package weighing over 10 kg and up to 25 kg. gross
2.50	1	-	2	-	Per package weighing over

TEXT								COMMENTARY
							25 kg. and up to 55 kg.gross	
1	-	2	-	4	-		Per package weighing over 55 kg. and up to 105 kg. gross	
2	-	4	-	8	-		Per package weighing over 105 kg. and up to 200 kg. gross	
3	-	6	-	12	-		Per package weighing over 200 kg. and up to 300 kg. gross	
4	-	8	-	16	-		Per package weighing over 300 kg. and up to 400 kg. gross	
5	-	10	-	20	-		Per package weighing over 400 kg. and up to 500 kg. gross	

TEXT					COMMENTARY
- 10	-	20	-	Per package weighing over 400 kg. and up to 500.kg.gross	
- 12	-	24	-	Per package weighing over 500 kg. gross	

Wood of all kinds including poles, iron of all kind, sheets of all kinds of metal, all kinds of pipes and elbows of any material, asbestos sheets, pressed cardboard sheets, windows, doors, empty tin cans, marble slabs, tires, and other goods that arrive in bulk or in separate pieces, are subject to storage charges at the rate of 1 Saudi qirsh daily per 100 kg. gross for the first ten days, 2 Saudi common qirsh daily for the second ten days, and 4 Saudi common qirsh daily for the third ten days or more. Fractions of 100 kg. shall be considered as 100 kg.

Imported postal parcels which are exempt from Customs duties under the Regulations are also exempt from storage charges, if these charges do

TEXT | COMMENTARY

not exceed 10 common qirsh.

b. Storage charges on transit goods be collected as follows:

a. Storage charges are payable on transit goods actually received by Customs, whether in its warehouses or in such places as it may designate for their storage, after the lapse of the ten-day period of grace, which shall include Fridays, but exclude holidays.

b. The period of grace shall be reckoned as of the date on which the delivery of the whole cargo of the means of transport is completed.

c. Storage charges to be collected per day on transit goods after the lapse of the said period of grace shall be the equivalent of half the rates prescribed in the list as storage charges, on the basis of the gross weight per package according to the schedule set forth in Article 61.

TEXT		COMMENTARY
ticle 65.	If the day following the ten days of grace for storage falls on a Friday, storage charges for that day shall be collected. If it is an official holiday, no storage charges shall be collected for the day or days of the holiday. Storage charges shall be due only as from the working day or Friday following the holiday.	
icle 66.	The merchant shall not be required to pay storage charges on the goods the withdrawal of which from Customs is delayed beyond the date of the issuance of the clearance, if such withdrawal is made during the days falling within the period of grace, since he is legally entitled to these days whether the packages remain in storage or are cleared. However, if the period of grace expires and the goods are not removed, they will be subject to storage charges according to the established	

TEXT | COMMENTARY

rates. Consequently, each time any portion of the goods is cleared, and until all the goods are removed, the merchant or his representative must sign for the cleared portion and note the date of the clearance on the back of the gate clearance form, in order that storage charges may be computed as they fall due for each day of the period of delay in removing the remaining goods.

Article 67. The Port Administration in Jiddah, and the Railroad Directorate in Dammam, by virtue of their pertinent instructions, are bound to make all arrangements and provide all means to insure sorting the goods and transferring them as quickly as possible to the Customs warehouses and the places designated for storage, so that the merchants will not have to pay storage charges because of the delay.

Any delay that is found to have

TEXT | COMMENTARY

occurred in sorting or transferring the goods and that results in the assessment of storage charges shall be the responsibility of the person who caused the delay and he shall be liable to penalty.

icle 68. The period of exemption from storage charges on goods unloaded from ships into dhows or any other means of conveyance shall start as of the date on which the last such means of conveyance carrying goods from the ship has been unloaded and all of the ship's cargo has been received.

icle 69. When packages are transferred from one Customs to another, the period of exemption from storage charges on the goods shall be renewed in each Customs.

icle 70. Storage charges shall remain due for collection on goods for a period of one year, after which the goods shall be considered abandoned. Under no circum-

TEXT | COMMENTARY

stances shall the storage charges exceed half the value of the goods.

Article 71. No storage charges shall be collected during periods of dispute between the Customs and those concerned regarding the goods imported.

If a delay in the withdrawal of the goods is the result of a dispute between merchants on the one hand and shipping or insurance companies or others on the other hand, then storage charges must be collected.

Storage charges shall not be collected for the period during which the goods remain in Customs because samples of them are sent by Customs for laboratory analysis or for examination by technical authorities.

No storage charges shall be collected for keeping tobacco, tumbak, and cigarette paper in the Customs area for the purpose of affixing banderole stamps

TEXT	COMMENTARY
thereon after the lapse of the first ten days and during the additional period fixed by Customs for this purpose. If the merchant fails to complete the process of affixing the stamps within the stipulated period, storage charges shall become due as of the day following the date of its expiration.	
...icle 72. Goods which are not destined for Saudi Arabia and which are unloaded in Saudi Arabia for compelling reasons or by mistake shall be kept in the Customs warehouses and the ten-day period of exemption from storage charges shall be applicable to them. After the expiry of that period, storage charges shall be computed on them at the equivalent of half of the rates prescribed in the schedule of storage charges set forth in Article 64 of Rules for Implementation of the Customs Regulations.	

TEXT		COMMENTARY
Article 73.	The Regulations governing storage charges shall be applicable to goods in transit which those concerned decide to withdraw from the Customs into Saudi Arabia. This means that these goods shall enjoy the ten-day period of grace after they are received in Customs. As a general rule, the regular storage charges shall be applicable to all goods in transit which are unloaded inadvertently or because of an emergency. This includes goods in transit which will be shipped to their final destination.	
Article 74.	If a court order is issued for the detention of any goods for any reason such as death of the owner, dispute over ownership, etc., the goods shall be delivered only after the verdict of the Court is issued and provided the delivery order is submitted by the shipping company, and the storage charges due according to	

TEXT	COMMENTARY
the Regulations are assumed by the person adjudged to be the owner of the goods.	
ticle 75. Items which come from abroad to the Customs warehouses and the entry of which is prohibited by an order issued by the local Government, must be returned abroad by their owners as soon as possible. Such goods shall be exempted from storage charges.	
icle 76. No storage charges shall be computed on goods that have fallen overboard until they are recovered from the sea and until those concerned are notified. They shall be granted the regular exemption period.	
icle 77. No storage charges shall be computed on goods that become damaged due to fire in the Customs warehouses. This exemption shall be effective from the time of the occurrence of the accident until the government investigations and contacts with the insurance companies in this	

TEXT

COMMENTARY

regard are completed.

Article 78.a. No storage charges shall be computed on any period during which the completion of processing formalities on goods is delayed owing to inevitable accidents such as rain, floods, or storms, or to taking inventory of warehouses, or for any other reason of force majeure or official formalities.

b. In cases where certain shipments have been subjected to storage charges for reasons beyond the control of the importers, the Director General of Customs shall investigate the matter on the basis of written requests to be submitted to him by the importers concerned. If the case is proven to his satisfaction, he shall be authorized to reduce or cancel the storage fees, or to collect a fine in lieu thereof from those who have caused its collection.

Article 79. After the expiration of the

TEXT	COMMENTARY
regular exemption period, storage charges on goods of value deposted in the vaults of the Department shall be computed at a rate of 5 common qirsh per package per day.	
ticle 80. When goods are released on deposit during the period of exemption from storage charges and the duties are settled later, such goods shall not be subject to storage charges since the consignment was actually withdrawn from the Customs area before the storage charges become due on it.	
icle 81. If goods are actually received by Customs and for some reason or other their owners do not find them at the time of clearing, the owners shall submit a petition to the Customs showing the number of packages they could not find after searching, their marks, numbers, and kind, and the name of the ship on which they arrived The Customs Director shall have this petition endorsed by the	

TEXT | COMMENTARY

employees responsible; he shall have an exhaustive search made for the packages; and he shall give the owner of the packages a reference number by which he can follow up the matter. If the packages subsequently are found, they shall be exempted from the storage charges due on them from the date the owner reported that they were missing up to the date they were found and the owner was notified accordingly.

Article 82. In order not to congest the storehouses, yards, and piers, Customs shall not permit the entry into the Customs area of goods destined for export unless the means of transportation is anchored in the harbor and ready to load. Prior to permitting the entry of the goods into the Customs area those concerned must submit the shipping permits issued by the shipping companies on whose means of transportation such exports are to be shipped.

TEXT	COMMENTARY
icle 83. Goods going to places inside or outside the Kingdom shall enjoy exemption from storage charges for a period of two days beginning from the day following the date of their entry into the Customs area.	
icle 84. Goods may not remain on the piers after the loading of the ship on which they were to be carried has been completed. In such instances, the owners of the goods must take them back to town immediately. The Customs Administration may, of its own accord, and six hours after notifying those concerned, order the removal of such goods to the warehouses or yards at the expense of those concerned. Storage charges shall then be assessed on these goods after the expiration of the stipulated period of exemption.	
icle 85. Storage charges on goods going to places inside or outside the Kingdom shall be collected on	

TEXT | COMMENTARY

each package per day, in accordance with the rates specified for imported goods as outlined in Article 64/a of these Rules for Implementation.

Porterage Charges

Article 86. The collection of porterage charges, whether by Customs or by the authorities concerned, shall be in accordance with the tariff set up for these charges. In Customs where there are regular porters, these shall be as follows:

1. On packages weighing from 1 to 5 kilograms, no porterage charges shall be collected.
2. On packages weighing over 5 kilograms and up to 25 kilograms, 2 common qirsh shall be collected.
3. On packages weighing over 25 kilograms and up to 50 kilograms, 4 common qirsh shall be collected.
4. On packages weighing over 50 kilograms, 8 common qirsh shall be collected.
5. Fractions of a kilogram shall

TEXT

COMMENTARY

be reckoned as one kilogram.

6. These charges shall be collected on both imported and exported packages.

Supervision Charges

:icle 87. Supervision charges as follows shall be collected for the Treasury's account on any operation which those concerned ask to have carried out within the Customs area and which is approved by Customs:

1. Special supervision, within the Customs area, of the opening of automobile crates and putting automobiles in running order: SR 4 per car.
2. Changing containers of or putting into sacks, within the Customs area, goods arriving in bulk or in sacks: SR 4 per day or fraction of a day.
3. Other operations such as weighing, inspection, etc.: SR 2 per hour.

cle 88. Upon written request submitted by those concerned, and for a

TEXT

COMMENTARY

charge as shown below, the Customs will approve the carrying out of the operations of unloading or loading, or both, or any other operation, outside the official working hours, that is, between the end of the official working hours and their resumption on the following day, or on Fridays and official holidays:

1. Steamers which are anchored to a buoy in the stream and work at night outside the official working hours: No additional charges for work outside the regular working hours shall be collected.
2. Dhows and barges which dock at the wharves to unload the cargo of a steamer outside the regular working hours: SR 25 per hour per steamer shall be collected from all of them and they shall be treated as one unit.
3. Steamers: SR 30 per hour or fraction of an hour per

TEXT

COMMENTARY

steamer for loading or unloading or both at the piers.

4. Steamers carrying livestock and animals: SR 15 per hour or fraction of an hour per steamer, for unloading.

5. Sailing ships and other means of maritime and land transportation: SR 5 per hour or fraction of an hour per sailing ship or other means of maritime transportation not mentioned elsewhere for loading or unloading or both.

6. Fueling and provisions of steamers: SR 15 per hour or fraction of an hour per steamer taking on liquid fuel or other supplies. This charge shall not be collected if the fueling or provisioning is carried out during the loading or unloading of goods for which a charge for work after regular working hours has already been paid.

TEXT | COMMENTARY

7. Loading steamers with petrleum outside the regular working hours: SR 30 shall be collected as charges for work outside the regular working hours on the entire operation.
8. Opening of the warehouses: SR 30 per hour or fraction of an hour from each merchant for the opening of each warehouse to clear goods or ship them on railroad cars or vehicles, including the opening of the gate.
9. Opening of the warehouses: SR 30 per hour or a fraction of an hour from each merchant for the opening of each warehouse to complete the formalities on dutiable goods and to withdraw them either on railroad cars or on vehicles.
10. Opening of the warehouses: SR 20 per hour or a fraction of an hour per warehouse, for the receipt of imported or exported goods.

TEXT	COMMENTARY
(Note): Opening of the warehouses for the above operations shall be decided by the Customs and only in cases of necessity or urgency.	
11. Opening of the cash office for the payment of duties after the official working hours: SR 10 per hour, for a maximum time of one hour, for payment on goods for which the formalities have been completed.	
12. Completing Formalities on Goods on which Duty Has Not Been Paid: SR 30 per hour or fraction of an hour from each merchant including the withdrawal or export of vegetables fruits, meats, and other perishable items, and animals.	
13. Exit and Entry of Ships' Passengers and Their Effects Before or After Working Hours or on Fridays and Official holidays: SR 50 per hour per steamer.	
14. Exit and entry of passengers	

TEXT | COMMENTARY

and their effects before or after the regular working hours, or on Fridays and official holidays: SR 25 per sailing ship or any means of transport other than a steamer.

15. Inspection of goods for export at Aramco's warehouse in Dhahran after regular working hours: SR 30 for each employee assigned to the job. Two employees shall be assigned each time, on a rotational basis.
16. Inspection of Aramco's goods placed in special vans for frozen goods at the Company's warehouses in Dhahran, outside regular working hours: SR 30 per employee working on a rotational basis.
17. Disembarkation and embarkation of airplane passengers with their personal luggage outside official working hours shall be exempted from additional charges.

TEXT	COMMENTARY
18. Clearance of goods received or to be shipped by air outside official working hours: SR 30 from each merchant.	
As for steamers, airplanes, and other means of transport carrying pilgrims during the pilgrimage season, these shall be exempted from payment of the charges for work outside the regular working hours in accordance with High Order No. 4860/1, dated 21 Ramadan 1376, April 21, 1957. The employees concerned shall receive their dues from the Government.	
[Arti]cle 89. It is understood that the work period outside working hours on Fridays and official holidays has the same number of hours as the regular working day. If continuation of work is desired after that time, additional charges for such work shall be paid at the same rates.	
[Arti]cle 90. After obtaining the consent of Customs, those concerned shall	

TEXT	COMMENTARY

pay the charge for work outside regular working hours to the Customs cash office against a special receipt.

Article 91. The Customs Director shall fix the number and names of employees and guards necessary for the foregoing operations on a rotation basis. The names of such employees shall be entered on lists upon which their signatures shall be obtained to signify their knowledge of these instructions and their agreement to carry them out.

Article 92.a. The Customs cashier shall keep a special register under the heading "charges for work outside regular working hours" for the amounts collected for the above mentioned operations, based on the special receipts. This register shall consist of two facing pages, one for receipts and the other for disbursements.

b. All receipts from overtime char-

TEXT	COMMENTARY
ges shall be deposited with the Saudi Arabian Monetary Agency and its branches. In the dependencies or towns where the Agency has no branches, these shall be remitted to the Finance offices as is the case with revenues.	
icle 93. At the end of each month the Accounting Section shall prepare lists of the receipts from overtime charges and of the amounts due to employees on the basis of the assignment lists approved by the supervisors of the work, in accordance with the requirements of Article 35 of the General Regulations for Government Employees.	
icle 94. After completion of the formalities of obtaining the signatures of the employees who have worked outside the regular working hours on the lists as well as the endorsement of the director of Customs concerned, the lists shall be submitted to	

TEXT

the Directorate of Customs for checking and referral to the Directorate General of Customs, to be audited and submitted to the Ministry of Finance and National Economy for the disbursement order.

Chapter VII

Contraband Goods and Items Subject to Special Provisions

Contraband Goods

Article 95. It is forbidden to import the following items:

1. Arms and parts thereof and military equipment and supplies, except those imported in the name of the Saudi Government.
2. Explosives and all varieties of potassium nitrate, except with permission from the Government and also compounds such as picrates (salts formed by picric acid, which are explosive) and potassium chlorate.
3. All kinds of fireworks, such

COMMENTARY

CHAPTER VII

CONTRABAND GOODS

The rules provide for a sizeable list of goods that are considered undesirable and are therefore banned from importation. These range from backgammon sets to watches bearing portraits of members of the Royal family. The strict religious tenets of Islamic law have had a considerable influence in determining what is prohibited, such as pictures and images that are "contrary to Moslem morality" and which include such diverse items as crucifixes and pictures of nudes. Most other countries have some restrictions on imports of socially undesirable goods. The U.S., for example, prohibits importation of immoral articles which include

TEXT

as skyrockets, firecrackers, etc.

4. All intoxicants, narcotics, qat, poppies of all kinds and any item consisting entirely or partially of heroin, morphine, cocaine, hasish, opium, or any other narcotic substance (except thos imported for medicinal purposes only, provided a permit is obtained from the Ministry of Health).
5. Ferro, Lais, Bisleri, and La Roche quinines, Vina Vita, Vial Tonic syrup, and all similar preparations which contain a definite proportion of wine, whether small or large, and anything in which there are semi-intoxicants.
6. Special preparations containing toxic substances, toxins, and dangerous medicines, unless licensed by the Ministry of Health.
7. All medicinal preparations, except for those persons who

COMMENTARY

obscene books, and books advocating treason and insurrection. See 19 USC Section 1305.

TEXT | COMMENTARY

are licensed by the Ministry of Health. The following items are excepted.

a. Linden leaves

b. Mint leaves

c. Marshmallow leaves

d. Camomile leaves

e. Castor oil in bottles

f. Cod-liver oil in bottles

g. Epsom Salt in sealed packets.

h. Talcum powder

i. Aspirin tablets

j. Alcox plaster

k. Zam-Buk ointment

l. Fruit salts

m. Krushen salts

n. Valda pastilles, and the like

8. All varieties of eau de cologne, may be cleared only after they have been analyzed in the laboratories of the Ministry of Health and the chemical analysis laboratory of the Ministry of Petroleum and Mineral Resources, Jiddah. If it is proven that they

TEXT | COMMENTARY

are not intoxicating, their entry will be permitted. But if they are intoxicating, their entry shall be absolutely forbidden.

9. Pornographic pictures and pictures of nudes, and the like and things which are made in the form of a cross or on which a cross is drawn, and pictures and images contrary to Muslim morality.

10. Printed matter and publications detrimental to Muslim beliefs and morality:
    a. Books, scriptures, and dictionaries specified in the list appended to the Rules.
    b. All books dealing with sex.

11. Watches and other merchandise bearing the portrait of H.M. the King, H.R.H. the Crown Prince, or any member of the Royal family, with the exception of copybooks and publications.

TEXT	COMMENTARY
12. Watches on which the Muslim creed, Quranic verses, or the like, are inscribed, as well as small flags resembling the Saudi flag on which is inscribed the Muslim creed or the name of God, and papers and boxes decorated with the Saudi flag.	
13. Goods on which the Mecca or Medina Mosques or both are pictured, with the exception of prayer rugs, utensils, publications, writing papers and envelops used by pilgrims, and rosaries the master bead of which contains a lense magnifying the pictures of the two Holy Mosques.	
14. Motion picture apparatus, cultural, agricultural, industrial, health films, and the like, with the exception of those imported by Government and private establishments provided the necessary undertaking is obtained from	

TEXT	COMMENTARY
those concerned to use them for educational purposes only.	
15. Phonographs, phonograph records, and other musical instruments, with the exception of cultural, agricultural, industrial, health records, and the like, and the machines necessary for their display imported by Government and private establishments, provided the necessary undertaking is obtained from those concerned to use them for educational purposes only.	
16. Games like backgammon, chess, and the like, except caroms and billiards.	
17. Games of chance and anything which is in the least objectionable and therefore subject to prohibition.	
18. Artificial pearls.	
19. False incense sticks, i.e. wooden sticks coated with the scent of the incense.	
20. Spoiled foods, and anything	

TEXT

COMMENTARY

that is harmful to public health.

21. All kinds of adulterated ghee, oil, and foods.
22. Government and private printed matter imported from abroad, except those authorized by a Council of Ministers' decision No. 687 of the Council of Ministers, dated 25 Dhu al-Qa'dah 1380, May 10, 1961.
23. Gold-colored coins and medals on which Quranic verses are written are prohibited in order to prevent their being used to defraud.
24. Blank invoices bearing the names of foreign companies abroad.
25. Hats.
26. Arms coming in with pilgrims shall be detained, registered in a special book, and given a serial number. The record shall show the kind of arms, their quantity, the serial number, the number of shots,

TEXT

COMMENTARY

and the name of the owner. The owner shall be given a receipt to enable him to reclaim them on his return in the presence of his guide or his agent, against his signature.

27. Prophylactic plastic sheaths.
28. Handkerchiefs and other commodities on which improper poems or expressions are inscribed.
29. Kaffiyah made of Khaki cloth or other material with a projecting front piece, known as vizored caps.
30. Husn Qasab or Husn Yusuf imported from India, which is crushed and used by women as a hair cosmetic.
31. Medicines that have no label or accompanying leaflet showing the method of their preparation, their components, and the quantity of each component.
32. Toy rifles used for training

TEXT

COMMENTARY

children in marksmanship, unless covered by a license from the Ministry of Interior.

33. Commodities bearing the Government's insignia composed of two crossed swords underlying a palm tree which stands between them with a long stem topped with palm leaves, shall be cleared only with permission from the Government. This does not include commodities decorated with an insignia which does not exactly represent the Government's insignia described above.

34. Telescopes used in photography

35. The entry of pictures in relief imported for sale shall not be permitted. However, if a picture in relief is brought in by a passenger as a present for his children, it shall be cleared, provided this is done on a one time basis and not on several trips, and provided the picture is not of such a

TEXT

large size as to attract attention. Anyone who imports more shall be instructed to return the excess to its point of origin.

ms Subject to Special Provisions

96. Special provisions shall apply in respect to the following items:

1. Nursery plants, plants, all kinds of fruits, vegetables, and seeds must be submitted to the Directorate of Agriculture before they are allowed in the country.
2. Live animals, poultry, and birds may not be withdrawn from Customs without permission from the Division of Veterinary Medicine.
3. Used clothes may not be withdrawn from Customs unless they are accompanied by a disinfection certificate from abroad, otherwise they will have to pass through the quarantine station.

COMMENTARY

ITEMS SUBJECT TO SPECIAL PROVISIONS

Items that possibly could become health or safety hazards are subject to various restrictions. These include plants, fruits, and vegetables, which must be inspected by the Department of Agriculture, and animals, which must be inspected by the Division of Veterinary Medicine. See 19 USC 1306 for some comparable U.S. provisions. Special provisions also apply to importation of alcohol, which is forbidden for internal use by Islamic law.

TEXT | COMMENTARY

4. Hunting arms may not be cleared unless the license provided for in the Regulations concerning them is submitted, and the number and date of the license are registered.
5. Customs formalities on tobacco, cigarettes, tumbak, jurak, and cigarette paper may not be completed until the importer produces the annual license, granted to him by the Ministry of Finance, authorizing him to trade in these items, and until the number and the date of the license are registered in the Customs records.
6. In general it is forbidden to clear alcohol except by special license from the Ministry of Health specifying the quantity authorized and the name of the importer. Alcohol used for lighting must be colored with a toxic substance as directed by the

TEXT	COMMENTARY
government committee concerned, in pursuance of High Order No. 11635, dated 1 Ramadan 1364, August 8, 1945.	
7. Fresh or preserved foods, and, in general, animal products, such as cheese, dairy products, butter, and cream as well as other preserved foods which may be harmful to health due to decomposition or decay shall, before being cleared from the Customs area, be submitted to the doctor in charge of food supervision or to the person acting for him.	
8. Invoices covering medicines must be sent to the Ministry of Health which will check them, ascertain that the medicines listed therein are of the permitted varieties, and make a notation thereon authorizing clearance. As for medicines imported in the name of clinics attached to foreign	

TEXT | COMMENTARY

legations in the Kingdom, which contain opium or other narcotics, the legation concerned shall be asked to send the clinic's physician to the Customs House to assist in opening the cases containing these medicines and checking their contents against the narcotics listed on the license issued by the Ministry of Health in Saudi Arabia authorizing the clearance.

9. Imported fresh, refrigerated, or frozen meats must be accompanied by a health certificate proving that they are free from diseases, and another certificate from an accredited government authority to the effect that the livestock was slaughtered according to Shari'ah,both certificates to be endorsed by the Saudi embassies or consulates, if any, at the points of export. In addi-

TEXT

tion, fresh meats shall, upon their arrival, be submitted to the doctor in charge, even if they are kept in cold storage.

10. The license plates of all vehicles the export of which is authorized must be withdrawn prior to such export.

Chapter VIII

mption from Duties on Re-Importation

le 97. As a general rule, import duties are payable on all locally produced and foreign goods that are exported and then re-imported for any reason. However, the following are exceptions to this rule:

The articles and goods specified hereunder shall be exempted from the payment of import duties if they are re-imported within six months from the date of export. The Director General of Customs may extend the period of grace to one year according to the circumstances of each case.

1. Automobiles and the like,

COMMENTARY

CHAPTER VIII

EXCEPTIONS FROM DUTIES ON RE-IMPORTATION

Articles 97 - 98

Generally, Saudi goods exported and re-imported are subject to duty. However, certain categories of goods re-imported within six months may be exempt from duty, such as automobiles and personal possessions of passengers who temporarily leave the country, and items sent abroad for repairs. The U.S. Tariff schedules are somewhat more liberal insofar as they exempt from duty most U.S. articles exported and re-imported that are not advanced or improved abroad. See Tariff Schedules of the United States (T.S.U.S.), Items 800-802.30. As to repaired articles

TEXT

such as bicycles and motorcycles ; typewriters, cameras, binoculars, and other personal effects belonging to passengers who leave Saudi Arabia temporarily, provided such items are necessary for personal use and are not intended for commerce, and provided the approval of the Customs administration is obtained in advance and full descriptions of the items are registered and distinguishing marks are placed on them. A certificate signed by the Customs Director must be obtained from Customs and it must show all descriptions and distinguishing marks in order that the items may be checked against it upon their return either through the Customs from which they were exported or through any other Saudi Customs.

2. Items sent abroad for repair

COMMENTARY

the U.S. places a duty on the value of the repairs. T.S.U.S.,Item 806.20, as does Saudi law.

TEXT	COMMENTARY
purposes, provided they are submitted to Customs and the descriptions of them registered, and provided a distinguishing mark is placed on them, if possible, and the owner is given a certificate to this effect. However, import duties and additional charges shall be collected on the costs of repair.	
3. Locally produced goods returned to Saudi Arabia without having left the Customs Area at the port of destination, provided the Customs ascertains that the goods returned are those that were exported.	
4. Empty cylinders, barrels, burlap sacks, and similar objects sent abroad empty to be filled with foreign goods and then re-imported. It is sufficient to register the descriptions and identifying marks on each for comparison with the statements made by	

TEXT	COMMENTARY
the Customs, and to put lead seals and distinguishing marks on them if possible to facilitate the identification of these objects when they are re-imported. 5. Goods imported into the Kingdom which, for any reason, are found not to be in demand in the local markets and the importer of which asks that they be re-exported to their point of origin for replacement by other new goods. The export of such goods shall be permitted after the authenticity of the request has been ascertained by the competent authorities, provided that the merchants concerned import similar goods in lieu thereof within the limits of their quality and quantity. These imported goods shall be exempted from Customs duties only, to the exclusion of charges and fees. Any in-	

TEXT

crease in the value of the goods shall be observed, and Customs duties shall be collected on such increase, in addition to those due on freight and insurance charges, with due regard to any increase in the rates of Customs duties that may be in force at the time of such re-import. However, additional charges and port fees shall be collected on the entire shipment.

le 98. Postal parcels returned from abroad shall be exempt from import duties if they did not leave the post office to which they were sent and if, on their return, the parcels are in the same condition as when they were exported.

Chapter IX

Goods Exempted from Customs Duties

le 99. Exemption from Customs duties shall be granted in accordance with the provisions of the following Articles, subject to the conditions set forth in each of

COMMENTARY

CHAPTER IX

GOODS EXEMPTED FROM CUSTOMS DUTIES

In addition to the large number of items that are duty free under the newly revised tariff schedules, certain broad categories

TEXT

them, and in accordance with the following general rules:

1. The bill of lading must be made out or endorsed in the name of the person who has the right to exemption.
2. Exemption from Customs duties does not under any circumstances entail exemption also from the regular Customs formalities or inspection, or from the additional charges, unless provision is specifically made to this effect.
3. Goods which are cleared and exempt from Customs duties in accordance with the provisions of the following Articles may not be used later for purposes other than those for which they were imported, or sold to persons or groups of persons not entitled to exemption, until Customs has been notified in order to assess thereon whatever should be collected of the duties and char-

COMMENTARY

of goods belonging to certain groups of people are also exempted. These include all articles belonging to the King, personal effects of diplomatic employees, and certain items brought in by tourists and pilgrims. One rather significant exemption applies to foreigners who are under contract to work for the government.

The United States and many other countries have a number of broad exemptions such as an exemption for articles imported for exhibitions and fairs. (See 19USC, Section 1751-1756 and 19 USC Section 144a) and certain types of gifts sent from abroad. (See 19 USC 1321).

TEXT	COMMENTARY

ges payable.

4.a. When it becomes evident that that certain foreign countries who have diplomatic representation with His Majesty's Government treat the members of Saudi diplomatic and consular corps in such a manner as to make their Customs exemptions include such items as may be sold by them to persons and organizations not entitled to Customs exemption, the principle of reciprocity would then dictate that exemption to the provisions of Paragraph 3, Article 99 of the Rules for Implementation of the Customs Regulations.

b. The principle of exemption on a basis of reciprocity shall be applied on the basis of a letter from the Ministry of Foreign Affairs.

:le 100. Articles belonging to H.M. the King shall be exempt from import duties and all additional charges,

TEXT | COMMENTARY

except porterage. They shall also be exempt from the inspection, opening, and other formalities.

Article 101. Foreign Employees of the Diplomatic and Consular Corps: Articles which are for the strictly personal use, within reasonable limits, of accredited ambassadors, ministers, charges d'affaires, counselors, secretaries, and attaches of embassies, consular employees, and those who are members of accredited foreign diplomatic and consular groups, shall be exempt from import duties and additional charges, except porterage, and from inspection formalities, provided that such persons apply themselves solely to their duties, do not do any other work, and do not engage directly or indirectly in commerce. This exemption shall be granted only to the extent that similar concessions are granted by the state which the official or group represents.

TEXT

COMMENTARY

2. Articles imported directly from abroad for official use, within reasonable limits and on a basis of reciprocity, in embassies, legations, and consulates shall be exempt. Articles in Customs warehouses that have been imported for another person who has no right to enjoy exemption may be exempted before they are cleared if they are sold to any of the parties mentioned in Paragraph 1 above, provided that before they are withdrawn from Customs the ownership of them is transferred to the name of the party who has a right to enjoy exemption.
3. Customs duties shall not be refunded on articles bought by the diplomatic and consular corps from local markets in the Kingdom, and goods imported by merchants to replace such articles shall not be exempted from duties. But what-

TEXT | COMMENTARY

ever foodstuffs, tobacco and other things these persons buy from captains of ships shall be exempt from duties if the applicant for exemption submits a letter about it or an invoice drawn up in his name.

4. The Customs Administration shall be notified of the names of the employees of the diplomatic and consular corps who have the right of exemption from Customs duties in accordance with the preceding rules. It shall list their names in a register and transmit them to the departments concerned for information and action accordingly.

5. Representatives of foreign countries shall submit a written statement, signed by the responsible official, and showing in detail items for personal use and those for use in embassies, legations, or consulates, and also the

TEXT

COMMENTARY

number of packages, their marks, numbers, contents, and value, and a declaration to the effect that the packages do not contain any contraband goods or articles which the Government forbids to enter the country. If Customs suspects that the packages of foreign legations contain liquor, it shall notify the Ministry of Foreign Affairs and the legation concerned so that each may send a representative to inspect the package or packages, if the legation so agrees. If the legation refuses to open the package and requests their return, its request shall be granted and it shall be permitted to export them unopened.

6. The mere possession of diplomatic passports does not entitle bearers thereof to exemption from duties, charges, or Customs formalities.

TEXT | COMMENTARY

7. Items and articles imported for persons other than those referred to in the preceding paragraphs, such as scientific or technical missions or others, may be exempted through courtesy if High Orders are issued concerning them or if a special Ministerial Order is issued by virtue of the powers granted to the Minister of Finance by H.M. the King.

8. The possession by Saudi citizens of diplomatic passports does not entitle them, within Saudi Arabia, to the right of exemption from duties and additional charges or to the privileges of exemption from opening and inspection.

Article 102. The following shall be exempt from import duties and additional charges:

a. Ordinary personal effects, even though new, brought in with passengers for their

TEXT	COMMENTARY
personal use. New effects must be of a reasonable quantity and not intended for sale, exchange, or presentation as gifts. In the event Customs is not convinced, it may collect duties and charges on the extra items.	
b. For each pilgrim, 50 kilograms of foodstuffs and two towels for pilgrimage rituals as well as the pilgrim's used personal effects.	
c. For each passenger, two hundred grams, i.e. one carton of cigarettes. This exemption shall not be granted to drivers, transit passengers, private couriers who travel frequently.	
d. For each pilgrim who enters the Kingdom for the purpose of performing the rites of pilgrimage and on a pilgrim's visa, one kilogram of tobacco.	
The following shall apply to excess quantities brought in by	

TEXT | COMMENTARY

pilgrims or passengers:

1. If the quantity is up to two kilograms in excess of what is prescribed for each passenger or pilgrim, Customs duties shall be assessed and collected thereon once and it shall be cleared after affixing stamps thereto.
2. If the excess quantity is over two kilograms but not more than five and the passenger or pilgrim declares it, Customs duties shall be assessed and collected thereon once. If he fails to declare it, double Customs duties shall be collected.
3, Any excess quantity over five kilograms must be included in a manifest otherwise, it shall be regarded as smuggled goods and shall be dealt with accordingly.

e. Furniture belonging to officials of the Ministry of Foreign Affairs who are assigned to

TEXT | COMMENTARY

the Ministry's headquarters shall be exempt from import duties. Likewise, employees transferred from the Ministry of Foreign Affairs headquarters to a foreign post, shall be permitted to export their vehicles and furniture to the location of their new post.

f. Vehicles brought in with Ministry of Foreign Affairs' employees transferred back to the Kingdom, shall be exempt from import duties and additional charges. It is to be observed, however, that none of the said employees may sell such vehicles before the lapse of two years.

..cle 103. Personal effects and household furniture of the persons described below shall be exempted from import duties and additional charges:

1. Persons coming to reside in the Kingdom of Saudi Arabia for the first time, provided that a certificate from the

TEXT

COMMENTARY

consulate of the State of which such a person or persons are subject, is submitted proving that they have entered the Kingdom for the first time, and provided that a permit is obtained from the Directorate of Public Security authorizing them to reside in the Kingdom of Saudi Arabia.

2. Saudi subjects who marry abroad and return to the Kingdom with their wives, provided that the furniture is brought in with them or within three months from the date of their entry into the Kingdom, is commensurate with the position of the husband, and is not imported for commercial purposes; and provided that upon their arrival they notify Customs by official letter, accompanied by the marriage certificate duly legalized by the Saudi embassy.

3. Foreigners who come for the

TEXT

COMMENTARY

first time to work for the Government under agreements or contracts, provided that the agreements or contracts concluded with them specifically provide for the exemption of these items from Customs duties and additional charges.

4. Students who are sent to study abroad, either at their own expense or at the expense of the Government, and then return to the Kingdom after completing their studies, provided that each student submits a certificate from the college or university where he was studying, duly legalized by the Saudi embassy or legation, attesting his affiliation to such college or university.

5. Saudis who are forced, under certain circumstances, to reside with their families outside the Kingdom for medical

TEXT | COMMENTARY

treatment or other reason, and then return to their country, provided that they have resided abroad for a sufficient period to justify their acquisition of such furniture.

6. All the above-mentioned items shall not include refrigerators, radios, fans, automobiles, or other similar luxury commodities.

7. All the items mentioned in the preceding paragraphs shall have been used by the persons concerned.

Article 104.a. Imports in the names of the Holy Mosque, the Mosque of the Prophet, mosques, waqfs, charitable institutions, and contributions to charities are exempt provided the exemption from duties is approved by the Council of Ministers.

b. Imports of the Carpet Institute in Medina, as well as imports of 'Ayn al-'Azizyah in Jiddah, shall be exempted from Customs duties.

c. Presents sent from abroad to the Two Holy Mosques shall be exempt

TEXT	COMMENTARY
from Customs Duties.	
icle 105. The following materials and farm implements shall be exempt from Customs duties and additional charges:	
1. Farm implements and machines described in detail in Item 01/06 of the Customs Tariff.	
2. Agricultural water pumps and their motors, hoses and pipes which fit such pumps, and the accessories and spare parts of agricultural pumps. (See Item 02/06 of the Customs Tariff.)	
3. Tractors and water well drilling rigs, whether imported separately or mounted on vehicles, provided such vehicles form an integral part thereof, and provided that an undertaking is obtained from the person concerned not to separate the vehicle and use it for other purposes.	
4. All kinds of agricultural seeds.	
5. Instruments and machines im-	

TEXT

COMMENTARY

ported for poultry and cattle farming which are described below:

a. Instruments for cattle farming and dairy:

1. Foreign varieties of cattle for breeding purposes.
2. Milk buckets and one-gallon cans.
3. Automatic drinking water taps.
4. Stable partitions.
5. Cattle shearing machines.
6. Special, numbered metal plates to be fixed to the ears of cattle for pedigree preservation purposes.
7. Special chains for fettering cattle.
8. Animal feed grinders and mixers.
9. Special nose rings for bulls.
10. Special buckets for young calves.
11. Special machines for milking cows.
12. Apparatus and measuring

TEXT | COMMENTARY

instruments for detecting milk adulteration.

13. Special partitions for keeping animal fodder, both fresh and dry, during the summer.
14. Milk filters and their accessories.
15. Milk separators.
16. Butter churns.
17. Butter and cheese forms.
18. Milk boilers.
19. Milk pasteurizers with coolers.
20. Butter strainers.
21. Cheese vats, metal.
22. Cheese and butter presses.
23. Special machines for measuring the percentage of fat in milk.
24. Butter cutters.
25. Special milk bottles and bowls.
26. Milk containers' washing apparatus.
27. Milk containers' sterilizing equipment.

TEXT | COMMENTARY

28. Cheese-making rennet.
29. Milk bottles fillers and cappers.
30. Cattle Vaccines, serums, medicines and veterinary examination instruments.

b. Poultry farming equipment:

31. Special hatching eggs, in accordance with certificates issued from accredited official departments.
32. Rearing chicks of foreign varieties, for improvement of stock.
33. Varieties of foreign poultry for breeding purposes, imported for specific projects.
34. Nests for raising poultry and chicks imported for specific projects.
35. Special wire fencing for poultry and chick enclosures.
36. All kinds of kerosene and electric incubators.
37. All kinds of kerosene and electric chick brooders.

TEXT	COMMENTARY
38. Feeders.	
39. Waterers, regular and automatic.	
40. Egg testing devices.	
41. Egg measures.	
42. Egg sorting machines.	
43. Special cases and baskets for the transportation of eggs.	
44. Special cases for the transportation of chicks.	
45. Electric, automatic timers.	
46. Thermometers and hygrometers.	
47. Egg laying coops for hens.	
48. Feed mixers and cutters.	
49. Feather picking machines.	
50. Numbered leg and wing metal bands.	
51. Poultry vaccines, serums, medicines, and examination instruments.	
The exemptions from duties of all of the items mentioned above in this Article should be based upon a certificate from the Ministry of Agriculture, the Departments re-	

TEXT

COMMENTARY

lated to it, or the agricultural commissions delegated by it, which the importer must obtain and submit to Customs at the time of clearance.

It is understood that the certificate shall define the required measurement of pipes, hoses, and belts necessary for pumps, and give full specifications of the other implements, machines, and motors mentioned above. The certificate shall also state that all these items are imported especially for farming, and shall record the amounts, specifications, and marks of the items as well as the names of the importers in order to ensure that the items are sold for and used in farming. If the Ministry of Agriculture finds out that the items mentioned above are used for a purpose other than that for which they were imported, it

TEXT

shall notify the Customs to collect the duties due thereon.

:le 106. Commercial Samples.

1. Commercial samples which are not fit as commodities for sale in the markets, such as small cloth cuttings, all varieties of buttons, oilcloth cuttings, etc., shall be exempt from duties.

2. Commericial samples which can replace commodities in the markets such as samples of stockings, handkerchiefs, undershirts, etc., shall be exempt from duties, provided they are damaged in a manner that will make them unusable. If the person concerned does not agree to the goods' being damaged they they shall be subject to duties.

However, if they are imported in small quantities the duties on which do not exceed ten Saudi qirsh then they shall be exempt from duties and it is not necessary to damage them.

COMMENTARY

Commercial Samples

The Rules provide for the importation of commercial samples but under strict limitations. If the samples are not fit for sale (e.g. small swatchs of cloth) there is no difficulty. However, if the sample is identical to the actual goods sold, it must be damaged, so as to make it unsaleable. This provides some obvious drawbacks to the use of samples as sales tools. A deposit of duties must be made on entry and this is refunded upon exportation. Samples must normally be exported within six months from entry. These provisions are generally more restrictive than comparable United States regulations which permit any commercial traveller to bring in samples under bond without formal entry or examination(19 C.F.R. Section 10.36). The United States also has special provisions governing the temporary importation of theatrical effects(19 C.F.R. Section 10.33),articles brought in by lecturers and scientists, and models of womens dresses, which do not appear to have parallels in Saudi customs regulations.

TEXT | COMMENTARY

3. Duties on commerical samples imported for purposes of display and eventual return and, likewise, duties on specimens and items imported for the purpose of display and sale, shall be collected on deposit. Detailed statements of such items shall be submitted showing the number of pieces, descriptions, numbers, and the value of each item. These statements shall be checked against the items imported and then approved by the Customs and the person concerned. Customs shall keep a copy of these statements against which the items shall be checked on re-exportation. The deposit collected shall be liquidated by finally collecting the duties on whatever items have been sold, and refunding of the deposit to the person concerned. Care should be exercised to have the Customs formalities carried out

TEXT

COMMENTARY

under the direct supervision of a representative from Customs. A period of six months shall be allowed for the display of samples and specimens. The period may be renewed for six more months upon the request of those concerned and the subsequent agreement of the authorities.

However, duties shall be collected on deposit for goods imported for display in permanent exhibitions. The deposit is goods for six months and may be renewed for one year after which the matter shall be referred to the Ministry of Finance for renewal or liquidation of the deposit.

4. The following shall apply to heavy and light equipment and instruments which are imported by contractors and firms entrusted with construction work or with the installation of stations or factories, and which are re-exported after

TEXT

COMMENTARY

completion of the work for which they were imported:

1. Every individual, contractor or the like must present to Customs, upon the importation of equipment or instruments for temporary use in the Kingdom, a statement of the pieces imported under the contract concluded between him and other individuals or organizations.
2. The contractor shall state the approximate period during which such equipment and instruments are expected to remain in the Kingdom for temporary use.
3. Customs duties and additional charges shall be collected on such equipment and instruments as a deposit valid for a period of six months. An undertaking shall be obtained from the person concerned to re-export them following the

TEXT	COMMENTARY
expiry of the six-month period. 4. If the contractor wishes to extend the said period, he must contact Customs and apply for such extension, giving the justifiable reasons; otherwise, the deposit shall be liquidated and transferred to the revenues. 5. The period may not be extended for more than one year, except by an order from the Ministry of Finance and National Economy and under certain circumstances. 6. The descriptions and the numbers of such equipment and instruments shall be shown on statements drawn up in duplicate, one copy of which shall be kept at Customs to serve as reference upon re-exportation and the other shall be given to the person concerned. 7. The deposit shall be refun-	

TEXT	COMMENTARY
ded only after ascertaining that the individual pieces of equipment and instruments and their descriptions were checked against the statements under which they had been imported, and making sure that such equipment and instruments were actually re-exported.	
8. Refunds shall be restricted to Customs duties collected, to the exclusion of additional charges, porterage and wharfage charges on the ground that services were provided when such equipment and instruments were unloaded at the wharves and transported. The additional porterage and wharfage charges shall be officially transferred to the revenue.	
9. Customs duties shall be definitively collected on equipment, instruments, and the like which remain in the	

TEXT | COMMENTARY

Kingdom and which the contractor decides to sell locally. They shall be deducted from the refundable deposit on the basis of the estimated values of the items as determined at the time of their importation into the Kingdom.

ticle 107. Factory advertising material imported for display and not for sale, whether made of paper or cardboard, or whether printed plates or glass, china, wood, or porcelain, etc., shall be exempt from duties if the duties thereon are found not to exceed SR 50. If the duties exceed this amount they shall be collected. This does not apply to illustrated or printed calendars. Catalogues and publications imported for free distribution to customers shall be exempted from Customs duties.

icle 108. All provisions and supplies of ocean-going naval and merchant ships, and also or airplanes and automobiles, shall be exempt from

TEXT	COMMENTARY
import duties, provided that the Customs is satisfied that such provisions and supplies are exclusively for use on board such means of transportation and are within reasonable limits in relation to the number of the crew and passengers and to the length of the stopover or the journey. Likewise, spare parts necessary for foreign vehicles which transport pilgrims into the Kingdom shall be exempt from import duties.	

Article 109. Qurans, scientific and religious books of all kinds, newspapers, magazines, and periodicals, and geographic, nautical, and astronomical maps, and plans of all kinds, shall be exempt from duties and additional charges after they are examined and inspected by the committee concerned.

Article 110. Small school notebooks, in recognized forms and sizes, real or artificial school slates, slate pencils, and chalk, shall be ex-

TEXT		COMMENTARY
	empt from Customs duties and additional charges.	
.cle 111.	Drugs, medicines, sterilized cotton wool, gauze, surgical bandages, adhesive plasters, disinfectants and insecticides for flies and for insects on plants, shall be exempt from import duties and additional charges. (See Customs Tariff, Chapter II, Paragraphs 1-3.)	
cle 112.	Containers imported for packing dates shall be exempt from import duties and additional charges.	
cle 113.	Gold imported in its raw form,ore, or in the form of ingots, residue, or fragments, shall be exempt from Customs duties and the additional charges. This exemption also applies to gold bars and foils, the cost of making of which does not exceed 1% of the cost of pure gold.	
:le 114.	Silver ingots, fragments, and residue shall be exempt from Customs duties and additional charges.	

TEXT	COMMENTARY
Article 115. Foreign gold, silver, and paper currency shall be exempt from Customs duties and additional charges.	
Article 116.a. Sailboats, steamships, airplanes, and cars which travel between towns of Saudi Arabia and foreign countries, regardless of their cargo, shall be exempt from Customs duties and the additional charges.	
Fishing boats which operate outside Saudi territorial waters and use a Saudi port as their base and which possess a license from the Department of Coast and Port Guards, as well as barges used in loading or unloading ships' cargoes, shall be exempt from import duties and additional charges.	
Yachts, launches, sailboats, small boats, etc., which are imported to operate in Saudi ports only, whether for pleasure or for transport, shall be subject to Customs duties and additional charges if they are unloaded at piers. If	

TEXT

they are not unloaded at piers, no wharfage, storage, or porterage charges shall be due on them.

b. Chemical compounds used in extinguishing fires shall be exempt from Customs duties and additional charges, whether they are in liquid, powder, or any other form designed to serve that purpose.

Chapter X

Customs Formalities on Imports

Part One

ertificate of Formalities-Import-Export Statement - Customs Declaration

See Customs Tariff, Section 212: Bill of Entry and Customs Declaration.)

cle 117. Customs certificates-Import-Export Statements and Customs Declarations (Bills of Entry)- must be submitted for all imported, exported, and transit goods. The certificates must be completed with all the specified data filled in by those concerned before the carrying out of Customs formalities on the goods is to be started.

cle 118. Alterations in the data entered

COMMENTARY

CHAPTER X

CUSTOMS FORMALITIES PART I

ENTRY OF GOODS

Saudi Customs rules require a Customs Declaration or Bill of Entry for all imported goods, including those in transit. However, the Saudis require further proof of the true cost of the goods in addition to the bill of entry. This includes copies of original invoices (translated into Arabic) and may also include copies of catalogs, insurance documents, and correspondence placing and confirming orders. The formal entry documents required are not unlike those required in the U.S., namely, the Customs entry record and the required invoices.

TEXT

on the certificates referred to in the previous Article are not permitted after the certificates have been submitted to Customs and entered in its books. The correctness or falsity of the statements shall be judged according to the entries on the certificate. If, prior to the issuance of the written orders for the inspection or weighing of the goods, the person submitting the certificate discovers any error in the data he may be permitted to correct it if Customs is convinced of the existence of good faith. Such correction must be accepted as authentic by the Customs director or by the person acting in his place.

Article 119. Upon presentation of the certificate to Customs, the importer shall show clearly on the Certificate of Formalities Bill of Entry the true cost paid or agreed to be paid for the goods, packed and ready for shipment at the port of

COMMENTARY

U.S. regulations provide for several different types of invoices to be used in different circumstances, such as the Special Customs Invoice (See 19 CFR Section 141.83). The Saudi requirement appears to only require the Standard Commercial Invoice similar to the U.S. Commercial invoice described in 19 CFR Section 141.83 (u). While U.S. regulations provide for waiver of the invoice requirements in certain circumstances (19 CFR Section 141.91 and 141.92) Saudi regulations apparently do not.

TEXT | COMMENTARY

export, in the currency of the exporting country or any other foreign currency, plus freight, insurance, and other expenses, to the port of discharge in Saudi Arabia.

cle 120. Upon clearing the goods, importers shall submit to Customs the original true invoices together with a translated Arabic copy thereof, and all documents confirming the correctness of costs including the frieght, insurance, and all other expenses. The Customs has the right to request the submission of the following:

1. The letter or telegram placing the order abroad.
2. The confirmation of the order and agreement on prices from the factory or export agents abroad.
3. Bank credits or transfer documents.
4. Supporting financial documents relating to the consignment which shows settlement with the bank for the balance or for

TEXT	COMMENTARY
the full amount. 5. Telegrams and correspondence regarding the consignment. 6. Catalogues or price lists if available. 7. Insurance documents. 8. Certificate of origin of the goods. 9. Confirmation by the exporting sources of the invoices submitted and their acknowledgment that the statements contained therein are correct. 10. Legalization of the invoices by by Saudi embassies, legations, or consulates abroad, if any, in accordance with the instructions in this matter. 11. Separate packing lists for each package. Invoices proven to be counterfeit or untrue shall be subject to the penalties mentioned in the Articles on smuggled goods in the Customs Regulations. Article 121. Customs shall examine all documents and correspondence connected with imported consignments found	

TEXT | COMMENTARY

by the importers to differ from the specifications already agreed upon, or which have some defects, or are of an inferior quality, or which, for any other reason, cause the importers and the exporters abroad to correspond resulting in the exporters' consenting to reduce the cost of the shipments by a specified percentage. If the Customs is convinced it will collect Customs duties on the basis of the cost less the reduction, whether the reduction was for the importers or for others, in accordance with the instruction from the original exporters abroad.

Any other disputes, other than that stated above, resulting in a reduction of the cost of the goods shall not cause a reduction in the Customs duties which in such cases shall be collected on the original cost prior to the occurrence of the reduction.

cle 122. The importer must put, on the Certificate of Formalities Bill of Entry, a statement showing clearly

TEXT | COMMENTARY

the number of packages, marks, numbers, weights or measurements, and a description of the goods for all kinds of imported goods whether the duty is specific or ad valorem. He must show, particularly for goods subject to specific duties, the quantities or weights according to the categories in the Customs Tariff

Article 123. Preliminary Inspection: Customs may if convinced of the necessity therefore because of exceptional circumstances, authorize owners of goods to inspect their goods in the presence of a representative of the Customs in order that the declaration on the Certificate Bill of Entry to be submitted shall be made correctly. This privilege must be requested in writing on the Certificates Bills of Entry before they are submitted to Customs. In such cases the Customs inspection will be completed at the same time.

Article 124. Temporary clearance on goods is forbidden whether they are commercial goods or for the Government. Customs

TEXT | COMMENTARY

formalities on the goods must be thoroughly completed and the goods inspected and the duties paid before they are withdrawn from the Customs Area.

.cle 125. Incorrect Declarations: If the Certificate Bill of Entry contains incorrect declarations regarding the quantity, kind, or weight of the goods, Customs shall specify a fine on the difference in proportion to the duties and the additional charges payable.

However, if the difference in weight or quantity does not exceed 5% then no collection of any fine shall be necessary. If the declaration showing the quantity, kind, weight, and value are incorrect and are such as would constitute an attempt to smuggle then the matter shall be referred to the Customs committee who will decide on the issue by enforcing the rulings set forth in the Articles on smuggled goods.

TEXT

Part Two

Unloading, Transportation, Receiving, and Delivering Goods

A. Unloading

Article 126. The Customs shall not permit the unloading of the cargo of any means of transportation until a request for unloading, signed by the captain of the ship or the agent of the shipping or transportation company, accompanied by the original manifest of the shipment endorsed by the agents of the shipping company at the port of origin or by the captain of the ship, has been submitted with two Arabic copies of it endorsed by the agent of the shipping company at the port of destination.

A period of delay not exceeding 36 hours shall be allowed for submitting the above mentioned codiments. However, mail boats which have a local agency may be permitted to unload their cargo before submitting the documents at the fixed time.

COMMENTARY

PART TWO

UNLOADING, TRANSPORTING, RECEIVING AND DELIVERING GOODS

A. Unloading

Goods may not be unloaded at the port until a request has been received from the master of the vessel, together with the original manifest along with two copies in Arabic signed by the local agent of the shipping company at the port of entry. Unloading is not permitted until the original manifest is compared with the two Arabic copies by the Manifest Section and found to correspond. Thus, the importance of a good Arabic translation cannot be over-emphasized. Although thi may appear burdensome, the same requirements are imposed by other countries. For example, the U.S. requires that ever arriving vessel which has a manifest which is in a foreign language, must be translated into English. 19 CFR Section U.S. Customs regulations also require applying for permission to unload by filing an application for a permit. (19 CFR Section 4.30).

TEXT

If ships arrive at night then the the 36 hour period of delay shall start at sunrise on the following day, except for holidays and the time taken for the carrying out of quarantine formalities.

Sailboats must submit the manifest and the two Arabic copies before the unloading of their cargo. Under compelling circumstances, Customs may permit sailboats to unload their cargo at the piers prior to the submission of the manifest, provided that the goods remain under the responsibility and guarantee of the captain of the ship and under Customs control, and provided that the manifest is submitted on the next day.

COMMENTARY

TEXT	COMMENTARY
the next day.	
Article 127. After the submission of the request referred to in the foregoing Article, it shall be transmitted to the Manifest Section for comparison of the original manifest with the two copies. If they correspond then permission to unload shall be granted. The original manifest shall then be returned to the shipping company and on of the two copies shall be kept at the Manifest Section. The other copy shall be sent to the Warehouse Division in order that the ship's cargo may be received.	

TEXT

COMMENTARY

If the ship's cargo contains items, such as inflammable material, etc., that must be unloaded in special places the shipping company must draw up two copies of an extract from the manifest covering such items, one copy shall be sent to the office at the pier which deals with these goods, and the other to the warehouseman.

icle 128. After permission to unload the goods has been obtained, ships anchored in the harbor may unload their cargoes of general goods.

icle 129. Unloading inflammable, corrosive, and explosive materials on ordinary goods is prohibited. These must be placed separately in boats and unloaded in the places set aside for them by the Customs.

TEXT

In connection with highly explosive materials, the Directorate of Public Security must approve of the places assigned for the unloading of such materials. Customs Directors may assign places for the unloading of certain kinds of goods which they think should not be mixed with other goods. They may stop the unloading at any time for one of the following reasons:

1. Congestion of the piers.
2. Failure to unload goods in the places assigned.
3. Failure or delay in presenting the manifest.

B. Transporting Goods.

Article 130. Imported goods shall be transported from the piers to the Customs warehouses, or to the places assigned for them, by the porter assigned for the job.

Article 131. In places where there are no piers at which the ships may dock, Customs shall have nothing to do with the operations of lighterage or unloading into boats. Shipping

COMMENTARY

B. Transporting Goods

Saudi customs takes no responsibility for the operations of lighters and the unloading of vessels in places where there are no piers for docking. Since the lack of development of Saudi ports has led to frequent use of lighters, to unload cargo from LASH vessels (lighter aboard ship), goods are often brought to the piers by this method. Saudi law does not appear to license lightermen.

TEXT

companies must make all the arrangements they think necessary for the safe unloading of goods from the ships into the boats and from the latter on the piers so that Customs may receive them into its warehouses or into the places it assigns for them.

C. Receiving and Storing Goods

icle 132. Actual receipt of the goods by Customs takes place only when the goods arrive at the gates of Customs warehouses or at the places assigned for storage, and when a careful inspection of the external condition of the packages has been made. Consequently, goods that have been unloaded remain under the control and responsibility of the shipping companies until they are actually received by the Customs warehouseman. In sailboats, the responsibility falls on the captains or the owners.

Entries

icle 133.1. The warehouseman assigned to receive the goods shall see that

COMMENTARY

U.S. Customs regulations, on the contrary, require cartmen and lightermen to be licensed and bonded, mostly as a method of improving port security. (See 19 CFR Part 112)

C. Receiving and Storing Goods

Customs does not exercise control over goods until they have been presented at the customs warehouse or place of storage. Inspection is then made. Damaged goods are segregated. The warehouseman then provides a receipt showing the total number of goods received. Permission may be obtained for delivery directly to the owners. Customs assumes no liability for the goods while in the Customs area or warehouse.

TEXT | COMMENTARY

they are entered on an up-to-date basis in the book set up for the receipt of goods as they enter the warehouses or as they are deposited in the places assigned for them after recording the route number thereon. He shall, with a representative from the shipping company, compare the packages received with the packages listed on the manifest.

2. Packages which do not bear any marks or numbers and packages which bear marks and numbers similar to those on other packages imported on the same ship, must be given a distinguishing mark by the shipping company concerned, and such a mark must appear on all the documents on which the goods are recorded.

3. Direct delivery goods shall be recorded daily in a handbook by the Customs man at the pier. After the unloading of each shipment he shall submit a memorandum to the pier man showing all the necessary

TEXT	COMMENTARY
information so that it may be recorded in the proper book.	
ticle 134. When items such as gold, silver, and precious stones are received they shall be deposited in special steel safes.	
Damaged Goods	
ticle 135.1. Packages which appear to be damaged shall be kept separate from the other packages, and shall be inventoried or weighed in the presence of a representative of the shipping company who, together with the receiving warehouseman, should sign in the column wherein such packages are recorded. The quantity or weight must be written on the packages and they shall be deposited in a separate room, called "Room for Broken Goods", in the same warehouse, and they shall be recroded in a special register that can be referred to when they are released.	
2. If the shipping company or the owner of the goods requests that these packages be examined before	

TEXT | COMMENTARY

the presentation of the Certificate Bill of Entry then the examination shall be made in the presence of the representative of the shipping company and the owner of the goods.

3. Shipping companies shall, in all instances, be responsible for the repair of damaged packages as Customs may regard necessary, so that such packages can be received in Customs.

<u>Packages Not Shown on the Manifest</u>

Article 136. Packages not shown on the manifest shall be opened and inventoried or weighed in the presence of the representative of the shipping company. A report on the results of this opening shall be prepared and referred to the Manifest Office so that it can add these packages to the copy of the manifest in its possession.

<u>Packages Unloaded by Mistake</u>

Article 137. If packages are unloaded by mistake and the shipping company requests that they be returned to their original destination then Customs

TEXT | COMMENTARY

must investigate the matter by examining the documents and the original manifest relating to the packages. If Customs is satisfied then the packages shall be returned to the means of transportation under Customs supervision.

icle 138. After receiving a ship's cargo the Customs warehouseman shall give the representative of this shipping company a receipt showing the total number of packages received. The receipt shall be approved by the piermaster or by the official acting in his place. A copy of the manifest is then returned to the Manifest Office showing in detail the total number of packages received, the packages that have not been unloaded, and the packages that are not shown on the manifest. The Customs Director may ask shipping companies to submit statements concerning discrepancies between packages actually received and packages shown on the manifest. Owners of goods who are authorized

TEXT

by Customs to receive their goods directly from the pier must give the receipts to the shipping company without the intervention of Customs.

Article 139. The Customs Administration shall assume no responsibility for any damage to the goods as a result of inevitable accidencts such as fire, rainwater, etc., within the Customs Area. While they are in Customs, whether in the warehouses or in the yards, the goods remain there on the responsibility of the owners who should take whatever precautions they deem necessary to insure their goods and to withdraw them promptly from Customs.
The owners of goods may bring in tarpualine to cover and protect their goods if they so desire.

D. Delivery

Delivery Order

Article 140.1. The bearer of a delivery order issued by the shipping company in his name is considered by Customs to be the owner of the goods, and

COMMENTARY

D. Delivery

The bearer of a delivery order is conside to be the owner of the goods and may clai them after the goods have cleared. The delivery order is negotiable. Due to the

TEXT

goods shall be delivered to him when he presents the delivery order signed by him and accompanied by the clearance.

The delivery order may be endorsed to other persons, in which case title to the goods shall pass to the person or persons to whom the delivery order has been endorsed.

2. In the event of loss of the delivery order, the person concerned must notify Customs immediately and must submit a copy of the delivery order issued by the shipping company.

No one other than the bearer of the delivery order may take samples of the goods stored in Customs or ask to have the incoming shipments examined.

3. Delivery of the goods to the bearer of a delivery order may not be refused except by a court order.

4. When goods stored in Customs are distrained, the distraint report must state that Customs may dispose of the distrained goods in

COMMENTARY

unique geographic and social characteristics of Saudi Arabia, imports are often brought across the border by land in caravans. Special regulations exist for entry of these goods since there is not always a customs checking point at every border crossing. Some unique features that are not generally of importance to Western nations are provided. For example, where goods are imported on animals of burden such as camels, a bond or deposit must be paid to insure re-exportation of the animal. If the animal bears no distinguishing marks, a wire is tied around its neck and sealed with lead. Convoys carrying rifles must register them, and the local Emir is notified.

TEXT

COMMENTARY

accordance with its Regulations if the goods are not withdrawn within the period specified. In the event of sale, Customs shall collect its duties, expenses, and other fees, and keep the balance in trust for a maximum period of five years pending a decision on the case.

5. Where there is a discrepancy between the particulars contained in the delivery order and those written on the manifest, the person concerned shall be asked to have the error corrected by the shipping company and to have the delivery order stamped and signed by the agent of the shipping company or his representative.

As a general rule, no goods whatsoever may be cleared from the Customs Area for any party until after the delivery order pertaining to the goods in question has been submitted by the persons concerned.

Imports by Land

TEXT

COMMENTARY

icle 141. Goods imported into Saudi Arabia by land must have a manifest or a cargo list prepared for them at the point of origin or at the last Customs Point in the neighboring countries prior to their crossing the Saudi frontier. They must be brought along recognized roads in the desert, without any deviation, until they arrive at the first Customs Office for the purpose of completing the Customs formalities there. If this Office is not authorized to collect Customs duties, it shall inspect the conveyance, take an inventory of the goods, prepare a list of them, and have the person in charge of the convoy sign the list. The list shall be attached to the manifest or statement, if any, and the goods accompanied by a Customs guard carrying the list, shall be sent to the nearest Customs Point, if the distance is less than ten kilometers, so that the duties may be collected. If, however, the dis-

TEXT		COMMENTARY
	tance is more than ten kilometers Customs shall secure a guarantee from a reliable person, the head of the convoy, the driver of the vehicle, or the owner of the goods to take the cargo to the proper destination.	
	If contact by wireless is possible, a message about the cargo shall be relayed to the Customs point which will receive the convoy.	
Article 142.	Convoys may not cross the Customs Lines at night between sunset and sunrise.	
Article 143.	Inspection and assessment of duties shall be effected in accordance with the rules in force. Those concerned shall be given a receipt voucher they can produce on request.	
	<u>Means of Transportation by Land</u>	
Article 144.1.	Cars: Fees shall be collected on foreign cars in the form of a deposit, or a bond shall be given on them until they eventually return within a definite period to be specified by Customs according	

TEXT

COMMENTARY

to the length of the journey. If the period elapses before the car has returned then the deposit collected shall be credited to the revenue account.

The Customs at the point of entry shall prepare a declaration showing the type of car, engine and chassis numbers, description, and the amount of the deposit collected or of the bond secured. In the event of departure, these particulars will be checked and, if they are found to agree, the deposit shall be refunded or the bond released.

2. Animals of burden: In the event of the transportation of goods on camels or donkeys and other foreign animals, fees shall be collected on the animals, in the form of a deposit or a bond, and their description and any distinguishing marks or brands shall be noted. If they do not bear any distinguishing mark, a wire shall be tied around their necks and sealed with lead. A declaration similar to the one

TEXT

COMMENTARY

on cars shall be prepared and the Customs at the point of departure shall compare the statements in question and refund the deposit in the manner outlined previously. The declaration shall be valid for a period of six months, renewable with the consent of the authorities concerned.

If the men of the convoy carry rifles or ammunition, these shall be taken from them and recorded, with full particulars, in a separate register. A receipt shall be issued for them and they shall be returned to their owners when the owners return against the delivery of the receipt.

The local Amir must be notified at the time of receipt of the arms and prior to their being released.

Typewriters, cameras, radio sets, et., coming in with passengers riding in cars, and claimed by their owners to be for personal use during their temporary stay in the Kingdom, shall be recorded with full descriptions and shall

TEXT

have a distinguishing mark placed on them, and fees shall be collected in the form of a deposit to be refunded if they are taken out of the Kingdom within six months.

Chapter XI

General Rules

Tare

icle 145. Tare is a deduction made from the gross weight of packages as an allowance for the weight of the containers or wrappers. It is made by finding the actual weight of the containers and wrappers, if the net weight is known, or by deducting the standard tare in accordance with schedule attached at the end of the Rules for Implementation.

Payment of Duties on Deposit

cle 146. As a general rule, duties may not be paid as a deposit during the official working hours except in cases where the Customs director or the person acting in his place thinks it desirable for the purpose of clearing out "direct

COMMENTARY

CHAPTER XI

GENERAL RULES

Since many Saudi duties are based on weight, deductions for packaging are provided for. A table of normal tare deductions is provided in the tariff schedules. Similar allowances are made in other countries as well. For the U.S. see, e.g. 19 CFR Section 159.12. Tare deductions are generally used in connection with agriculture and tobacco products.

Provisions are made for a reduction in duty for goods damaged in transit, so as to reflect their reducted value. In the case of Ad Valorem duties, the value is simply reduced. Where specific duties are involved, a deduction proportionate to the amount of damage is granted. This is more liberal than in the United States where only reduction in Ad Valorem duties

TEXT

delivery" goods or "goods in the process of unloading", or in cases where the person concerned is adked to submit the original documents on his shipment, or where disagreement has arisen for some good reason between the merchant and Customs. In this case, duties may be collected in the form of a cash deposit to avoid delaying the shipment in Customs. However, the estimator must set the deposit at a figure 10% higher than the amount fixed by Customs to cover the duties.

In the case of "goods in the process of unloading" and "direct delivery goods", the deposit shall be liquidated immediately after the withdrawal of the shipments. The person concerned must call at Customs immediately to have the deposit liquidated within a period not exceeding one week from the day the shipment was withdrawn. (Failing this, Customs shall credit the deposit as revenue to

COMMENTARY

is permitted unless part of the shipment becomes completely worthless so as to be considered a non-importation. (See 19 CFR Section 158.12).

Direct Delivery Goods

Saudi regulations, like those of many other countries, provide for the direct delivery of goods without the normal delays involved with customs clearance. Deposits may be accepted where full impor documentation is not immediately availabl However, only certain designated goods are eligible for treatment under this section. These generally include bulk agricultural products and raw materials.

One advantage of the direct delivery procedure is that parts of a shipment can be delivered immediately without the necessity of the entire shipment being unloaded, inspected, and assessed. This is particularly important in a developing economy such as Saudi Arabia where there are many large capital projects in progress and where frequent delays are

TEXT

the revenues account.)

In cases where the person concerned is asked to submit documents, Customs shall allow him that period of time which it considers sufficient for obtaining the documents. If the period expires and the required documents are not received from the person concerned, the deposit shall be credited as revenue to the revenues account.

Evaluation of Damaged Goods

icle 147. If it is found that a shipment was damaged or injured while on the way, the controller of the Valuation Division, jointly with a Customs inspector and the piermaster, or those acting in their places in the various Customs offices according to their different organizations, shall examine the shipment, prepare a statement on it, and estimate the decrease in its value with respect to its condition. If the shipment is subject to duties according to value (ad valorem), these shall be

COMMENTARY

experienced due to lack of available materials.

Unclaimed and Abandoned Goods

Goods left unclaimed for more than one year are subject to public auction. Customs duties are assessed against the purchase based on the auction price. The goods may not be sold at a price lower than the duties, and the provisions are substantially similar to those in the U.S. (See 19 CFR Section 127.11 et seq.). Sale of unclaimed goods is handled by the manifest office. (See Section 214 *infra*).

Postal Parcels

Procedures are available for importation through the mails. However, dutiable articles may not be sent in sealed letters. Unlike the U.S. where there is a distinction between formal (usually where the value exceed $250.00) and informal mail entries (19 CFR Section 142.12), all mail importations are treated the same by

TEXT

collected, after the approval of the Customs director has been obtained, on the basis of the estimate made by the committee.

If the shipment is subject to specific duties, a statement shall be prepared by the committee of officials giving a detailed description of the condition of the goods and showing the amount of the damage sustained. A deduction from the Customs duties proportionate to the amount of the damage shall be granted to the merchant in accordance with the dicision of the committee. This decision shall not go into effect until after the approval of the Customs director has been obtained.

In any case, the statement must be made in a number of copies, one of which must be attached to the Customs documents.

It is permissible to deduct 2 1/2% on shipments of gas, gasoline, and gas residues which come in containers as an allowance for shor-

COMMENTARY

the Saudis.

Perishable Goods

Perishable goods are considered unclaime unless withdrawn immediately. (In the U.S. perishables may be sold generally after three (3) days. (See 19 CFR Section 127.28 (c)). They are subject to auction in the same manner as other unclaimed goods.

Tobacco Products

Certain provisions are made for segregat imports of tobacco products and for the affixing of stamps. See 19 CFR Section 11.1 et seq. for comparable U.S. provisi

TEXT | COMMENTARY

tages, empty containers, and evaporation.

Perishable Goods

icle 148. Throughout all stages of completion of Customs formalities all sorts of facilities should be made available for items of perishable goods such as vegetables, fruit, fresh and frozen meats, and other items that are subject to deterioration in order that the goods in question can be cleared as soon as possible.

Goods Damaged by Sea or Rain Water

cle 149. If wet goods or goods damaged by rain water are subject to ad valorem duties, the necessary reduction in the value of the goods shall be made in accordance with the results of the inspection made by the controller of the Valuation Division, the Customs inspector, and the piermaster. If the goods in question are subject to specific duties, these shall be reduced in proportion to the amount of the damage, according to the

TEXT

COMMENTARY

procedure explained in Article 147.

Items Imported for Promotional Purposes

Article 150. Items imported for promotional purposed shall be subject to the following provisions:

1. Duties on items subject to specific duties, shall be collected in full.
2. Items which are subject to ad valorem duties and which serve as substitutes for items displayed in the markets, such as pocketknives, watches, lead pencils, wallets, ashtrays, fountain pens, etc., shall be allowed a reduction not exceeding 30% of their actual value, provided Customs has made sure that they have been imported for advertising and that they bear the name of the factory or merchant who imported them and that they are in a reasonable quantity and not for sale.
3. Samples distributed for advertising, provided they come in

TEXT | COMMENTARY

sizes difference from the standard commercial size, may be allowed a maximum reduction of 50% of their actual value.

Items and samples which are imported to be distributed for advertising purposes and which are shown on the invoices to be of no commercial value shall have duties collected on them on the basis of their value as fixed by Customs, after the deduction referred to above has been completed.

Special Provisions for Certain Kinds of Goods

Duty-Free Goods

le 151. Items exempted from duties shall be subject to the same clearance formalities required for goods in general. A Certificate of Formalities (Bill of Entry) must be submitted to the Manifest Office to identify the consignee and then to the warehouses to confirm the arrival of the shipment. After it is endorsed accordingly it shall be submitted to the Customs direc-

TEXT | COMMENTARY

tor who will authorize the exemption. A notification for clearing the shipment must be sent to those granted the exemption, and they must be requested to advise the Customs of their receipt of the shipment.

Article 152. The value of goods imported by the Government shall be estimated on the basis of the original invoices after the transportation costs, insurance and freight have been added.

Article 153. Before Customs formalities are started, untanned and undried hides must be taken to the Quarantine Office for its approval of the clearance of these items from the sanitary point of view.

Article 154. Formalities on money bags, whether imported or exported, must be completed in the presence of the person concerned or of someone acting in his place, and also in the presence of a representative from Customs. Formalities shall be completed on the responsibility of the

TEXT | COMMENTARY

person concerned. If the money bags are not shown on the manifest, the importer must submit an application for clearance from Customs signed by the shipping company, and such an application shall serve in the place of the manifest insofar as formalities are concerned. If it is found necessary to examine money bags imported by banks then such examination shall take place at the office of the bank in question.

Medicines and Shipments Containing Alcohol

cle 155. No kind of medicine or medical product imported for trade or for hospital use may be cleared except those which bear a license from the Ministry of Health.

Narcotics for Medical Use

cle 156. No quantity of narcotics imported for medical use and arriving at Customs may be cleared or exported until after the necessary authorization has been obtained from the Ministry of Health. Likewise,

TEXT

COMMENTARY

no shipment of narcotics may be allowed to pass in transit by land, sea, or air unless the person concerned submits to the Ministry of Health a copy of the export license which accompanies the shipment.

Direct Delivery Goods

Article 157. Direct delivery goods shall be subject to all the formalities pertaining to other goods. The following, however, shall be done:

1. Customs authorizes those concerned to have their shipments withdrawn, without its intervention, directly from the piers by the porters assigned for this purpose, either after the whole shipment has been unloaded or while the goods are being unloaded, without having to wait for the whole shipment to be unloaded. In this latter instance goods are referred to as "goods in the process of unloading".
2. The official charged with the

TEXT | COMMENTARY

supervision of the piers shall enter these shipments in a handbook daily, and shall take down all the necessary particulars of every shipment after it is unloaded and submit in memo form to the pierman who will enter them in a special book.

3. The person concerned shall submit the Import Statement (Bill of Entry) and Customs Declaration attached to the delivery order form, or to a written request carrying the approval of the shipping company and accompanied by the delivery order, with all the particulars required, to the official charged with the supervision of the piers, so that he may indicate on the papers in question the first and final dates of unloading. The person concerned shall then submit the certificate to the controller of the Valuation Dision to obtain permission to withdraw the

TEXT

COMMENTARY

shipment in accordance with the provision for "direct delivery goods", and to have the Valuation Division authorize the inspection and weighing of the goods as required in such a way that the operations of inspection and weighing are distributed properly for the whole shipment.

4. Customs shall collect duties on a definite basis in accordance with the invoices submitted. The clearance document shall show the weight, number, or measurements so that Customs will not allow anything in excess thereof to pass through the gates when clearance is made. If, at the time of clearance, there appears to be an excess over the quantity shown on the clearance documents, the excess may not be withdrawn until the applicable duties have been paid thereon.

5. The Customs director may, at the request of the person concerned,

TEXT

COMMENTARY

authorize the collection of duties in the form of a deposit on goods imported under the provisions for "direct delivery goods" pending submission of the documents, or for any reason which the Customs regards as justifying such an action, provided the merchant undertakes, in writing, to accept the decision regarding the valuation of the goods and the fixing of the duties which Customs may take if it is not satisfied with the papers submitted by the person concerned. Customs may credit the deposit to the revenues account if merchants do not submit the documents within the period fixed by Customs.

The duties shall be computed on the basis of the tariff in effect at the time the deposit is paid, as though the duties were paid on a definite basis.

6. The provisions for "direct delivery goods" shall apply to

TEXT | COMMENTARY

the following goods: rice, flour, potatoes, sugar in bags, lentils, grains, fresh fruit and vegetables imported in bulk or in containers, cement, gypsum, lime, construction lumber and lumber in bulk, vehicles, interlaced steel rods, rods, beams, all kinds of steel pipe, cement pipe, metal sheets, empty drums, coal, live animals, any package exceeding two tons in weight, and also any shipment of machinery exceeding fifteen tons in weight.

Unclaimed- Abandoned- Goods

Article 158. Abstention from or delay in submitting the Certificate of Formalities (Bill of Entry) or failure to appear at Customs to withdraw the goods within one year from the date of unloading, entitles Customs to sell the goods at auction, and the following procedures shall be carried out prior to the sale.

Article 159. Packages which are not withdrawn by their owners within a period of

TEXT

COMMENTARY

three months from the date of unloading shall be transferred from the Customs Area to the warehouse used for neglected goods after these have been weighed and their weight shown on them. Broken or torn packages shall have their contents inventoried or weighed and shall be registered on the records. Customs shall notify the Manifest Office of the particulars of such goods.

cle 160. The Manifest Office shall write to the shipping companies asking if they issued delivery orders to the owners of these goods. It must notify the chambers of commerce to advise those concerned of the existence of these shipments and ask them to withdraw the goods as soon as possible.

Goods Abandoned for One Year

cle 161. The man in charge of the warehouse used for neglected goods shall notify the Manifest Office of any shipments which have been left in his custody for a whole year. The Manifest Office shall review this

TEXT

COMMENTARY

notification and submit it to the Customs director who will authorize the initiation of the formalities of inspection and valuation and fix a date for opening the packages. The Manifest Office shall announce the date fixed for opening the packages at least thirty days in advance and notifications shall be sent by official mail to the persons concerned who are known to Customs. Notifications shall also be sent to the shipping companies concerned, the local authorities, the municipality, and the Chamber of Commerce, if there is one, so that they may send representatives to attend the operation of opening the packages. The packages shall be opened at the appointed time and shall be valued by the Customs estimator in the presence of a senior Customs official and an inspector. A report shall be prepared bearing the names of the attending representatives and their signatures. If no one appears on behalf of the local

TEXT | COMMENTARY

authorities, the municipality, the Chamber of Commerce, or the shipping companies then Customs shall proceed with the opening operations alone. After the opening and valuation operation is over, the date of the sale of the goods shall be published, and the sale shall not take place until at least eight days after the day on which the notice was published.

Customs shall notify the local authorities, the municipality, the Chamber of Commerce, and the shipping companies concerned to attend the sale. If no one appears then Customs shall proceed with the sale at auction under the supervision of one of its senior officials.

The goods shall be put up at public auction and sold at highest price offered. If the members of the sale commission agree to that price, the sale shall be awarded to the highest bidder and the goods shall be delivered to him against his immediate payment of

TEXT

COMMENTARY

the price. However, if no one bids at the auction, or if the price tendered is not agreeable to the members of the commission, the sale of the goods shall be suspended and the goods shall be put up at another auction. Duties and expenses shall be deducted from the sale price in the following order:

1. Selling expenses, including advertising expenses.
2. Customs duties and additional charges computed on the basis of the sale price, after deduction of the selling expenses in respect of items subject to ad valorem duties.
3. Freight and other incidental charges supported by documents presented by the shipping companies.
4. Porterage charges.
5. Storage charges.

The balance shall be kept with the Customs Cash Office in the form of a deposit to be paid on request to the person entitled to it. If

TEXT | COMMENTARY

this deposit is not claimed within a period of five years, it shall become the property of the Government.

ıcle 162. If the items abandoned are of the type subject to specific duties, they may not, under any circumstances, be sold at a price lower than the amount of the duties applicable, after consideration has been given to the condition of the goods at the time of inspection and after reduction of the duty according to such condition. If they cannot be sold at a price equal to the amount of duties plus the selling expenses referred to above, the goods shall become the property of the Government and shall be distributed to the Government departments, asylums, hospitals, or other charitable institutions, and shall be charged to the State.

:le 163. The owner of the abandoned goods described in Article 161 may, prior to the consummation of the sale or the signing of the of-

TEXT	COMMENTARY

ficial report transferring the title of the goods to the Government, withdraw the goods from Customs after payment of the Customs duties and storage and additional charges, including all expenses incurred.

<u>Perishables and Goods Subject to Shrinkage</u>

Article 164. Perishable goods and goods subject to shrinkage such as fruit, liquids, etc., shall be regarded as unclaimed if they are not withdrawn immediately.

Customs shall appoint an estimator to inspect the shipment jointly with the pierman and to decide whether its sale must be immediately effected or may be postponed.

If it is decided that it should be sold, then the sale shall be made at auction after notifying the person concerned and the representatives of the local authorities by telephone, and also after notifying one of the

TEXT

COMMENTARY

senior Customs officials.

Customs duties and charges and other expenses on the goods shall be deducted from the proceeds of the sale, and the balance shall be kept on deposit to the credit of the person concerned.

If the damage is so great that the goods cannot be sold then the goods shall be examined by the Ministry of Health doctor and if he decides that they are not fit for consumption the owner shall be asked to return them immediately or else they shall be destroyed and a report prepared thereon.

When such shipments are destroyed and the containers are left over, the person concerned shall be asked to complete the formalities on the containers and pay the duties and charges required, or else they shall be sold at public auction.

Relinquished Goods

cle 165. Goods relinquished by their owners in writing and, likewise, minor items found in the warehouses or

TEXT | COMMENTARY

on the piers and the source of which is unknown shall be sold at public auction for the account of the Government.

Chapter XII

Postal Parcels

Article 166. Upon the arrival of postal parcels, the Post Office shall notify Customs to delegate an official who will supervise the unloading of the packages at the piers and see that the seals on the bags are intact.

Article 167. The Customs official at the pier shall make a note showing the number of bags and shall give it to the Post Office employee so that he can take the bags out through the gate.

Article 168. Parcel bags may not be opened in the post office except in the presence of the Customs official who is authorized to receive the parcels. The sound condition of the seals on the bags and the number of bags as shown on the note prepared by the official at the pier must be confirmed and checked.

TEXT | COMMENTARY

ticle 169. The parcels shall be delivered to the Customs official in accordance with a statement prepared in two carbon copies, one of which goes to the Customs representative and the other remains at the Post Office.

ticle 170. If one of the parcels is found to be broken or damaged and it is suspected that the contents are short, it shall be inventoried in the presence of the Customs representative and a report shall be made on it, and such parcel shall be taken to Customs by its employees.

icle 171. The Department of Posts shall prepare two copies of the original manifest and these copies shall be sent to the Customs director who will forward one to the warehouseman in charge of postal parcels and the other to the Auditing Division.

icle 172. The Customs warehouseman in charge of postal parcels shall register the copy of the manifest in the book kept for this purpose.

icle 173. The Post Office shall send the

TEXT

COMMENTARY

dispatch notes, together with the Customs certificates and postal forms, to the Customs warehouseman in charge of parcels and he will endorse the forms and return them to the Post Office which will send them to the persons concerned so that they may call at the Customs Deaprtment and receive the parcels in question after completing the Customs formalities on them.

In instances where parcels are sent to persons not residing in the place where the parcels are received, the persons concerned may request that the parcels be sent to them at their places of residence, provided such places have Customs that are authorized to assess duties, so that duties can be assessed and the parcels can be delivered to their owners.

If such places do not have Customs authorized to assess duties and the persons concerned request that their parcels be delivered at their places of residence, then Customs shall examine and evaluate the

TEXT

COMMENTARY

parcels in the presence of the Post Office employee who, in this instance, represents the person concerned in the matter of opening the parcels, assessing the Customs duties and charges payable on them and delivering them to the Post Office in accordance with a statement prepared in two copies showing the contents of each parcel and the duties and charges payable thereon and signed by the employee concerned in the Post Office.

Such parcels shall be delivered by the Post Office to their owners at their places of residence upon the collection, prior to delivery, of the duties payable to Customs and the transmittal of these duties to the Customs which forwarded the parcels.

Should the addressee protest the amount of the duties charged then the parcels shall be returned to the Customs through which they came and the person concerned shall take up the matter with

TEXT		COMMENTARY
	Customs.	
	If, while an inventory of the contents of the parcels is being made by Customs, it is found that some parcels contain sealed envelopes these envelopes may not be opened except in the presence of the addressee.	
Article 174.	Parcels addressed to H.M. the King, or to members of the diplomatic corps who enjoy exemption, shall be exempt from opening.	
	<u>Assessment of Customs Duties on Parcels</u>	
Article 175.	Customs duties shall be assessed in accordance with the provisions of part 1/214 of the Customs Tariff. (See Articles 51 and 120 of the Rules for Implementation).	
	<u>Items of Commercial Value Imported Other than through the Official Postal System</u>	
Article 176.	It is forbidden to send dutiable items inside letters or sealed envelopes, whether by ordinary or registered mail. The Post Office shall, in accordance with its Regu-	

TEXT	COMMENTARY
lations, forward such letters and envelopes to Customs so that it may take the necessary action in this regard.	
All goods of value which are subject to import duties and which arrive in this manner or in any manner other than through the legal postal system shall be considered, in principle, as smuggled goods, and shall be subject to confiscation and to the penalties prescribed in the Articles on smuggling.	
No fine shall be collected on any letter that carries on its cover the following words: "To be submitted to Customs and may be opened by Customs".	
icle 177. Contraband items may not be sent by mail. If such items are seized then they shall be subject to the penalties prescribed in the Regulations.	
icle 178. Insured packets imported from abroad shall be subject to the Customs formalities applied on ordinary parcels. Senders of	

TEXT

COMMENTARY

insured packets that contain precious stones, gold or silver articles, etc., must list a desription of the contents of the packets and the actual weight of each kind of stone and metal separately on the accompanying Customs certificates.

Parcels Returned by Request of the Department of Posts

Article 179. Parcels which are not received by their addressees and which, on request of the senders, the Department of Posts asks that they be returned shall be delivered to the Post Office together with the necessary receipt and shall be exempted from storage Fees. Likewise, parcels that cannot be delivered to their owners shall be returned to the Post Office, which will take the necessary action in accordance with the Postal Regulations. The entries shall be closed in accordance with the receipts issued by the Post Office.

TEXT | COMMENTARY

Unclaimed or Relinquished Parcels

icle 180. The Post Office must get in touch with Customs regarding any parcels which it decides to sell, in order that Customs duties and charges may be computed for the Customs account. The balance remaining from the selling price shall be disposed of by the Post Office in accordance with its Regulations. But Customs has priority in collecting its duties from the proceeds of the sale. As regards goods that are subject to specific duties and goods that cannot be sold, the instructions regarding sale at public auction shall be applied. (See Article 161)

Exported Parcels

icle 181. Exported parcels shall be subject to the same procedure applied in the case of items exported regard- of whether they are foreign or local. They must be presented to Customs so that it may examine their contents and make a note to that effect on the postal form.

TEXT

COMMENTARY

Parcels Returned to the Kingdom

Article 182. Parcels returned to Saudi Arabia shall be considered as though they were imported for the first time, and duties and charges shall be collected on them. Parcels which are returned intact and which have not left the Post Office to which they were sent shall be exempted from import duties and additional charges. This includes storage charges but excludes porterage charges.

Article 183. Parcels containing items sent abroad for repair shall be subject to import duties only which are to be applied to the repair costs provided the parcels are handled in accordance with the instructions given in Article 97, Section 2.

Articles Imported for Transit

Article 184. Postal parcels in transit which are unloaded on their way abroad shall be exempt from import duties and additional charges, including storage charges, provided

TEXT | COMMENTARY

the Post Office describes them as such and lists them in transit manifests. Customs must make sure that their condition at the time of re-export is the same as it was at the time of import.

Chapter XIII

Tobacco

ticle 185. Tobacco, tumbak, cigarettes, cigars, jurak(honeyed tobacco smoked in hubble-bubbles), and cigarette paper shall be treated in the same way as goods in general. The following must, however, be observed:

1. Shipments of tobacco and tumbak, when received must be kept away from other goods in a separate place.
2. Cigarette paper, tumbak, and all kinds of tobacco may not be withdrawn until banderole stamps have been affixed to them.
3. The Treasury shall issue banderole stamps to importers against payment of their value,

TEXT

COMMENTARY

provided an account for such stamps is kept at the Customs through which they have been issued showing the quantities received affixed to cigarette and tobacco packets or to cigarette paper.

4. Importers must keep books to record these stamps in the manner prescribed by the Customs and these books shall be subject to periodic inspection by the Customs.
5. The importer must submit a report on all banderole stamps that have become mutilated or are accidentally destroyed and this report is to be accompanied by all the necessary certificates. In this instance the importer may purchase new stamps from the Treasury.
6. Banderole stamps shall be affixed in the factories making the tobacco, cigarettes, and cigars, so firmly and so securely that they cannot be removed

TEXT	COMMENTARY
and used again. 7. Varieties of tumbak, tobacco, and cigarette paper to which banderole stamps cannot be affixed at the place of export shall not be released from the Customs Area until after the stamps have been affixed to them carefully and under Customs supervision so that such stamps may not be misused. 8. Banderole stamps shall be affixed on the basis of the categories described in Article 63. 9. Clearance on tobacco, tumbak, cigarettes, cigars, and cigarette paper shall not be permitted until after the importer has produced a license authorizing him to trade in these items. 10. Anyone who forges banderole stamps or uses them again with the deliberate intent of embezzlement shall be subject to the penalties prescribed in the Customs Regulations.	

TEXT	COMMENTARY
11. All tobacco, tumbak, cigarettes, cigars, and cigarette paper found to be in a condition not in harmony with the provisions of these Regulations shall be seized by the authority concerned. A report on the case shall be prepared and forwarded with the seized goods to the nearest Customs office so that the Customs committee may study the matter and take the necessary action thereon.	
12. Tobacco, tumbak, cigarette paper, and jurak may be transported from one town to another within the Kingdom only in accordance with a "raftiyah" from Customs and after the annual license authorizing trade in these items has been checked and the packages have been tied with wire and sealed with lead. Also, consideration should be given concerning the areas to which export of such items is prohibited by the relevent orders.	

TEXT

Chapter XIV

Passenger Division

ticle 186. The division in charge of searching passengers shall complete Customs formalities on the following;

1. Passengers' luggage on arrival and departure.
2. Minor items arriving with passengers.
3. Perishable and easily damageable goods arriving after the official working hours.
4. Items imported by sailors and salesmen on ships.
5. Ordinary goods that demand prompt processing such as cattle, birds, and meats that are listed on the manifest and which need to be cleared during working hours or after the official time schedules.
6. Ship supplies.

icle 187. The Passenger Division shall be authorized to complete Customs formalities on items referred to to it such as those described in Article 186. However, if such items are found difficult to

COMMENTARY

CHAPTER XIV

PASSENGER DIVISION

Passengers,except Pilgrims, are required to complete a customs declaration upon arrival. A double duty is assessed on any undeclared items. A special division handles inspection of passengers' luggage. However, when passengers attempt to bring in commercial goods, the same entry and documentation requirements that apply to commercial shipments must be complied with (i.e. the Bill of Entry). This is similar to the provisions in U.S. law contained in 19 CFR Section 148.5. Oral declarations, as permitted in the U.S. (19 CFR Section 148.12) are not provided for in the Saudi regulations.

TEXT | COMMENTARY

evaluate they shall be kept in custody until they are turned over to the estimator concerned.

Article 188. Examiners in this Division shall evaluate minor items and any other items shall be referred to the estimator concerned.

Article 189. On arrival, passengers shall submit a declaration on the dutiable articles they carry and the formalities shall be carried out accordingly. However, pilgrims arriving during the pilrimage season shall not be required to submit the said declaration upon arrival and departure.

Article 190. Goods of a commercial nature which are to be cleared through the Passenger Division must have a Customs certificate (Import Statement and Customs Declaration) submitted for the goods by the owner along with the original invoice and all the other documents. Formalities on such goods shall be the same as those on ordinary goods and clearance shall be obtained in

TEXT	COMMENTARY
the usual manner.	
ticle 191. In general, pilgrims are forbidden to bring with them merchandise not shown on the manifest. If they do so, however, the amount of the duties payable shall be doubled.	
ticle 192. On arrival, each passenger must declare, on the Passenger's Declaration, the articles he has brought with him for his own use or as gifts, except his ordinary clothes, showing the number, kind, description, and value of all such articles. If the Customs official finds that the passenger's statement is true then Customs duties and additional charges shall be collected from the passenger on the items in his possession that are dutiable. But if, upon inspection of the passenger's luggage, the Customs official finds that there are items not shown on his declaration, then double the amount of duties shall be collected. If the items not shown on his declaration are placed among his luggage in a manner that arouses	

TEXT

suspicion and are hidden in a manner that suggest a deliberate attempt to smuggle then, in such cases, the goods shall be subject to the penalties prescribed in the Articles on smuggling.

Article 193. Arms and ammunition carried by passengers shall be kept in custody if they are shown on the declaration. A deposit receipt shall be issued and the arms and ammunition shall be given back to their owners when they return or when the owners submit a permit authorizing their withdrawal. However, if arms and ammunition are not declared they shall be confiscated and the owners shall be sent to the police who will take the necessary action on the case.

Chapter XV

Aircraft Regulations and Related Procedures

Article 194. As a general rule, aircraft coming into Saudi territory from abroad may not land except at the airports assigned for that purpose and in the presence of a Customs

COMMENTARY

CHAPTER XV

AIRCRAFT REGULATIONS

Routine provisions exist for controlling the landing of aircraft and inspection of passengers. Inspection is also required prior to departure of aircraft. Aircraft

TEXT

representative.

cle 195. The airport authorities must notify the airport Customs of the arrival of each plane, whether from abroad or from the interior, in time to allow Customs to appoint the necessary officials for inspection.

However, no such notification is needed in the case of aircraft operating on a regular schedule, provided Customs has already been officially notified of such schedules.

:le 196. Immediately upon his arrival, the pilot must submit the following documents to the director of the airport Customs:

1. The log book so the director of the airport Customs can review it and make sure that the airplane has not landed in Saudi territory prior to its arrival at the airport. If Customs learns that the airplane, has landed in some place without the landing's being attended by any Customs officials then the

COMMENTARY

other than regular scheduled flights, must provide advance notice to customs officials. (See 19 CFR Section 6.2 (6) for comparable U.S. provisions). Saudi regulations are silent on a number of areas such as crew purchases, unaccompanied baggage, and repairs and equipment made to the aircraft abroad. U.S. law, for example, exempts certain repairs or equipment purchased abroad from duty when purchased for safety reasons (19 CFR Section 6.7 (c)). Some esoteric areas, as the dutiable status of wrecked aircraft that may be salvagable, also are not dealt with in the regulations. (U.S. Customs has dealt with this problem in Treasury Decision 55063 (1), March 4, 1960).

TEXT		COMMENTARY

pilot will have to submit a written statement giving the reasons for such landing.

2. A Manifest in two copies, regardless of whether the aircraft carries any cargo or not.

Article 197. Passengers may not leave the airport until the formalities on their luggage and personal effects have been completed, and goods from abroad or from within the Kingdom may not be unloaded from the airplane without the authorization of the director of the airport Customs or the person who is acting in his place. Such goods must be moved to the places assigned by the Customs director and they are to be checked against the manifest relating to them. The warehouseman shall give the airline company representative a receipt for the goods.

Article 198. Upon the arrival of an airplane from abroad and after the passengers have disembarked and their personal effects have been unloaded, the Customs officials at

TEXT	COMMENTARY
the airport shall inspect the craft and all of its seats and cabins after securing, prior to starting the inspection, a written statement from the pilot, or the person acting in his place, showing whether the airplane contains anything not mentioned in the papers. After that the Customs officials shall do the following:	
1. Search those among the incoming passengers suspected of smuggling.	
2. Search the personal effects of those mentioned in 1., above.	
3. Detain any merchandise that the passengers may have with them so that the necessary action may be taken in respect thereof in accordance with the Regulations.	
cle 199. Any goods carried on the aircraft but not shown on the manifest shall be subject to the provisions of the Customs Regulations even though the goods are only goods in transit.	

TEXT		COMMENTARY
Article 200.	Any contraband articles found in the aircraft shall be confiscated and such articles as well as the individual responsible for the act, shall be subject to the provisions of the Regulations.	
Article 201.	Foodstuffs and simple personal effects belonging to the crew and found in the airplane shall be exempt from duties. However, if Customs discovers that there is an excess of such foodstuffs and effects, it shall assess duties on such excess in accordance with the Regulations.	
Article 202.	Airplanes and other means of transportation running only between towns situated within the Kingdom shall, with their passengers and their luggage, be exempt from inspection by Customs. However, in the event suspicion arises and inspection becomes necessary, Customs shall take the necessary action to cope with such a situation. In the case of airplanes, and other conveyances which arrive from abroad and which, on their	

TEXT | COMMENTARY

way, pass through Saudi towns and carry passengers with alien passengers, all of the passengers on board shall be subject to Customs inspection.

icle 203. The inspection of an airplane shall be carried out by the appropriate Customs official at the airport where the airplane to be inspected has landed, jointly with an employee from the Aviation Department. In the event such employee is absent or unavailable, the Customs official shall carry out the inspection alone.

cle 204. In the event contraband or dutiable articles are discovered when Customs inspects the airplane,,a report shall be prepared to that effect showing the number, contents, and full description of the articles. It shall be signed by the Customs official who conducted the inspection, by the Aviation Department employee who assisted him, if one were present, and by the pilot.

TEXT

COMMENTARY

Article 205. The manifest of goods shipped from one town to another within the Kingdom must be approved by the Customs at the point of origin and checked by the receiving Customs. The goods shall be delivered to the owners after being inspected, and the owner's signature shall be obtained on the manifest against the owner's receipt of the goods. Should packages be discovered which are not included on the manifest then the necessary steps shall be taken to identify them and to determine the procedure to be followed in respect thereof.

Article 206. Military aircraft shall be exempt from inspection unless special orders are issued in this respect. In cases when special orders are issued, the text of the orders issued shall be applied.

Procedures for Aircraft Departure

Article 207. The airport authorities must notify the airport Customs prior to the departure of any plane for the interior or for abroad early enough to enable Customs to appoint the

TEXT

COMMENTARY

necessary officials to inspect the airplane and to complete the Customs formalities for its passengers and cargo. Inspection shall be quick and thorough and shall be conducted in such a manner as will not cause delay in the departure of the airplane on schedule.

The notification referred to above shall not be needed in the case of aircraft operating on a regular time schedule, provided Customs has already been notified of the official schedules of such aircraft.

cle 208. No one is permitted to board any airplane or ship any goods on it except by authorization from Customs. The pilots of the aircraft or the agents of the airline companies must submit two copies of the cargo manifest and the passenger manifest prior to the departure of the airplane, so that they can be checked and it can be made sure that the Customs formalities have been completed on the passengers and on the goods ex-

TEXT

ported.

Article 209. The pilot of the airplane must secure the departure authorization from the Customs representative who in this case, will stamp the log book and one copy of the manifest with the Customs stamp and sign his name on the copy and return the log book and the manifest copy to the pilot.

Article 210. A declaration similar to the one used for incoming passengers shall be used for outgoing passengers. Inspection of the luggage of passengers scheduled for departure shall be conducted in the Customs building at the airport.

Article 211. Pilots of aircraft shall be held responsible to Customs for any goods hidden in the airplane which are not shown on the manifest or which are contraband goods.

Chapter XVI

Manifests

Article 212. Captains of steamships and sailboats, pilots of aircraft, and others in charge of other means

COMMENTARY

CHAPTER XVI

MANIFESTS

A special Manifest Office has been estab-lished for the purpose of checking manif and to investigate shortages. Where pac

TEXT

of transportation arriving from foreign countries must submit the original manifest of the cargo they are carrying. As for the Arabic copies, they may be submitted within a period not exceeding 36 hours after their arrival.

cle 213. The Manifest Office shall check the copies of the Arabic translations with the original text to insure that the translation is correct and identical to the original.

cle 214. The Manifest Office shall check the manifests and delivery orders when they are submitted; close the manifests after the shipments are withdrawn; inquire of the shipping and transport companies, when there is shortage in the goods imported, about the reasons for such shortage; request information from these companies about goods that are not claimed by owners after the lapse of three months; inquire whether delivery orders were issued to the owners of such goods or not; advertise such ship-

COMMENTARY

are lost and insurance claims paid to the owners, the shipper must pay customs duty on the value of the lost item. A fine of ten percent (10%) of the customs duty on the missing item is levied on the captain of the ship. A decision to fine a captain is appealable to the Commercial Court within five (5) days from the date of notification. Shortages on bulk goods of less than five percent (5%) do not result in fines. Goods not listed on the manifest may result in a fine against the master of the vessell of up to three (3) times the duty.

Option Goods

Provisions are made for goods to be delivered at optional ports designated by the consignee. A somewhat comparable provision exists in the U.S. Customs Regulations (19 CFR Section 4.86).

TEXT	COMMENTARY

ments in the official gazette asking the owners thereof to withdraw the goods promptly, and check up on notifications on goods that remain unclaimed for a full year, thus becoming abandoned by virtue of the Regulations in order that the procedures outlined in Article 161 relating to advertising them and opening, evaluating and selling them at public auction may be applied.

In case there is a discrepancy between the descriptions in the delivery orders and those in the manifests, the person concerned or his representative shall be asked to have the error corrected by the shipping company, and the agent of the shipping company or his representative shall stamp and sign the delivery order in question.

Article 215. The shipping and transport companies shall be responsible for effecting actual delivery of all the packages shown on the manifests of their ships upon arrival

TEXT

COMMENTARY

of such ships at Saudi ports.

If the packages received are short, they shall be registered on the books of receipt and on the manifests relating to the, and these must be approved by the representative of the shipping company.

Shipping companies shall be allowed a period of time not exceeding three months to bring the missing packages that were unloaded by mistake in nearby ports. A period of six months shall be allowed for bringing the missing packages from distant ports. If the period allowed elapses before the missing packages arrive, the Customs duties and charges due thereon shall be collected from the shipping companies on the basis of the original invoices, if these are available, or on the basis of the evaluation by Customs of the missing packages as compared to other similar ones before they are cleared from Customs.

Packages which for one reason or another have not been shipped and

TEXT | COMMENTARY

which the shipping companies have decided not to ship, supporting their decision by official documents and certificates satisfactory to Customs, shall have their relative manifest entries closed on the basis of such documents.

When packages are lost from the ships for unknown causes and the shipping companies declare that they have paid the value of such packages to their owners, the shipping companies shall be required to pay the Customs duties and additional charges due on these packages. However, if the captain of the ship declares that due to a casualty resulting from force majeure some of the packages have been lost, and he submits official reports to Customs confirming this fact and convincing to Customs, the manifest entries relative to such packages shall be closed on the basis of these reports.

In cases where it is decided to collect Customs duties from the shipping companies on missing

TEXT

COMMENTARY

packages, the following shall be complied with:

1. Captains of ships shall be fined 10% of the Customs duties on each missing package, provided that this fine does not exceed thirty riyals per package.
2. As regards shipments of cement, shortage not exceeding 5% shall be disregarded; but the shipping company shall be answerable for any shortage in excess of this percentage.
3. Sacks of grain, flour, and similar items shall be subject to the provisions of paragraph 2 above.
4. As regards shipments of iron, wood, pipes, elbows, and similar items, the shipping company shall not be answerable for any shortage not exceeding 5% of the weight of the shipment.
5. The captain shall submit a certificate in regard to packages which fall off the ship's tackle into the sea while they are being unloaded in the stream or

TEXT | COMMENTARY

at the piers. Such certificate shall be approved by the Coast Guard officer assigned to the ship, if the ship is in the stream, and by the Customs representative if the ship is anchored at the pier. The same applies to those packages which the ship is forced to throw overboard. These certificates shall suffice to account for all such packages, and the shipping companies shall not be accountable for the shortage.

All the preceding cases mentioned in paragraphs (2) to (5) shall be handled as follows:

First: The manifest entries for the entire shipment shall be closed on the assumption that the shortage in the shipments is a probable occurrence. The manifest shall not be left open.

Second: The shipping companies shall not be required to pay any fine or Customs duties on any such shortage.

Third: The foregoing measures

TEXT

COMMENTARY

shall not prejudice the right of the consignee vis-a-vis the shipping or insurance companies.

Fourth: Customs shall give to those concerned, upon their request, certificates confirming the shortage, if they submit their request in writing. These certificates shall be given on the basis of the official records, without any responsibility on the part of the Government in connection with the issuance of such certificates.

Fifth: It is understood that Article 215 deals with whole packages which prove to be missing when the shipment is received. In this case the shipping companies shall be accountable for the missing packages in accordance with Article 215 of the Rules for Implementation. If they do not produce them within the specified time, or fail to account for them, then the provisions of Article 215 shall be applied, and, consequently, the captain of the ship shall penalized for his failure to con-

TEXT | COMMENTARY

trol and safeguard the goods in his custody.

Sixth: For bulk goods, a fine shall be imposed for any shortage exceeding 5%, in accordance with Paragraph 3-1 above, and each one hundred kilograms of bulk goods shall be regarded as one package.

Seventh: The Customs director shall notify the captain's shipping company of his decision imposing the fine which shall be payable within five days from the date on which the notification of such decision is served on the ship's agent, unless those concerned appeal the Customs decision to the Commercial Court prior to the expiration of this time limit. If a shortage is discovered in the cargo of sailboats, launches, and similar vessels, the captain of the ship (under the guaranty of the owner of the goods or his agent) must bring such shortage from the point of origin within the legal period, or else he must produce, again within the legal

TEXT

COMMENTARY

period, a certificate showing that, for one reason or another, the missing packages had not been loaded or that they had been delayed.

If neither the missing goods nor the certificate is produced, the captain of the ship or his guarantor shall be required to pay the duties imposed. In case Customs does not trust the captain or his guarantor, it may collect the duties on the missing goods in the form of a deposit to be kept until the documents are brought within the fixed period. If the documents are not presented, the deposit shall be credited to the Revenues Account.

If the missing goods are received within the legal period, or if the necessary certificate is obtained from the customs at the point of origin, the missing goods shall not be made subject to any restrictions. However, if it is proved later that the quantities received are not the same as those missing,

TEXT | COMMENTARY

or that the certificate issued by the Customs at the point of origin is not valid as a result of its being forged by the ship's master or for any other reason, then in both instances, the shortage shall be considered subject to the Articles on smuggling.

Article 216. The owner of goods which for some reason or another are partially or wholly damaged or missing may demand an official certificate from Customs confirming the shortage or the damage in his goods, and Customs shall issue such certificate without any delay on the basis of its official records. It shall not, however, bear any responsibility that may result from the issuance of such certificates.

Article 217. If the shortage in goods shipped in bulk and entered in the manifest does not exceed 5%, no fine shall be inflicted. But if the shortage exceeds 5%, an explanation from the shipping company shall be requested, and if such an explanation is not satisfactory, the shipping company

TEXT | COMMENTARY

or the ship's master shall be required to pay the duties and charges payable on the shortage in addition to the fine prescribed under Article 215.

icle 218. In the case of packages in excess of those shown on the manifest or packages arriving without any manifest, the master shall pay a fine not less than the Customs duties and not more than three times the amount of such duties for every package not listed in the manifest. If the excess packages include packages which bear marks and numbers identical with those shown on other packages listed in the manifest, then those packages on which the higher duties are payable will be considered as the ones not listed in the manifest. If, in the case of goods in bulk. the excess quantity does not exceed 10%, no fine shall be imposed.

cle 219. If the manifest of imported goods includes goods that are to be unloaded in different Saudi ports, the shipping companies must prepare,

TEXT | COMMENTARY

for each port, a separate manifest extracted from the original manifest. Likewise, if goods are to be unloaded at different places in a single Saudi port, a manifest extracted from the original manifest shall be prepared for each place separately.

Article 220. Customs must designate for the shipping companies the items to be unloaded in the places assigned for them.

Article 221. Shipping and transport companies must submit original manifests for goods in transit and trans-shipped goods separately. If transit and trans-shipped goods are entered and described in the manifest of imports, the shipping companies must extract separate manifest for these two types of goods from the original manifest.

Article 222. The original manifest must show the following:

Name of the ship.

Date of arrival of the ship.

Saudi port of call.

Number of packages.

TEXT	COMMENTARY

Kinds, marks, and numbers of packages.

Number of the bill of lading.

Consignor.

Consignee.

Type and weight of goods.

Exporting country.

Exporting country.

Total number of packages, in figures and words.

The manifest must contain spaces to show the number and date of the company's clearance document, the date the goods were cleared, and the number of the Customs clearance document. A special space must be provided for remarks, and any modifications in the way of comments, erasures, or additions in the margin or between the lines, on the original manifest, must be approved by the shipping company or the master of the means of transportation, and all the supporting documents must be presented to Customs. Customs may reject translated manifests if any errors are discovered in them, and

TEXT | COMMENTARY

the shipping company must replace such manifests with correct ones

Article 223. No amendments may be made in the manifest after it has been submitted to Customs except by a written request from the agent of the shipping company to the Customs Director and such request is to be supported by adequate documentary evidence to satisfy Customs.

Article 224. Sailboats, carrying firewood, charcoal, fish, sheep, etc., and coming from coasts that do not normally have Customs Stations, shall have a report prepared on them in which the statement of the head sailor shall be recorded. Permission shall then be granted to unload the goods on the pier under the responsibility of the head sailor or his representative and under Customs guard. After the goods have been unloaded, they shall be inventoried in the presence of representatives from Customs, the port, the Coast Guard, and the head sailor, and a manifest

TEXT	COMMENTARY
shall be prepared on the basis of the report mentioned above.	
icle 225. In the case of ships, sailboats, and aircraft which, as a result of force majeure such as a storm or a shortage in fuel or supplies, are forced to anchor or land at Saudi seaports or airports, Customs may ask to examine their manifest regardless of the length of their period of stay, and, during such period, they shall remain under Customs control.	
icle 226. There is no objection to unloading goods that arrive at Saudi ports under manifests showing that they are consigned to foreign ports if unloading goods to dispose of them in the Saudi port where the ship has arrived is requested by the owner who is on board the ship or by the head sailor on his behalf, or by his agent at the Saudi port, and this is to be done after it is made sure that the agents are in possession of an official authorization to that effect approved by the port or local authorities.	

TEXT | COMMENTARY

Customs shall retain such an authorization or a copy thereof. In the Manifest Office such shipments shall be handled in the following manner:

1. In case the whole shipment is diverted, the documents shall be attached to the manifest and a note shall be made in the space provided for "Remarks", to the effect that the shipment was diverted to a Saudi port.
2. In case only a portion of the shipment is diverted, the shipping company shall be required to prepare an extract from the manifest. If the conveyance is a sailboat, the head sailor shall be required to prepare a manifest at the port to be submitted to Customs showing the quantity of goods diverted to the Saudi port.

Option Goods

Article 227. Definition: Option goods are goods that are shipped by boat to various places according to the wish

TEXT

COMMENTARY

of the persons concerned. A notation must be made on the manifest at the port of export, to the effect that the goods are sent to various Saudi and foreign ports, such as, for instance, "option goods for Jiddah, Port Sudan, Musawwa", or "option goods for Bahrain, Dammam, Kuwait."

Handling: The masters of ships or the shipping company agents must, on the basis of the instructions issued to them by the shipping companies at the port of origin, indicate the exact destination of this category of goods as soon as the ship carrying the cargo arrives at a Saudi port, regardless of whether such goods are destined for the Kingdom or to some other foreign port.

Therefore, if option goods are destined for a Saudi port, they shall be unloaded in that port and the manifest shall be considered as wholly relating to the port of unloading . However, if the goods are destined for a foreign port

TEXT | COMMENTARY

and Customs is satisfied with the documents received from the shipping company agents or the ship masters, the number of option packages shall be subtracted from the total number of packages listed on the manifest.

Shipments for which credits were opened in Saudi Arabia must be unloaded in this country.

Article 228. In the event of the arrival of sailboats carrying goods destined wholly or in part for other Saudi ports, as shown on the ship's manifest. a bond shall be taken on the goods destined for these ports until a certificate from the Customs of destination is presented.

Article 229. Ships carrying goods destined for a foreign port, or ships arriving empty for the purpose of loading cargo may not stay at the port of arrival more than two weeks except for reasons beyond their control, such as repairs, damage, unfavorable winds, or failure to take on sufficient cargo.

TEXT | COMMENTARY

The period of stay may not be extended except by permission from the Coast Guard, and such permission will not be granted unless the reasons advanced are found to be valid and convincing.

In the event permission is not given, the ships must leave the port without delay. During the period of stay, the ships in question shall remain under control and shall be inspected prior to their departure by the Customs and the Coast Guard.

cle 230. If a ship stops at a Saudi port for some reason that arouses the suspicion of Customs, Customs may demand the immediate submission of the manifest and inspect the ship as may be necessary. However, such inspection may take place only by written order of the Customs Director and in the presence of a senior Customs official and a representative from the Coast Guard. The report prepared by the Customs official must contain the statements made by the

TEXT		COMMENTARY
	ship's master or his representative in the event of his absence, and he must be asked to sign such a report.	
Article 231.	If the masters of the means of transportation refuse to submit the legal manifest, or if they do not have it with them, or if they depart or attempt to depart without the permission of Customs, or if they commit an act contrary to Customs Regulations, the masters shall be fined SR 25 to SR 125. If the ships fail to anchor at the places assigned for the, or,if goods are shipped, unloaded, or trans-shipped without permission from Customs or not in the presence of its employees, or if the submission of the manifest is delayed and no evidence is given to prove that there is justification for the delay, the master of the ship shall be fined not more than SR 25. In the event importation or exportation is attempted in a manner	

TEXT

contrary to the established rules, the ship's master shall be fined not more than SR 12 even if the goods in question are exempt from import and export duties.

The manifest procedures shall apply to all types of means of transportation.

Chapter XVII

Transit and Trans-shipment

icle 232. Transit goods are goods that pass through the territories of Saudi Arabia. Their passage is merely a part of a complete trip that begins and ends outside the borders of the Kingdom. They are addressed to a certain person in a certain place outside the Kingdom, and the original invoices, the bills of lading, the manifests, and the packages as well bear a notation to the effect that the goods are goods in transit.

cle 233. There are two types of transit:

1. Direct transit.
2. Indirect transit.

The term "direct transit" is applied to the following:

COMMENTARY

CHAPTER XVII

TRANSIT AND TRANSHIPMENT

Although Saudi Arabia consumes a large amount of the goods that enter from abroad, many shipments are destined for other countries. An Inter-Arab Transit Agreement covers many of the details for handling goods in transit, including the sealing of goods and vehicles of commerce carrying them.

Companies transporting goods through Saudi territory must be bonded and licensed by the government. In order to tranship goods a written request must be made. An extract from the manifest, showing the goods to be transhipped, must be sent to the manifest office within 36 hours.

TEXT

A. Trans-shipped goods: Foreign goods that are transferred from one ship to another, either directly or through maritime means of transportation, without their being unloaded at the piers.

B. Transient goods: Goods unloaded at piers or airports and kept until they are shipped by other means of transportation to their ultimate destination.

The term "indirect transit" applies to goods unloaded at the piers and stored in the warehouses, then withdrawn for shipment abroad to their ultimate destination.

C. Transient goods transported by vehicles across the Kingdom, which are not unloaded within the Kingdom, shall be considered direct transit goods. These goods shall be exempt from the usual Customs and inspection formalities except as provided for in the Inter-Arab Transit Agreements and without prejudice to the right of the Directorate General of Cus-

COMMENTARY

Most countries have regulations governing transhipment of goods in bond, and exempting them from customs duties. Becaus the only transhipment of any signifigance in the U.S. involves goods going to or from Canada and Mexico, this is not as important a problem in the U.S.. See 19 CFR Section 123.31 et seq..

U.S. Customs regulations make a number o provisions for in transit goods, such as commerical travelers' samples, and professional tools (19 CFR Section 10.68); and baggage (19 CFR Section 18.13). Generally, U.S. law permits transportati in bond of any merchandise, except explo and contraband, without appraisement or payment of duties (19 USC Section 1553). Use of a TIR Carnet is permitted (i.e. Transport International Routier), as set out in the Customs Convention on International Transport of Goods Under Cover of TIR Carnets (TIAS 6633). Saudi Arabi is not a member of the Convention.

TEXT

COMMENTARY

toms to act as it may deem necessary in emergencies or in cases arousing suspicion.

D. Vehicles acceptable under the Inter-Arab Transit Agreement must meet the following specifications and conditions:

First: General Conditions:

1. The vehicles must be in good condition and must carry a license plate.
2. The vehicle must be so adapted as to allow the fixing of the lead seal on its box.
3. The box of the vehicle must not have any concealed compartment or one difficult to detect that can hold goods.
4. The box must only have hinges, pins, or nuts, that are secured from the inside.

Second: Conditions in Respect of Vans

1. The sides, bed, roof, and all parts comprising the section designed to hold goods must be so secured as to make it im-

TEXT	COMMENTARY
possible to disassemble them from the outside and put them back in place without leaving any visible traces of this act.	
2. The box must not have any aperture other than the door.	
3. The door opening must be equipped with a simple locking device that can provide, once it is lead-sealed, adequate security to prevent the possibility of removing or changing the goods without breaking the seal or using force, or without leaving any visible traces of such acts.	
Third: Conditions in Respect of Open Vehicles	
1. The sides and the bed of the box must be firmly secured to the chassis of the vehicle.	
2. The sides and the bed of the box must not be gridded, but completely closed to a height of not less than 70 centimeters from the bed.	
3. The sides must have a single opening only, designed for	

TEXT

COMMENTARY

loading and located on the rear.

4. The driver's compartment and the box must be separated by a clearance for the canvas cover.
5. The box must be provided with welded rings for tying the canvas. These rings must be fixed by means of hinges or nuts secured to the interior of the box, provided the distance between each ring and the next does not exceed 50 centimeters, and provided the rings are placed in line with the approximate level of the bed of the box and along all its sides.
6. The vehicle must be provided with a canvas which meets the following conditions:
   a. That it consist of one piece. Joined canvases may be accepted, provided the seam is sewn twice by machine, i.e. consists of two rows of stitches 15 to 25 millimeters

TEXT | COMMENTARY

apart.

b. That it be provided with metal loops on the edges which permit the insertion of a rope, provided that the number of these shall not be less than that of the rings fixed to the box.

c. That it be provided with a strong rope made of one piece.

Fourth: Lead Sealing

Goods transported under the Inter-Arab Transit Agreement shall be subject to lead-sealing. This shall be effected by the use of the reinforced tape (a rope and wire twine) and the Customs lead seal as follows:

1. Vans shall have their doorlocks sealed with the Customs lead seal by means of reinforced tape or wire.
2. With regard to open vehicles, the reinforced tape must be inserted in all the loops of the canvas and in all the rings

TEXT | COMMENTARY

surrounding the box, and must be firmly knotted with the rope knot and have both ends sealed with the Customs lead seal.

Lead-sealing in the preceding manner shall not apply to the following:

1. Large packages which cannot be covered with the canvas and which can be lead-sealed individually.
2. Goods imported in bulk which can be described accurately in the manifest, such as iron rods and lumber planks. The lead seal may be broken at the transited country if suspicion arises or if the above conditions are not fulfilled. The Customs office in the transited country, may add another lead seal to that affixed in the country of export. If it is proven that the lead seal has been broken, any Customs office may conduct a thorough examina-

TEXT | COMMENTARY

tion of the goods and prepare a report on its findings, a copy of which shall be attached to the manifest after a notation to that effect in the remarks column is made.

Fifth: Transit cards pertaining to transiting trucks, which are granted by the authorities of the country where the trucks are registered, shall be carried in the trucks. In the Kingdom of Saudi Arabia, these cards are granted by the Customs authorities upon obtainment of a certificate from the Traffic authority attesting that the trucks are suitable for transportation across the desert.

Sixth: Each vehicle must carry with every shipment the transit manifest prepared in the country of origin.

E. For each vehicle, a standard manifest shall be prepared in the country of origin for the goods it carries, in accordance

TEXT

COMMENTARY

with the form established by the signatories of the Inter-Arab Transit Agreement.

F. Transit cards shall be prepared for vehicles transporting goods under the Inter-Arab Transit Agreement, in accordance with the form established by the signatory countries.

G. Anyone engaged in transportation across Saudi territory under the terms of the Inter-Arab Transit Agreement, whether he be a Saudi company, or a Saudi individual, or a subject of the other signatory countries of the Inter-Arab Transit Agreement, must be duly bonded and permitted to engage in transportation by the competent Saudi authorities; he must obtain an official license from the Directorate General of Customs, subject to the following provisions.

1. A permanent license shall be issued to those companies

TEXT

COMMENTARY

or persons who can prove that they have transported between the Arab countries not less than one thousand tons annually during the previous three years.

2. A temporary license valid for a period of two years shall be issued to new companies and individuals, if they undertake to transport an average of not less than one thousand tons annually for two years.
3. The license shall be withdrawn from companies or persons who fail to transport one thousand tons annually for three years subsequent to the issuance of the license, unless this is due to compelling reasons acceptable to the authorities empowered to grant this license.
4. Companies or person wishing to obtain licenses must pay a cash deposit, submit a

TEXT

COMMENTARY

bank guarantee, or bring a solvent, responsible guarantor, acceptable to the Directorate General of Customs, for one hundred thousand Saudi riyals. Whenever the need arises, the Directorate General of Customs shall make the necessary recommendations for the adjustments of the value of this guarantee.

5. In normal cases, the license shall remain valid so long as the cash deposit is in the hands of the authorities concerned, or so long as the bank or personal guarantee is in effect for an indefinite period. If the guarantee is limited to a specific period, the validity of the license shall lapse upon the expiry of the period of the guarantee. The competent authorities shall, however, have the right to reconsider

TEXT

COMMENTARY

the formalities and conditions necessary for the renewal of such expired license.

6. The said license shall be granted only if the applicant is registered at the competent departments in accordance with the rules in force.

H. The person who carries out Customs formalities in respect of vehicles operating under the Inter-Arab Transit Agreement must:

1. Hold an official Customs broker's license.
2. Hold the license provided for in Paragraph G, or an accredited power of attorney from the holder of such license and act at the latter's responsibility.

I. The preceding provisions shall be applied with due regard to the principle of reciprocity and without prejudice to the

TEXT | COMMENTARY

regulations, orders, and agreements in force in the Kingdom.

Trans-shipment

ticle 234. The trans-shipment of goods shall take place in accordance with a written request from the shipping companies. The shipping companies shall, within a period not exceeding 36 hours, submit to the Manifest Office an extract from the manifest in two copies showing the goods to be trans-shipped. A copy of the extract shall be kept in the Manifest Office and the second copy shall be forwarded to the Customs Director for approval and issuance of the necessary instructions to the Pier Division.

Entries

The representative of the shipping company concerned shall keep a book in which to enter the trans-shipped packages as shown on the manifest. He shall show beside each package the name of the ship on which it arrived, the name of

TEXT | COMMENTARY

the company to which the ship belongs, and the date of shipment. Those books shall be under Customs control and, as and when entries are made therein, shall be examined by the Pier Division which will make a notation on the second copy of the manifest referred to it by the Customs Director to the effect that the goods listed therein have been shipped. It shall then forward this copy to the Manifest Office which will attach this copy to the copy in its possession and close the entries on it.

Article 235. Goods unloaded at the piers and re-shipped by the shipping companies from the pier, on board a ship or any other means of transportation, to their ultimate destination before they are received at Customs shall be dealt with in the following manner:

1. The shipping company shall submit two copies of the original manifest to the Manifest Office

TEXT

so that it may check the description on the original manifest and keep one copy in its files.

2. The second copy shall be submitted to the Customs Director for his approval and for him to designate the packages which he thinks should be inspected or investigated or make a notation for release without opening.
3. Then it shall be submitted to the Valuation Division for assessing the storage and porterage charges and overtime pay which may be due thereon.
4. Then to the Accounting Department and the Cash Office for collecting whatever amount may be payable under (3).
5. Then to the Pier Division so that it may authorize shipment and make a notation on the second copy of the manifest to the effect that the goods have been shipped and then return this copy to the Manifest Office

COMMENTARY

TEXT

6. The representative of the shipping company shall keep a record book that will be subject to examination by Customs.

Indirect Transit Goods

Article 236. Indirect transit goods are goods that are unloaded on the piers and received by Customs into its warehouses. In the case of these goods a Certificate of Formalities (Bill of Entry) for transit goods will be required instead of extracting two copies from the manifest, and the following procedure shall be applied:

1. The person concerned shall prepare the Certificate(Bill of Entry) and attach it to the delivery order and the shipment authorization given to him by the shipping company that owns the means of transportation on which the goods will be shipped.
2. The above-mentioned papers shall be submitted to the Manifest Office and then to the warehouseman who will make a notation on them acknowledging

COMMENTARY

INDIRECT TRANSIT GOODS

Goods may be unloaded at piers for reshipment. Goods must, generally, go through customs even where reshipment is involved unless special authorization from customs is obtained. If goods are destined for another Saudi port duty in the form of a deposit may be collected, until payment of actual customs duties at the port of destination is received. Goods from foreign countries destined for other foreign countries, and arriving on ships or airplanes are not subject to customs duties.

TEXT | COMMENTARY

receipt and showing the date of receipt.

3. These papers shall then be submitted to the Customs Director who will authorize shipment and designate the packages which he thinks should be examined or investigated or make a notation for release without opening.
4. Then they shall be submitted to the Warehouse Division for carrying out the instructions of the Customs Director.
5. Then to the Valuation Division for assessing the storage or porterage charges, or overtime pay, which may be due thereon.
6. Then to the Accounting Department and the Cash Office for collecting the amounts payable and the charges referred to above, and for issuing the necessary clearance. After this, the clearance shall be submitted to the Warehouse Division which will authorize shipment

TEXT | COMMENTARY

under the supervision of Customs.

Authorization for shipment in sailboats shall not be granted except by special permission from the Customs Director and after a deposit, fixed by Customs, has been made. This deposit shall be refunded upon the submission, within a period to be specified by Customs, of an official certificate from the Customs at the port of destination, regardless of whether the goods are shipped to a Saudi or foreign port, confirming arrival and unloading of the goods at that port. In the case of ships and airplanes, however, it will be sufficient to present the bill of lading.

General Rules

Article 237. As a general rule, re-shipment of goods that are unloaded at the Customs piers are not permitted except after they have been received by Customs, as is the case with imported goods. However, the

TEXT | COMMENTARY

Customs Director may authorize the shipping companies to ship goods of this type before they are received into the Customs warehouses.

Customs may inspect all transit and trans-shipped goods.

Any prohibited goods found to have been misrepresented shall be subject to seizure, and penalties shall be imposed accordingly.

icle 238. In the case of transit goods coming from a foreign port to a Saudi port and destined for another Saudi port, import duties shall be collected at the first port of call in the form of a deposit to be refunded to the person concerned upon the arrival of the goods at the Saudi port of ultimate destination.

In case the quantity is short when it arrives at the Saudi port, duties shall be collected on the missing packages and the fine referred to in Article 215 shall be imposed, unless the shortage is

TEXT | COMMENTARY

proved to have been due to force majeure.

Article 239. In the case of transit goods which arrive from foreign ports and are destined for other foreign ports, but are on ships which discharge their cargo at a Saudi port and call at other Saudi ports before they arrive at the foreign port of ultimate destination, duties shall be collected on such goods in the form of a deposit if they are shipped on sailboats or in small vessels, and this deposit shall be refunded upon the receipt of an official certificate from the foreign port of destination confirming the arrival of the goods at that port. Should a shortage be discovered in the quantity of the goods received at the foreign port, the duty on such shortage shall be collected from the amount of the deposit, unless the shortage is proved to have been due to force majeure. However, if the goods are shipped on board ships or airplanes, no

TEXT

COMMENTARY

deposit shall be collected and it will be sufficient to look over the bill of lading.

icle 240. If it is found from the official certificates that transit goods shipped to Saudi or to foreign ports have been exchanged on the way, the case shall be considered a case of smuggling and shall be subject to the penalties prescribed in the Regulations.

icle 241. Transit goods received in Customs warehouses shall be subject to porterage charges in consideration of their being moved to the warehouses and their being issued therefrom. However, if the goods are not received by Customs but remain on the piers until they are shipped away, porterage charges thereon shall be collected at the rate applicable. Storage charges on transit goods shall accrue after the lapse of ten days if the goods are received in the warehouses and after the lapse of two days if they are unloaded at

TEXT | COMMENTARY

the piers.

Export and Re-Export

Article 242. If local goods are exported or foreign goods re-exported abroad, the proper export certificate (Export Statement and Customs Declaration) must be submitted, with the necessary particulars filled in by those concerned, to the Customs Director who will authorize the export, and then to the Valuation Division which will stamp it and register it in a special book, and then give it a serial number and endorse it for inspection.

The goods may not enter the Customs Area except when the means of transportation on which the goods will be shipped is anchored in the port and a shipment authorization is submitted. Goods for export shall be permitted to enter the Customs Area for the purpose of inspection and valuation. The Pier Division shall supervise the process of export and confirm it

TEXT

COMMENTARY

on the Export Statement.

icle 243. If goods are to be exported from a Saudi port to another Saudi port, the same procedures as outlined above shall be followed and the person concerned shall be given a "raftiyah" (advice note) showing all the particulars of the goods. This "raftiyah" shall be submitted to the Customs at the point of destination.

When local goods are exported on sailboats not represented by an agency at the port of shipment, a bond equivalent to the value of the goods shall be taken until a Customs Certificate has been submitted confirming the arrival of the goods at the other Saudi port.

cle 244. Goods exported from a Saudi port to another Saudi port lose their nationality if they pass through a foreign port, except in cases of emergency when it is proved that the goods have not been unloaded at the foreign port and the Customs at the point of destination is con-

TEXT | COMMENTARY

vinced by documents that the goods in question are the same goods exported from the Saudi port. Goods for export which enter the Customs Area and are not exported within two working days, excluding the days on which they are received and any official holidays, shall be subject to the applicable storage charges.

Moneybags

Article 245. When moneybags are to be exported, they shall be brought to Customs accompanied by the Export Certificate and the shipment authorization. After proper inspection, the packages shall be sealed with red wax in the presence of the person concerned, and an official shall be assigned to take them to the ship, the post office, or the airplane.

Export By Land

Article 246. Export from Saudi Arabia shall be permitted after the formalities have been completed, either at the Customs point located at the border

TEXT | COMMENTARY

if it is authorized to carry out the formalities, or at the nearest Customs point within the Kingdom. In the latter instance a "raftiyah" shall be issued authorizing passage through the Customs point at the border, and checking shall be made in the usual manner.

icle 247. Export of the following items shall not be permitted unless they are accompanied by a certificate from the Ministry of Health: Sheepskins, goatskins, cowhides, camel hides, mule skins, donkey skins, intestines whether salted or dried, horns, hair, woven camel hair, empty jute bags, cloth rags, used cotton, sheep, goats, camels, cows, mules, donkeys, shells, mother-of-pearl, cuttle-fish, and shark bone.

<u>Transportation of Goods Inside the Kingdom By All Means of Transportation</u>

cle 248.1. All goods carried by any means of transportation from Saudi towns situated on or near the borders of the neighboring kingdoms to other

TEXT

Saudi towns situated either on the borders or inland and, likewise, goods carried from Saudi towns on the coasts near the borders either to Saudi towns situated on the borders or to neighboring towns not situated on the borders, must follow the desert routes presently recognized until such routes are defined officially, and a "raftiyah" must be obtained for such goods from the Customs at the point of origin.

2. All goods shipped by aircraft within the Kingdom shall be registered on the aircraft manifest in accordance with Article 208.

3. Tobacco, tumbak, jurak, and cigarette paper shipped between towns in the Kingdom by land, sea, or air must be accompanied by a "raftiyah".

Chapter XVIII

Smuggling

Part One-General Provisions

Definition

Article 249. The following shall be considered

COMMENTARY

CHAPTER XVIII

SMUGGLING

Saudi law provides for harsh treatment o[f] smugglers. The use of fraud to avoid pa[y]

TEXT

guilty of the offense of smuggling:

1. Any person who uses fraudulent means to evade payment of all or part of the Customs duties on goods.
2. Any person who uses fraudulent means to bring in or export contraband items or items subject to special regulation.

Attempt to Smuggle

cle 250. Attempts to smuggle are equivalent to actual smuggling and the penalties imposed for both offenses are the same.

Complicity

cle 251. The accomplice in smuggling shall be liable to the same penalty as the principal offender. Complicity in smuggling consists of taking part in the act of smuggling, either directly or indirectly, with the free choice and consent of the accomplice.

Judicial Police Officials

le 252. While performing their duties, Customs officials are considered

COMMENTARY

ment of customs duties may be considered as smuggling. Saudi law, like that of the U.S. (19 CFR Section 162.22) and other countries, provides that vehicles, boats, and other instruments of commerce used for the specific purpose of smuggling may be seized. Rather explicit formalities relating to searches are provided for.

A special group of quasi-judicial boards, known as Customs Committees, have been established for the purpose of dealing with smugglers, and disposing of contraband goods. Six regional committees have been set up to cover the principal border and port areas. The Customs Committees can decide if arrested smugglers are to be released on bond (Article 258), and have jurisdiction over infractions committed by customs employees. Decisions are made by majority vote, except in the case of a tie vote, the chairman's decision prevails. The operations of the Customs Committee appear to contain most elements of due process found in western administrative tribunals, although no

TEXT

as judicial police officials.

Part Two- Seizure and Search

Articles to be Seized

Article 253. Smuggled articles and, likewise, any means of transportation such as boats or animals that have been used to carry such articles, with the exception of ships and aircraft, unless these have been hired for the specific purpose of smuggling, shall be seized. To be seized, also, are such items as have been used to conceal smuggled articles or facilitate their passage. However, no goods may be detained without indicating in the report that such goods are seized goods.

Seizure Report

Article 254. Officials performing an act of seizure must take the offenders, together with the articles seized, to the nearest Customs Office to prepare the report required, and under no circumstances may the writing of the report be delayed. The report must show the date and

COMMENTARY

specific provisions for representation by counsel are provided. The Committees must issue a written decision containing a summary of the facts, and the reasons for the decision. A limited appeal, within 15 days to the Administrative Governor, is permitted.

Convicted smugglers are subject to fines and imprisonment. Since imprisonment for debt is permitted, those who cannot pay the fines may be incarcerated. The Saudi system differs from the U.S. system mainly in the use of administrative tribunals to handle what is in the U.S. a criminal process governed by the courts. This is because Islamic law, as noted in our earlier discussion (See Saudi Arabia Legal System,Page 9) is basically a religious law, which was not geared to dealing with transgressions of a commercial nature. The Saudis have therefore supplemented the "Shariah" law with various administrative tribunals.

TEXT

COMMENTARY

hour of its being opened and closed; the place in which the seizure took place; the date and hour of the seizure; and the name, surname, nationality, occupation, and place of residence of the offenders. If this information cannot be obtained because the offenders refuse to give it, this fact must be mentioned in the seizure report. Also, if the offender escapes and cannot be located, this fact must be mentioned in the report which, in this case, is to be filed against an unknown person. The report must show all the facts and information which will facilitate the search for the accused and lead to his discovery. In case the offender is employed on a ship or on any other means of transportation, the name and type of conveyance, the name of its master or driver, and the name of the company acting as its agent must be mentioned.

The names, surnames, positions,

TEXT | COMMENTARY

and places of residence of the seizors must be stated. The report must give a summary of the case, the reasons for the seizure, the circumstances surrounding it, and a minute description of the articles seized. If the item seized is hashish, then the labels numbers, marks, and any other thing that may be written or drawn on the wrappers of the pieces of hashish themselves must be shown. If there is nothing shown on the wrappers then this fact must be stated in the report. A full description of the kinds of seized arms or ammunition must be made. It should be mentioned, for instance, that the rifles are military rifles or that they are hunting rifles and that the cartridges are filled with pellets. The value of the articles seized must be estimated and shown in the report which is to be sent to the Customs Committee, and such value will be the basis for computing

TEXT | COMMENTARY

the fine to be imposed.

In the event there are informers, their names must not be stated in the seizure report or contravention report; rather, the phrase "in accordance with secret information received from a person known to us" must be mentioned.

The report must be prepared in the presence of the accused persons and they shall be asked to sign it. This, together with the statements made by the accused persons, should be shown in the report. It must be stated, also, if they agree or refuse to sign the report.

Seizure reports must be written clearly and without any abbreviation. There should be no blanks or empty spaces between the words, and comments and remarks may be written only in the margin of the page and must be signed or initialed by those who sign the report; otherwise, they shall be considered void.

There should be no insertions or

TEXT | COMMENTARY

additions between the lines. Anything of this sort shall be considered void. If it is necessary to delete certain words, their number must be shown in the margin of the page or at the end of the report, and such deletions must be signed by those who sign the report. The seizure report, with all the relative documents, must be sent within twenty-four hours from the date on which it was prepared to the Customs Committee concerned in order that it may investigate the case and take the necessary action thereon. Directorates of Customs that have Customs Committees must send a copy of the report to the Directorate General of Customs accompanied by their remarks, without thereby delaying or suspending the proceedings of the case.

In addition to the above, the Directorates of Customs should, upon seizing hashish, opium, intoxicants, contraband goods, or

TEXT

arms or ammunition, send a copy of the seizure report to the Administrative Governor of the town in order that the offenders may be brought to trial. However, such trial shall not interfere with the right of the Customs committees to look into the smuggling charges.

Search:

1. Search of Houses, Shops, and Stores

icle 255. If the house, shop, or store to be searched is located within the limits of the Customs Control Zone, which is ten kilometers from the sea coast or the land borders, the search shall be conducted in accordance with written instructions from the Customs Director. The search shall take place in the presence of a senior Customs official and a representative of the Administrative Governor, and it shall not be made except for the purpose of looking for and seizing contraband goods or goods smuggled to evade the payment of duties.

COMMENTARY

Search:

Despite the absence of constitutional safeguards relating to searchs and seizures in Saudi law, the Saudi customs regulations are nevertheless tempred with moderation in the exercise of search powers by customs agents. If a building is located in what is known as the "customs control zone" which is a ten kilometer area from the boarder or port the search can be conducted by customs officials in accordance with written instructions from the Director. Outside the zone the Coast Guard or police must be present. Even ships anchored in port can only be searched with a written order from the Customs director or at the request of the master. Depending on the location of the ship, search authority is divided between customs and the Coast Guard .

TEXT

The Customs men may request the assistance of the Coast Guard or the police if they find it necessare to do so.

However, if the house, shop or store is located outside the limits of the Customs Control Zone,the search must be made in the presence of the Coast Guard or the police.

2. Ships Anchored in Port

No ship anchored at a Saudi port may be searched until after a written order has been obtained from the Customs Director. Customs officials may board any ship without prior formalities if a writtent request is submitted by the master. If the request is verbal it must be confirmed by two witnesses for the search to proceed.

When Customs receives some secret information about the presence of

COMMENTARY

The rules specifically deal with attempt to bribe or bestow gifts on Saudi Custom icials, a practice not unkown in the Mid East, and rigid procedures are set out t control these activities. The powers of Saudi Customs officials are not unlike t of their American counterparts.(See e.g. 19 C.F.R. Section 162.21). Although Saud makes no provision for search warrants c tained from a judicial officer, as is do in the US(See 19 U.S.C. Section 1595) .

The Saudi system has a built in provisic for rewarding those who inform on smuggl as well as those who actually seize the Informers can receive as much as 30% of value of the goods and duties after cert deductions and those who actually seize goods may receive as much as 50%. In the of narcotics, a flat cash award of SR 3 per kilo is provided for. Other countrie including the U.S. reward informers but not provide incentive payments to govern officials lest they become overzealous i enforcing the law and engage in abuses i order to supplement their incomes.

TEXT

smuggled goods on any of the ships anchored at a pier (a ship anchored at a pier is one so close to the pier that it is not possible for a floating boat to circle around it), the ship may be searched by Customs officials alone and to the exclusion of others, and Customs shall have the right to keep or dispose of the articles seized. However, Customs Directors may request the assistance of Coast Guard technicians, such as engineers and stokers, who are able to discover secret hiding places in which smuggled goods are likely to be concealed. If the secret information about the presence of smuggled goods on one of the ships anchoring at the pier is received by men of the Coast Guard, then these men shall have the right to search the ship in the presence of the Customs official assigned for this purpose. Also, in this case, the Coast Guard may retain the seized articles and, in all cases, the report, the ac-

COMMENTARY

United States law speciffically precludes any United States officials from receiving a reward or payment. 19 U.S.C. Section 1620; 19 C.F.R. Section 161.11(B). Informers in the United States may recover 25% of the net amount recovered by the government up to a maximum amount of $50,000. (19 C.F.R. Section 161.13).

TEXT | COMMENTARY

cused persons, and the goods smuggled shall be referred to the Customs Committee.

3. Search of Ships Anchored Outside the Port in the Roadstead

The search of ships and boats not anchored at a pier, and the seizure of smuggled goods carried on them, shall be made by the Coast Guard or by the Port Police.

4. Precautionary Measures Toward Ships in General

Precautionary measures, such as the posting of guards around the ship, may be taken to prevent the concealment of smuggled goods or their infiltration into the Kingdom.

Insubordination, Resistance, and Violence

Article 256. The seizure report must show every act committed by the offenders against the seizors while they are performing their duties, such as attempts to escape or prevent the seizure of smuggled goods, resistance, insubordination, violence,

TEXT

COMMENTARY

or any attempt at bribery, whether by offering gifts or by making promises. In this instance, a copy of the report must be sent to the Administrative Governor. Gifts in cash or otherwise must be sent, together with the copy of the seizure report, after they have been placed in a bag and sealed with red wax with the seal of the official or the department to which he belongs.

Custody of Seized Goods

cle 257. If possible, seized goods must be kept in the warehouse assigned for the purpose. In the case of ships carriages, cars, animals of burden, etc., the Customs Director shall entrust their custody to a Customs guard, with the exception of ships whose custody shall be entrusted to the Coast Guard. Valuables shall be kept in the Customs vaults.

Explosives shall be sent to the warehouses assigned for them, and each article seized must be kept

TEXT | COMMENTARY

separately and must bear a label containing a summary of the facts of the seizure. Receipts must be obtained from the warehouseman who has custody of the articles, and must be delivered to Customs for purposes of record.

At the beginning of each month the warehouseman must forward a statement of all the articles seized and kept in his custody.

In the case of narcotics, Customs shall send a statement on them to the Ministry of Health so that it may take whatever quantity is needed for medical purposes and destroy the remaining quantity after the case has been closed.

Part Three- <u>Arrest of Offenders Involved in the Offense</u>

Article 258. Offenders who have a permanent and known place of residence in Saudi Arabia may, after the seizure report has been written, be set free against a guaranty given by a reliable party, unless they

TEXT

COMMENTARY

are persons who have previous criminal records and unless they are accused of smuggling hashish, opium, or intoxicants. A person shall be considered as having a previous record of smuggling if he had been convicted of smuggling during the five years preceding the occurrence of the latest offense.

Offenders who do not have a permanent, known place of residence in Saudi Arabia must be referred to the Customs Committee so that it may decide, within 24 hours from the time of their arrest, whether or not they should be kept in detention under remand. If the Committee decides to confirm their detention under remand, it shall specify the amount of the bail which the accused has to pay in order to be released. However, the amount of such a bail must not exceed the amount which the Committee decides may be imposed as a fine.

TEXT	COMMENTARY

The Committee may, in lieu of bail, accept a responsible guarantor, and under no circumstances may the period of detention under remand exceed seven days.

Voluntary Payment of the Fine

Article 259.1. If the accused wishes to pay the fine and relinquish by a written statement, the articles seized, or if he submits to the former and refuses the latter, the seizors may accept this arrangement and confirm it in the report and indicate the amount received. In both instances he shall be released without the need of a bond for him.

2. However, this does not preclude the necessity of getting all the information required, such as the name of the accused, his surname, occupation, and place of residence, so that these particulars may be registered in the criminal record book and so that it may be easy to summon him to appear before the Customs Committee looking into the

TEXT	COMMENTARY

matter of confiscation, whenever, such action is required.

3. The provisions outlined in paragraph I shall not apply if the seizors learn that the accused has a previous record of smuggling.

4. Relinquishment of the articles seized does not apply to contraband items, since these are by nature subject to confiscation. If the items seized are narcotics, the acceptance of the accused of paying the fine and relinquishing the items seized does not excuse him from having to be taken to the Administrative Governor to stand trial.

cle 260. All kinds of penalties imposed by Customs Committees on smugglers are outlined in the Articles on Smuggling in the Customs Regulations.

As regards the various kinds of narcotics, like hashish, opium, etc., a fine of SR 500 shall be imposed on each kilogram up to three kilograms, and anything over

TEXT | COMMENTARY

three kilograms shall be subject to a fine of SR 300 on each kilogram, in accordance with telegraphic Royal Order No. 9307, dated 19 Ramadan 1372(June 1, 1953).

This is in addition to the exemplary penalty which is imposed by the administrative authorities in accordance with the Regulations prohibiting trading in narcotics, and which amount to from 50 to 300 sovereigns and imprisonment from five months to two years. (See decisions of the Consultative Council No. 103, dated 5 Ramadan 1369(June 21, 1950) and No. 14, dated 25 Safar 1370(December 6, 1950) and Decision No. 70 of the Council of Ministers dated 14 Rajab 1374(March 8, 1955).)

For all kinds of intoxicants, a fine of SR 500 shall be collected on each dozen bottles up to three dozen. Anything over three dozen shall be subject to the collection of SR 300 on each dozen.

TEXT

COMMENTARY

Part Fourt-Rewards in Cases of Seizure

General Rule

cle 261. Fines collected and money obtained from the sale of seized articles shall be distributed in accordance with the provisions given hereinafter. The distribution of rewards in cases of seizure shall be made in proportion to the part played by each of the seizors and according to each seizor's position and grade.

Seizors Who Are Not Customs Officials

cle 262. Rewards due to seizors who are not employees of the Customs Department shall be paid to them through the department to which they belong, after the necessary deductions have been made from the total amount of the fines collected.

Part Five-Customs Committee-Jurisdiction

cle 263. The Customs committees shall have jurisdiction in all cases of smuggling or attempts to smuggle, and

PART FIVE-CUSTOMS COMMITTEE JURISDICTION

As discussed at the beginning of this chapter, the Customs committees perform a special function in Saudi law. Since

TEXT

the minutes of the meetings of the Committee shall be considered authentic unless they are impeached on grounds of forgery. (See Article 51 of the Customs Regulations.)

Areas under the Jurisdiction of Customs Committees

Article 264. The Jiddah Committee shall have the power to examine all smuggling offenses committed in the Directorate of Customs for the Hijaz, its branches and subsidiaries.

The Dammam Committee shall have the power to examine all smuggling offenses committed in the Directorate of Customs for the Eastern Province, its nearby branches and subsidiaties.

The Tabuk Committee shall have the power to examine all smuggling offenses committed in the Directorate of Customs for the Northern Area and in its nearby subsidiaries.

The Northern Frontiers Committee shall have the power to examine

COMMENTARY

the Shariah law does not specifically provide for customs related offenses, such as smuggling, the Shariah court system, which might otherwise have jurisdiction over crimes of a related nature, is replaced by administrative boards comprised of civil servants. This is in keeping with the tendency of the Saudi judicial system to remove jurisdiction over violations of "decree" law (i.e. laws not directly originating from the Koran and the Al-Sunna) from the traditional Qadi courts to administrative bodies. Similar tribunals exist for resolving labor disputes, disciplining civil servants and military personnel. The decentralized nature of the Customs Committees is consistent with the histori tendency of the Saudi judicial system to place decision making power in the hands of local officials, most notably the Emir Jurisdiction over customs offenses is als more likely to involve foreigners. By vesting authority in the Customs Committe rather than the Shariah courts, foreigner are protected from the harsher corporal punishments, such as floggings, that coul

TEXT

all smuggling offenses committed in the Directorate of Customs for the Northern Frontiers and its nearby branches and subsidiaries.

The Jaizan Committee shall have the power to examine all smuggling offenses committeed in the Directorate of Customs for the Southern Area and its nearby branches and subsidiaries.

The Qaryat Committee shall have the power to examine all smuggling offenses committed in the Directorate of Customs for the Borders and its nearby branches and subsidiaries.

Customs committees shall be formed in Customhouses that are far away from the locations of the Directorates.

Formation of Customs Committees

[Arti]cle 265. Customs committees shall be organized in the Directorate General of Customs, in the Directorates of Customs and in Customs Branch Offices, in the following manner:

COMMENTARY

be administered under the Hanbalite law.

It should be noted that although the Customs Committees have quasi-judicial functions, none of the members are required to be attorneys. The rules do not provide for the legal representation of parties appearing before the Committees, but there would apparently be no prohibition, and retention of a Saudi lawyer would be advisable. The services of an attorney would also be useful in case an appeal of the decision is taken to the Administrative Governor.

TEXT		COMMENTARY
1. Directorate General of Customs		
a. Assistant to the Director General of Customs	Chairman	
b. Inspector General of Customs or his deputy	Members	
c. Director, General Accounting	Members	
d. Director, General Auditing	Members	
e. Director, Customs Cases	Members	
f. Customs expert, if any	Members	
g. Controller General Tariff and Valuation	Members	
2. Directorate of Customs for the Eastern Province		
a. Director of Customs of his assistant	Chairman	
b. Customs expert, if any	Members	
c. Chief Accountant	Members	
d. Chief Auditor, if any	Members	
e. Chief Controller, if any	Members	

TEXT	COMMENTARY
f. Customs inspector, if any)	
g. Director of the Customs) Members	
concerned, or his assistant)	

Note: It is to be observed that the Director of the Customs concerned means that of the customhouses where the formalities requiring consideration by the Customs committee are initiated.

3. Directorate of Customs for the North
   - a. Director of Customs — Chairman
   - b. Chief Accountant)
   - c. Director, Tabuk Customs) Members
   - d. Customs inspector, if any)
4. Directorate of Customs and Finance for the Northern Frontiers Area:
   - a. Director of Customs — Chairman
   - b. Chief Accountant)
   - c. Chief Auditor, if any) Members
   - d. Director, local Customhouse)
   - e. Customs inspector, if any)
5. Directorate of Customs for the South
   - a. Director of Customs or his assistant — Chairman
   - b. Chief Accountant)
   - c. Director, Local Customs) Members
   - d. Accountant, Local Customs)

TEXT	COMMENTARY
e. Customs inspector, if any — Member	
6. Directorate of Customs for the Frontiers, Qaryah	
a. Director of Customs or his assistant — Chairman	
b. Chief Accountant; c. Director, local Customhouse; d. Customs inspector, if any — Members	
7. Jiddah Customs Committee	
a. Director of Customs, or his assistant — Chairman	
b. Head, Valuation Division; c. Head, Accounting; d. Head, Manifest Division; e. Customs Inspector — Members	
8. In Customhouses that are far away from the locations of the Customs Directorates, committees shall be formed as follows:	
a. Director, Customhouse — Chairman	
b. Accountant; c. Director of Munici-	

TEXT | COMMENTARY

pality or the)
person acting)
for him.) Members
d. Director of)
Police)

9. Each committee shall appoint an employee of its choice to perform secretarial work, number decisions, and arrange them in its files.

10. All these committees shall look into cases of smuggling and contraventions committed at Customhouses by the employees or merchants, as well as all occurrences relevant to Customs. They shall make their decisions in accordance with existing instructions and these Rules, and their decisions shall be conclusive.

11. In addition to investigating cases of smuggling and the like, Customs committees formed at the Customs Directorates or other Customhouses shall act as disciplinary boards and shall con-

TEXT

COMMENTARY

sider acts committed by employees in violation of their duties, and shall apply the provisions stipulated in the General Regulations for Government Employees in their respect, provided that their decisions, as disciplinary boards, shall not be effective except after they are submitted to the Directorate General of Customs and the latter is notified of the action to be taken.

12. In cases where the chairman or one of the members serving on a committee is a party thereto, one of the members shall be elected by ballot to act as chairman instead of the permanent chairman, and such elected chairman shall have two votes in his capacity as chairman without having a vote as a member. Where a member is a party to a case, this shall entail that he shall not sit on the committee in his official capacity and not replacement for

TEXT | COMMENTARY

him shall be elected.

13. In the event that a fundamental difference arises among the members of a committee as to interfere with the proceeding of a case, and if a case is so important that the committee cannot look into it, the case shall be submitted to the Directorate General of Customs for consideration.

Investigation Before Customs Committees

Summoning the Accused

[Art]icle 266. The accused shall be requested to appear before the Customs committee to present their defense. The request shall be made by means of official correspondence sent to the Administrative Governor who will summon them. If they appear, the committee shall proceed to interrogate them and shall prepare a report on their statements and remarks and on the testimony of the seizors and witnesses if necessary. As regards cases connected with the

TEXT | COMMENTARY

Coast Guard, the Directorate of the Coast Guard must be notified of the day fixed for the hearing of the case, so that it may send its representative if it deems it necessary.

Decisions of Customs Committees

Article 267. After it has examined the cases referred to it, the Customs committee must formulate decisions thereon. The decision must be written on paper stamped with the Customs stamp, and the pages must be numbered serially. Each Directorate must give the decisions issued by its committee a serial number to be renewed at the beginning of each year.

Deliberations

Article 268. The decisions shall be issued on the basis of a majority vote. If, however, the votes are equal, the opinion of the Chairman of the committee shall prevail. The decisions must be dated and signed by the members of the committee who have attended the examination and the deliberations.

TEXT

COMMENTARY

Form of the Decisions

icle 269. The decisions must contain a summary of the case and must show the reasons on which the conviction or the acquittal was based. The text of the verdict must contain a clear description of the articles to be confiscated. The decisions of the committees shall be considered authentic unless the particulars contained therein are impeached on grounds of forgery.

Transmitting Decisions to the Coast Guard

icle 270. As and when issued, decisions on cases connected with the Coast Guard shall be transmitted by the Customs Director to the officer in charge of the division making the seizure for the latter's own information. The Directorate of the Coast Guard shall be notified of all decisions connected with it as soon as such decisions become final.

Notification of the Decisions

icle 271. A copy of the decision, signed by the Director General of Customs or

TEXT

COMMENTARY

his representative, shall be sent by registered mail or delivered against a receipt to the Administrative Governor on the day on which it was written or on the following day.

In case the accused persons are unknown, notification shall be made by publication in the official gazette.

Objection to the Customs Decisions

Article 272. Decisions of the Customs committee may be challenged within 15 days from the date the decision was transmitted. In this instance, the accused shall submit the objection to the Administrative Governor. If the objection to the decision of the committee is not submitted within the period specified, the decision shall become final, and the challenge can in no way be accepted.

Execution

Article 273. Pecuniary fines imposed by Customs committees or by the courts which review the objections raised against the decisions of such committees

TEXT

COMMENTARY

may be executed through imprisonment for debt in accordance with the last paragraph of Article 53 of the Customs Regulations which provides for an imprisonment of one day for every five Saudi riyals, provided the whole period of imprisonment does not exceed three months. The Administrative Governor under whose jurisdiction the Customs committee falls shall be notified to take this action. Orders issued for imprisonment shall be drawn up in two copies and shall be given a serial number and recorded in a special register. The prison administration shall keep one copy and return the other, signed by the director of the prison, to the Customs to be placed in the file on the case.

In urgent cases, precautionary attachments may be laid prior to the issuance of the final decision, in accordance with an order from the Administrative Governor.

The Directorates of Customs shall

TEXT | COMMENTARY

conduct the necessary investigations concerning the property owned by the convicted person in order that the fines can be collected.

Sale or Destruction of Seized Items

Article 274. When the decision calling for the confiscation of seized items becomes final, Customs shall proceed to sell these items unless they are contraband, in which case they shall be destroyed.

Seized arms and ammunition shall be sent to the Ministry of Defense.

Perishable Items

Article 275. Even though their confiscation may not have become final, perishable items shall be sold without delay, as outlined in Article (60) of the Customs Regulations.

Method of Sale

Article 276. Seized articles shall be sold at public auction in accordance with the usual procedures.

Rewards

Article 277. Rewards shall be distributed in the following manner:

TEXT	COMMENTARY
1. Confiscated goods on which two duties have been collected: a. Customs duties and subsidiary charges due on the confiscated goods shall be paid to the Customs Cash Office. b. The second duty, plus the value of the smuggled goods after they are sold, shall be distributed, after deducting transportation charges and other expenses, if any, in the following manner: 30% to the informers 30% to the seizors and their helpers. 20% deposit to the Reward Fund 20% to the Treasury If there are no informers, the distribution shall be made as follows: 50% to the seizors and their helpers, 20% to the Reward Fund 30% to the Treasury. 2. Confiscated goods the owners of which are unable to pay the two	

TEXT

COMMENTARY

duties and are imprisoned in lieu thereof, or on which goods the two duties are not collected as a result of an order issued to that effect, and smuggled goods the smugglers of which have not been discovered, shall be sold and the Customs duties and subsidiary charges due and other expenses, if any, shall be deducted from the sale price, and the balance shall be distributed in the ratios quoted previously.

3. In the case of smuggled goods regarding which an order has been issued only to collect the duty payable thereon and to return such goods to the individual concerned, and also in the case of confiscated goods which cannot be sold at the price stipulated and which have to be destroyed or delivered to charitable institutions in accordance with the Regulations, gratuities shall be paid from the Treasury

TEXT | COMMENTARY

to the seizors and informers at the rate of 30% of the Customs duty payable.

icle 278. In the event of the seizure of smuggled gold or silver money or paper currency, in connection with which decisions have been issued prohibiting their import or export, such goods shall be confiscated only, and the rewards shall be distributed as follows:

1. 20% of the value of silver money and paper currency to the informers and seizors, to be divided among them equally,
   20% to the Reward Fund,
   60% to the Treasury.
2. Gold money
   a. 10% to the informers and seizors
      10% to the Reward Fund,
      80% to the Treasury.
   b. As regards Saudi gold money, in the event it is seized while being smuggled out of the country, a part thereof shall be divided equally among the informers and seizors:

TEXT | COMMENTARY

25% to the informers and seizors
10% to the Reward Fund,
65% to the Treasury.

Article 279. In the event of the seizure of narcotics such as hashish, opium, and the intoxicants mentioned in Article 50 of the Regulations, rewards shall be paid from the Treasury and divided equally among the informers and seizors:

1. For each kilogram of narcotics up to three kilograms SR 500
   For each kilogram in excess of three kilograms SR 300
2. Intoxicants of all kinds and different sizes:
   For each dozen up to three dozen SR 500
   For each dozen in excess of three dozen SR 300

These rewards shall be paid to the persons entitled to them regardless of whether the fines due have been collected from the smugglers or whether they have not been collected as a result of their inability to pay, their imprison-

TEXT

COMMENTARY

ment, etc.

ticle 280. With the exception of those items mentioned in the previous article, all materials and items which are forbidden according to Article 51 of the Customs Regulations, and which are included in Article 95 of the Rules for Implementation, shall, if seized while being smuggled, be destroyed and the gratuity shall be distributed out of the fine collected from the smuggler in the following manner:

30% of the amount to be divided equally among the informers and seizors,

20% to the Reward Fund,

50% to the Treasury.

In the event the amount of the fine cannot be collected from the smuggler because of his inability to pay and his imprisonment in lieu of the fine, or because of failure to locate him, or for any reason, the informers and seizors shall be paid 30% of the estimated value of the smuggled goods from the

TEXT | COMMENTARY

Treasury.

Article 281. Items the import of which is prohibited, such as intoxicants, playing card, etc., or items in regard to which orders were issued prohibiting their import, shall, if they are shown by name on the manifest of the means of transportation, or if they are accompanied by passengers who declare them in their statement to the Customs, be merely confiscated and destroyed. However, if they are not shown on the manifest, or if they are concealed by the passengers in their baggage and are not declared, they shall be confiscated and a fine equal to their value shall be collected from the shipping company or the passenger, respectively.

Discrepancies in the Description of Goods Shown on the Manifest

Article 282. Goods which are being cleared by their owners and which, upon inspection or examination, show differences in kind, quantity, measurements, weights, or strength,

TEXT | COMMENTARY

etc., that would result in the loss of a portion of the Customs or Government duties shall be dealt with in the following manner:

If there is a discrepancy in the description of the kind of goods, whether in part of in whole, a fine equal to the amount of the Customs duties that would have been lost as a result of such discrepancy shall be imposed.

If the weight, measurements, or quantity is in excess of that shown on the invoices, the fine shall be overlooked if the difference does not exceed 5%. But if the difference exceeds 5%, a fine equivalent to the amount of the duty which the Government would have lost as a result of the discrepancy in the description shall be collected.

The Director General of Customs or any person delegated by him in writing may lower the percentage of the fine to not less than one-quarter in the above cases of

TEXT | COMMENTARY

discrepancies in the description of goods.

However, if the differences or the the discrepancies in the description are such that Customs considers them to be tantamount to the offense of smuggling or attempted smuggling, the goods shall be subject to the Articles on smuggling and shall be confiscated.

The fines collected under this Article shall be distributed as follows:

60% of the fine to the official who discovered the error as a reward,

20% of the fine as a reward to the checkers of the statement and the checker of the invoices,

20% to the Reward Fund.

These fines shall be deposited in the Reward Fund at the Customs and shall be paid to the persons entitled to them once at the end of each month. A special record shall be kept for these fines in which the name of each official entitled

TEXT

COMMENTARY

to the fine shall be entered on a separate page together with the amounts of the fines payable to him. At the end of each month these fines are totaled and reported on a statement. They shall then be paid to the persons entitled to them after their signing the statement.

(Prohibition of Importation of Spiritous Liquors, Narcotics, and Contraband Goods, and Sealing of Ships' Stores Containing Intoxicants and Tobacco.)

ticle 283. All ships, aircraft, and other means of transportation which anchor or land at any Saudi port, are absolutely forbidden to have among their cargoes destined for Saudi ports, whether shown on the manifest or not, any alcoholic drinks, wines, or other kinds of intoxicating drinks, or narcotics, or contraband goods. The stores of all ships and other means of transportation arriving at Saudi ports shall be subject to the following

TEXT | COMMENTARY

measures:

1. The doors of the ships' stores containing alcoholic drinks and tobacco shall be sealed with lead, red wax, or the like during the time such ships are anchoring at Saudi ports, and this is to be done by representatives from Customs and the Coast Guard, if the ships are anchored at the pier. However, if the ships are anchored in the stream, the representative of the Coast Guard shall perform this task alone. In both cases, a report shall be prepared to that effect, to be cosigned by the captain of the ship.
2. Ships are permitted to be supplied with such quantities of tobacco as may be commensurate with the number of their crew and the period of their stay at the port.
3. While anchoring at Saudi ports, ships are not permitted to keep any quantity of alcoholic

TEXT | COMMENTARY

drinks outside their stores for purposes of consumption on board.

4. The master or first mate of the ship must receive the affixed seals from the representatives mentioned previously, and must not break them until after the ship has left the port.
5. For every Customs seal affixed to the stores and broken before the departure of the ship from the port, the master shall pay a fine of not less than SR 1000. This fine shall be collected from him in accordance with a decision issued by the Customs Director and transmitted to the shipping company to which he belongs. The shipping company may submit its objection to the Administrative Governor within five days. If it does not do so then the decision shall go into effect and the shipping company shall have to pay the fine immediately to the Customs Cash Office. Any master who

TEXT	COMMENTARY

repeats this offense shall have the fine doubled each time.

6. Any ship that arouses suspicion must be inspected by the Customs men and the Coast Guard and, in the event of the seizure of intoxicants therein, these shall be confiscated and destroyed, and the master shall pay a fine of SR 1,000. In the event of repetition the fine imposed on him shall be doubled.

   Warships may not be inspected, except by special permission from the higher authorities, in accordance with Article 9 of these Regulations.

7. Likewise, if intoxicants or tobacco are seized in the town, and the accused persons declare that they have obtained them from a ship anchoring at the port, the master of such ship, if proved guilty, shall pay a fine equivalent to the one imposed on the smuggler.

TEXT

Chapter XIX

Completion of Formalities and Withdrawal of Shipments

General Instructions on the Method of Completing Customs Formalities and Withdrawal of Shipments

icle 284. In order to complete the Customs formalities on imported shipments, the persons concerned must follow these steps in the order they are given:

I- The Manifest

The person concerned shall submit the certificate of formalities (Import Statement and Customs Declaration), duly filled in with the particulars required and signed by him, to the Manifest Office together with the delivery order, so that the particulars contained therein may be checked against the manifest. After it has made sure that these particulars are correct and that there are no restrictions preventing the delivery of the goods, the Manifest Office shall make a note to the effect that a preliminary check-up has been made.

COMMENTARY

CHAPTER XIX

CUSTOMS FORMALITIES

This section sets out in detail the procedures that must be followed in entering the goods, having them valued by customs, paying the customs duties, and withdrawing the goods. The details must be closely followed to avoid difficulties. Since, as previously discussed (See page 184), most customs duties have been reduced to 3% ad valorem in 1974, by Royal Decree M/44 (See p.187), determining value is one of the principal tasks of Saudi Customs officials. A schedule of duties on Saudi items that have not been reduced to 3% or been exempted can be found on page 193. It must be remembered that a copy of the original invoice, translated into Arabic, is required.. A representative sample of the shipment is generally inspected. Where the goods are identical this will usually be a 10% sample. The Valuation Division

TEXT

If there is a discrepancy, however, the person concerned shall be asked to have the Delivery Order corrected signed and stamped by the shipping company.

II- The Warehouseman

The person concerned shall submit to the warehouseman the certificate (Bill of Entry) and the Delivery Order, so that the warehouseman may note on the certificate, (Bill of Entry), in the space provided for that purpose, that the packages are in conformity with his records, and show the date of receipt, the condition of damaged packages, and packages without marks, and the quantity, marks, and numbers of the packages.

III- The Valuation Division

The person concerned shall submit the Certificate of Formalities (Bill of Entry and Customs Declaration) showing, in the spaces provided for statements by the merchant, the details and descriptions of all the items, and the value of each item, as well as the

COMMENTARY

of Customs determines the value of the goods by viewing a sample in connection with the entry documents. The rules do not devote much attention to classification. However, since, unlike the United States for example, most duties are now at one level (3% ad valorem), the question of classification is really only of importance when the goods that are above 3% ad valorem are involved. The tariff classifications and tariff numbers for all of the goods not exempt or 3% ad valorem are set out in the schedule that appears on page 193 et. seq.. Unlike the U.S. Tariff Schedules (19 U.S.C. 1202) that provide detailed headnotes aiding in interpretation, classification, and valuation, the Saudi Customs Schedules provide little guidance for interpretation. They do, however, contain certain footnoted references to particular decrees dealing with certain types of goods. Each chapter also contains some headnotes dealing with the scope and contents of the chapter.

Value is defined in the General Provisions

TEXT

Delivery Order, the original invoice, along with a true copy thereof translated into Arabic and signed by him, all the other documents authenticating the values, the freight and insurance documents, and the packing list to the Valuation Division, which shall perform the following:

a. Make a preliminary check of all the documents to ascertain that marks, numbers, and quantities of packages are the same on all documents, and that the relevant documents are duly filled in. The number of attachments shall be entered on the Certificate(Bill of Entry).

b. Stamp the Certificate(Bill of Entry), as well as all the attachments thereto, with the number and date stamp, and enter them in a special book.

c. The documents shall be referred to the employee concerned in the Valuation Division who shall review the documents

COMMENTARY

for the Customs Tariff No. 1191(6/4/1393H) which is set out in its entirety herein on page 189. The definition of value is the actual price paid or agreed to be paid for the imported goods at the port of origin, plus freight and transport and additional expenses, which include commissions and bookeeping expenses.

Saudi value is a C.I.F. value, including shipping and transportation costs, compared the U.S. which uses an F.O.B. value based on export value. For example, the usual U.S. custom value is the price at the time of exportation to the U.S., at which such or similar goods are freely sold in the principal markets of the country of exportation, in usual wholesale quantities in the ordinary course of trade for exportation to the U.S.. Added to this is the cost of packaging, when not included in the price (see 19 U.S.C. Section 1401a). When export value cannot be ascertained, U.S. Customs utilizes the United States value. This is the price which similar goods are sold or offered for sale in the United States for domestic

TEXT

and the notations made on them by the warehouseman, and examine the invoice. If the goods are of one category and have a uniform price, he will make a notation for selecting packages for inspection or investigation, equivalent to 10% of the shipment, or less for large shipments. He shall carry out this after the Tariff and Valuation Controller, or his representative, has given his approval. If the invoice shows different kinds of goods, he shall, when making a notation for inspection or investigation, select packages from the different kinds so that the entire shipment may be represented. He shall also make a notation for inspecting all the damaged packages.

If the particulars of the invoices are so incomplete that particulars for every package cannot be checked separately,

COMMENTARY

consumption, packed for delivery, in the usual wholesale quantities, and in the ordinary course of trade, less commission, transportation, insurance and customs duties (id.). The U.S. also provides for a constructed value and special "American selling price" values in certain circumstances.

Where there is a dispute over classification or values, the general provisions of the Customs Tariff provide for an appeal to a committee established by the Minister of Finance and National Economy. Interestingly the provisions refer to a "Proces verbal" report of the dispute to be drawn up by the Customs official to be referred to the Minister of Finance and National Economy. This is a document known in French law which consists of the report of a public officer, of events which occurred and verbal statements which were made in his presence, and of his own actions. This would appear to preclude the importer himself from submitting a formal statement of his own, stating the grounds for his disagreement, as is done in the U.S. by

TEXT

he shall make a notation for inspecting the entire shipment. In all cases, the numbers of the packages that are to be inspected or investigated must be shown both in figures and words. If the packages bear marks without numbers, the number of packages for selective inspection by the Pier Division must be shown.

d. The Certificate (Bill of Entry and Customs Declaration) shall be returned to the person concerned, and the remaining documents shall be retained by the Valuation Division for checking. Then the person concerned shall take the Certificate (Bill of Entry) to the Customs Director who will assign the examiner who will inspect his consignment.

IV- <u>Procedures for Inventory</u>

The Examiner shall put his name and the number of the Certificate (Bill of Entry) on the packages that are to be inspected and are

COMMENTARY

filing an official "protest" (See 19 C.F.R. Section 174.11 et. seq.). The review committee is empowered to release the merchandise under bond, while the matter is under consideration.

TEXT

COMMENTARY

brought to the inspection hall. He shall ask the Opener to open these packages in his presence, but the person concerned shall have the right to bring an opener of his own choice if the shipments are such that they will require special care in opening them. However, if the items that are to be opened are of a dangerous nature, such as explosives, they shall be opened by workers to be brought by the person concerned and under his responsibility. The person concerned, or his employee, shall sort out the contents of the packages that are to be inspected or investigated (inspection means taking an inventory of all the contents of the packages and showing their kinds, quantities, and measurements or weights, while investigation means ascertaining the kind only, without need for counting or weighing), separate them over the counter provided for inspection, then return them into the packages after

TEXT | COMMENTARY

the inspection operation has been completed. The Examiner shall fill out a special form in which he shall enter all the contents of the packages he has inspected or investigated, showing:

a. The mark on the box
b. Its number
c. Description of the contents (kind of goods)
d. Quantity or weight of goods.
e. Measurements: length, width, and thickness
f. Description of the goods according to their nature, such as the horsepower of an engine, or the number of a motor. In the case of cars mention shall be made of whether or not they are equipeed with a radio or an air-conditioner, the model of the car, its tonnage, or the number of passengers. In the case of refrigerators, mention shall be made of the volume.

In general, the names of the

TEXT | COMMENTARY

goods shall be entered, although they may be subject to the same duty, but come under different names, and the total amounts shall be shown both in figures and words. The Examiner shall attach the form, after he as signed it, to the Certificate of Formalities (Bill of Entry), leaving a carbon copy thereof in his book.

The Examiner himself shall sort out the samples representing the shipment, and shall affix the number of the Certificate (Bill of Entry), his signature, and the date on the samples themselves. Such samples shall be entered in a special book at the warehouse or the inspection hall, and sent by the person concerned, to the Valuation Division, along with the Certificate of Formalities (Bill of Entry), after the inventory form has been approved by the pier master, or the person acting on his behalf, who shall have the right to repeat the inspection or in-

TEXT

COMMENTARY

vestigation of the shipment.

If the goods are such that a sample thereof cannot be forwarded, the Valuator shall examine them and estimate their value on location. While the merchant or broker is held up by the inspection operation, the Valuation Division shall check the invoices as to conformity of the copies of the invoices with the originals, check the calculations in the invoices, additions, deductions or additions, and conversions or foreign currencies into Saudi currency according to the last average exchange rate published by the Saudi Arabian Monetary Agency.

V- Procedures for Valuation

a. The person concerned shall take the sample, the Certificate of Formalities (Bill of Entry), and the inventory form to the Valuation Division for inspection of the sample, verification against the Examiner's statement, and estimation of

TEXT | COMMENTARY

the value.

If samples are sent for analysis or other purposes, the following shall be observed:

1. The samples shall be well wrapped and sealed with red wax or lead.
2. Eau de Cologne and liquid substances shall be placed in cartons to be covered by cloth, and then the covers shall be sealed with red wax or lead.

Samples may not be sent with the person concerned, but shall be sent by virtue of an official memorandum showing the marks and origin of the samples and routed through the official delivery log book.

b. The sample shall be returned to the person concerned after valuation, so that it may be returned to the warehouse and checked out in the book of samples. At the same time, the Certificate of Formalities

TEXT	COMMENTARY
(Bill of Entry) and the inventory form shall be forwarded, after valuation, to the Valuation Division so that they may be attached to their relative invoices and documents.	
c. The Valuation Division shall check the result of the inspection against the information in the invoices or packing lists, and shall make a notation on the invoices or their copies to the effect that the checking did take place. It shall also insert excesses, whether in weights, quantities, or measurements, on the merchant's statements, in the space provided for the Customs remarks on the Bills of Entry and Customs Declaration so as to provide a basis for the collection of Customs duties. All the papers shall then be forwarded to the Valuator concerned to decide whether the values of invoices are to be accepted as correct.	

TEXT

COMMENTARY

If the Valuator has good reasons for not being satisfied, he may deterime the value on the basis of the nearest equivalent value ascertainable. A written acceptance of that value shall be obtained from the person concerned, or his representative, on the Certificate.

d. The papers shall be returned to the Valuation Division for assessing duties on the Bill of Entry and the Customs Declaration, on the basis of the result of the valuation.

e. The Clearance shall be written down on the basis of the particulars recorded on the Bill of Entry. It shall be detached and attached to the papers, and all the foregoing formalities shall be approved by the Customs Director.

VI- Procedures for Paying the Duties to the Cashier

The person concerned shall go to the Cashier to pay the duties due

TEXT

COMMENTARY

and so that the Cashier may sign the Clearance and the Bills of Entry after issuing a payment receipt showing the total sum of the duties and giving the merchant a copy of the Bill of Entry showing all the particulars. The Cashier shall also give the person concerned the Clearance and the Delivery Order.

The remaining copies of the clearance shall be filed as follows:

1. The first copy with its attachments shall be sent to the Auditing Division at the Directorate General of Customs.
2. The second copy shall remain with the Accounting Division of the Customhouse concerned.

Distribution for all the preceding operations shall take place on the day following the payment of the duties.

VII- <u>Procedures for Withdrawals from Warehouses</u>

a. The person concerned shall present the Clearance and the Delivery Order to the Warehouse-

TEXT | COMMENTARY

man in order to receive his shipment.

b. The Warehouseman shall ask the Porter to take the shipment outside the warehouse gates, and shall give the person concerned a card for each carload or truckload showing the number of packages, the marks and numbers, the name of the driver, and the number of the car or truck.

c. The Warehouseman shall close those entries in the Receipts Book which represent the portion issued, and shall return the Clearance and the card to the person concerned.

d. The person concerned shall receive his goods and proceed to the Customs gate for clearance. He shall present the Clearance and the card to the Gateman for completion of the clearance formalities.

e. The marks, numbers, and number of packages shall be checked against the particulars written

TEXT | COMMENTARY

on the Clearance and the card. The Gateman shall verify some of the packages and make the notations required for clearance.

One of the functions of the Gateman is to make sure, at the time of clearance, that no storage charges are due on the goods, as follows:

1. There shall be written on all Customs Clearances the date on which unloading was completed and following which the ten-day period of grace, including Fridays, is to be reckoned. After reckoning this period, the goods shall be subject to a storage charge; and if the ten-day period ends on a holiday, the holiday period shall be added to the period of grace.
2. If a merchant completes the clearance formalities on his goods and obtains a Clearance before the expiry of the ten-

TEXT | COMMENTARY

day period of grace, he shall be entitled to the balance of the period of grace prescribed by the Regulations.

3. If a merchant completes the clearance formalities on his goods after the period of grace has expired and a storage charge becomes due on his shipment, and if the date on which the Clearance was written is the same as that on which the shipment was withdrawn from the Customs Area, then the Valuation Division would have determined whether storage charges were due and would have collected them along with its duties. In this instance the Gateman shall order the clearance of the shipment.

4. If the date of withdrawal of the shipment falls after the date of the Customs Clearance, then the Gateman shall make sure that the goods were not subject to storage charges

TEXT

COMMENTARY

and were cleared during the period of grace, in which case they come under the provision of Paragraph 2; or, if they were subject to storage charges and the Valuation Division had collected storage charges up to the date on which the Clearance was written but the merchant delayed the withdrawal of his shipment until the following day, the Gateman shall ask the person concerned to go to the Valuation Division to pay the storage charges due, so that the Valuation Division may make a notation on the Clearance to the effect that the charges have been collected up to the date of withdrawal.

5. In the case of shipments that are withdrawn over several days, it must be ascertained whether every partial withdrawal occurs within the

TEXT | COMMENTARY

period of grace, or the storage charges due thereon have been collected by the Valuation Division, or a storage charge has become due thereon after the Clearance has been written. In this last instance, parts of the shipment shall not be cleared before the storage charges due thereon have been paid.

VIII- The Warehouseman shall secure the signature of the merchant, or that of his representative, on the copy of the card to indicate that he has received that portion of his shipment.

IX- The merchant shall be allowed to have his goods cleared through the Customs gates. Cards shall be entered in a special log at the gate.

The Gateman shall stamp the cards with a "Cleared" stamp and deduct the quantity cleared on the reverse side of the Clearance. He shall

TEXT

also enter the serial number of the card against which the goods are cleared, and shall return the Clearance to the person concerned so that he may receive the balance of the shipment. However, if the entire shipment is cleared against a single card, both the card and the Clearance shall be stamped and retained at the gate, and the signature of the merchant, or that of his representative, shall be secured on the card or the Clearance to indicate clearance through the gate.

X- The Pier Officer shall collect all Clearances and Delivery Orders after he has verified them against the records at the Gates and made sure that they are in order. He shall then forward them to the local Customs Director who must arrange to send them to the Directorate of Customs and from there to the Directorate General of Customs.

COMMENTARY

TEXT | COMMENTARY

Chapter XX

The Connection of Customs with the Directorate of Coast Guard

Supervision within the Customs Area

The Coast Guard shall be charged with the supervision from the sea of ships and boats anchored at the piers in the Custom ports. On land, and on the piers as well, the Customs guards shall be the ones who shall carry out the supervision.

Only authorized Customs guards shall undertake to guard, supervise, perform inspection work, and effect seizures in the Customs Area, which includes the piers and warehouses, and all the building therein. In cases of necessity, assistance shall be sought from the Coast Guardsmen or policemen.

Unloading

Ships or boats anchored in the stream or at the pier may not unload their cargo before obtaining permission from the Customs. The piers on which they unload their cargo shall be assigned by Customs.

Inspection

The Coast Guard alone shall have the right to inspect ships anchored in the stream without obtaining permission from the Customs. They

TEXT

COMMENTARY

may also perform such inspection in compliance with a request from Customs if the Customs receives information about the ship. However, if it is required that ships anchored at piers in Customs areas be inspected the approval of the Customs must be obtained and the inspection must be attended by a senior Customs official. Likewise, if Customs desires to inspect a ship anchored at the piers, it shall seek the assistance of the Coast Guard experts who will supply information about hiding places and passageways on the ship.

Outside the Customs Area

The Coast Guard shall be charged with the supervision of the Customs Line and the district lying under Customs control and situated beyond the Customs Area wherein the Customs offices are located. They shall prepare seizure reports concerning smuggled and prohibited goods, arms, and narcotics, and forward them to the nearest Customs Area which shall consider the cases of smuggling and refer the accused to the Customs committees. The Coast Guard may not interfere within the Customs area unless they are in possession of special information. In such cases they shall submit their information secretly to the

TEXT | COMMENTARY

Customs director who will make the necessary arrangements for the seizure.

Travel Order and Export Manifest

The Directorate of Coast Guard and Ports shall not permit the departure of ships and sailboats unless they are in possession of a travel order from the Customs and an export manifest.

Ships Operating in Saudi Waters

The Department of Coast Guard shall notify Customs of any ships that arrive from abroad and operate in territorial waters, and likewise of any ships which remain for over a year, in order that import duties may be collected on them.

Ships Stores

Before Customs authorizes supplying ships with provisions, the shipping companies shall be required to specify, by means of statements approved by the Directorate of Coast Guard or the Passports Department, the number of crew and passengers carried, the first foreign or Saudi port at which the ship will anchor, and the period of travel required to reach that port.

Jetsam: Sunken goods, Flotsam and Goods Cast up on the Coasts, Discovered by the Coast

TEXT

COMMENTARY

uard or Salvaged from the Bottom of the Sea

report on such goods shall be prepared by he Coast Guard and the goods shall be forarded, with the report, to the nearest ustoms which will carry out the provisions f the relevant Regulations.

eddlers

he Coast Guard shall not permit peddlers o board ships unless they are in possession f a license from the Customs Administration. hey shall direct these peddlers to the ustoms in order that Customs duties be colected on anything they buy from the ships.

Chapter XXI

nstruction for the Dammam Port Customs

. The Customs Area

n the Dammam Port Customs, the Customs Area ncludes the causeway, the port, and the adoining region extending from the coastline o the Customs yard, including the railway arshalling yard.

. Customs Working Hours at the Piers

uring the preliminary stage of operations nd until the Railroad acquires cars, trains nd passenger cars in sufficient number, ustoms supervision shall be conducted in two hifts. The first shift starts at 5:00 a.m.

TEXT | COMMENTARY

and ends at 5:00 p.m., the second shift starts at 5:00 p.m. and ends at 5:00 a.m. the next day. Later it is expected that work will be performed in three shifts following an agreement among the Customs, the Railroad, and the Coast Guard.

Working Hours at Inland Customs

Customs formalities for goods subject to duties, whether the goods belong to merchants or companies, shall take place during daytime, between 8:00 a.m. and 4:00 p.m.

3. Transportation of Employees

The Railroad shall transport all employees of the Dammam Port Customs from Dammam to the Customs offices and to both piers, and shall carry them back to Dammam after working hours. Customs employees are entitled to ride in passenger trains, within the Customs Area, to go over the two piers. They shall not have the right to ask for special trains for their transportation.

4. The Manifest

1. Representatives of shipping companies shall submit manifests of ships to the Customs Administration, on behalf of the shipping companies, in the following manner:

TEXT | COMMENTARY

A. The original manifest with two Arabic copies thereof.

B. An extract of the original manifest showing transit goods.

C. An extract of the original manifest showing goods that are of a dangerous nature.

D. In the case of goods that are to be unloaded from the ship into barges to be taken to Ras Tanura, Ras al-Mish'ab, al-Khobar, or any other port in the Kingdom, shipping agents shall make out the appropriate form in three copies. One copy shall remain with the Damman peirmaster and two copies shall be sent to the Customs at the point of entry, after they have been stamped and signed by the piermaster, for the purpose of verification and so that one copy may be returned bearing the result of the verification and the remarks.

2. Aramco must submit the following:

A. An extract of the original manifest showing dutiable goods for Aramco.

B. An extract of the original manifest

TEXT | COMMENTARY

showing Aramco goods exempt from duties.

3. Goods other than the above, whether for the Government or merchants, shall remain in cars or be stored away until the Customs formalities are completed thereon. However, cars loaded with such goods shall be taken to the marshalling yard.

5. Unloading of Ships

Ships shall be permitted to unload their cargoes directly into railroad cars, under Customs surveillance, after the manifests referred to in the foregoing section have been submitted.

The Customs Administration may authorize ships to unload their cargoes prior to the submission of the manifest, provided the shipping companies undertake to submit the manifests before the departure of the railroad cars from the Customs Area, early enough to enable the Customs to perform the necessary verifications.

6. Delivery Receipt

The unloading of the ships shall be performed under the surveillance of the Customs in the presence of a representative from the shipping company and a representative from the Rail-

TEXT

COMMENTARY

road. The latter shall prepare a statement to show the cargo and number of each car. A copy of this statement shall be given to the shipping company representative as a receipt from the Railroad for the goods delivered. The Customs representative at the pier shall be given another two copies for the purpose of checking the cars against them and to enter them in a special register. He shall make a notation on one of them to show that the checking work has been done, then deliver it to the train conductor who will submit it to the Customs officer at the Customs yard.

The Customs representative at the pier shall deduct the number of packages from the original quantity and show this number on the reverse of the extract or copy of the manifest, so that when the whole number of packages has been unloaded he shall send it to the Customs, together with the statements previously attached thereto, for the purpose of verification. The shipping company shall appoint one of its employees to participate with the Railroad in the delivery of the goods to Customs and to check them against the manifest.

TEXT | COMMENTARY

7. Shortages

In accordance with the Customs Regulations, the shipping companies shall be held responsible for any shortage in shipments when they are unloaded from the ship into the railroad cars.

However, the responsibility for any shortage that may be discovered in the goods after they have been shipped on railroad cars and until they arrive at Customs shall fall on the Railroad.

8. Overages

In the event of the existence of goods not shown in the manifest or in excess of the quantity shown in the manifest, they shall be considered as being off the manifest and shall be delivered to Customs which shall apply the Customs Regulations thereto.

9. Defective Goods

Packages which, upon being unloaded, appear to be defective or damaged, must be so described in the Railroad statement. This statement shall be signed by the shipping company representative who shall also take the necessary measures for repairing them and protecting the contents until they are received by the Customs from the Railroad representa-

TEXT

COMMENTARY

tive in accordance with a report showing their weight or their quantity.

10. Loading

Goods may not be loaded on ships before the Customs formalities have been completed and and export clearance has been given on them. The Customs employee at the pier shall verify the exported goods against the clearance given for them. In order to avoid delaying ships at the piers, when all of the goods in a hold have been unloaded from the ship, goods may be loaded into that hold, and there is no objection to performing the operations of both loading and unloading at the same time on this basis, provided this does not delay or hinder in the least the operation of unloading. Goods may be loaded into a hold containing other cargo destined to another port, with the agreement of Customs.

If the loading operation is to be performed outside the working hours fixed by the Law, a written notification must be submitted to Customs to this effect.

11. The Warehouses

Warehouses for storing goods on which Customs duties have not been fully paid may be built within the Customs Area subject to the terms

TEXT | COMMENTARY

and conditions to be determined by the Minister of Finance. The application shall be submitted, together with the plan, to the Customs director in Dammam who will study it with the Railroad and refer it to the Ministry with his suggestions.

It is understood that any land reserved at the present time for exclusive use in the Aramco enterprise, and located within proximity of the present Customs installations in Dammam Port within an area the radius of which if five kilometers from the base of the causeway, which may be needed by the Government for expanding the installations of the Dammam Port, the Customs, or the Railroad, shall be placed at the disposal of the Government whenever such need arises, provided such expansion does not interfere with any Aramco installations or facilities then existing. If further additions are required in the future, the Government and Aramco shall come to an agreement concerning this matter.

12. <u>Customs Formalities</u>

In general, certificates of formalities, (Bills of Entry) like those in use in the Directorate of al-Hasa Customs, shall be

TEXT

COMMENTARY

submitted with the delivery order, for all imported goods, whether dutiable or exempt from duties. They must show the number, marks, and numbers of the packages; the kind, weight, and value of the goods; and they must be accompanied by the original invoices and a single copy of each.

If copies of invoices are not submitted, the original invoices shall be retained by the Customs with the certificate of formalities (Bill of Entry).

Due to the large imports by Aramco of goods exempt from duties, the following shall constitute an exception to the general rule referred to previously:

This Company shall submit invoices for such packages as may be designated by the Customs director.

It is understood that the Customs may, at any time it deems fit, examine all the invoices pertaining to exempted goods.

13. Formalities on Goods Exempt from Duties

These goods shall be divided into two classes:

A. Those exempted from duties and all additional charges:

B. Those exempted from duties but subject to the additional charges.

TEXT

COMMENTARY

In the case of the goods mentioned in A, the consignee or his agent must submit to Customs at Dammam Port the certificates of formalities (Bills of Entry) together with all other documents, including the delivery order, in order to obtain the clearance. Then the clearance papers shall be delivered to the Customs employee at the pier. The Customs employee at the pier shall verify the goods shipped on railroad cars and deduct them on the back of the clearance. If the whole consignment is shipped on railroad cars, he shall attach the clearance to the Railroad statement and deliver it to the train conductor who shall deliver it to the Customs Officer at the Customs yard when the train arrives there. The Customs officer at the pier shall stamp the statement and the clearance with a special stamp: "Exempt from duties". If the goods shipped on railroad cars do not constitute the whole consignment, he shall retain the clearance and, in this instance, he shall only stamp the Railroad statement and deliver it to the

TEXT

COMMENTARY

conductor who shall forward it to the Customs office. He shall attache the clearance to the statement only when the whole consignment shown thereon has been shipped to the Customs yard. Goods shown under B, in accordance with the Customs Regulations, shall be subject to the formalities mentioned in A. Furthermore, if the original invoices are not submitted, and the Customs is not satisfied with the documents presented, Customs may order that such goods be brought to the Customs yard for completion of the Customs formalities.

14. Goods Subject to Customs Duties

After these goods have been shipped on railroad cars, they shall all be sent to the Customs yard. When they arrive at the Customs yard, they shall remain on the cars for a period not exceeding six hours, during which time the owners of the goods or their agents shall be given an opportunity to complete the Customs formalities. During this time it shall be sufficient to take the packages that are to be examined and weighed to the Inspection Hall.

TEXT | COMMENTARY

In the case of the other items contained in packages or boxes, only the number of packages or cases selcted for inspection shall be taken to the Inspection Hall for completion of the Customs formalities. If the owners of the goods or their agents fail to complete the Customs formalities during the six-hour period referred to above, the goods shall be taken to the Customs warehouses and the railroad cars shall be relieved of their cargo.

If the goods belong to Aramco and it wishes to have them stored in its private warehouses within the Customs Area, it shall be permitted to do so, provided that the doors to its warehouses are all locked with two locks the key to one of which shall be in the hands of Customs, and that the goods in storage be subject to Customs control. Until the time such warehouses are erected in accordance with the terms and conditions to be approved by the Ministry of Finance, Aramco's goods shall be subject to the same formalities required on dutiable commercial goods. It is understood that Aramco workmen shall be permitted to perform their duties within the Company's storehouses during the official working hours.

TEXT

COMMENTARY

15. Porters

The Railroad shall assign from ten to twenty workmen, according to need, for internal Customs operations such as stowing the goods in the warehouses, transporting them to the Inspection Hall, opening them and returning them to the warehouses, and the Railroad shall undertake to pay their wages. The Customs director shall notify the Railroad in the event any of the porters is absent or leaves without permission, and the Customs may inflict penalties on these porters and notify the Railroad of such action.

In addition to the foregoing, the Railroad shall provide the porters necessary to unload the cargoes of the railroad cars in the Customs Areas and carry them to the warehouses and reload them after the Customs formalities have been completed thereon.

Porters and Railroad workmen operating within the Customs Area shall be subject to the instructions issued by the Director of the Dammam Port Customs in the interests of the operations.

16. Porterage Charges

These shall be collected in the manner and at the rates set forth by the Railroad and ap-

TEXT

COMMENTARY

proved by the Ministry of Finance. The Railroad shall provide the Customs Administration with the equipment which the Railroad and the Customs consider necessary for the transportation and protection of the goods. It is expected that the equipment required shall consist of fork lifts, carts, protecting tarpaulins, etc.

The Railroad shall show, on the back of the Delivery Order, the amount of the porterage charges to be collected, and the Customs shall collect them on behalf of the Railroad.

17. Wharfage Charges

These shall be collected by the Railroad in the manner and at the rates to be determined by the Railroad and approved by the Ministry of Finance.

18. Shift Workers

Inasmuch as the working hours fixed by law are eight hours, and because the working conditions in the Dammam Port Customs require that employees work day and night, and that some employees must carry on their work for 12 hours per shift, such employees shall rereceive remuneration for the four hours during which they have worked in excess of the hours

TEXT

COMMENTARY

officially set for them.

In order to avoid burdening the State Treasury with remunerations due to such employees as a result of performing work for the benefit of companies and individuals, it has become necessary to collect shift charges from all individuals, companies, and shipping companies which request Customs to perform duties for them outside the regular working hours.

The Customs Administration shall specify the rates to be applied for shift charges subject to the approval of the Ministry of Finance.

19. Movement of Railroad Cars

Trains shall leave the Customs zone only after Customs has completed its formalities and authorized their departure from the Customs zone.

20. Guards

The Directorate of Customs for the Eastern Province shall provide the necessary guards for the Customs zone.

CHAPTER XXII

Agreements with Certain Companies and Organizations

1. Customs Formalities for Petroleum Companies in the Eastern Parts of Saudi Arabia

"In return for the obligations assumed by the Company under this contract, and for the payments required from the Company hereunder, the Company and enterprise shall be exempt from all direct and indirect taxes, imposts, charges, fees and duties (including, of course, import and export duties), it being understood that this privilege shall not extend to the sale of products within the country, nor shall it extend to the personal requirements of the individual employees of the Company. Any materials imported free of duty may not be sold within the country without first paying the corresponding import duty."

2. Customs Formalities for the Former Pacific Western (Oil) Corporation, Now Getty [Oil] Company

Article 49 of Decree No. 14/1/49/3156, dated 22 Rabi' II 1368 [20 February 1949] provides for the following:

"Neither the Company nor any property imported into, used or held for use in said Neutral Zone or in Saudi Arabia in connection with, or incidental to operations by the Company hereunder or produced, sold or exported as a part of or as a result of such operations shall be subject to any taxes or charges whatsoever by or on behalf of the Government; and the Company and all activities carried on incidental to developing and exploiting said concession and drilling for, producing, refining, processing, transporting, selling and exporting oil and other petroleum and gas products and by-products in connection therewith and importing materials, equipment and supplies for use incidental thereto, or for use or incidental to the exercise of rights granted to the Company hereunder or the performance by the

Company of its obligations hereunder, and all of the aforesaid property of the Company shall be free from all taxes, imposts, duties, excises, tariffs, restrictions on import or export or charges of any kind; provided, however, that the Government may impose, with respect to the ownership or operation by the Company, within said Neutral Zone or Saudi Arabia, of automotive, aeronautical or marine equipment, fees, at the same rates charged within Saudi Arabia in respect of the ownership and operation of such equipment by others, for the annual registration or licensing of such equipment; and provided further, that such freedom from taxation shall not pertain to the personal property of employees of the Company or to what is sold for their personal requirements, but that neither such employees nor their property nor property so sold or such sale thereof shall be taxed at any different rates than are applied in the Neutral Zone and Saudi Arabia in respect of others or their property or such sales; provided further that, insofar as the Company may operate or have facilities outside the said Neutral Zone, it shall be subject to municipal taxes in those municipalities in which such operatons are conducted or in which such facilities are located of the same nature and at the same rates as all other persons or corporations conducting operations or having facilities in such municipalities; and provided further, that any materials or property imported free of duty may not be sold within either said Neutral Zone or Saudi Arabia without first paying the import duty which would be payable in respect thereof if imported for such sale."

3. Customs Formalities for the Trans-Arabian Pipe Line Company

(The Trans-Arabian Pipe Line Agreement)

Articles four [and five] of Decree No. 4589, dated 2 Muharram 1369 [24 October 1949], provides for the following:

"No import tax, export tax, transit tax, transfer tax or financial charge of any sort shall be levied on petroleum, naphtha, ozokerite, natural gases, whether in a crude state or any form of derivatives thereof, whether intended for a consignment in transit or utilized for the industrial operation of the undertaking.

"If the said products, crude or refined, are marketed locally for consumption in Saudi Arabia, with the consent of the Government, or if they are utilized for requirements other than those of the undertaking they will be subjected to the same duties and fiscal charges as are leviable on similar products in Saudi Arabia.

"The conditions of the sale of such products in the local market will form the subject of an arrangement between the Government and the Company.

"The Company shall be entitled to import into Saudi Arabia free of Customs duties, Municipal dues, or other dues (which duties, Municipal dues, or other dues (which duties and/or dues are hereinafter collectively referred to as "import dues") all equipment, materials and other things which may be necessary for the works of the undertaking and for its transportation purposes, including all equipment for offices, houses, hospitals or other buildings, which will be the property of the Company and used for its operations (all which equipment, materials and other things are hereinafter collectively referred to as "materials").

"Materials imported free of import dues if they should be sold by the Company for use in Saudi Arabia shall be liable to the import dues leviable at the time of such sale on similar materials, and such dues shall be paid by the Company.

"The Company shall be entitled to re-export free of dues materials free of import dues.

"In view of the exceptional nature of the undertaking, the Government will cause special facilities to be granted to the Company, if necessary, for the import of materials at points convenient to the Company, and will permit the import and export of materials at all times, whether by day or by night, and on public holidays. The Company for its part undertakes to erect and maintain any special buildings that may be necessary for this purpose and to pay the additional fees of Customs officials prescribed by regulations.

"All things and materials imported or exported by the Company's employees for their personal use, or imported by the Company for sale to its employees, shall be liable to the import dues in force.

"No refund of the duties paid on materials purchased locally by the Company will be made."

4. Text of Article 8 of the Agreement Concluded between the Saudi Arab Government and the Japan Petroleum Trading Company Ltd., pertaining to exemption:

"The Government grants the Company total exoneration from import duties on materials, machinery, utensils and other property which the Company may need to bring into the country, having direct and immediate relation to its work of exploration, exploitation, manufacture, refining and transport, or to the works it is under obligation to undertake and maintain for their operations or for the protection of workmen and of installations; it being understood that this privilege shall not extend to the personal requirements of individual employees of the Company. Furthermore, should the Company intend to sell or transfer within Saudi Arabia any materials imported free of duty, the Company shall before such sale or transfer make a declaration thereof to the Customs Department and shall, unless such materials are sold or transferred to another concessionaire entitled to the same exemptions, pay on demand such import duty as may be assessed by the Director General of Customs in accordance with the then prevailing Customs law."

5. Dhahran Airport Agreement

This is the text of Articles 9 and 10 of the Air Base at Dharan Agreement which [Articles] pertain to Customs and which were issued in letter No. 1/2/8/646, dated 13 Ramadan 1370 [18 June 1951], of HH the Minister of Foreign Affairs. The Agreement shall be valid for a period of five years from 13 Ramadan 1370 (18 June 1951) as provided therein.

Article 9" (a) The Saudi Arabian Government will accord exemption from Customs duties, taxes and all Government charges on materials, equipment and supplies necessary for the construction, maintenance, supply and operaton of the Airfield, provided that the Mission will submit to the appropriate authorities of the Saudi Arabian Government the official bills of lading and manifests on the material, equipment and supplies imported for the operation and maintenance of Dharan Airfield.

"(b) - The Saudi Arabian Government accords the military personnel of the Mission personal exemption from Customs duties and Government charges for themselves or their personal effects which may be brought in for their personal use provided that such effects will be subject to submission of official bills of lading and manifests and provided that quantities of such effects will be within reasonable limits and that no such articles will be sold unless the appropriate authorities of the Saudi Arabian Government are informed in order that the applicable taxes may be collected. Civilians of United States nationality who are attached to the Mission will also be accorded exemption from Customs duties, taxes and Government charges for themselves or on their personal effects which may be brought in for their personal use provided that such effects will be within reasonable limits and that no such articles will be sold unless the appropriate authorities of the Saudi Arabian Government are informed in order that the applicable taxes may be collected.

"(c) - It is understood that the Mission will inform the appropriate authorities of the Saudi Arabian Government of anything the Mission may intend to sell in order that the applicable taxes may be collected.

"(d) - Subject to the provisions of paragraph 6 (b), the Mission may withdraw from Saudi Arabia any of those items which have been brought in after notifying the Saudi Arabian Government; if the United States has no special interest in using such items in some other place outside Saudi Arabia, these items will be offered for sale to the Saudi Arabian Government at a fair price. In case the Saudi Arabian Government does not wish to buy these items they may then be exported free of any export charges."

"Article 10 - The Mission is permitted to receive its military mail and to send it to and from Dhahran Airfield exempt from Customs duties provided that parcel post will be in accordance with the terms of paragraph 9 (a)."

6. Exemptions of the World Health Organization

[This is] in accordance with the General Agreement concluded between the Saudi Arab Government and the World Health Organization for providing technical assistance.

4- Exemptions

a. Exemption of international members from taxes and Customs duties, and anything connected therewith, such as quarantine, etc.

b. Exemption from Customs duties, additional charges, etc. of the furniture and materials brought by the group.

7. Customs Instructions for the Railroad in the New Dammam Port:

1. The unloading of ships shall be in accordance with the regulations in force at the Port.

2. The Railroad Department shall not permit the unloading of any shipment arriving by sea except after presentation of the original manifest of the shipment with four Arabic and four foreign language copies. The Railroad Department shall compare the copies of the manifest with the original, and delivery and receipt shall be effected in the presence of the representative of shipping company concerned.

The Railroad Department may permit ships that have local agencies to unload their cargo prior to the presentation of the manifest, and the Railroad shall receive the cargo pending the presentation of the manifest within 36 hours at most.

3. The Railroad Department shall send to the Dammam Port Customs a number of copies of the manifest agreed upon by Customs and the Railroad.

4. The Railroad Department shall notify Customs of the dates of arrival of ships, dhows, and sailboats, and the dates when they finish unloading, due to the importance of these dates in calculating storage charges which may become due on the goods after they have been loaded on railroad cars.

5. According to these new Regulations, the Railroad shall be considered responsible for unloading goods and issuing the necessary receipt therefor to the shipping companies. It shall also be responsible for transporting these goods under guard and storing them in the Customs Area until their owners receive them after Customs formalities have been completed thereon.

6. After the goods have been unloaded, the Railroad shall forward to Customs a copy of the manifest showing receipt of the goods, or a detailed memorandum showing the following:

a. Total number of parcels in the manifest;

b. Number of missing parcels;

c. Number of excess parcels;

d. Total actually received;

e. Marks and numbers of the missing parcels;

f. Marks and numbers of the excess parcels.

The copy of the manifest or the foregoing statement must be approved by the representative of the shipping company concerned and by the Railroad representative in the Port.

In view of the fact that the preparation of the statements required in 5 and 6 of this Article may take some time, the Railroad shall advise that they be sent within a maximum period of one week after the departure of the ship.

7, The Railroad shall take into consideration the condition of goods of the same category such as cement, flour, timber and pipes, etc., and shall load them on separate cars, whenever this is possible, in order to facilitate their inspection, completion of formalities thereon, and their prompt clearance.

8. It is advisable to load Aramco goods which are shown by appropriate marks to be exempt from duties in separate cars, whenever this is possible, and not to mix them with other goods, so that their inspection and clearance may be effected promptly, according to the practice followed.

9. The Railroad shall keep records in which it shall enter successively all parcels delivered to it, with their marks and numbers, entries or issues, in accordance with supporting documents.

10. The Railroad and its employees shall be held responsible for any packages that are shown missing in the statements submitted by the Railroad to Customs as outlined above in Secton Six, in accordance with the regulations concerned and the results of the tally.

11. The Railroad shall be responsible for any deterioration or damage that might happen to the goods due to the acts or negligence of its workers and porters or that is caused directly by them,

and it shall suffer the consequences of such damage according to the regulations in effect. However, it shall not be responsible for damages incurred as a result of force majeure, such as fire, etc.

12. The Railroad shall be held responsible for packages which are in good condition when received but which later are found to be in bad condition--short. However, the Railroad shall not be responsible for damages in respect of the contents of the packages if their outward appearance is intact.

13. Packages that arrive broken or in bad shape shall be placed within a fenced area inside the warehouse. They shall be weighed and their weight shall be marked thereon in the presence of representatives from the shipping company, Customs, and the Railroad. Their condition must be described in the manifest and they must be hauled in vans whenever this is possible.

14. In storing inflammables and explosives, the regulations in force must be followed.

15. Goods that are not shown on the manifest shall be stowed away separately pending their inspection by Customs, the Railroad, and a representative of the shipping agents, to ascertain their contents.

16. The Railroad shall write the route number of the ship on each package while it is being stored in the warehouses or yards, and, in general, it shall give serial numbers to the manifests, each of which shall represent the number of the route referred to.

17. The Railroad shall assign whenever possible separate places in the warehouses and yards for the cargo of each ship.

18. The Railroad shall notify Customs immediately of any parcels that are fragile, perishable or subject to shrinkage, if their owners do not receive them directly. If they are not withdrawn

promptly, they shall be considered as unclaimed; and Customs shall appoint an estimator to inspect them and determine whether they should be sold immediately or whether the sale can be postponed. Any duties and expenses payable to Customs and the Railroad shall be deducted from the sale price, and the balance shall be credited to the person concerned.

19. The Railroad shall assign special places in the warehouses for Customs inspections and weighing, and it is advisable that these places be enclosed. The Railroad shall provide all assistance to Customs men in order to perform their duties inside the warehouses.

20. Railroad employees shall not on their own initiative open any package or box inside the warehouses or in the Customs yards. Such opening may be carried out only on inspection in the presence of the Customs employees concerned, the Railroad representative, and the owner or his agent.

21. The Railroad shall enter on special records the samples that are sent to Customs for evaluation, and ensure their return to the relative boxes or packages.

22. No goods shall be withdrawn from the Customs Area before Customs has completed formalities and issued Customs clearance thereon. Likewise, the Railroad shall not permit cars loaded with goods coming from the pier or from Customs, to pass outside the Customs Area, prior to the completion of the formalities, even though the cargo on these is exempt from duties.

23. Customs has the right to make from time to time a partial inventory of the goods stored in the warehouses or in the yards, and it may make a complete inventory at the end of each year.

24. On behalf of the Customs department and the Railroad, Customs shall conduct the necessary investigations on any package that is found in the process of inventory to be in excess or missing according to the Railroad records. The person responsible shall be punished in accordance with the regulations concerned.

25. Goods may be stored in the warehouses or yards for one full year after which they shall become unclaimed and Customs shall apply on them the regulations for abandoned goods. When such goods are sold, any Customs duties, Railroad, and other charges that are due shall be deducted from the sale price, and the balance of the amount shall be credited to the owner.

26. In cases of an emergency in the warehouses or other storage places, the Railroad shall take prompt action to protect the goods in storage, without obtaining prior permission from Customs. However, it shall notify Customs at once.

27. The Customs employees concerned shall have access to Customs warehouses and yards to check on the conditions of the work and to attend the inspection of and complete the necessary Customs formalities on the goods, to insure that the Customs Regulations are fully enforced.

28. Cases of smuggling and theft occurring at the piers, on the causeway, or in the Customs area, shall be referred to Customs after investigation, together with the seized goods and the accused, so that the necessary action may be taken in accordance with the Regulations.

29. When the Customs employees are relieved of their duties at the two piers, in pursuance of a Decision to that effect, the Coast Guard and the Railroad shall be entrusted with the supervision of the

Port and the control of whatever is unloaded from the ships, except contraband goods and articles, and dutiable articles. The Railroad shall send all such unloaded articles and their owners to Customs, with a representative who shall carry a memorandum showing the kinds and quantities of such articles so that Customs may take the necessary action in their regard. Likewise, the Railroad shall not permit passengers and their belonging to pass from the piers out of the Customs Area outside official working hours.

30. An extract from the manifest of goods unloaded from ships into dhows or launches and destined for Ras Tanura, Ras al-Mish'ab, al-Khobar, etc., shall be drawn up by the shipping companies upon request from the Railroad. The Railroad shall send a copy thereof to Customs and two copies to the Customs stations at the point of destination. One of the two copies showing receipt of the goods must be returned. The means of transportation shall not be permitted to leave before approval by the Dammam Port Customs and before the Railroad checks the packages.

31. The export of goods from both piers shall not be permitted prior to the completion of customs formalities thereon and the submission of an export manifest therefor to be approved by Customs.

32. The Railroad and Customs shall cooperate in carrying out the instructions, each within its limits, to insure the prompt withdrawal of shipments and avoid their delay.

33. If the shipping companies request the return to their intended destination of packages unloaded by mistake and if it has been proved to Customs, after examination of the documents and the original manifest concerned, that they belong to other locations, Customs

shall notify the Railroad to re-load them on the ship which will carry them off to their intended destination.

34. The Railroad shall first make a notation on the delivery orders, and later on the Import Statement and Customs Declaration [Bill of Entry] prior to clearance of the goods, to show that the goods are in its custody in the warehouses or in the storage yards. The Railroad shall also mention the date on which the unloading was completed, the condition of the goods if they are not intact, and the route number.

35. The operations of transit, trans-shipment, and ship chandlery are not permitted unless Customs formalities on the goods have been completed thereon.

36. Customs must be notified of goods relinquished in writing by their owners, of minor items found in the warehouses, storage yards or the pier, the source of which is unknown, and of sweepings, so that they may be handled as abandoned goods.

37. The Railroad shall be held responsible for the goods from the time they are unloaded from the ships or other conveyances into Railroad cars. The goods shall remain in custody of the Railroad and under its guard till they are given out to their owners after the necessary formalities have been completed thereon.

38. Upon approval of H.E. the Minister of Finance of these instructions, the Railroad and Customs, shall decide on the method according to which all the goods stored at present in the Customs warehouses and yards shall be delivered to the Railroad, and their custody transferred thereto after signing a statement of transfer prepared by Customs from its records and verified against the goods that actually exist in the warehouses and yards during the process of handing over.

39. Customs inspection of goods or persons is the duty of Customs employees. Customs employees at Customs gates shall check the cleared goods against what is shown on the clarance certificates, and carry out inspections as required. They shall also inspect suspected persons and means of transport. Customs shall assign the necessary personnel to inspect, during the day, non-dutiable Company [Aramco] goods of the same category which Customs thinks can be cleared without being taken into the Customs yard. If the Railroad thinks that it needs to continue work at night to clear the goods of the same category referred to, it shall notify Customs which shall provide the necessary personnel for their inspection and clearance. The Railroad shall see to it that these cars stand on the main line adjacent to the station because of the presence of lights and to save the employees the risk of walking at night between the railroad tracks.

40. Employees of the Railroad and Customs who are on duty must respect all regulations, instructions, and orders pertaining to Customs and the Railroad. Any disputes arising between Customs and the Railroad as a result of the applicaton of these instructions shall be referred to the Ministry of Finance to determine the action to be followed.

41. The Railroad shall work on fencing the lines from the shoreline to Customs and lighting the track as well as possible at night to afford better protectin of the goods, and it shall provide telephone communications between the Railroad, Customs, and its other offices, to enable the taking of prompt decisions on matters connected to the Railroad and Customs.

42. After the regular working hours, the Customs warehouses shall be locked with two locks, one key to which shall be kept with the Customs officer and the other with the Railroad controller. The warehouses shall be opened during the regular working hours in the presence of the Customs employee and the Railroad controller who locked them, and they shall not be opened or locked after or before such time, nor shall they be opened at night.

43. The Railroad shall maintain all Customs warehouses, the piers used by it, the scales, cranes, and carts used in unloading and transportation.

44. The Railroad shall provide the transporation and unloadi facilities, and the porters and openers required for work in the Customs area until the goods are delivered to their owners.

8. Instructions Pertaining to the [Jiddah] Port Administration

After reviewing decision No. 208 dated 4 Dhu al-Qa'dah 1379 [30 April 1960] of the Council of Ministers, communicated to H.E. the Minister of State for Finance and National Economy under No. 22649 on 6 Dhu al-Qa'dah 1379 [2 May 1960], pertaining to the non-renewal of the Government's agreement with Hajj Abd Allah Alireza Company for the operation of the Port of Jiddah upon its expiration,

The following was decided:

1. A directorate, to be called the Port Directorate, shall be established at the Jiddah Port under the supervision of a director who shall be called the Director of the Port and who shall report to the Ministry of Finance and National Economy.

2. Upon the expiry of the term of the agreement, namely, on 29 Rabi' I 1380 [20 September 1960], the Director of the Port shall, in condjunction with the Committee concerned, receive from Hajj 'Abd Allah Alireza and Company the vehicles, equipment, furniture, and everything belonging to the Government which are in the custody of that company according to the records.

3. The operations covering transportation of packages of goods from the piers to the warehouses and open yards, unloading them at the warehouses or open yards, and moving packages to the inspection halls, as well as opening, closing, restowing such packages and then transporting them outside the gates of the Customs warehouses after completion of the Customs formalities in respect thereof and payment of the payable duties and charges, shall be put up for general public tender.

Likewise, the operation of loading lumber and iron from underneath the ships' tackle or from barges and small boats, and their transportation to the open yards designated by Customs within the Customs Area, as well as the sorting of such goods, shall be put up for general public tender.

Also to be put up for general public tender is the operation of cleaning the Customs Area, Jiddah, covering the warehouses, open yards, roads, and piers.

4. The term of [each of] the contracts to be awarded for the three operations mentioned in Paragraph 2 shall be fixed at one year, renewable for another year and so forth, unless it is abrogated by either party two months prior to its expiry.

5. The Director of the Port shall be responsible for all the operations performed, beginning with the unloading of packages through the completion of the relevant Customs formalities and the reception of the goods by the owners from the warehouses or open yards.

6. The Director of the Port shall extend every facility to the Customs officials concerned with the inspection and weighing operations; he shall also extend every facility to Customs inspectors to enable them to perform search operations.

7. An imprest of SR 200,000 shall be appropriated to the Directorate of the Port, so that it may be able to make urgent disbursements, provided the Financial Regulations are observed.

8. Documents pertaining to employees' salaries, contractors' charges, and other expenditures shall, after verification, be submitte to the Ministry of Finance for disbursement [of the sums involved] in accordance with the present procedure.

9. The Directorate of the Port shall provide all floating bu and other equipment necessary to guide ships, barges, rafts, vessels, and large sailboats, into the piers and from there into the open sea. It shall also provide the pilots, sailors, and workers necessary for such operations. Agents of shipping companies shall, however, have t right to select the pilots and notify the Directorate of the Port the

10. The Directorate of the Port shall entrust the contractor awarded the bid with the operations of unloading and loading of goods of any kind and weight within the Customs Area in Jiddah, whether the ships or other vessels are anchored at the bridge, or at the quay, away from the piers near the shore. Attached to unloading and loadin operations shall be the storing of goods in Customs warehouses, their stowage therein, and their withdrawal therefrom after completion of t formalities and settlement of duties and supplementary charges in accordance with the regulations.

11. The Directorate of the Port shall provide the means of transport [necessary] for the above operations, maintain them, and replace damaged items, in accordance with the condition [of each].

12. The Directorate of the Port shall maintain the bridge, piers, and dock.

13. The Directorate of the Port shall continue to employ the present employees who are necessary for the performance of the work at their current salaries and classifications, and shall also keep other costs within the limits of the present rates until the expiry of the 1379/1380 fiscal year.

14. In conjunction with the committee provided for in Decision No. 208 of the Council of Ministers, dated 4 Dhu al-Qa'dah 1379 [30 April 1960], the Directorate of the Port shall prepare the necessary budget for its employees according to their salaries and grades and in conformity with the General Regulations for [Government] Employees, as well as for other disbursements, for approval in the 1380/1381 fiscal year.

15. The Directorate of the Port shall cooperate with Customs, the Coast Guard, Quarantine offices, Passport offices, etc., within the jurisdiction and in accordance with the regulations of each.

16. The Directorate of the Port shall operate the existing cranes at the Port.

17. The Directorate of the Port shall give priority to ships in the order of their arrival at the Port.

18. The Port employees, workers, pilots, or guides, shall not be permitted to board ships, boats, etc., prior to their arrival at the piers, except by express permission from the Coast Guard and after completion of the formalities pertaining to the Port police and the Quarantine. The unloading or loading of the goods on ships anchored at the pier or elsewhere or on the high sea shall take place only with the express permission of the Customs Director.

The Director of the Port shall specify the piers at which packages of goods, livestock, and other imports may be unloaded.

19. No cargo arriving by sea shall be unloaded before applying to Customs. The application should be signed by the ship's master or by the agent of the shipping company, and attached to the original manifest pertaining to the cargo and two Arabic copies thereof. The Directorate of the Port shall, prior to the commencement of unloading, ascertain that Customs has officially approved the unloading in writing. Customs shall, after checking the manifest, send a copy thereof to the Directorate of the Port to be sent to the Customs warehouses which shall receive the ship's cargo accordingly.

Customs may permit mail ships which have local agencies to unload their cargo prior to the presentation of the manifest, and the Directorate of the Port shall receive the cargo pending the presentat of the manifest within 36 hours at most. If the cargo includes items such as inflammable material, etc., that must be unloaded in special places, the shipping companies shall submit an extract from the manifest therefor in Arabic in two copies, and send one to the Directorat of the Port and the other to the section where such items will be unloaded. The representative concerned of the Directorate of the Por shall endorse the Directorate's copy showing that the items in questi have been sent to another place.

20. Unloading inflammable, corrosive, caustic, or explosive materials with ordinary goods is prohibited. They shall be placed in sailboats and barges, separately, and unloaded in the places assigned to them by Customs. With regard to highly explosive materia however, they shall be unloaded only under conditions and in places t be agreed upon with the Directorate General of Public Security and the Ministry of Defense.

21. The Directorate of the Port must avoid, as much as possi

leaving goods on the pier, and must see to it that the ships' cargoes are unloaded on the means of transportation and carried away at once to the Customs warehouses or to the places assigned to them. It shall be permissible, however, to unload directly on the quay, but this should not prevent the prompt removal [of the goods] to the warehouses or open yards.

22. The Customs Director may stop the unloading at any time, particularly if the shipping company fails or delays to submit the manifest. He must, within 24 hours from such failure or delay, prepare an official report stating the reasons that made him stop the unloading.

23. Packages of imported goods shall be carried from the piers to the Customs warehouses or to the places assigned to them by the contractor on the means of transport provided by the Directorate of the Port.

24. The Directorate of the Port shall notify ship agents of the necessity of delivering packages of goods at the piers in the presence of a representative of the shipping company; it shall secure his signature on the result of the delivery [operation] after recording any shortages or overages in accordance with the provisions of Article 15 of the Customs Regulations and Article 215 of the Rules for Implementation; and shall issue the necessary receipt on the basis of the result of the actual delivery, provided the Customs employees concerned shall participate to effect the necessary tally [with the manifest]. The Directorate of the Port shall most strictly comply with this procedure and shall take the necessary legal notion against ship agent who do not deliver goods in accordance with the above instructions.

25. The Directorate of the Port shall notify the Customs concerned of packages short, landed or received in excess of the manifest, as well as of packages damaged or not in good condition, so that the

Customs may, in turn, demand the necessary clarifications from the shipping companies.

26. The Directorate of the Port shall write the ship's route number on each package when received, and this number shall be written in serial order by the Manifest Office on each manifest submitted to it.

27. Upon receiving the goods in the warehouses, the Director of the Port shall request the contractor to stow the goods pertaining to each boat or ship separately, and mark the route number on all pac The marks and numbers must be written clearly in order to find them easily in the stocks and the height of the stacks and the width of th pathways must be suitable.

28. In the case of packages bearing no numbers or marks, or bearing marks or numbers identical to marks or numbers of other packages arriving on the same ship, the Directorate of the Port shall ask the shipping company concerned to place a distinguishing mark thereon and show such mark on all the documents in which the goods are recorded. Packages which outwardly appear not to be in good condition shall be isolated from the rest of teh packages and a statement to this effect shall be secured from the ship's master or the representative of the shipping company. They shall be weighed and their weight shall be noted thereon prior to their deposit in the place assigned to them in the warehouse. If the packages are importe for Government departments, they shall be examined in the presence of representative from the Government department concerned. The shippin companies shall, in all cases, be under obligation to make such repairs to the said package as may be deemed necessary by the Directo of the Port to enable it to receive them.

29. The Directorate of the Port shall receive large-size

packages, cars, machines, crates of furniture, and the varieties of iron bars, pipes, timber, building materials, etc., outside the Customs warehouses.

30. The Directorate of the Port shall notify Customs and the person concerned at once of any perishable or fragile goods and of goods subject to shrinkage. If the owners of such goods do not receive them directly or fail to withdraw them immediately, they shall be considered unclaimed, and Customs shall delegate an estimator to inspect the consignment and decide whether it should be sold at once or whether the sale may be postponed.

31. If the shipping companies request the return of parcels unloaded by mistake to their original destination, and if, upon examining their documents and original manifest Customs is satisfied that they are destined to other places, the Directorate of the Port shall be notified to re-load them on the ship under Customs supervision.

32. All samples that Customs requires [to be evaluated] shall be sent to the Valuation Section for inspection. They shall then be returned to the packages and all this shall be recorded in a book called "The Sample Book". If such samples are not returned after completion of the formalities, the Directorate of the Port shall request Customs to return them.

33. The Directorate of the Port shall endorse the bills of entry and Customs declarations prior to the clearance of the shipments showing that packages of goods are at hand in the warehouse or at another place, the date the unloading was completed, their condition in case they are not intact, the number of the warehouse, the route number, and the name of the boat or ship.

34. The Directorate of the Port must not clear any goods from the warehouses, piers, or other locations, except by virtue of a Customs Clearance.

35. Simultaneously with the collection of Customs duties, Customs shall collect port charges for the account of the Directorate of the Port in accordance with the current tariff. Crane charges shall be collected by the Directorate of the Port in accordance with past practice, and shall be remitted to the Saudi Arabian Monetary Agency.

36. The Directorate of the Port shall make out cards for the load of each car or carriage, showing thereon the quantity of packages and their marks and numbers, the clearance number, the da of issue, the car or carriage number, and the name of the driver. Loaded cars and carriages shall be allowed to go out only after the officer at the main gate has received those cards, checked them against the clearance, and deducted them from it.

37. The Directorate of the Port shall not allow any packages of goods to be taken out of the warehouses after completion of formalities thereon unless the means of transport that will carry them are at the warehouse gate.

38. Clearance Certificate submitted to the Directorate of the Port after the date of issue shown therein shall be returned to Customs to confirm their validity and collect any storage charges that may be due. Customs shall indicate on each Clearance Certificat the extent of its period of validity.

39. The Directorate of the Port shall not permit the shipping of any goods, in general, whether exported, transit, or transshipped, without prior authorization from Customs. Such authorizatio shall be in the form of clearance certificates in respect of the first two cases and orders for the last case.

40. Goods found in the warehouses or other storage spaces

and are not recorded in the receipt books, shall be investigated by Customs and the Directorate of the Port, to ascertain the reasons for the failure to record them, and to take the necessary action under the Regulations.

41. The Directorate of the Port shall notify Customs of any goods relinquished in writing by their owners, and likewise of minor items found in the warehouses, storage spaces, or at the piers, the origin of which is unknown (sweepings), so that they may be treated like abandoned goods.

The Manifest Office shall also be notified of packages not withdrawn by their owners within three months from the date on which their unloading was completed. This applies similarly to seized goods, fetsam, and prohibited goods. These items shall be deposited in the warehouse for abandoned (unclaimed) goods which shall be accessible to Customs employees only. Nothing shall be deposited therein except after it is weighed, and its description and kind shown. The contents of the warehouse of abandoned goods shall be dealt with by Customs employees in accordance with the Customs Regulations.

42. The contractor shall be responsible to the Directorate of the Port for any deterioration or damage that might happen to the goods due to the acts or negligence of his workers and porters or that is caused directly by them. The Government shall not be responsible for damages occurring as a result of force majeure such as fire, rain, etc.

43. Goods in Customs areas shall remain under the responsibility of their owners who must withdraw them promptly. The Directorate of the Port shall be responsible only for the packages of goods that are proven to have been lost after they were received and a receipt therefor was given to the shipping company. It shall likewise be

responsible for the goods it receives in good condition but which later are proven to be damaged or short. The Directorate of the Port however, shall not be responsible for damages in respect of the conte of packages if their outward appearance is intact.

44. The Directorate of the Port shall, in the presence of the shipping company and the Customs employees concerned, inventory and weigh unloaded packages which are not in a good condition, prepar a report to this effect, and deposit these packages in the warehouse for broken goods.

45. The Directorate of the Port is obligated to watch over the goods while they are unloaded, transported, stored, inspected, cleared, and, in general, as long as the goods are in the Customs area, from the time they are received from the ships or vessels. It shall ask Customs to appoint guards over the goods received outside the customs warehouses. After the official working hours, the warehouses shall be inspected and then locked with two different keys, one to be kept with the Directorate of the Port and the other with the Chief of Customs Guards stationed at Customs. The guards shall b instructed to check that the [doors] are well locked and the locks and warehouses are in safe condition. Goods received outside the war house shall be handed over, and this shall be recorded daily in a han over report. If the padlocks, doors, windows, or ceilings are found be broken, or if there is shortage in the goods received outside the warehouses, the Directorate of the Port shall at once ask Customs to conduct an investigation and make a total inventory of the warehouse or goods. The Customs shall, at any rate, have the right to take par tial or complete inventory at any time without giving any reasons.

46. The Directorate of the Port shall caution shipping companies not to unload broken or damaged packages at the same time a intact packages, but to postpone the unloading thereof until the

entire shipment is unloaded, so that the packages may be inventoried and weighed in the presence of their representatives and of a representative of the Directorate of the Port and Customs.

47. The Directorate of the Port shall draw the attention of shipping companies to take into consideration the condition of the packages to be unloaded and to provide the suitable nets and containers necessary for the unloading of such packages, so that these may not be affected by impact and damaged as a result of failure to use suitable containers for unloading. Shipping agents shall be allowed a maximum period of three months within which to comply with the above.

48. The Directorate of the Port shall draw the attention of the shipping companies to issue strict instructions to stevedoring contractors to exercise care in transporting packages from the holds by means of nets or containers, so as not to cause any damage thereto through misuse [i.e. mishandling]. Stevedoring contractors shall be responsible to the Directorate of the Port and shall be answerable for any wrongful act.

49. Customs inspection of goods or persons is the exclusive right of Customs.

50. At the request of the Government, Customs may open the warehouse for night work.

51. The Directorate of the Port shall notify those concerned not to smoke inside the warehouses or keep any open flame near them. If a fire breaks out [at a warehouse] the warehouse must be opened even though it is locked, and the director of Customs shall be notified at once. As for the means of extinguishing fires, these shall be the responsibility of the Directorate General of Fire Brigades, Ministry of Interior.

52. The Directorate of the Port shall authorize only the persons concerned or competent officials to enter the warehouses or gain access to the goods. It shall not permit any person who has no business in the warehouses to enter them.

53. Customs and the Directorate General of Inspection shall have the right to inspect and reexamine goods, both inside and outside the warehouses, at any time.

54. The Directorate of the Port shall keep, in the Customs Area, books for recording the goods stored and issued, which books shall be subject to Customs inspection.

55. The Directorate of the Port shall keep its accounts in accordance with the financial regulations in force.

56. In matters concerning its budget, the Directorate of the Port shall contact the Ministry of Finance and National Economy. As regards Customs operations and business with other departments, it shall have the power to contact them directly.

57. The Directorate of the Port shall draw up the necessary reports upon the occurrence of accidents or damage to piers or buildir

58. The Directorate of the Port shall insofar as it is concerned, see to it that the Customs Regulations and the Rules for Implementation are complied with.

Tariff of the Directorate of the Port

As Amended by Ministerial Order No. 9249, dated
15 Ramadan 1374 [8 May 1956]

Riyals	Unit of Measurement	Categories of Goods
30	per ton	Airplanes
30	per ton	Boats
30	per ton	Electric appliances
30	per ton	Refrigerators
30	per ton	Wireless [equipment]
30	per ton	Radio sets
30	per ton	Glass panes
30	per ton	Glassware
30	per ton	Films, not banned
30	per ton	Medicines
30	per ton	Washing tube and hypo
30	per ton	Fire-arms
30	per ton	Cars packed in crates
100	each	Ordinary tank-truck
100	each	Auto bus
90	each	Ordinary truck
40	each	Five-passenger car
40	each	Box and pick-up cars
30	each	Small jeeps
5	each	Motorcycles
8	each	Horse carts
30	per ton	Gold Silver ingots
30	per ton	Explosives
30	per ton	Fuses
30	per ton	Silk and silk cloth
30	per ton	Incendiary materials
30	per ton	Nylons
30	per ton	Woolen cloth
30	per ton	Tumbak, processed and raw
30	per ton	Perfumes in barrels and demi-johns
30	per ton	Eau de Cologne
30	per ton	Perfumes in small Essences containers
30	per ton	Shoes
30	per ton	Ready-made clothes, including:
30	per ton	Stockings cotton, woolen,
30	per ton	Flannels and silk
30	per ton	Men's scarves
30	per ton	Handkerchiefs
30	per ton	Women's headscarves

Riyals	Unit of Measurement	Categories of Goods
30	per ton	Sundry haberdashery, including:
30	per ton	thread and cotton spools
30	per ton	Pressure kerosene stoves
30	per ton	Padlocks
30	per ton	Scissors
30	per ton	Flashlights
30	per ton	Cigarette lighters
30	per ton	Flashlight batteries
30	per ton	Buttons, mother of pearl porcelain, and glass
30	per ton	Razors
30	per ton	Razor blades
30	per ton	Mirrors
30	per ton	Coffee kettles and parts: brass and copper
30	per ton	Knives
30	per ton	Pocket knives
30	per ton	Rosaries, of all kinds
30	per ton	Necklaces: glass and amber
30	per ton	Beads, of all kinds
30	per ton	Flatirons
30	per ton	Hair Cream
30	per ton	Vaseline
30	per ton	Hair oil
30	per ton	Indian trays
30	per ton	Metal rings
30	per ton	Metallic pressure kerosene lamps
30	per ton	Kohl tubes
30	per ton	Cups
30	per ton	Censers
30	per ton	Dinner pails
30	per ton	Typewriters and printing equipment
30	per ton	Iron and steel rods
30	per ton	[Iron] beams
30	per ton	Motors and machines
30	per ton	Mechanical equipment
30	per ton	Kulandi ware [brass]
30	per ton	Asphalt
30	per ton	Oils
30	per ton	Powder for removing colors (bleaching powder)
30	per ton	Clay pipes
30	per ton	Sanitary appliances
30	per ton	Paints
30	per ton	Jurak [honeyed tobacco]
25	per ton	Books
25	per ton	Printed Matter
25	per ton	Posters
25	per ton	Maps
25	per ton	Printed Quranic verses: Mecca, Medira, etc.

Riyals	Unit of Measurement	Categories of Goods
25	per ton	Asbestos sheets
25	per ton	Gypsum slabs
25	per ton	Cylinders containing gases
25	per ton	Liquids, including acids
25	per ton	Furniture
25	per ton	Wooden furniture
25	per ton	[Prefabricated] windows
25	per ton	Prefabricated doors
25	per ton	Prefabricated houses
25	per ton	Perambulators
25	per ton	Children's toys
25	per ton	Sidecars for motorcycles
25	per ton	Sidecars for bicycles
25	per ton	Leather suitcases
25	per ton	Tires
25	per ton	Tubes
25	per ton	Timber, of all kinds
25	per ton	Cotton sewing threads
20	per ton	Medical instruments
20	per ton	Surgical instruments
20	per ton	Hospital equipment
20	per ton	Currency, Nickel
20	per ton	Solder
20	per ton	Lead
20	per ton	Lathing tools
20	per ton	Marble
20	per ton	Mosaic
20	per ton	Alabaster
20	per ton	Tiles
20	per ton	Screws
20	per ton	Bolts
20	per ton	Sundry washers
20	per ton	Lamps
20	per ton	Lanterns
20	per ton	Globes
20	per ton	Thermos bottles
20	per ton	Heavy oil
20	per ton	Kerosene
20	per ton	Gasoline
20	per ton	Asphalt
20	per ton	Fly spray
20	per ton	Grease
20	per ton	Motor oil, of all kinds
20	per ton	Tin sheets
20	per ton	Copper sheets
20	per ton	Cotton textiles
20	per ton	Yarns
20	per ton	Threads: Hemp, wool, and silk
20	per ton	Wool
20	per ton	Tanned hides
20	per ton	Galvanized iron sheets
20	per ton	Zinc sheets
20	per ton	Matches

Riyals	Unit of Measurement	Categories of Goods
20	per ton	Woolen carpets
20	per ton	Cotton carpets
20	per ton	Woolen rugs
20	per ton	Cotton rugs
15	per ton	Insecticides, of all kinds
10	per ton	Printing paper
10	per ton	Wrapping paper
10	per ton	Writing paper
10	per ton	Soap
10	per ton	Threads in bales
10	per ton	Twine in bales
10	per ton	Cotton, raw and processed
10	per ton	Green tobacco bales
10	per ton	Tumbak sticks
10	per ton	Straw mats
10	per ton	All kinds of mats made of palm lea
10	per ton	Foodstuffs of all kinds
10	per ton	Coffee beans
10	per ton	Spices
10	per ton	Cardamom
10	per ton	Vegetables
10	per ton	Fruits
10	per ton	Canned foods, of all kinds
10	per ton	Biscuits
10	per ton	Confectionaries, of all kinds
10	per ton	Varieties of foods, cereals, and groceries not mentioned in the following paragraph or elsewhere:
8	per ton	Cement
8	per ton	Gypsum
8	per ton	Bran
8	per ton	Lime
8	per ton	Fertilizer, farm or chemical
6	per ton	Rice
6	per ton	Wheat
6	per ton	Flour
6	per ton	Barley
6	per ton	Beans [ful]
6	per ton	Lentils
6	per ton	Pearl millet
6	per ton	Corn
6	per ton	Sugar
6	per ton	Tea
6	per ton	Ghee
6	per ton	Sesame cake (tukh)
6	per ton	Dates
2	per head	Livestock
1/2	per head	Sheep
1/2	per sack	Mail sacks, of all kinds
30	per ton	Other goods not mentioned in this tariff, excluding all kinds of foo stuffs, which fall under this chap
30	per ton	Jewels
30	per ton	Jewelry

Riyals	Unit of Measurement	Categories of Goods
30	per ton	Cameras
30	per ton	Watches, of all kinds
30	per ton	Perfumes
30	per ton	Rose [Water]
30	per ton	Essences
30	per ton	Empty cans
30	per ton	Cigarettes
30	per ton	Cigarette paper

1. As a royal grant and on the basis of Decision No. 7442, dated 6 Rajab 1374 [28 February 1955], of the Minister of Finance, half a riyal shall be collected on goods bleonging to sailors.

2. An additional charge of SR 15 per ton will be collected for loadi heavy packages for which a fifty-ton crane is used.

3. The rates listed above are payable for the transporation [of good to the [Customs] warehouses or open yards, for stacking and sorting them in these places after their being unloaded from the ships on the means of transport; for the removal of the goods, in whole or in part, from the warehouses or yards, to the inspection halls for inspection, and for carrying them outside the warehouse gates for delivery to the owners. They do not cover the loading of goods on the conveyances provided for their transport to the town after they are cleared,

SAUDI ARABIAN REGULATIONS RELATING TO THE BOYCOTT OF ISRAEL

Saudi Arabia is one of the thirteen nations participating in the boycott against Israel. As a result of this boycott certain documentation is required by the Saudi government before imported goods can be entered. The boycott not only pertains to goods manufactured in Israel, but also to goods from other countries that contain Israeli components. It also applies to goods shipped on Israeli vessels or insured by Israeli companies. In order to regulate the possible flow of boycotted goods, the Saudi government requires that each shipment of imported goods be accompanied, not only by a commercial invoice and bill of lading, but also by a certificate of origin, steamship certificate, and insurance certificate. In contracts with the government of Saudi Arabia certain language is required, the text of which is set out below:

Ministry of Finance Circular
on Inclusion of Boycott Clauses
in Contracts. (January 21, 1979)*

Greetings,
Further to the Ministry's circular note No. 17/11901 of 12/7/98H on provisions which must be included in contracts signed by government entities in implementation of Israel boycott regulations. In order to avoid discrepency in the English version when copy of the contract is in English, the following text shall be included in provisions: Standard government contract clauses.

1) In connection with the performance of this contract, the second party (contractor/supplier) acknowledges that the import and customs laws and regulations of the kingdom of Saudi Arabia shall apply to the furnishing and shipment of any products or components thereof to Saudi Arabia. The second party (contractor/supplier) specifically acknowledges that the aforementioned import and customs laws and regulations of the kingdom of Saudi Arabia prohibit, among other things, the importation into Saudi Arabia of products or components thereof: (1) originating in Israel; (2) manufactured, produced or furnished by companies organized under the laws of Israel, and

* unofficial U.S. Embassy translation. Unclassified cable, U.S Embassy,Jedda

(3) manufactured, produced or furnished by nationals or residents of Israel.

2) The first party (the Saudi government agency concerned) in its exclusive power, reserves its rights to make the final unilateral and specific selection of any proposed carriers, insurers, suppliers of services to be performed within the kingdom of Saudi Arabia or of specific goods to be furnished in accordance with the terms and conditions of this contract. These provisions are to be included in all contracts you sign with foreign or local firms for their compliance.

With warm regards,
Minister of Finance and
National Economy

Muhammad Aba Al-Khayl

Forms for the certificates needed for exports to Saudi Arabia are set out in the following list of requirements for shipment to Saudi Arabia. 1)

Appearing at the end of this chapter is the complete text of Regulations for the Boycott of Israel, issued in November, 1962.

1) Source, Royal Consulate General of Saudi Arabia

Effective June 21, 1978

Requirements for Shipment to Saudi Arabia

I. Commercial Invoice

II. Certificate of Origin must state the following:

To the extent that the goods as described in the Certificate of Origin attached herewith are not solely and exclusively products of the country of origin indicated therein then the declaration in the form appearing below must be appended to the Certificate of Origin.

NAME OF SUPPLIER/MANUFACTURER

The undersigned ______________________________ does hereby declare on behalf of the above named Supplier/ Manufacturer, that certain parts or components of the goods described on the attached Certificate of Origin are the products of such country or countries other than the country named therein is specifically indicated hereunder:

Country of Origin:	Percentage of Value of Parts or Components Relative Total Shipment
1. ______________	______________________________
2. ______________	______________________________
3. ______________	______________________________

Dated at: ________________
Signature

Sworn to before me, this ____ day of _____ 19 __.

NOTARY SEAL

III. STEAMSHIP CERTIFICATE must state the following:

1. Name of Vessel ______________________

2. Nationality of Vessel ________________

3. Owner of Vessel _____________________

The undersigned does hereby declare on behalf of the owner, master, or agent of the above named vessel that said vessel is not registered in Israel or owned by nationals or residents of Israel and will not call at or pass through any Israeli port enroute to Saudi Arabia.

The undersigned further declares that said vessel is otherwise eligible to enter into the ports of the Kingdom of Saudi Arabia in conformity with its laws and regulations.

Dated at __________on the ___ day of _____19__.

Sworn to before me, this ____day of _____19______.

NOTARY SEAL

Signature of vessel's owner or agent

IV. INSURANCE CERTIFICATE must state the following:

1. Name of Insurance Company ___________________
2. Address of its Principal Office______________
3. Country of its incorporation_________________

The undersigned ______________________ does hereby certify on behalf of the above named insurance company that the said company has a duly qualified and appointed agent or representative in the Kingdom of Saudi Arabia whose name and address appears below:

NAME OF AGENT/REPRESENTATIVE   ADDRESS IN SAUDI ARABIA

____
Signature

Dated at ______on the _________day of _________19___.

NOTARY SEAL
&
SIGNATURE

V. BILL OF LADING

While compliance with the boycott regulations is not in itself difficult, it may run counter to specific laws relating to boycotts in the country of exportation. Since many Saudi imports originate in the United States a brief discussion of the rules relating to participation in the boycott is required. Compliance with the boycott may result in violations of a number of U.S. laws including, but not limited to, the Internal Revenue Code, the Export Administrat Act of 1969 as amended, the Securities Acts of 1933 and 1934, various antitrust statutes, including the Sherman Act and Clayton Act and the U.S. Civil Rights Statute contained in 42 USC 1981 et. seq., as well as state and even municipal regulations.

Tax benefits that can be forfeited due to participation in the boycott include the foreign tax credit, the use of domestic international sales corporations (Discs) and foreign tax deferrels. Tax benefits can be denied when a party enters into an agreement to: [1)]

1) Refrain from doing business with a boycotted country or companies, and nationals of the country;
2) Refrain from doing business with a U.S. person engaged in trade with a boycotted country, its nationals or its companies;
3) Refrain from doing business with persons of certain races, nationalities or religions, or to refrain from selecting corporate directors of certain races, nationalities or religions.
4) Refrain from employing persons of a particular race, religion, or nationality; and
5) Refrain from shipping goods on a carrier or insuring goods with an insurer who is from the boycotted country.

If any of the above agreements are made as a condition of doing business or a condition of sale of goods with or to a Saudi company, adverse tax consequences could result to a U.S. firm. Guidelines provided by the Treasury Department provide that,

> " Merely providing at the time of import a certificate as to the content and shipper of goods,... does not in itself constitute an agreement under §999(b)(3).

---

1) See I.R.C. §999

The Internal Revenue Code also imposes strict reporting requirements[1] for U.S. persons operating in a boycotted country and requests to cooperate in the boycott, as well as instances of participation, must be reported. Criminal penalties are involved for violations of this section.

Perhaps even more restrictive that the provisions of the Interna Revenue Code are the 1977 amendments to the Export Administration Act The act imposes severe criminal penalties for undertaking various act intended to comply with, or further the boycott. This would include the refusal to do business with an Israeli firm pursuant to an agreem with the Saudi government. Many of the acts that result in tax penal under the Internal Revenue Code, result in criminal penalties under t Export Administration Act, such as discriminating against U.S. employ officers or directors and furnishing information to the Saudi governm about the race, religion, sex, or national origin of its employees. [2] Regulations implementing the amendments to the Export Administration were issued in January, 1978.[3)]

The Export Administration Act amendments and regulations do perm a U.S. firm to furnish information to comply with the import document requirements of Saudi Arabia, such as the information requested on th forms previously illustrated requiring information as to the country origin, name of shipping company, and insurers.[4)]

1) I.R.S. Form 5713 may be used for reporting.
2) The amendments to the Export Administration Act appear in Volume U.S.C. Appendix.
3) 43 Fed. Reg. 3508 (1978). See also 15 C.F.R., Part 369.
4) 15 C.F.R.369 .3(b)

However, this information can not be in a "negative" form, so as to further the boycott. In other words, it is permissable to certify the country(s) of origin of the goods, but not to certify that no portion of the goods are manufactured in Israel. Retrictions relating to shipment on Israeli vessels, or vessels that stop at Israeli ports, are not prohibited,[1)] apparently on the theory, that a sovereign nation may regulate vessels entering its ports that are owned by nationals of states with which they may be at war or have no diplomatic relations. Thus it appears that the Saudi documentation forms, illustrated previously, may not necessarily be in violation of at least the Internal Revenue Code and Export Administration Act, as amended.

No attempt will be made to discuss all of the possible implications that are involved in trading with Saudi Arabia under the U.S. antitrust and civil rights laws. However, those planning business operations and extensive trade relations with the Saudis should review the recent antitrust suit brought by the U.S. government against the Bechtel Corporation[2)], where Bechtel was charged with refusal to deal with blacklisted persons as subcontractors.

---

1) 15 C.F.R. 369.3(b)
2) U.S. v. Bechtel Corporation, Civ.No.C.76-99(N.D.Calif.,filed January 16, 1976)

Kingdom of Saudi Arabia
Office of the Prime Minister

Royal Decree No. 27 of 25/6 (November 23, 1962)

With the Help of God, may He be exalted.

We, Su'ud bin 'Abd al'Aziz Al Su'ud,
King of the Kingdom of Saudi Arabia,

After perusal of Article 19 of the Council of Ministers Statute promulgated by Royal Decree No. 38 on 22/10/1377 (May 12, 1958), and on the basis of Council of Ministers' Resolution No. 312 of 21/6/1382 (November 19, 1962),
And on the basis of the presentation made to us by the Prime Minister,
Make the following decree:

1. We approve of the Code of Regulations for the Boycott of Israel in the form attached hereto.
2. The Prime Minister and the Ministers, each in his appropriate capacity, shall implement this Decree.

Kingdom of Saudi Arabia
Office of the Prime Minister

Decree No. 312 of 21/6/82 (November 19, 1962)

The Council of Ministers,

After perusing the Prime Minister's Office document No. 21304 of 7/11/81 (April 12, 1961) relating to the project for the directives of the Regional Office for the Boycott of Israel and to the project for the Unified Code of Regulations for the Boycott of Israel that it is proposed be promulgated in the Kingdom.

And on the basis of the Committee on Organizations' recommendation No. 40 of 9/3/1382 (August 10, 1962), Resolves as follows:

1. To accept the Code of Regulations for the Boycott of Israel in the form attached hereto.
2. To draw up a draft Royal Decree on the matter, a copy of which is attached hereto.
3. To approve the directives of the Regional Office for the Boycott of Israel in the form attached hereto.

Done according to the above,

His Highness, the Amir Fays
Prime Minister

CODE OF REGULATIONS FOR THE BOYCOTT OF ISRAEL

Article 1.
A. All persons, whether natural or legal, are prohibited from concluding, whether directly or through an intermediary, any covenant with any entities or persons resident in Israel, of Israeli nationality, or working for the account or interests of Israel, wherever they may reside. This shall apply when the object of the covenant consists of commercial dealings, financial operations, or any other transaction of whatever nature.

B. Domestic and foreign companies having interest, branches, or general agencies in Israel shall be considered to be in the category of entities and persons with whom dealing is prohibited under the preceding paragraph, as determined by the Council of Ministers or by the authorities authorized by it to do so in accordance with the recommendations of the Conference of Liaison Officers.

Article 2.
A. The introduction or importation of Israeli goods, merchandise, and products of all kinds, or of financial documents or other negotiable instruments into the Kingdom is prohibited, as is exchanging them or trading in them.

B. Considered as Israeli are goods and merchandise made in Israel or into the manufacture of which any percentage of Israeli products of any kind has entered, whether such goods and merchandise have arrived directly or indirectly from Israel.

C. Considered as being in the category of Israeli goods are merchandise and products transshipped from Israel or made outside of Israel with the object of exporting them either for the account of Israel or for that of any of the persons or entities stipulated in Article I.

Article 3.
In cases determined by decision of the Minister of Commerce and Industry, the importer must provide a certificate of origin in which the following are clearly stated:

A. The country in which the merchandise was made.
B. That no material consisting of Israeli products in any percentage has entered into the manufacture of the merchandise.

Article 4.
The competent authorities, who are to be appointed by decision of the Minister of Commerce and Industry, have the duty to take the measures necessary to prevent goods designated by the Conference of Liaison Officers from being exported to foreign countries that have been shown to re-export them to Israel.

Article 5.
The provisions found in Articles 2,3, and 4 apply to merchandise entering or exported from free zones in the Kingdom and to merchandise landed on or transiting the territory of the Kingdom with the object of exporting such merchandise either to Israel or to any persons or entities resident in Israel. These provisions shall be applied with due regard to the provisions of the international agreements to which the Kingdom of Saudi Arabia is a party.

Article 6.
It is forbidden to offer for sale, sell, purchase, or possess the goods, merchandise, and products referred to in Article 2. In the application of this present Article, any transaction carried out by donation or barter shall fall within the category of sale and purchase.

Article 7.
A. Any person contravening the provisions of Articles 1, 2, and 5 shall be punished by imprisonment for a period of not less than three years or more than ten years and with a fine of not less than five thousand or more than fifty thousand Saudi riyals.

B. Any person contravening the provisions of Article 3 or Article 6 shall be punished by imprisonment for a period of not less than three months or more than three years and by a fine of not less than five hundred or more than five thousand Saudi Arabia riyals, or by one of these two penalties.

C. If the delinquent party of one of the foregoing offenses is a legal person, the monetary penalty shall be enforced against that member or those members of the legal person who committed the offense.

D. In all cases, the effects distrained shall be ordered to be confiscated, as shall be the means of transport used in the commission of the offense, if the owners of the latter were aware that the offense was being committed.

Article 8.
Exemption from the penalties provided for in Article 7, except for that of confiscation, shall be granted to any of the delinquent parties, if there are more than one, who undertakes to inform the Government beforehand of the persons taking part in any of the aforementioned offenses, if such information in effect leads to the discovery of the offense.

Article 9.
A. A resume of any adjudgment of guilt under the provisions of this Code of Regulations shall be published in large type in the press at the expense of the person found guilty. In addition, also at his expense, the same resume in large letters shall be affixed to the front of the commercial establishment, factory, store, or other place in which he operates, for a period of three months.

B. The removal, concealment in any way, or destruction of such resume shall be punished by imprisonment for a period of not more than three months and a fine of not more than two hundred Saudi riyals, or by one of these two penalties.

Article 10.
A reward shall be paid through administrative channels to any person, whether or not a Government employee, who seizes or facilitates the seizure of the effects involved in the offenses indicated in this Code of Regulations. The reward shall consist of 20 percent of the value of the effects ordered to be confiscated. In the event that the reward is due to more than one person, it shall be distributed among them, each receiving a share in proportion to the effort he has expended, as decided by the Minister of Commerce and Industry.

Article 11.
A. Officials appointed by the Ministers of Commerce and Industry, Finance, Defense and Aviation, and Interior shall investigate and substantiate the the commission of the offenses specified in this Code of Regulations or in the

decisions implementing it.

B. After offenses have been investigated and confirmed, the Ministry of Commerce and Industry shall be the authority competent to refer the case to the body that is to try them.

Article 12.

1. The offenses specified in this Code of Regulations shall be referred to a body composed of:

   1. The head of the Council on Inequities
   2. A legal advisor from the Council on Inequities
   3. A legal advisor from the Council of Ministers.

2. The decisions of this body are to be considered as effective only after they have been approved by the Prime Minister.

Article 13.

Regulations and decisions conflicting with the provisions of this Code of Regulations are abrogated.

Article 14.

It is the duty of the Prime Minister and the Ministers, each in his appropriate capacity, to implement this Code of Regulations. The Code of Regulations is to be considered as coming into force as of the date of its publication.

APPENDIX I

CHAMBERS OF COMMERCE & INDUSTRY IN SAUDI ARABIA

1. IN Riyadh:
Chamber of Commerce and Industry
Khazan St., P.O. Box 596 Riyadh,
Saudi Arabia
Telephone: (011) 22600, 22700
Telex: 20054 Tejaryah SJ
Telegraph: Tejaryah Saudi Arabia
President: Sheikh Mohammed Al-Furaih
Sec. Gen.: Saheh Al-Toami

2. IN Jeddah:
Chamber of Commerce and Industry
Kabel St., P.O. Box 1264, Jeddah
Saudi Arabia
Telephone: (021) 31059,25659,23535,24824
Telex: 40069 AL GHURFA SJ
Telegraph: ALGURFA Jeddah Saudi Arabia
President: Sheikh Ismail Abudawood
Gen. Mgr.: Sari I. Islam

3. IN Dammam:
Chamber of Commerce and Industry
P.O. Box 719, Dammam, Saudi Arabia
Telephone: (031) 25218, 21134
Telex: 60086 CHAMBER SJ
Telegraph: ALGURFA Dammam Saudi Arabia
President: Sheikh Saad Al-Moajil
Gen. Mgr.: Abdullah Al Duhailan

4. IN Mecca:
Chamber of Commerce and Industry
P.O. Box 1086,Mecca, Saudi Arabia
Telephone: (022) 25775
Telegraph: Algurfa Mecca, Saudi Arabia
President: Sheikh Mohammed Al-Bogary
Gen. Mgr.: Mohammed Saeed Korban

5. IN Medina:
Chamber of Commerce and Industry
Government Offices Bldg., P.O. Box 443, Medina, Saudi Arabia
Telephone: (041) 25190
Telegraph: IQTISAD
President: Sayed Habib Mahmood
Gen. Mgr.: Mohammed Saeed A.K. Shalaby

APPENDIX II

SAUDI FACTORIES WHOSE PRODUCTS ARE SUITABLE FOR SAUDI GOVERNMENT PURCHASING

March 27, 1978

(Informal translation of Arabic names)

Foodstuffs	Product
1. Badra P.O. Box 1678 Jidda Phone: 20857	candy, biscuits
2. National Food Industries Co. P.O. Box 1797 Jidda Phone: 53607, 53549	macaroni
3. National Co. for Food Products P.O. Box 1033 Riyadh	tomato pasta and juice, canned vegetables
4. Bin Zagr and Coro Co. P.O. Box 9852 Jidda Phone: 27529	"Sun-Kwik" drinks
5. Saudi Danish Milk Co. P.O. Box 5043 Jidda Phone: 42756, 46894	dairy products
6. Bin Amar Project for Milk Production Tarig al-Hijaz (Durma, Shifa Section) Riyadh Phone: 32871, 71409	milk
7. National Dairy and Ice Cream Factory P.O. Box 78 Dammam Phone: 43916	dairy products
8. National Modern Factory for Date Packing P.O. Box 188 Medina Phone: 23895	dates
9. National Est. for Date and Derivative Packing P.O. Box 466 Medina Phone: 21674	dates
10. Al Matrud Est. for Agricultural Processing P.O. Box 97 Al Khobar Phone: 43916	milk, eggs, poultry

Animal Feed	Product
1. Poultry Fodder Factory Jidda Phone: 20496	poultry feed
2. Animal Protein Factory P.O. Box 1195 Jidda	proteins for animal food
3. Saudi Arabian Feed Co. P.O. Box 173 Dammam Phone: 22923	poultry feed
4. Arabian Co. for Poultry P.O. Box 1039 Jidda Phone: 28277	poultry feed
5. Saudi Co. for Agricultural Development P.O. Box 967 Al Kharj Phone: 67974	poultry feed
Mineral Water	
1. Saudi Co. for Mineral Water P.O. Box 2572 Riyadh	bottled water
2. Safa Water Factory P.O. Box 1925 Jidda Phone: 52940,56755	bottled water
Furniture	
1. Arabian Factory for Mattresses P.O. Box 3436 Riyadh	spring mattresses
2. Saudi Factory for Spring Mattresses Abdullah Al Faisal Building Jidda	spring mattresses
3. Arabian Factory fo Spring Mattresses (Dammam Branch) c/o P.O. Box 3436 Riyadh	spring mattress frames and beds
4. Saudi Modern Factory for Furniture P.O. Box 894 Riyadh Phone: 28336	desks and beds
5. Abanumi Industrial Est. Industrial Estate Riyadh	furniture

Engineering Products	Product
1. National Car Manufacturing Co. P.O. Box 104 Jidda Phone: 22222	Mercedes truck assembly
2. Saudi Cable Co. P.O. Box 2824 Jidda	electrical wires and cable
Building Materials	
1. Saudi Marble Co. P.O. Box 1187 Jidda	marble products
2. National Quarries Co. (Jidda) c/o P.O. Box 789 Riyadh	granite
3. Saudi Arabian Amiantit P.O. Box 589 Dammam	asbestos pipe
4. Riyadh Aluminum Factory P.O. Box 115, Industrial Estate Riyadh	doors and windows
5. Saudi Aluminum Co. (SALIMCO) P.O. Box 2802 Riyadh	doors and windows
6. Dammam Aluminum Factory P.O. BOx 466 Dammam	doors and windows
7. Gharnateh Aluminum Factory of Riyadh P.O. Box 359 Riyadh	doors and windows
8. National Factory for Aluminum P.O. Box 2792 Riyadh Phone: 39517	doors and windows
9. National Co. for Pressing and Industrializing Wood P.O. Box 5913 Riyadh Phones: 83668,84609	chip board
Textiles	
1. Saudi Textile Co. P.O. Box 3549 Jidda Phone: 20185,27977	ghutras (head covers), towels

2. National Cloth Factory — pilgrim towels
   P.O. Box 559, Mocca Rd.,Kilo 14
   Jidda Phone: 22994

3. Towel Factory — pilgrim towels
   P.O. Box 608
   Mecca Phone: 21527

4. Ahmed and Saleh Kaki Co. for Textiles and Tents — tents, trampolines, bathing suits
   P.O. Box 2506
   Jidda Phone: 31749,31555

5. Saudi Co. for Ready Made Clothes — clothing
   P.O. Box 378
   Jidda

6. Automatic Carpet Factory — prayer rugs
   P.O. Box 1041
   Jidda Phone: 21831

7. Saudi Arabian Carpet Factory — prayer rugs
   P.O. Box 2371
   Jidda Phone: 32310

<u>Chemical Products</u>

1. Saudi Plastics Factory — plastic containers and housewares
   P.O. Box 79
   Riyadh Phone: 28686

2. National Plastic Factory — plastic household utensils
   P.O. Box 244
   Riyadh

3. Saudi Co. for Plastic Manufacturing — plastic housewares
   P.O. Box 1159
   Jidda

4. Riyadh Plastic Factory — plastic containers
   P.O. Box 359
   Riyadh Phone: 26359

5. Saudi Co. for Insecticides — insecticides
   P.O. Box 3592
   Riyadh Phone: 21187,24791

6. International Pharmaceutical Products Co. Ltd. — tablets
   P.O. Box 252
   Jidda

7. Bin Zagr and Unilever — Lux and Lifebuoy soap
   P.O. Box 54
   Jidda Phone: 23769

8. National Industries Co. (RIALCOM) P.O. Box 1394 Riyadh	auto batteries
9. Saudi Plastic Products Co. P.O. Box 2823 Riyadh Phone: 28228	plastic pipes
10. Basic Chemical Industries Co. P.O. Box 1043 Dammam Phone: 26178	soda acid, cloride, hydrochloric acid, sodium hydrochloride
11. National Factory for Polystyrene P.O. Box 5398 Jidda Phone: 26528	plastic egg trays, meat trays, cups and baskets

Paper Products

1. Banawi Factory for Paper Products P.O. Box 922 Jidda Phone: 21750	Kraft paper bags and boxes
2. National Co. for Paper Products P.O. Box 538 Dammam Phone: 24222	plastic bags, napkins
3. Sawazir Factory for Diapers P.O. Box 67 Mecca Phone: 23441	baby's paper towels
4. National Est. for Paper Products P.O. Box 422 Riyadh	paper products
5. Arabian Co. for Continuous Forms c/o Abdul Rahman Al-Turki Est. Dammam Phone: 23193,23192	computer paper
6. Al Hilal Est. for Printing P.O. Box 349 Dammam Phone: 44444	forms, paper
7. Al Shark Press P.O. Box 977 Jidda Phone: 53723	calculating machine paper
8. Safari Bag Co. for Corrugated Paper Board P.O. Box 4720 Jidda Phone:44926	corrugated paper
9. Mohamed Ali Maghrebi P.O. Box 71 Jidda Phone: 22636	envelopes

10. Mohamed Ali Maghrobi
P.O. Box 71
Jidda Phone: 22870
school notebooks

11. Saudi Est. for Envelope Industry
Dhahran St.
Dammam Phone: 22287
envelopes

12. Al Nasr Industrial Co.
P.O. Box 2151
Jidda
pencils, carbon paper, typewriter carbons, paper clips, pens, chalk

Prefabricated Houses

1. Saudi Factory for Prefab Structures (Saudi Prefab)
P.O. Box 3461
Riyadh Phone: 67880
prefab houses

2. Saudi Prefab Construction and Industrial Est.
P.O. Box 1723
Riyadh Phone: 25553
precast slabs

3. Saudi Co. for Construction of Cement Houses (SAPRICO)
P.O. Box 2918
Riyadh Phone: 61817,21335
precast houses

4. Payez and Steiger Construction Co.
P.O. Box 5180
Jidda
prestressed, precast slabs

5. Beton and Badcock
P.O. Box 250
Riyadh
precast structures

6. Ready Made Houses (MABCO)
P.O. Box 1549
Riyadh Phone: 39486
precast hollow-core slabs

Paint

1. Hemple Marine Paint Co.
P.O. Box 1077
Dammam Phone: 26670,26677
paint

2. Saudi Arabian Sherwin Williams
P.O. Box 21
Dammam
paint

3. United Industrial Co. Ltd.
P.O. Box 1477
Jidda Phone: 28031
paint

4. International Co. for Chemical Industry and Trade P.O. Box 1555 Jidda Phone: 32007	paint and thinner
5. Saudi Paint Co. P.O. Box 2549 Riyadh Phone: 24523	paint
6. Arabian Danish Paint Co. P.O. Box 562 Riyadh	paint
7. Al Waha Commercial Est. Pigments Factory P.O. Box 479 Al Khobar	paint

Guard Rails

1. Saudi Italian Factory for Guard Rails Medina Rd., Kilo 40 Jidda	guard rails

Metal Products

1. Al Mutlag Furniture Factory (Dammam) c/o P.O. Box 1321 Riyadh Phone: 28800 (Riyadh) 41226 (Dammam)	sofa sets (wooden)
2. Industrial Projects Co. P.O. Box 1723 Riyadh Phone: 25553	desert coolers, metal ovens, desks, chairs, file cabinets
3. Hasr Al Hamid for Trade and Industry P.O. Box 927 Riyadh Phone: 3;428,31432	metal furniture
4. Al Hijaz Metal Factory P.O. Box 867 Mecca	telephone poles, metal furniture
5. Al Anwar Factory Industrial Estate Riyadh	telephone poles, lamps
6. Al-Rabiaan Est. for Trade and Industry Riyadh Phone: 62907	carts, buckets, shovels, pots,trowels
7. Saudi Co. for Aluminum Products (ALUBCO) Industrial Estate Dammam	aluminum products

8. Al Rajhi Factory for Agricultural Pumps P.O. Box 2474 Riyadh	vertical pumps
9. Al Zamil-Soule Steel Buildings Co. P.O. Box 270 Dammam Phone: 29452	steel structures
10. Zaza Factory for Production of Pumps Industrial Estate Riyadh	pumps
11. Kaif Est. for Refrigeration & Purification Amir bin Al-Aas St. Riyadh	air conditioners (central units), suction fans, heating units, wa[illegible] purification units, and water storage tanks.
12. Arabian Refrigeration Factory P.O. Box 83 Al Khobar Phone: 42567	air conditioners (window and central units)
13. Modern Mejd Factory for Hot Water Heaters P.O. Box 2456 Riyadh	electric water heaters
14. Electric and Gas Heater Factory P.O. Box 533 Riyadh Phone: 27358	water heaters (electric),
15. Saudi Casting Co. Industrial Estate Riyadh	manhole Covers

APPENDIX III

LIST OF SAUDI STANDARDS

Sr. No.	Name of Standards	Date of approval	Date of publication
1	Labelling of pre packaged foods	24.11.93H (1973)	30.1.94 (1974)
2	Steel bars for the reinforcement of concrete	15.2.99H (1979)	
3	Wheat Flour	6.4.96H (1976)	3.6.96H (1976)
4	Methods of test for wheat flour	6.4.96H (1976)	3.6.96H (1976)
5	Asbestos-cement pressure pipes and their joints	12.10.96H (1976)	10.11.96H (1976)
6	Methods of testing asbestos-cement pipes	12.10.96H (1976)	10.11.96H (1976)
7	Macaroni, spaghetti and vermicelli	12.10.96H (1976)	10.11.96H (1976)
8	Methods of test for macaroni, spaghetti and vermicelli	12.10.96H (1976)	10.11.96H (1976)
9	Corrugated asbestos-cement sheets used in roofing and cladding	12.10.96H (1976)	10.11.96H (1976)
10	Methods of test for corrugated asbestos-cement sheets	12.10.96H (1976)	10.11.96H (1976)
11	Electric water heaters for household use	12.10.96H (1976)	10.11.96H (1976)
12	Electric fires for household use	12.10.96H (1976)	10.11.96H (1976)
13	Methods of test for electric fires for household use	12.10.96H (1976)	10.11.96H (1976)
14	Pipes for portable water of unplasticized plastic (polyvinyl chloride)	12.10.96H (1976)	10.11.96H (1976)
15	Methods of testing of pipes for portable water of unplasticized plastice (polyvinyl chloride)	12.10.96H (1976)	10.11.96H (1976)
16	The international system of units SI part 1,Base, supplementary and derived quantities and units	12.10.96H (1976)	17.11.96H (1976)

Sr. No.	Name of Standards	Date of approval	Date of publicat[ion]
17	The international system of units part 2, Rules for the use of basic, supplementary and derived units of the international system and their decimal multiples and submultiples	12.10.96H (1976)	17.11.96H (1976)
18	Conversion of toleranced dimensions from inches into millimeters and vice versa	12.10.96H (1976)	10.11.96H (1976)
19	Lubricating oils for internal combustion engines	12.10.96H (1976)	17.11.96H (1976)
20	Methods of sampling lubricating oil	12.10.96H (1976)	17.11.96H (1976)
21	Measuring of viscosity by saybolt universal viscometer	12.10.96H (1976)	17.11.96H (1976)
22	Determination of water in petroleum products by Dean and Stark method	12.10.96H (1976)	17.11.96H (1976)
23	Determination of strong (mineral) acid number in petroleum products	12.10.96H (1976)	17.11.96H (1976)
24	Determination of pour point of petroleum products	12.10.96H (1976)	17.11.96H (1976)
25	Determination of flash and fire points for petroleum products by cleveland open cut apparatus	12.10.96H (1976)	17.11.96H (1976)
26	Methods of sampling for edible oils and fats	12.10.96H (1976)	17.11.96H (1976)
27	Lead-acid batteries	12.10.96H (1976)	17.11.96H (1976)
28	Methods of test for lead-acid batteries	12.10.96H (1976)	17.11.96H (1976)
29	Edible Maize oil	9.4.97H (1977)	24.10.97H (1977)
30	Physical and chemical methods for testing edible oils and fats	9.4.97H (1977)	24.10.97H (1977)
31	Methods of sampling for meat and meat products	27.10.97H (1977)	10.01.98H (1977)
32	Methods of sampling of prepackaged fruit and vegetable products	27.10.97H (1977)	10.01.98H (1977)
33	Tungsten filament lamps for general lighting service	27.10.97H (1977)	21.03.98 (1978)

Sr. No.	Name of Standards	Date of approval	Date of publication
34	Methods of test for tungsten filament lamps for general lighting service	27.10.97H (1977)	21.03.98H (1978)
35	Evaporative air coolers (Desert Coolers)	27.10.97H (1977)	21.03.98H (1978)
36	Methods of test for evaporative air coolers (Desert Coolers)	27.10.97H (1977)	21.03.98H (1978)
37	Steel carbon dioxide cartridges for fire extinguishers	27.10.97H (1977)	21.03.98H (1978)
38	Methods of test for steel carbon dioxide cartridges for fire extinguishers	27.10.97H (1977)	21.03.98H (1978)
39	Mechanical tests of welded joints	27.10.97H (1977)	21.03.98H (1978)
40	Pasteurized milk	27.10.97H (1977)	10.01.98H (1977)
41	Methods for sampling milk and milk products	27.10.97H (1977)	21.03.98H (1978)
42	Methods for the physical and chemical analysis of milk	27.10.97H (1977)	10.01.98H (1977)
43	Methods of microbiological examination of liquid milk	27.10.97H (1977)	10.01.98H (1977)
44	Mutton and goat meat, fresh chilled and frozen	27.10.97H (1977)	10.01.98H (1977)
45	Methods for physical and chemical analysis of meat and meat products	27.10.97H (1977)	10.01.98H (1977)
46	Canned shrimps (Prawns)	27.10.97H (1977)	10.01.98H (1977)
47	Canned tuna	27.10.97H (1977)	10.01.98H (1977)
48	Methods of sampling for fish, chill fish and their products	27.10.97H (1977)	10.01.98H (1977)
49	Methods for physical and chemical analysis of fish, shellfish, and their products	27.10.97H (1977)	24.01.98H (1978)
50	Margarine and methods of analysis	27.10.97 (1977)	21.03.98H (1978)
51	Switches for domestic purposes	27.10.97H (1977)	21.03.98H (1978)

Sr. No.	Name of Standards	Date of approval	Date of publicatio
52	Methods of test for switches for domestic purposes	27.10.97H (1977)	21.03.98H (1978)
53	Graphical symbols for electrical installation	27.10.97H (1977)	21.03.98H (1978)
54	PVC-Insulated flexible cords with circular copper	27.10.97H (1977)	21.03.98H (1978)
55	PVC-Insulated cables with circular copper conductors	27.10.97H (1977)	21.03.98H (1978)
56	Methods of test for PVC-Insulated cables and cords with circular copper conductors	27.10.97H (1977)	21.03.98H (1978)
57	Domestic storage type water heater for use with gas	27.10.97H (1977)	5.04.98H (1978)
58	Methods of test for domestic storage type water heater for use with gas	27.10.97H (1977)	5.04.98H (1978)
59	Gas fired domestic heaters part I. Radiant portable heaters	27.10.97H (1977)	25.05.98H (1978)
60	Methods of test for gas fired domestic radiant type portable heaters	27.10.97H (1977)	25.05.98H (1978)
61	Portable steel cylinders for liquefied petroleum gases (LPG)	27.10.97H (1977)	25.05.98H (1978)
62	Methods of test for portable steel cylinders for liquefied petroleum gases	27.10.97 (1977)	25.05.98H (1978)
63	Fire estinguishers part 1-steel portable carbon dioxide fire extinguishers	27.10.97H (1977)	25.05.98H (1978)
64	Methods of test for portable fire extinguishers	27.10.97H (1977)	25.05.98H (1978)
65	Nonautomatic double-pan balance with base of ordinary accuracy	27.10.97H (1977)	25.05.98H (1978)
66	Calibration of Nonautomatic double pan balance with base of ordinary accuracy	27.10.97H (1977)	25.05.98H (1978)
67	Nonautomatic weighing instruments	27.10.97H (1977)	25.05.98 (1978)
68	Methods for calibration of nonautomatic weighing instrument	27.10.97H (1977)	25.05.98H (1978)
69	Cheese-hard-semi-hard-soft	27.10.97H (1977)	24.01.98H (1978)

Sr. No.	Name of Standards	Date of approval	Date of publication
70	Methods for the analysis of cheese	27.10.97H (1977)	24.01.98H (1978)
71	Vegetable shortening and vegetable oils and fats	27.10.97H (1977)	24.01.98H (1978)
72	Methods of test for permitted additives in edible oils and fats	27.10.97H (1977)	24.01.98H (1978)
73	Benzoic acid, sodium benzoat and potassium benzoat used in food preservation	27.10.97H (1977)	24.01.98H (1978)
74	Methods of test for benzoic acid, sodium benzoat and potassium benzoat used in food preservation	27.10.97H (1977)	24.01.98H (1978)
75	Hermetically sealed tin cans used for canning foodstuffs	27.10.97H (1977)	25.05.98H (1978)
76	Methods of test for hermetically sealed tin cans used for canning foodstuffs	27.10.97H (1977)	13.08.98H (1978)
77	Grey cast iron pressure pipes	27.10.97H (1977)	13.08.98H (1978)
78	Methods of testing grey cast iron pressure pipes	27.10.97H (1977)	13.08.98H (1978)
79	Aluminum products part 1. sheets, strips, plates, bars and structural sections	27.10.97H (1977)	13.08.98H (1978)
80	Testing methods of aluminum products part 1. sheets, strips, plates, bars, and structural sections	27.10.97H (1977)	13.08.98H (1978)
81	Fire extinguishers-part 2-portable bromochlorodiflouromethane fire extinguishers	27.10.97H (1977)	13.08.98H (1978)
82	Radiators of motor cars	27.10.97H (1977)	
83	Methods of test for radiators of motor cars	27.10.97H (1977)	
84	Liquefied petroleum gases (LPG) for household use (mixture of commercial propane and butane)	27.10.97H (1977)	
85	Methods of testing liquefied petroleum gases for household use (commercial propane-butane misture)	27.10.97H (1977)	
86	The international system of units (SI part 3:A selection of the decimal multiples of basic supplementary and derived units	27.10.97H (1977)	

Sr. No.	Name of Standards	Date of approval	Date of publicati[on]
87	Methods of test for concrete (cement) building bricks and blocks	27.10.97H (1977)	
88	Orange juice, concentrated orange juice and orange juice powder	28.2.98H (1978)	
89	Orange nectar, diluted orange juice and orange drink	28.2.98H (1978)	
90	Methods of test for fruit juices	28.2.98H (1978)	
91	Boiled linseed oil for paints	4.4.98H	
92	Methods of test for boiled linseed oil for paints	4.4.98H	
93	Commercial weights of medium precision from 1 gram to 50 kilograms	4.4.98H	
94	Calibration method for commercial weights of medium accuracy from 1 gram to 50 kilograms	04.04.98H (1978)	
95	Dried milk	04.04.98H (1978)	
96	Methods for the analysis of dried milk	04.04.98H (1978)	
97	Raw milk	03.05.98H (1978)	20.08.98H (1978
98	Sterilized milk	03.05.98H (1978)	20.08.98H (1978
99	Carbonated water and beverages	03.05.98H (1978)	20.08.98H (1978
100	Methods of test of carbonated water and beverages	03.05.98H (1978)	20.08.98H (1978
101	Honey	15.07.98H (1978)	
102	Methods of test for honey	15.07.98H (1978)	
103	Methods of microbiological examination	15.07.98H (1978)	
104	Salts of sulphurous acid used in preservation of foodstuffs	15.07.98H (1978)	
105	Methods of test for salts sulphurous acid used in preservation of foodstuffs	15.07.98H (1978)	

Sr. No.	Name of Standards	Date of approval	Date of publication
106	Permitted food additives in edible oils and fats	15.07.98H (1978)	
107	Tensile Testing of steel	25.02.99H (1979)	
108	Methods of physical and chemical tests of canned vegetables	25.02.99H (1979)	
109	Microbiological methods for testing canned vegetables	25.02.99H (1979)	
110	Canned green beans	25.02.99H (1979)	
111	Canned green peas	25.02.99H (1979)	
112	Domestic electric fans	25.02.99H (1979)	
113	Methods of test for domestic electric fans	25.02.99H (1979)	
114	Electric irons for household use	25.02.99H (1979)	
115	Methods of test for electric irons for household use	25.02.99H (1979)	
116	Fresh, cooled and frozen cow and buffalo meats	23.03.99H (1979)	
117	Frozen chickens	23.03.99H (1979)	
118	Methods of test for valves of liquefied petroleum gas cylinders.	23.03.99H (1979)	
119	Valves of liquefied petroleum cylinders	23.03.99H (1979)	
120	Methods of test for pressure regulators of valves for liquefied petroleum gas	23.03.99H (1979)	
121	Pressure regulators of valves for liquefied petroleum gas cylinders	23.03.99H (1979)	
122	Methods of testing of gasoline the high lead content in gasoline	23.03.99H (1979)	

APPENDIX IV

DAILY NEWSPAPERS IN SAUDI ARABIA

AL-JAZIRAH	P.O. BOX 354, Riyadh
AL RIYADH	P.O. BOX 851 Riyadh
AL-NADWAH	Mecca Establishment for Printing,Mecca
AL-MADINAH	P.O. BOX 807 Jeddah
OKADH	P.O. BOX 1408, Jeddah
AL-BILAD	Al-Bilad Establishment for Press,Jeddah
AL-YAWM	P.O. BOX 565, Dammam
RIYADH DAILY	P.O. BOX 851, Riyadh (English)
ARAB NEWS	P.O. BOX 4556, Heddah (English)

WEEKLY MAGAZINES

AL-YAMAMAH	P.O. BOX 801, Riyadh
IQRAA	Bachashab Bldg., Jeddah
SAUDI ECONOMIC SURVEY	P.O. BOX 1989, Jeddah (English)

PRINCIPAL GOVERNMENT OFFICIALS

King and Prime Minister-- Khalid bin Abd al-Aziz Al Saud

First Deputy Prime Minister- Crown Prince Fahd bin Abd al-Aziz Al Saud

Second Deputy Prime Minister- Abdallah bin Abd al-Aziz Al Saud

Defense and Aviation Minister-- Sultan bin Abd al-Aziz Al Saud

Public Works and Housing Minister- Mitab bin Abd al-Aziz Al Saud

Municipal and Rural Affairs Minister- Majid bin Abd al-Aziz Al Saud

Interior Minister- Nayif bin Abd al-Aziz Al Saud

Foreign Affairs Minister-- Sa'ud bin Faisal bin Abd al-Aziz Al Saud

Finance and National Economy Minister- Muhammad Aba al-Khayl

Information Minister-- Muhammad Abdo Yamani

Industry and Electricity-- Ghazi Abd ar-Rahman al-Quasaibi

ABOUT THE AUTHOR

LESLIE ALAN GLICK was born in New York City and graduated from Cornell University and Cornell Law School, where he was on the staff of the Cornell International Law Journal. He has practiced law in the Washington D.C area since 1971 where he has specialized in international trade and maritime law. His clients have included shipping companies and multinational corporations doing business in the Middle East. He is the author of numerous articles on international trade and business law and he has served as Vice-Chairman of the Private International Law Subcommitee of the Federal Bar Association. He resides in Potomac, Maryland.